The Forgotten Front

The Macedonian Campaign 1915-1918

Jon Lewis

Helion & Company Limited

To my wife Josée
We met in Jugoslavia over five decades ago and have frequently
returned to the Balkans, including visits to the scene of the
action in Greece and North Macedonia.

Helion & Company Limited
Unit 8 Amherst Business Centre
Budbrooke Road
Warwick
CV34 5WE
England
Tel. 01926 499 619
Email: info@helion.co.uk
Website: www.helion.co.uk
Twitter: @helionbooks
Visit our blog at blog.helion.co.uk

Published by Helion & Company 2023
Designed and typeset by Mach 3 Solutions (www.mach3solutions.co.uk)
Cover designed by Paul Hewitt, Battlefield Design (www.battlefield-design.co.uk)

Text © Jon Lewis 2023
Images open sourced unless otherwise credited
Maps based on sketches by the author drawn by George Anderson
© Helion & Company Ltd 2023
Front cover: Serbian Drina Division embarking for Salonica from Corfu, April 1916. (RMN – Grand Palais/Opérateur H)

Every reasonable effort has been made to trace copyright holders and to obtain their permission for the use of copyright material. The author and publisher apologize for any errors or omissions in this work and would be grateful if notified of any corrections that should be incorporated in future reprints or editions of this book.

ISBN 978-1-915113-73-3

British Library Cataloguing-in-Publication Data.
A catalogue record for this book is available from the British Library.

All rights reserved. No part of this publication may be reproduced, stored in a retrieval system, or transmitted, in any form, or by any means, electronic, mechanical, photocopying, recording or otherwise, without the express written consent of Helion & Company Limited.

For details of other military history titles published by Helion & Company Limited contact the above address or visit our website: http://www.helion.co.uk.

We always welcome receipt of book proposals from prospective authors.

Contents

Acknowledgements		v
Note on Names and Places		vii
Preface		ix

Part I: Macedonia: Background and the Balkan Wars — 11

1	Macedonia: The First 2,500 Years	13
2	The Balkans in the Nineteenth Century	17
3	The Balkan Wars 1912-13	21
4	The Third Balkan War	23

Part II: The Macedonian Campaign 1915–1918 — 31

1915-16

5	Alliances and Misalliances	33
6	From the Dardanelles to Salonica	37
7	The Defeat of Serbia	45
8	The Allies Arrive in Salonica	52
9	The Allied Expedition to Serbia, October–December	59
10	Consolidation and Reinforcement	65
11	Tensions between the Allies and Pressure on Greece	76
12	Defeat of Romania	82
13	The Bulgarians Strike First	87
14	The Allies Re-enter Serbia	94
15	Autumn Campaigns on the Vardar and Struma Fronts	100
16	Allied Interventions in Greece	107

1917

17	Stocktaking and Perplexity	114
18	The Italians in Albania	120
19	Preparations for a Spring Offensive	124
20	First Battle of Doiran	133
21	The Failed Offensive	143
22	Disaffection and Disarray in the Serbian Army	150
23	Dethronement of Constantine	156
24	Summer of Discontent	163
25	Malaria – The Enemy Within	170
26	Allied Actions and Initiatives Summer and Autumn 1917	176
27	Recall of Sarrail	182

1918

28	On the Defensive	187
29	Greek and Other Reinforcements	195
30	Guillaumat Completes his Mission	201
31	Franchet d'Espèrey Picks up the Reins	210

32	Final Offensive: Decisions and Preparations	218
33	Final Offensive: The Battle of Dobropolje	227
34	Final Offensive: Second Battle of Doiran	237
35	Final Offensive: Pursuit and Rout	247
36	Armistice	260
37	Aftermath	267
38	Conclusions	276

Appendices

I	Composition of the Allied Army of the East 1915–1918	284
II	Post-War Careers	285
III	Diary of Signaller Bailey	287

Bibliography 293

Index 296

Maps

The Macedonian Front 1915–1918.	vi
1. The Balkans 1800-1913.	18
2. Serbia 1914-1915.	24
3. Anglo–French Campaign October–December 1915.	60
4. From Vardar to Struma and Entrenched camp.	66
5. The Romanian Campaign August–December 1916.	83
6. Monastir and Kaymakcalan 1916.	88
7. The Struma Front.	101
8. Albania 1915 – 1918.	121
9. Macedonian Theatre West of the Vardar.	125
10. Doiran Battlefield April-May 1917, September 1918.	134
11. Battle of Dobropolje September 1918.	219
12. Armies, 15 September 1918.	228

Acknowledgements

John Skinner, whose grandfather also served on the Macedonian Front, has followed this project through right from the start. I am deeply grateful to him for his encouragement and informed commentary over the years.

The DVDs and publications of the Salonica Campaign Society have been of great value in their coverage of the British part of the Campaign, and tribute must be paid both to the SCS and the *Association Nationale pour le Souvenir des Dardanelles et Fronts d'Orient* in France for their work in keeping the memory of the campaign alive well into the 21st Century.

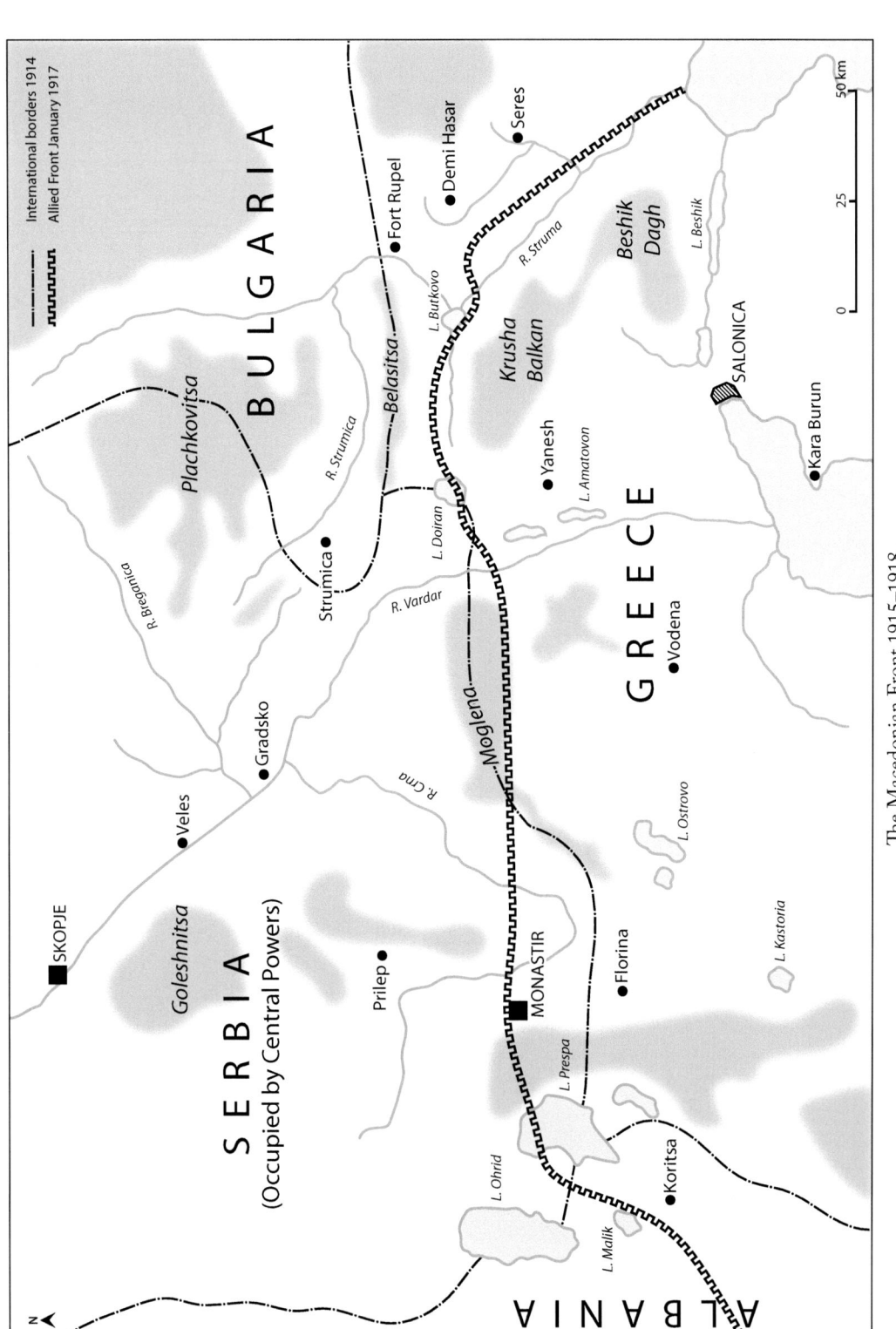

The Macedonian Front 1915–1918.

Note on Names and Places

The First World War Campaign fought in the Balkans is sometimes referred to as the Macedonian Campaign, and sometimes (mainly by British sources) as the Salonica Campaign.

Historically, Macedonia is the whole of the area embraced by the current Greek Region of Macedonia plus that of the present-day Republic of North Macedonia, which at the time of the Macedonian Campaign was part of Serbia. In the pages which follow these two parts will be referred to as 'Greek Macedonia' and 'North Macedonia'.

Salonica is one of the names given to the major town in Greek Macedonia which remained the headquarters of the Allied Army of the East throughout the Campaign.[1] The British component of the Allied Army of the East was called the British Salonica Force (BSF), and at the time the British Government and military used the term 'Salonica Front' rather than 'Macedonian Front.'[2]

However since the Allied Army was spread out along a three hundred kilometre front covering virtually the whole of Greek Macedonia's northern border, the wider term is more geographically consistent, and is the one used by later historians.

Salonica (sometimes with a 'k') was the name given to the town in the nineteenth and early twentieth century. The town had also been known, depending on the language of the speaker as Salonique, Salonicco, Selanik, and Solun.

In fact the correct name is the original one, the one given to the town on its foundation in 315 BC, Thessaloniki. Philip II of Macedonia had given this name to one of his daughters in honour of a victory (*niki*) over Thessaly which he had achieved at the time of her birth in about 342 BC.

The town was founded by Cassander, who had married Thessaloniki to advance his pretentions to the Macedonian crown which he subsequently achieved. Cassander also founded a number of towns in his own name but these have vanished from the pages of history. The one he founded in the name of his wife, however, has lasted and is now the second city of Greece.[3]

One of the first actions of Prince Constantine of Greece when he took the town from the Ottomans in 1912 was to restore the historical name of Thessaloniki to the town. In this account however I shall use 'Salonica', since this (or Salonique) is the name by which it was known to the hundreds of thousands of Allied soldiers who passed through it at the time.

Regrettably, naming complications don't finish here. When the Macedonian Campaign began Greece had been masters of Greek Macedonia for only two years. All the towns, villages, mountains and rivers still had the Turkish or Slavic names they had been known by during the long Ottoman occupation, and these were the names used on the maps of the time and throughout the Campaign. None of these is to be found on a present-day map, for as soon as the war was over a

---

1   The rather inappropriate name by which the Army was known throughout the Campaign, the 'Allied Army of the East' (*L'Armée Alliée de l'Orient*)-- was carried over from the force which the French had originally destined for Gallipoli and which was diverted to Macedonia in October 1915. The Allied Army of the Balkans would have been more appropriate.
2   There was some logic in this since the BSF's area of operation throughout the campaign was the immediate hinterland of the town of Salonica between the Vardar and Struma rivers and up to the Bulgarian–Serbian border.
3   Mark Mazower, *Salonica City of Ghosts* (London: Harper Perennial, 2005), pp.15–17.

local Greek government committee was set up to suppress all the old names and replace them with Greek ones.

Many of the place names in the present day Republic of North Macedonia, however, have remained unchanged.

Finally, since three members of the Allied Army of the East were not original members of the 'Entente' I have used the term 'Allies' in line with the general convention. On the other side I have used 'Central Powers' rather than 'Quadruple Alliance.'

Preface

In October 1915 three Allied divisions, one British and two French, disembarked at Salonica. Most of this small force had been withdrawn from the Gallipoli debacle, and its task in Macedonia was to advance up the Vardar River into Serbia where the Serbians were fighting a desperate rearguard action against the combined armies of Bulgaria, Austro-Hungary and Germany. The Allied force was too late; it never made contact with the Serbians, and by mid-November had to fight its way back to Greece harried by the victorious Bulgarians. But its intervention might have helped the Serbian army to avoid encirclement and destruction. Miraculously around 150,000 Serbian soldiers made their way in winter over the Albanian mountains to the Adriatic, from where in due course the majority were shipped around Greece to join the Allies in Salonica.

The 'Allied Army of the East', now expanded to fifteen divisions – five British, four French, and six Serbian – was put under the command of General Maurice Sarrail. By the end of 1916 with a further strengthening of the British and French presence, and contributions from Italy and Russia, the Army had grown to twenty divisions. Its objectives were to prevent the Central Powers from breaking into Greece, to bring Greece and its army into the Allied camp, and to prepare for actions and advances into Bulgaria and enemy-held Serbia from the south.

While the first two of these objectives were met following the forced abdication of King Constantine of Greece in June 1917, territorial gains in 1916 and 1917 were limited. The Serbians consolidated a strong position to the west of the Moglena mountain range, and with the French advanced into Serbia as far as Monastir. The new Greek formations won their spurs in a mountain assault to the east of the Moglena. The British fought successful actions in the Struma valley but suffered costly reverses against the virtually impregnable Bulgarian defences west of Lake Doiran on two occasions in 1917, and again in 1918.

In September 1918, with General Franchet d'Espèrey now in charge, French and Serbian forces finally punched their way through the Bulgarian lines in the centre of the Moglena mountains and supported by the rest of the Allied Army on their flanks, advanced at a phenomenal pace towards the upper Vardar and Skopje, splitting the enemy forces into two. Within 15 days the Bulgarians capitulated. This was followed shortly and inevitably by an armistice with Turkey. The First World War was won and lost on the Western Front, but the defeat of Bulgaria in September 1918 was a major factor, recognised also by the German High Command, in bringing it to a close before the end of the year. Up to this point the extension of the war into 1919 still seemed eminently possible; both sides were planning on this basis.

* * *

My grandfather Edward Bailey died in 1953 at the age of 75. I was ten at the time and remember very little about him except that he once gave me a football.

A photo of his unit in front of the pyramids on the upstairs landing of my grandparents' house, and a glass case with his war medals, showed that he had served in the First World War and spent time in the Mediterranean. I knew nothing else about his army career until, upon my mother's death in 2008, a diary which her father had kept of his war service was unexpectedly found among her papers.

It ran to nearly 200 pages of notebook and was headed:

> Notes kept of my journeys and visits to various places during my soldiering experiences in the War of Wars 1914–1918.

My mother had never mentioned her father's time in the 'War of Wars' at all, the next war following too quickly behind it, and she had never shown me her father's diary. Perhaps she didn't know she had it.

I found that my grandfather had enlisted with 4th Devon Territorials on 29 October 1914, one of nearly 900,000 men who volunteered for service in the war before the end of October.[1] He was a 37-year old shopkeeper with three children. He makes no comment about his decision to enlist, and restricts his feeling on leaving his home, shop and family to; 'Advertised business for sale, very sad to part with it, thought it was the best thing to do.'

As it turned out, his was to be an unusually varied war experience. After a year on the Home Front he trained as a signaller and volunteered for overseas service. On 3 January 1916, now with 22nd Battalion, the Rifle Brigade, he left Liverpool for the Mediterranean. During 1916 he served in Egypt, Cyprus, and on four separate Aegean islands as a signaller. In December 1916 he arrived in Salonica, where 22nd Battalion and three other ex-garrison battalions were combined to create 228th Brigade. He spent the rest of the war on the Macedonian Front. A more complete summary of his war service is given in Appendix III.

My grandfather was neither a writer nor a historian. His 'notes' cover the day-to-day activities and concerns of a private soldier, largely unaware of the wider picture.

But they have provided the framework from which, including visits to the scene of the action, I could begin to understand the history of the British Salonica Force to which my grandfather was attached, and then, slowly, the composition, purposes and actions of the whole Allied Army of the East, of which the BSF was a component. The book which has resulted aims to cover the whole Macedonian Campaign, and the respective parts played by the French, British, Serbs, Italians, Russians and Greeks, both in the field and at General Staffs and Government level.

Treatment of such a wide-ranging and complex subject has allowed little space for many eyewitness reports from the battlefront. Nor, in the account of military engagements, have I frequently gone down much further than brigade level. My objective has been to tell the story of the entire Macedonian Campaign, not to write a detailed military history.

In view of the central role he played in setting me off on this project, however, I have quoted from my grandfather's 'notes' from time to time and given 228th Brigade slightly more coverage than would be strictly necessary in an objective account of the campaign.

---

1   Between volunteers (2,675,149) and conscripts/attested (2,277,623) very nearly five million men enlisted for military service from August 1914 to the end of the war. (UK Parliamentary Papers 1921, General Annual Reports on the British Army). My grandfather had no idea of this of course in October 1914, but as a sporting man would have been pleased to been in the first 20%, and perhaps the first 5% of married men of his age with young families.

Part I

Macedonia
Background and the Balkan Wars

1

Macedonia: The First 2500 Years

(Map 1)

Historically the land of Macedonia ran from Skopje in the north to Mount Olympus in the south. Since the 1912-13 Balkan wars this area has been divided in the middle, and still is, with the southern half forming Greek Macedonia, and the northern half finally recognised, even by Greece, as the Republic of North Macedonia.

Between the two World Wars North Macedonia was part of the Kingdom of Yugoslavia. In 1946 following the abolition of the monarchy it became one of communist Yugoslavia's six constituent republics.

After the death of Tito and following the collapse of Yugoslavia, each of these six republics – Slovenia, Croatia, Bosnia-Herzegovina, Serbia, Montenegro and Macedonia – became an independent country.

For most of its long history however Macedonia has not been separated in this way. Until the end of the nineteenth century it was essentially ruled as a geographical entity.

A Macedonian state and kingdom was already in existence in the seventh century BC, with its capital at Aegae, today's Vergina. Following a period when it fell under the domination of the Persian Empire, Macedonia sought greater integration with the Greek states, being admitted to the Olympic games around 480 BC, and hosting Greek artists and philosophers.[1] At the end of the fifth century BC King Archelaus I moved the capital from Vergina to Pella, built strongholds and straight roads through his territory and reformed the army.[2] He also rebuilt the town and temple of Dion, dedicated to the god Zeus.[3] He died in 399 BC. The forty years of unrest which followed were ended with the accession of Philip II in 359.

If Philip had never had a son, he would still keep a place among the great men of the classical world. The army which he created, and which Alexander inherited and developed, was centred on a pike-armed infantry phalanx interacting with a highly trained and flexible cavalry arm.[4] Moreover, it was a professional standing army, unlike the conscript armies of his adversaries. The Macedonian phalanx was to remain invincible until the arrival of the Romans.

Philip campaigned successfully in Thrace, Illyria and as far away as the Dobrujah. In 338 BC he swept down from Macedonia and thrashed the Athenian and Theban armies at the battle of

---

1   Michael Grant, *The Classical Greeks* (London: Weidenfeld and Nicolson, 1989), p.235.
2   Thucydides, *History of the Peloponnesian War* translated by Rex Warner (Harmondsworth: Penguin Books Ltd, 1954), p.190.
3   There is very little of Pella left to see. Dion, on the other hand, remained more or less untouched by succeeding generations, has been fairly comprehensively excavated in recent years, and is a magnificent site to visit. Pella is only about 20 km east of Thessaloniki, while Dion is about 80 km south-east just below Mt Olympus, the seat of the gods.
4   Over 2250 years later General Franchet d'Espèrey was once again to use cavalry with devastating effect in Macedonia.

Chaeronea, his eighteen-year old son leading the cavalry. The subsequent Congress of Corinth confirmed his hegemony over the whole of classical Greece bar Sparta. By this time Philip was in control of an area extending from the Danube to southern Greece.[5]

Two years later, like the majority of his predecessors, he was assassinated and at the age of twenty Alexander became King of Macedonia. After re-establishing Macedonia's control over Greece in a lightning campaign involving the complete destruction of the city of Thebes, he turned his attention to Asia.

At Granicus near Troy in 334, and the following year at Issus with an army of 35,000 men he inflicted heavy defeats on Persian armies twice the size.[6] Besieging and conquering Tyre and Gaza on the way he then moved on to Egypt where he founded Alexandria, as Plutarch would have it 'the most lasting of all his achievements.' He returned in 331 to complete his conquest of the Persian Empire with a crushing victory over the forces of the hapless Darius at Guagamela on the upper Tigris.[7]

Alexander spent two years consolidating his hold on the Persian Empire, occupying Babylon, Susa and Persepolis and setting up structures of government. Then in 329 he set out to reach the 'Outer Ocean' which he and his former tutor Aristotle believed to be beyond the Hindu Kush. His army, now amounting to 120,000 men (including many from the conquered territories), crossed Afghanistan into India. Further battles and victories ensued, but his army would go no further, and following a final battle in Taxila in 326 returned via the Indus river. Alexander died of a fever in 323 in Babylon having maintained and built on his father's inheritance, and having conquered vast swathes of Asia, but with most of his plans and ambitions still unrealised.[8]

Confusion and bloodshed over the succession was inevitable. His generals in Susa collectively held the military power, but Antipater, Alexander's regent in Macedonia, held the power back at home.

Finally an agreement was reached whereby Alexander's generals divided up the conquered territory between them, while Antipater's son Cassander took Macedonia and Greece.[9]

Cassander's reign in Macedonia is counted from 316. He ruled with brutal efficiency, maintained control of Macedonia and Greece, and died in 296. The son of Antigonus, one of Alexander's generals, then seized control and adopted the title of King Demetrius I. With short interruptions the Antigonid dynasty was to provide most of Macedonia's kings until it was finally conquered by the Romans.[10]

Apart from the Samnites and the Carthaginians only the Macedonians made Republican Rome fight three wars before they were subdued. The first of these was provoked by the Macedonian alliance with Hannibal in 215. Hostilities were renewed in 200, and then again in 172 when the famous Macedonian phalanx was finally broken by the Roman legions at the Battle of Pydna in 168 BC.

The kingdom of Macedonia had lasted for over five hundred years. It had become master over most of continental Greece and acquired a mighty Empire in the east, and in one form or another

---

5   Robin Lane Fox, *The Classical World* (London: Allen Lane, 2005), pp.192–193.
6   Issus is close to the Mediterranean at the point where today's Turkey turns south into Syria. The remarkable mosaic discovered in Pompei and now in the Archaeological Museum of Naples of Alexander the Great in action against the Persians supposedly depicts the battle of Issus.
7   Peter Green, *A Concise History of Ancient Greece* (London: Thames and Hudson, 1974), p.170.
8   Lane Fox, *Classical World*, pp.230–235. An excellent map of the conquests of Alexander is given on pp.32–33.
9   Cassander's wife was Thessaloniki. See Note on Names and Places above.
10 J. Boardman, J. Griffin and O. Murray, *The Oxford History of the Classical World* (Oxford: OUP, 1968), p.319.

maintained control of both until finally dispossessed by the Romans. Military supremacy ensured its dominance over this period but was never an end in itself as with Sparta.

As with Rome later on, the Macedonians were impressed by the culture they discovered in the lands they conquered and were not backward in absorbing and imitating. Above all they adapted to the Greek language and took it into the lands which were eventually to form the Eastern or Greek half of the Roman Empire. Some idea of the sophistication of Macedonian art can be gained today from the rich grave-goods found in the Macedonian tombs at Vergina in the late 1970s.[11]

After their victory at Pydna the Romans left the Macedonians a fair amount of freedom to conduct their internal affairs. This degree of autonomy was removed after the Macedonians rose up once again in 149 BC and had to be put down with force. At this point Macedonia was formally annexed and become a Roman province.[12]

The Romans made Thessaloniki the capital of the Province of Macedonia. The inland town of Pella had served the Macedonian kingdom, but the port of Thessaloniki was for the Romans a far more logical place to develop as the centre of their affairs. It was expanded with a street layout conforming to the classical Roman grid system and fortified with walls which much later would withstand Ottoman assaults for many years.

From this point Macedonia, strategically placed between Italy and the Roman provinces in Asia Minor and beyond, became an intrinsic and indispensable part of the Roman Empire. One of the great Roman roads, the Via Egnatia, was started in 146 BC, and ran from Durres in Albania to Thessaloniki and in due course onward to Constantinople.[13] With the effective division of the Roman Empire into four parts by Diocletian in 286 AD, Thessaloniki became one of the imperial capitals, the seat of the tetrarch with responsibility for the Balkans and Illyria.[14]

In the middle part of the first century AD St Paul preached in Macedonia and subsequently kept up a correspondence with his converts in Philippi, Thessaly and Thessaloniki.[15] It could be argued that the Macedonians were therefore the first Europeans to receive the message of Christ.

On the fall of the Western Roman Empire in 476 AD, Macedonia remained part of the Eastern or Byzantine Empire, and for a period of two hundred years even provided the Byzantine Emperors. The most famous of these was Basil Bulgaroktonos, the Bulgar-slayer. He reigned from 976 to 1025 and extended the boundaries of the Empire into Mesopotamia, Georgia and Armenia, as well as wiping Bulgaria off the map. His final battle against the Bulgarians was at the base of the Belasitsa mountains in 1014.[16] Just over 900 years later, at the end of the Macedonian Campaign of which this book is the subject, a British–Greek force overran retreating Bulgarian forces in the same place.

Basil's exploits turned out to be the highpoint of the late Byzantine Empire. Constantinople remained a town of untold riches, but under increasingly incompetent and fragmented management. Then in the late thirteenth century, seemingly out of nowhere, came the Ottoman Turks. By

---

11 Four royal tombs were discovered in the 1970s within the Great Tumulus next to the remains of the former Macedonian capital of Vergina. Two had been partially despoiled, but two were discovered intact, with grave furniture and treasure as they had been left over two thousand years before. These may be visited today beneath the tumulus which has been turned into an underground museum with imagination and sensitivity. Of the numerous sites and monuments available to today's visitors to Greece, this is one of the most wonderful and least expected.
12 Michael Grant, *History of Rome* (London: Weidenfeld and Nicolson, 1996), pp.113–124.
13 The Via Egnatia is still the main west–east road running through Thessaloniki, and still bears the same name.
14 John Julius Norwich, *Byzantium, The Early Centuries* (London: Penguin Books, 1990), p.33.
15 The exact spots where the Saint preached are sacred territory. One such is in Veria, (or Berea as the New Testament has it; Acts 17,13) only ten miles west of Vergina as it happens, where a thoroughly tasteless modern altar has been set up to confound and dismay the pilgrim.
16 John Julius Norwich, *Byzantium, The Apogee* (London: Penguin Books, 1993), p.261.

1360 they had taken most of the Byzantine Empire, including Thrace and Macedonia. Following a four year siege the people of Thessaloniki could read the writing on the wall with increasing clarity and surrendered in April 1387.

The Ottoman Sultan Murad I treated his new subjects with leniency. The Turks established a garrison, but otherwise mainly allowed business to carry on as usual, in particular interfering little in the religious life of the city.[17]

Unfortunately for Thessaloniki the Ottomans were badly defeated by Tamburlaine the Great in 1402, and in the ensuing confusion the Byzantines regained possession of the city, which was then subjected to an intermittent siege during which half the population slipped away. Finally in 1430 the Ottoman Emperor Murad II offered an 'honourable surrender,' which was turned down by the Orthodox Archbishop under pressure from Venetian mercenaries. The sack when it came was complete and devastating, and most of the remaining population of the town was killed or enslaved. The Venetians got away.[18]

The Ottoman rule of Macedonia was to last for over 400 years. As it turned out this may have been the most peaceful period of its history. Apart from savage reprisals against the Greek population at the time of the Greek wars of independence in the 1820s, Macedonia suffered, from the conclusion of Murad's bloody siege in 1430 right up to the moment the Greek army entered Thessaloniki in 1912, little more than infrequent Venetian raids. There were occasional internal disturbances, usually caused by the Janissary Corps until this body was finally disbanded in 1826.

Until 1430 the language and culture of the Macedonian capital was Greek. During the long period of Ottoman dominance this changed. In order to repopulate the city which he had sacked, Murad resettled many Turks from Asia Minor. By the end of the century the population was rising to around 15,000, not much more than a third of its level at the start of the century, and Greeks only made up around half of this total.

In 1492 a development at the other extremity of Europe, in Spain, was dramatically to affect the ethnic mix of Thessaloniki; in line with other European nations, Spain banished its Jewish population, and the Ottoman Empire had no hesitation in taking them in. By 1530 the population of the city had expanded to 30,000, of which half were Jews, and only a quarter Greeks. And as a result of this massive Jewish settlement, and quite unlike the major towns of adjoining Ottoman provinces, Muslims never reached anything like a majority of the population of Thessaloniki.[19]

If the city was cosmopolitan, so was the Macedonian countryside, where waves of Slavic and Bulgarian invaders had already been settled for centuries and were now joined not only by Turks but also by refugees seeking the calm of the Ottoman Empire from troubled lands to the north and the east.

When Greece achieved its independence in 1832 Macedonia remained within the Ottoman Empire, so did Thessaly which did not revert to Greece until 1881. Therefore, by the early twentieth century Macedonia had never been part of Greece.

In the heyday of the Macedonian kingdom of Philip II and Alexander it had been master of Greece, but never politically united with it. During the period of the Roman Empire Macedonia was a province in its own right, administered separately from Greece, and during the long years of the Byzantine Empire this division remained. And when the Greeks finally took possession of (Greek) Macedonia following victory in the Balkan wars of 1912–1913, ethnic Greeks were in a minority within the territory.

---

17   John Julius Norwich, *Byzantium The Decline and Fall* (London: Penguin Books, 1995), pp.341–345.
18   Mazower, *City of Ghosts*, pp.26–30.
19   Mazower, *City of Ghosts*, pp.46–56.

2

The Balkans in the Nineteenth Century

(Map 1)

By the early sixteenth century all of the Balkans had been overrun by the forces of the Ottoman Empire, whose relentless progress towards the heart of Europe was checked only at the gates of Vienna in 1529.

The Ottoman ambitions, like those of the Romans before them, were mainly economic and territorial. They were generally tolerant on matters of religion. But during a presence of nearly four hundred years a degree of Islamisation was inevitable, the consequences of which are still being felt today.

The Ottoman hold on their European provinces did not go unchallenged. Between 1568 and 1878 conflict between Turkey and Russia was almost continuous, usually over control of the lands around the Black Sea.

By the mid nineteenth century it was clear that the Ottoman Empire was in decline. In 1853 the Russian Tsar Nicholas I was credited with coining the expression, much used since, 'the Sick Man of Europe'. The Ottomans were on the losing side in three of the Russo–Turkish wars of the nineteenth century, and after their crushing defeat in the last of these were faced with the humiliating terms of the Treaty of San Stefano in 1878. Under this Serbia, Montenegro and Romania were to gain their independence, and an autonomous Bulgarian state stretching from the Danube to the Aegean, taking in all of Thrace and nearly all of Macedonia was to be created.[1]

The Treaty of San Stefano which the Russians subsequently claimed was only a draft was initialled by the Ottomans and the Russians in March 1878. Almost immediately however British-led consternation at the emergence of a mega-Bulgaria clearly under the tutelage of Russia resulted in a meeting of the Great Powers at the Congress of Berlin in June.

The Treaty of Berlin, signed by Britain, France, Germany, Austria, Italy, Russia and the Sublime Porte (as the Ottoman Empire was then known in the councils of Europe) essentially left the provisions for the independence of Serbia, Montenegro and Romania unchanged. But it radically reduced the size of the San Stefano proposals for Bulgaria by withdrawing Thrace and North Macedonia, dividing the remainder into two federated entities, a Bulgarian north and a Roumelian south, and defining the whole as an autonomous state still theoretically under the suzerainty of the Sublime Porte. The 'San Stefano' Bulgaria had covered 176,000 square kilometres; the Congress of Berlin reduced it to 96,000.[2]

Macedonia, Thrace, Albania and, tellingly, the province of Kosovo remained within the Ottoman Empire. Agreement was reached that Thessaly would be ceded to Greece in 1881.

---

1   Sean McMeekin, *The Ottoman Endgame* (London: Allen Lane, 2015), p.3 and p.22.
2   Misha Glenny, *The Balkans 1804–1912* (London: Granta Publications, 1999), p.147.

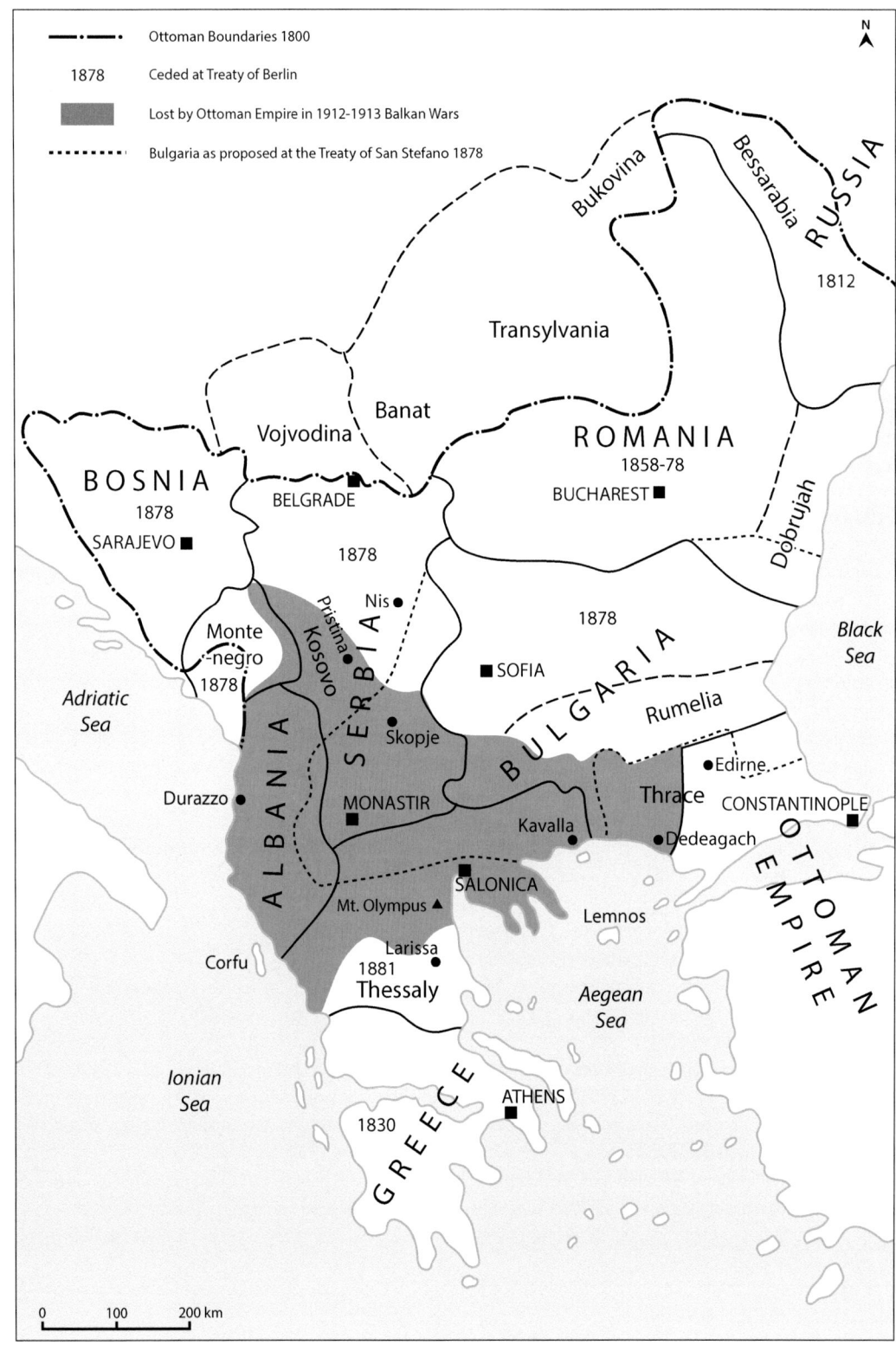

Map 1. The Balkans 1800-1913.

The 'larger' Bulgaria held up tantalisingly at San Stefano and then withdrawn was to remain the main Bulgarian political and military objective up to and beyond the 1912–1913 Balkan wars, and through two World Wars. Despite this today's Bulgaria is almost exactly the size determined at the Treaty of Berlin a hundred and fifty years ago.

The clause in the Treaty of Berlin with the longest and bloodiest consequences was the decision of the Great Powers to allow Austria to occupy and administer Bosnia-Herzegovina, although notionally under the suzerainty of the Ottoman Empire.

Britain, whose territorial ambitions were not European, but who would not have wished to return empty-handed, picked up the suzerainty of Cyprus from the disintegrating Ottoman Empire.

The Russians took the opportunity (they had fought for it) to take over much of the east coast of the Black Sea, including Batum which was to become a free port.

Finally the Great Powers, then as now could not resist inserting a Human Rights clause into the final document. The Turks were asked under Article LVII to promise that religious liberties would be respected throughout their (remaining) domains, a rather gratuitous and insensitive request given that the Ottoman record on this issue over the past six hundred years was far cleaner than that of their interlocutors.

The geographical expression of Serbia which emerged from these talks was far less than its people might have hoped. Macedonia remained in Ottoman hands. The province of Vojvodina which had been wrested back by the Austrians from the Ottomans in 1690 remained part of the Austro-Hungarian Empire. This meant that the Serbian capital Belgrade, situated in the extreme north of the country on the southern banks of the Danube, was in easy artillery range of the Austrians on the other side, a vulnerability which was to prove acute later on.

Also, more symbolically, the new Serbia had not been given Kosovo, which remained for the time being under Ottoman control. The defeat of the Serbian army under Prince Lazar by the Ottomans under Sultan Murad I (both died in the conflict) at the Field of the Blackbirds in Kosovo on 15 June 1389 had remained indelibly fixed in the collective Serbian memory for five hundred years. For them this was core Serbian territory and then – as now – they considered it theirs.

Three years after the Treaty of Berlin both Serbia and Romania proclaimed themselves kingdoms, as did Montenegro in 1910. In 1908 Bulgaria threw off the last vestiges of Ottoman suzerainty and declared full independence. In the same year to the dismay of Russia and Serbia, Austria annexed Bosnia-Herzegovina and incorporated it fully into the Austro-Hungarian Empire.[3]

An inevitable result of the 1878 Turco–Russian war and the determinations of the Treaty of Berlin was the growth of nationalism. During the hundreds of years of Ottoman rule the citizens of the Empire had tended to define themselves by religion and language rather than by national provenance, but this was now to change.

In 1893 a grouping called the Internal Macedonian Revolutionary Organisation (IMRO) emerged, aimed at securing a 'Macedonia for the Macedonians'. But who were the 'Macedonians?' Ottoman Macedonia defined as the provinces of Salonica, Monastir and Uskub (Skopje) had been a melting pot for different ethnic groupings for many centuries. IMRO was fundamentally Bulgarian, anti-Greek and anti-Turk, and engaged in terrorist attacks and substantial guerrilla operations against the Ottomans.[4]

The Greek response to IMRO ran on more traditional religious lines. In 1870 the Ottomans, trying to satisfy those of their Christian citizens who preferred the Slavonic liturgy to the Greek liturgy had authorised the establishment of an Exarchate to meet this mainly Bulgarian requirement. As an autonomous and alternative branch of the Orthodox church, this represented a major

---

3   A.J.P. Taylor, *The Struggle for Mastery in Europe 1848–1918* (Oxford: OUP, 1954), p.276 and p.451.
4   McMeekin, *Ottoman Endgame*, pp.44–45.

setback for the Greek Patriarchate which had held monopoly control over all forms of Orthodox worship since the days of Byzantium.[5]

By the end of the nineteenth century the Exarchate had almost as many adherents as the Patriarchate in Macedonia, and the Greeks, egged on by representatives of the Greek nation (Ottoman Macedonia had had a Greek consul as early as 1835), were fighting an openly vicious rearguard action.

A more critical parallel development was what came to be known as the Young Turk revolution.

On his succession in 1876 Sultan Abdul Hamid II, under pressure from the western powers, had announced a programme of political reform and issued a constitution. Two years later he reneged on all this and suspended the constitution. The aim of the Young Turks, initially a secret society of disaffected civilians and army officers, was the re-instatement of the constitution and the modernisation of the political and administrative structures of the Ottoman Empire. In the early 1890s they set up a Committee of Union and Progress (CUP).

The movement, based principally in Ottoman Macedonia, gathered strength. In July 1908 Abdul Hamid was obliged to restore the constitution, and the CUP leader Major Ismail Enver was rapturously received in Salonica. The Young Turk Revolution however exposed divisions in Ottoman society and ruling circles, and there was a conservative backlash. During a period of political confusion during which Abdul Hamid was deposed and replaced by his brother, Bulgaria took the opportunity in 1908 to declare its full independence, with its Prince discarding his nominal suzerainty and adopting the title of Tsar Ferdinand.[6] In the same year Austro-Hungary took the opportunity (with Russian connivance) to annexe Bosnia-Herzegovina, the act which perhaps more than any other was to provoke the crisis of 1914.

The Balkan Wars of 1912-13 however were to radically change the political landscape, and the CUP's programme and ideals were overtaken by events. Ottomanism moved inexorably towards Turkish nationalism, to entry into the First World War on the side of the Central Powers, to ultimate defeat and the eventual emergence of Kemal Ataturk, hero of Gallipoli and father of modern Turkey.

---

5   In fact, the Slavonic liturgy had an impeccable Macedonian ancestry. Saints Cyril and Methodius who created the Cyrillic alphabet which in its modern form is still in use today in much of Eastern Europe, who translated the Greek liturgy into Slavic, and who were personally responsible for bringing the Christian message to much of the Balkans and central Europe in the ninth century, were born in Thessaloniki, long before the Ottomans had entered the stage.
6   Eugene Rogan, *The Fall of the Ottomans* (London: Penguin House, 2015), pp.1–9.

3

The Balkan Wars 1912-13

(Map 1)

The dismembering of the Ottoman Empire in Europe had begun in the 1820s with the liberation of Greece. Incessant Russian pressures over the following fifty years, interrupted only for a short period by the Crimean war, led to the comprehensive victory of the Russians over the Turks in 1878 and the establishment of four new independent or quasi-independent states in the Balkans at the Treaty of Berlin.

Over the next thirty years Serbia, Montenegro and Bulgaria consolidated their national identities and began to look south and west at the remaining swathe of Ottoman territory in Europe. Greece, meanwhile, encouraged by her recent acquisition of Thessaly, began to look further north. In 1912 Italy defeated Ottoman forces in North Africa and captured Libya. The time seemed ripe for military actions in the Balkans.

In late 1912 an alliance was formed between Serbia, Montenegro, Bulgaria and Greece, an unlikely group of bedfellows brought together by common interests. Within two months the allies had overrun all of Macedonia and most of European Turkey and shared out the spoils.

Significantly, Greek forces led by Prince Constantine had taken Salonica, arriving just a few hours before the Bulgarians. A peace conference was convened in December in London without any positive result. The allies then returned to the field and completed their work at the one end by taking an extra part of eastern Thrace including the city of Edirne, and at the other end by taking Epirus and the city of Ioanina.

The London conference reconvened and recognised the status quo on the ground with the exception of Albania which had been taken by Serbia but upon which the Great Powers had elected to confer a separate national identity.

Frustrated by her loss of Albania, Serbia plotted with Greece for a larger slice of Macedonia at the expense of Bulgaria. Dissatisfied herself with the territorial outcome of the war, Bulgaria re-opened operations in June 1913 against Greek and Serbian positions in Macedonia. This new conflict, known separately as the Second Balkan War, saw Greece, Serbia, Romania, and subsequently Montenegro and Turkey herself in alliance against Bulgaria.

Bulgaria lost, was obliged to cede part of Dobrujah to Romania, accept a less satisfactory share of Macedonia with Greece and Serbia, and suffer the loss of eastern Thrace and Edirne which the Ottomans had won back during this second conflict. Although well outside the battle zone, Turkey ceded Crete to Greece at the same time.

In territorial terms Turkey in 1913 retained from its European Empire only eastern Thrace and the city of Edirne, one of the four imperial capitals. Bulgaria gained part of Macedonia and western Thrace with access to the Aegean through the inferior port of Dedeagach (Alexandroupolis today), having had to return Kavalla to Greece. .

Greece gained Epirus and southern Macedonia within frontiers which are almost identical to those of today. Montenegro's territory was expanded slightly to the east. Serbia, no doubt to her enormous satisfaction, regained Kosovo after 526 years, and almost all of the territory which is now the Republic of North Macedonia. Albania, also essentially within today's frontiers, was born as an independent country. A treaty in Bucharest gave international recognition to the results of the Balkan wars in August 1913.[1] The pieces were now in place for the greater conflict shortly to begin.

---

1 A.J.P. Taylor, *Struggle for Mastery*, pp.483–498. David Fromkin, *Europe's Last Summer* (London: Vintage, 2004), pp.84–86.

4

The Third Balkan War

(Map 2)

By 12 August 1914 the five major powers of Europe were at war. Germany had long foreseen the problem of fighting on two fronts. The Schlieffen plan, considerably modified by Moltke, envisaged the crushing of France within six weeks by means of a massive pincer movement through the low countries and around Paris, and then rushing most of the victorious troops on Germany's excellent rail network to the Eastern front. Russia in the meantime, supposedly slow to mobilise, would be held by limited forces strengthened by the Austro-Hungarian allies.[1] To succeed it was obvious that this plan would have to be implemented at lightning speed, and within weeks of the outbreak of war the forces of the Entente were facing those of the Central Powers on two already well-established fronts in France and Eastern Europe.

Far from these centres of conflict, and unconnected with their purposes, the Austro-Hungarian army was simultaneously waging war on Serbia.

Austro-Hungary had been given the go-ahead to 'occupy' Bosnia-Herzegovina and 'administer it on behalf of the Sultan' in 1878 by the Great Powers at the Congress of Berlin. But in October 1908 Austro-Hungary formally annexed the territory and made it a constituent part of their Empire. This was naked imperialism without even the 1938 Sudetenland or 2014 Crimean pretence of ethnic absorption; the largest element in the racial mix of Bosnia was Serb, and just as with the Bosnian crisis at the end of the twentieth century, the Bosnian Serbs wanted incorporation into Serbia. Serbia, now doubled in size after the Second Balkan war, was outraged, and following the annexation of Bosnia by Austro-Hungary a nationalist paramilitary organisation called *Narodna Odbrana* sprang up to champion the Serbian cause in Bosnia.

In September 1908 however Russia, Serbia's main sponsor, had made a secret agreement with Austro-Hungary not to oppose the annexation of Bosnia if the Austrians supported Russian designs on the Straits.[2] As a result Russia persuaded a very unwilling Serbia to accept the situation, which she did in the form of a formal note to the Austrian Government in March 1909.

In 1911 a more extremist grouping was formed. This was *Ujedinjenje ili Smrt*, 'Union or Death' but subsequently known as the 'Black Hand', a secret society whose members were mainly ultra-nationalist Serbian army officers. The most influential of these was Colonel Dragutin Dimitrijević, who went under the code name of 'Apis'.[3] Apis was no stranger to extreme political dissent, having taken part in the assassination of the unpopular King Alexander of Serbia and his wife in 1903, and the replacement of the Obrenović dynasty (for the second time) with the Karadjordjević dynasty.[4]

---

1   Ian F.W. Beckett, *The Great War* (New York: Routledge, 2013), pp.61–65.
2   A.J.P. Taylor, *Struggle for Mastery*, pp.449–451.
3   Apis survived the Serbian defeat at the hands of the Austro-German armies in 1915 and re-appeared as a troublemaker in the reconstituted Serbian army on the Macedonian Front.
4   Glenny, *Balkans*, p.188.

Map 2. Serbia 1914-1915.

The aim of the Black Hand, which over three years infiltrated the ranks of Narodna Odbrana, was the direct rule by Serbia of all the lands in which Serbs lived.[5]

Unconnected with the Black Hand was a looser movement in Bosnia itself, *Mlada Bosna*, Young Bosnia. This had no formal membership but was motivated by on-the-ground hatred of Austrian rule and the economic plight of the Bosnians. The key adherents to *Mlada Bosna*, Gavrilo Princip and his associates, although mostly Bosnian Serbs, were seeking the unification of all south Slav races, and not the Serbian hegemony sought by the Black Hand.[6]

In the late nineteenth and early twentieth century assassination was the favoured form of political protest; between 1894 and 1913 no less than twenty monarchs or heads of state lost their lives in this way.[7] Unsurprisingly, despite the difference in their end objectives, both the Black Hand and *Mlada Bosna* saw assassination as the best way of achieving them. In this, Apis had form.

Until they learnt that Archduke Franz Ferdinand would be coming to Sarajevo in June, Princip and his group had settled on General Oskar Potiorek, the Austrian Governor of Bosnia as their target. There was logic in this; the murder of Potiorek would certainly have de-stabilised Hapsburg rule in Bosnia.[8] It was also unlikely to have unleashed a world war.

In early 1914 Princip and his two main partners, Cabrinović and Grabez, were in Belgrade. They had a mission but lacked the means to fulfil it. Then a man called Milan Ciganović, sympathetic to their cause, secured a supply of grenades and revolvers from Major Voja Tankosić, a senior member of the Black Hand. The conspirators were given basic training in the use of the weapons. Then, using a route borrowed by the Black Hand from *Narodna Odbrana* they were smuggled back into Bosnia with their arms. They arrived in Sarajevo in the first week of June, where the assassination team was expanded to seven. Others were involved in the preparations, the concealment and distribution of the weapons – the Austrian authorities finally rounded up twenty five suspects, mostly Bosnian Serbs, but also four Bosnian Croats and one Bosnian Muslim.[9]

The Archduke, heir to the Austro-Hungarian Empire following the suicide of his cousin Rudolf in 1899, arrived with his wife in Sarajevo on 25 June 1914. They spent two days on various engagements including military inspections and a war game. Their visit was planned to finish on 28 June following an official reception. It was their wedding anniversary. The Archduke and his wife were taken in an open car through Sarajevo accompanied by General Potiorek. As they drove into town Cabrinović threw a bomb at the Archduke's car, which exploded further down the convoy, injuring one of the Archduke's attendant officers.

Following the reception Franz Ferdinand decided to go to visit his officer in the hospital. This non-programmed event caused the driver to take a wrong turning, and then to have to reverse in order to get back en route. As bad luck would have it Princip was right on the spot, and with the car virtually stationary shot the Archduke at point blank range.[10] A second shot aimed at Potiorek was deflected, hitting and killing the Archduke's wife. Princip attempted to kill himself, first with his pistol, then with cyanide, but was unsuccessful.[11]

The Archduke, who was 51 at the time of his death, was not well-loved by his uncle the Emperor, partly for his radical ideas on restructuring the Empire, and, ironically, giving its Slavic components

---

5   Fromkin, *Last Summer*, pp.123–124.
6   Tim Butcher, *The Trigger* (London: Vintage, 2015), p.188.
7   Fromkin, *Last Summer*, p.221.
8   Butcher, *Trigger*, p.275.
9   Butcher, *Trigger*, 251–257, 268–269.
10 Fromkin, *Last Summer*, p.116 and pp.132–136.
11 The death sentence in the Austro-Hungarian Empire could not be given to offenders under the age of twenty. Princip, just short of this, was condemned to twenty years' imprisonment. He died in prison of tuberculosis four years later, long enough to appreciate the international carnage which his act had unleashed.

a stronger voice within it, although he had stepped back somewhat from this before his fateful visit to Sarajevo.[12]

On his death the succession passed to his nephew Karl who became Emperor in 1916 when Franz-Joseph finally died after an extraordinary 68 years on the throne. Karl, who during his brief tenure made unsuccessful attempts to negotiate a separate peace with the Entente, was deposed at the end of the war, the last of the Habsburgs.

The activities of secret societies, particularly those run by ranking military officers, were unlikely to remain very secret in Serbia; before Princip and his companions departed on their mission the Serbian Prime Minister Pašić got wind of it and gave instructions that they were to be stopped on the border. These instructions were not carried out. He may also have sent a circuitous message to the Austrians to warn them of the potential danger.[13]

Like Churchill later on, Bismarck was given to sententious remarks and pithy sayings which have since appeared in anthologies of aphorisms. None of them could have been more prescient than one attributed to him at the Congress of Berlin in 1878:

> Europe is a powder keg and its leaders are like men smoking in an arsenal. A single spark will set off an explosion which will consume us all. I cannot tell you when that explosion will occur, but I can tell you where. Some damned foolish thing in the Balkans will set it off. (*wird er durch irgendeinen Unsinn auf dem Balkan aufgeloest werden*).

Following the assassination of the Archduke the Austrians drew a long breath, made a number of consultations including the one which secured the 'blank cheque' from Germany and then, on 23 July 1914, in the unstated but evident belief that the Serbian Government had condoned the assassination plot, presented Serbia with a ten point ultimatum. A reply was requested within forty-eight hours.[14] At this point the rest of Europe held its breath.

Points 1-4 of the ultimatum dealt with Austrian demands for the Serbian government to suppress anti-Austrian propaganda and publications, to dissolve terrorist organisations, not to teach terrorism in schools, and to sack any public figures involved in anti-Austrian activities or declarations.

Points 7-10 asked the Serbs to arrest two named persons, to prevent arms from crossing the border, to furnish explanations for anti-Austrian declarations by 'high Serbian officials', and to tell the Austro-Hungarians when all these steps had been taken.

The harshest demands were contained in points 5 and 6; firstly to 'accept the collaboration in Serbia of representatives of the Austro-Hungarian government for the suppression of subversive activities directed against the territorial integrity of the Austro-Hungarian monarchy' and secondly 'to take judicial proceedings against accessories to the plot of 28 June with delegates of Austro-Hungary taking part in the investigation'.

Sir Edward Grey, used perhaps to a milder sort of diplomatic language found this to be an unusually severe set of demands for one sovereign state to make of another, particularly given that

---

12 Rebecca West, *Black Lamb and Grey Falcon* (London: Macmillan, 1941), pp.332–344. Miss West's long and minutely detailed account of the life and character of the Archduke presents a dark and damning picture of a man with almost no redeeming features. Many people in Austro-Hungary must have been mightily relieved when he was unexpectedly disposed of. She also describes (pp.372–73) reprisals taken by the Croat and Muslim populations of Sarajevo – and other Bosnian towns where they were in a majority – against the local Serbs over the days following the assassination while the authorities stood back. A foretaste of the ethnic violence never far beneath the surface in Bosnia.
13 Fromkin, *Last Summer*, pp.126–127.
14 A.J.P. Taylor, *Struggle for Mastery*, pp.522–523.

the assassin was, in fact, Bosnian. Winston Churchill wrote to his wife that the ultimatum was 'the most insolent document of its kind ever devised.'

It is difficult to imagine a more conciliatory or cooperative reply than that which the Serbs made, within the required time-frame, to these demands.

Those made in points 1-4 were accepted immediately. With regard to points 7-10 Serbia agreed to take the action requested if Austria provided them with the details, that they would do all in their power to stop the passage of arms across the border, and that they would notify Austro-Hungary of all actions taken in line with the ten demands.

With regard to Points 5 and 6 Serbia replied that it would accept any collaboration consistent with the principles of international law and good neighbourliness. Finally, that if Austro-Hungary had any further issues, Serbia would be happy for them to refer these to the Permanent Court of Justice at the Hague, or to the Great Powers.[15]

Kaiser William when he received a copy of Serbia's reply said he thought it was totally reasonable, writing in the margin; 'A great moral victory for Vienna, but with it every cause for war is removed. The few reservations which Serbia makes in regard to individual points can in my opinion be cleared up by negotiations.' He was in favour, he told Jagow, his foreign minister, of Austria 'temporarily occupying Belgrade as a pledge'.[16] He may well have expected this message to be passed on, but it was not.

The Austrians however, armed with the blank cheque, had already decided that, whatever the reply, they were going to teach the Serbs a lesson and declared war on them on 28 July, three days after receiving the Serbian reply. The Serbs, no doubt expecting this outcome, had already initiated mobilisation on 26 July and a few days later evacuated the Royal Court, the Government and the Treasury to Niš. Bismarck's prescient prediction had come true. But as Chairman of the Congress which had agreed to the 'occupation and administration' of Bosnia by the Austro-Hungarian Empire, he himself bears a lot of responsibility for setting up the 'damned foolish thing' in the first place.

The Third Balkan war opened on 12 August 1914.[17] Of the six Austro-Hungarian armies, two, the Fifth and Sixth were allocated to the Serbian Front together with part of the Second Army which was later to be allocated to the Russian Front. Commanding the war with Serbia was General Potiorek, he who had been accompanying the Archduke in his car on that fateful morning in Sarajevo. His plan was to invade Serbia from Bosnia with the Fifth and Sixth armies, while the Second army which was strung along the northern banks of the Sava and Danube would make massive artillery demonstrations against Belgrade, Sabac and other Serbian positions south of the river. The Fifth Army was drawn up between Bijeljina and Ljubovija, and the Sixth Army south of Vlasenica along the Drina. The plan was for the Fifth Army to take Valjevo by 18 August, and for the Sixth Army then to march on Niš via Užice along the west Morava river.[18]

The Serbian forces were also divided into three principal armies. The First, to the south east of Belgrade, from Smederevska Palanka to Topoli, the Second to the south of Belgrade in the Lazarevac area, and the Third to its left positioned from the mouth of the Kolubara to the Bosnian border. A smaller fourth army was based on Užice to the south. Further troops were held in North Macedonia should Bulgaria enter the war on the side of the Austrians (eminently possible given their

---

15   Fromkin, *Last Summer*, pp.307–16, gives the complete text in translation of the Austro-Hungarian Ultimatum and the Serbian reply.
16   Martin Gilbert, *The First World War* (London, Weidenfeld and Nicolson, 1994), p.24.
17   Map 2 shows the movements of Serbian and opposing armies in the much greater conflict of 1915, but the small area in north-western Serbia where the Third Balkan War took place can also be identified on this map.
18   Dusan Babac, *The Serbian Army in the Great War* (Solihull: Helion and Company, 2016), p.30.

very recent defeat in the Second Balkan war at the hands of the Serbian-led coalition). Nominally the Serbian supreme commander was Prince Regent Alexander, but the actual commander was Voivode Putnik, a veteran of the First and Second Balkan wars of the two previous years.

In terms of operational manpower the two sides were fairly equally balanced. The Serbs had the support of the Montenegrin army,[19] which however had its own objectives on the coast of southern Bosnia and the bay of Kotor. The Austrians were better equipped with transport and artillery, and of course had far greater reserves. At the start of the war the population of the Austro-Hungarian Empire was twelve times that of Serbia.

Marshal Putnik had expected the main Austrian thrust from the north, across the Sava and Danube. In fact, it came across the Drina, another major river which runs south-north into the Sava and forms the frontier between Bosnia and Serbia for much of its length.

The Austrians had opened their campaign on 29 July with the bombardment of Belgrade. The following night the railway bridge between Belgrade and Semlin on the other side of the Sava was blown up by Serbian forces under the orders of none other than Major Tankosić who had provided Princip and his companions with weapons. Austria had demanded his arrest as part of their Ultimatum, but that was before they declared war. The Austrian bombardment continued for two weeks. It was supported by guns from heavy armed monitor ships patrolling the rivers. No serious attempt however was made to build pontoon bridges across the river and invade Belgrade, many of whose inhabitants had fled.[20]

On 12 August the Fifth and Sixth Austrian armies crossed the Drina on a sixty mile front and advanced twenty kilometres into Serbian territory. Having quickly reacted to the unexpected direction of attack, Putnik's Second and Third armies turned westwards and established a defensive line from Sabac to Krupanje. A vicious battle ensued on 15–19 August for control of the Cer mountain, in the centre of this line, but finally the Austrians were routed and forced to retreat back across the Drina. Unobserved perhaps from the capitals of Europe, the battle of Cer represented the first Allied victory against the Central Powers following the opening of hostilities.[21]

On 6 September the Serbian First army crossed the Sava at Srem and established a brief bridgehead on Austrian territory but withdrew to support the Second and Third armies as Potiorek made another attack across the Drina, this time establishing strong positions to the east of the river albeit with heavy losses. Bitter fighting ensued throughout September, the casualties mounted, particularly on the Austrian side. The Serbian armies regained some strategic positions from the Austrians, however, lacked the strength to force them over the Drina again.

In the meantime the smaller 'Užice' army had linked up with the Montenegrins and was advancing on Sarajevo, only to be repulsed by the end of October following the diversion of Austrian forces.

Despite the approach of winter Potiorek consolidated his forces, his communications and his supply lines, and launched a new attack on the Serbian First and Third armies on 5 November. By 14 November all three Serbian armies were forced back to Valjevo and then to the Kolubara river, where a fierce battle was fought and won by the Austrians. The Serbs withdrew even further east, counting on help from the weather and the lengthening Austrian supply lines, but getting ever closer to their own key rail link to Niš, the temporary capital, and their main ammunition centre of Kragujevac.

To the north the Austrians entered Belgrade on 3 December. Potiorek's aim was now to encircle the Serbian forces with his Fifth Army moving south from Belgrade, while his Sixth Army was to force the Serbian left northwards.

---

19 Babac, *Serbian Army*, p.40.
20 Glenny, *Balkans*, pp.312–313.
21 Glenny, *Balkans*, p.315.

But with their backs to the wall, the Serbs now counter-attacked, forced their way through the Austrian centre, and re-crossed the Kolubara on 9 December. In danger of having his own forces split by the Serbian advance, Potiorek ordered a retreat. On 15 December the Serbs re-entered Belgrade, and on the same day the Austrians withdrew their last soldiers from Serbian territory.[22]

Generals Mišić and Stepanović, subsequently to play key roles in the Macedonian Campaign, were both promoted to the rank of Voivode. Potiorek unsurprisingly was relieved of his command.

The campaign had been particularly savage and the losses on both sides were enormous. Of the 450,000 troops used by the Austrians during the campaign, just over half were killed, wounded or reported missing, while Serbian casualties amounted to 170,000.[23] Given the disparate sizes of populations and available manpower however, Serbia's losses were more significant, and her weakened army took many months to recover. But she had repelled the aggressors, and against all odds and expectations emerged the undisputed winner of this Third Balkan war.

---

22 Babac, *Serbian Army*, pp.45–69.
23 Cyril Falls, *Official History of the Great War, Macedonia. Vol. 1, From the Outbreak of War to the Spring of 1917* (London: HMSO, 1933, Reprint by Naval and Military Press, 2013), pp.20–21.

Part II

The Macedonian Campaign 1915–1918

5

1914-15
Alliances and Misalliances

On 18 March 1913 King George I of Greece was assassinated in Salonica by a man called Alexandros Schinas. George had been the second of Greece's kings. At the end of the Greek war of independence in 1832, the three 'Tutelary Powers', Britain, France and Russia had decided at the Convention of London that Greece should become a constitutional monarchy, and that the king should be Otto, second son of King Ludwig of Bavaria. Otto reigned for thirty years before being deposed by the Greek National Assembly. In a referendum on who should replace him, the Greeks gave a 95 percent preference to Alfred, the second son of Queen Victoria. However the Convention of London had prohibited the monarchy to any member of a royal house of one of the Great Powers. Finally the choice fell on Prince William of Denmark who took the title of George 1 at the tender age of 17 in 1863.

He was only a few weeks away from his Golden Jubilee when he was assassinated. He had been a popular king, and during his reign the territory of his kingdom had doubled, first with the addition of Thessaly (from the Ottoman Empire) and the Ionian Islands (a gift from Great Britain), and then, following the victories in the Balkan wars, Epirus, Greek Macedonia, Crete and the islands of the North Aegean. Short of eastern Thrace and the Dodecanese Islands, the geography of Greece at the death of George I was more or less as it is today.

When the king visited Salonica in 1913, it had only been part of Greece for a year. Unfortunately the mingle-with-the-people approach he had long favoured in Athens proved lethal in the still unstable and multi-ethnic environment of Macedonia.

He died before the outbreak of the War, but his sympathies were pro-Entente – Edward VII had been his brother-in-law. However his son and successor, King Constantine, had a closer rapport with Germany; his military training had been in Germany, and he was married to the Kaiser's sister. When war broke out in 1914 he decided to stay neutral and await developments. The assassination of King George turned out to be a major setback to the Allied cause in the Balkans. Had he remained head of state during the war, and had Greece swung behind the Allies in 1914, the Campaign on the Macedonian Front would have taken a very different shape.

Eleutherios Venizelos, Greece's towering political presence in the pre-war and war years had been Prime Minister since 1910. His sympathies were firmly with the Allied Powers. When war broke out however the main political ambitions of both King and Prime Minister were, although from different directions, very similar; the acquisition by Greece of European Turkey including Constantinople, and of the western seaboard of Asia Minor.

* * *

By mid-August 1914 seven European countries were at war, on the one side Germany and Austro-Hungary, and on the other side Britain, France, Russia, Serbia, and as a result of her invasion by Germany, Belgium. In both camps the race was now on to secure the active participation of Europe's so-far uncommitted nations.

Following their collaboration in the Second Balkan War, Greece and Serbia had signed on 1 June 1913 a Treaty of Alliance and Military Convention in case of attack by a third power. Bulgaria was specifically cited, but the agreement was not limited to Bulgaria. In case of such hostilities Greece committed to provide an army of 90,000 men, and Serbia an army of 150,000. These were initial troop sizes, to be provided respectively in Greek and Serbian Macedonia; they were to be supplemented by 'the rest of their military forces' as soon as they became available. Greece would also mobilise her fleet in the common interest.[1]

Despite the existence of this Treaty, of which he must have been aware, Kaiser Wilhelm sent a message to King Constantine via the Greek Minister in Berlin on 4 August 1914 asking him to ally himself to the Central Powers in a 'united crusade against Slav domination in the Balkans.' Despite being an Honorary Field Marshal in the German army he not only turned down his brother-in-law's request but a fortnight later, in rare agreement with Venizelos, offered the services of his army and navy to the Allies for action against Turkey.[2] A crusade against Slavdom was not his main priority. A campaign against the Ottoman Empire to achieve his territorial ambitions in continental Turkey and Asia Minor could very well be, and he may have agreed with Venizelos that his chances of this were greater at that time with the Allies than with the Central Powers.

For although Turkey was at that point unaligned, both Constantine and Venizelos could see which way the wind was blowing more clearly than the Allies. This offer of 19 August was followed by another on 9 September. Both were made on the condition of Bulgaria entering the war on the Allied side, or at least declaring her neutrality.[3]

Objectively Constantine and Venizelos may have been right in their calculations. But the Russians, who regarded Constantinople and the Straits as theirs in any post-war share-out of the spoils, leaned on the British Foreign Secretary Grey to refuse the Greek offer. At that stage Grey's preferences, based on whatever historical contacts and personal feelings he and the Foreign Office may have entertained, were for alliances with Turkey and Bulgaria. Events were soon to prove that with regard to Turkey the Germans had got in first.

Russia was to block another almost identical offer from Greece on 1 March 1915, and for the same reason. In August 1914, the Allies were not at war with Turkey, but in March 1915 they very definitely were. Churchill was furious with Grey, writing to him 'No impediment must be placed in the way of Greek cooperation. If Russia prevents Greece from helping, I will do my utmost to prevent her from having Constantinople.'[4]

With regard to Bulgaria, possible territorial offers made by the Allies were more than trumped by the Central Powers who could virtually promise the fabled frontiers of the Treaty of San Stefano, the 'greater Bulgaria' stretching from the Danube to the Aegean to Albania, taking in all of Thrace and most of Macedonia, promised to Bulgaria in March 1878 and then taken away at the treaty of Berlin later that year.

Italy, at this stage theoretically an ally of the Central Powers through the Triple Alliance of 1882, had yet to declare her hand. Prime Minister Salandra however had made it very clear in his 'sacred egoism' speech of 16 October 1914 that the defining factor in Italy's decision was to be self-interest rather than treaty obligations. The aim of his foreign policy, he declaimed, was to remove from the equation *ogni sentimento che non sia quello della illimitata e esclusiva devozione alla patria*

---

1   Commandant M. Larcher, *La Grande Guerre dans les Balkans* (Paris: Payot, 1929), Annexe 2, p.263. Serbo–Greek Treaty of 1 June 1913.
2   Alan Palmer, *The Gardeners of Salonika* (NY: Simon and Schuster, 1965). Reissued edition (London: Faber and Faber, 2009), p.20.
3   Larcher, *Grande Guerre*, p.28, quoting from Churchill, *The World Crisis Book 1* (London: Thornton Butterworth, 1923).
4   John Laffin, *The Agony of Gallipoli* (Oxford: Osprey 1980), p.27.

nostra, dal sacro egoism per l'Italia (any consideration other than the exclusive and unlimited devotion to our native land, a sacred egoism for Italy).[5]

On 23 May 1915, having decided that her sacred interests lay in territorial aggrandisement in the Trentino, South Tyrol, Triestino and Istria, parts of the Dalmatian Coast, and ports in the Adriatic, and having negotiated with the Allies in this sense at the (secret) Treaty of London in April 1915, Italy declared against the Central Powers, and threw 35 divisions into the Allied equation.[6]

Italy's interests however did not coincide with those of Serbia, whose ambitions were in due course to unify all the south Slav peoples, including those of Istria and Dalmatia. Representations by the Serbian Government were made to the French Government and on 2 July a note of protest was passed to the British Government.[7] Italy's relationships with Serbia and in due course also with Greece were to remain uneasy throughout the war as their interests in the Adriatic often overlapped.

Nevertheless Italy in due course was to participate fully in the Macedonian Campaign with its 35th Division an integral part of the Allied Army of the East from 11 August 1916 until the end of the war. The presence of the Italian XVI Corps in Albania also discouraged any attempted incursions by the Austro-Hungarians into northern Greece, or much further down the Adriatic coastline than Durazzo.

German involvement in Turkey went back many years. From 1885 a German Military Mission had been reorganizing their army along German lines and providing up to date weapons, and already, ominously, had been strengthening shore defences on the Dardanelles. In 1889 the Kaiser had made a state visit to Constantinople, and another in 1898 when he announced 'May the Sultan (Abdul Hamid) and his 300 million Muslim subjects scattered around the earth who venerate him as their Caliph, be assured that the German Kaiser will be their friend for all time.'

The Germans were building and mainly financing the Bagdad railway, and the Heraz to Medina railway. The deposition of Abdul Hamid in 1909 scarcely caused this process of rapprochement to miss a beat. From 1910 the Germans were again flexing their diplomatic, military and financial muscle in Constantinople, and when the 'Young Turks' came to power in 1913, their efforts intensified.[8]

They provided a government loan after Britain had refused it. They trained Turkish officers at their military academies, Britain and France did not. Their powerful diplomatic presence was augmented in 1913 with a strong military mission in the form of General Liman von Sanders and his staff. The new thirty-two year-old Turkish Minister of Defence Enver Pasha gave his German advisors more or less free rein in reorganising his armed forces, and in July 1914 asked for a secret military alliance with Germany.[9] The massive German investment in Turkish affairs began to pay off immediately the war started.

Since 1912 the German battle cruiser *Goeben,* one of the most powerful ships afloat, had been cruising in the Mediterranean as part of the German Mediterranean fleet under Admiral Souchon. On 3 August 1914, the day Germany declared war on France, Souchon was ordered by Grand Admiral von Tirpitz to steam for Constantinople. Avoiding all attempts at intervention by the British and French fleets, *Goeben* and her sister ship the light cruiser *Breslau* arrived at the mouth of the Dardanelles on 10 August. The German military mission had already primed Enver to let them pass through to the Sea of Marmara, despite an old (1871) Treaty between the Great Powers

---

5   Antonio Salandra, *I Discorsi della Guerra* (Roma Tipografia del Senato,1915).
6   Mark Thompson, *The White War* (London: Faber and Faber, 2008), p.64.
7   Babac, *Serbian Army*, p.81.
8   McMeekin, *Ottoman Endgame*, pp.24–32.
9   Laffin, *Gallipoli*, pp.4–6.

which forbade any foreign warship access through the Straits while Turkey was at peace. This was, if not exactly a declaration of war (which Churchill maintained), a very strong declaration of intent.

The immediate outcome was that the Admiralty refused to hand over two dreadnought battleships ordered by Turkey (and already paid for), when the Turks came to collect them in August.[10] Since it was believed that these two ships were to be used to take back the islands of Lemnos, Imbros and Lesbos lost to Greece in 1912, this move may have forestalled future problems, but it effectively closed the door on the Allies ever supplanting the Germans in winning Turkey to their side.[11]

In order retrospectively to justify the contravention of the 1871 Treaty, the Germans made a fictitious sale of the two ships to the Ottoman navy – but the crews remained German, and Souchon remained in charge. For two months the Germans strengthened their grip on military and State affairs in Constantinople. By end September in conflict with all treaty rights the Turks and their German advisors were preventing any shipping from using the Dardanelles. This was the moment if any for the British and French fleets to force the Straits and join up with the Russian Black Sea fleet in the Sea of Marmara. At that time the Dardanelles defences were incomplete and piecemeal, and the only two Turkish munition factories at the time were on the Bosphorus.[12] Then on 28 October 1914 the *Goeben* and *Breslau* sailed into the Black sea and bombed Odessa, Sebastopol, and other Russian ports. This was stage-managed aggression of the most overt kind. On 2 November Russia declared war on Turkey. Britain and France followed 3 days later.

The Central Powers' position in the Balkans and the Black Sea was considerably strengthened by having Turkey on their side as long as they could secure and then maintain supply lines with their new ally. The importance of the supply lines was two-way, firstly to provide munitions and materiel to the Turks, and secondly to relieve some of the effects of the British naval blockade.[13] By mid-November a British force was ashore at Basra and marching on Baghdad. In the Mediterranean however action was limited to a token and pointless bombardment of the outer forts of the Dardanelles on 3 November, which led to an immediate strengthening of the forts and gun emplacements in the Straits, and the laying of mines directed by a force of four German officers and 160 soldiers and experts.[14]

* * *

By mid-1915 therefore, the intense competition between the two sides to draw the uncommitted nations into their camps had resulted in the two biggest fruit, Turkey and Italy, having been picked from the tree. Three strategically positioned Balkan nations, Bulgaria, Romania and Greece however remained dangling. Allied assumptions up to this time had been that all three of these smaller fruit would fall onto their side of the fence. However, in order for the Central Powers to secure overland communications with their Turkish ally, they needed to control, through conquest or alliance, either the routes through Serbia and Bulgaria, or those through Romania. But Romania, with her historic ambitions to incorporate Transylvania, part of the Habsburg domains since 1699, was scarcely worth courting by the Central Powers, and indeed preserved her neutrality until she declared for the Allies in August 1916. For the Central Powers an alliance with Bulgaria after having crushed Serbia was a much more promising route to follow, and so it proved.

---

10   Glenny, *Balkans*, p.319.
11   Laffin, *Gallipoli*, p.7.
12   Laffin, *Gallipoli*, p.10.
13   Alexander Watson, *Ring of Steel* (London: Penguin Random House, 2014), p.207 passim.
14   Gilbert, *First World War*, p.105

6

1915
From the Dardanelles to Salonica

As the war in France hardened by the end of 1914 into stalemate with horrendous casualties, plans for the opening of new fronts in the Mediterranean began to emerge. At first all such plans were immediately undermined by the refusal of the Generals on the Western Front, particularly Joffre, to release manpower for peripheral enterprises.

Over Christmas 1914, Colonel Hankey, Secretary to the Committee of Imperial Defence, drafted a paper proposing ways to 'break the remarkable deadlock which has occurred in the Western Theatre of war.' He suggested making common cause with Bulgaria and Greece against Turkey. Success at the Dardanelles he said 'Would give us the Danube, and a line of communication for an army penetrating into the heart of Austria.' Alternatively there was 'the possibility of some cooperation with Serbia against Austria.'[1]

Coincidentally on the same day Lloyd George, at that time Chancellor of the Exchequer, was submitting a weighty document to the War Council. His plan was to mount a general offensive against Austria through Salonica together with Serbia, Greece and Romania. That his plan was given far less attention than it deserved by the War Office was because he was presenting it as a replacement for, not as an adjunct to, the main war on the Western Front. The Balkans would thus become the main theatre of war for the British, the French and the Belgians being 'easily' able to hold their own against Germany after the withdrawal of the Austrians to defend their Balkan frontiers. This, combined with a concurrent attack on the Ottoman Empire through Syria would serve to 'knock away the props' under Germany.[2]

This was several steps too far for the Army Chiefs of Staff, who put it around that Lloyd George had 'discovered the Balkans on an atlas', a charge which the French picked up with amusement.[3] This was unjust since Lloyd George was far more widely travelled in Europe (though not in the Balkans) than many of his cabinet colleagues. Foreign Secretary Grey only went abroad once or twice during his 11 year tenure, and then only to France on business.

The idea of belated action against Turkey however was given extra impetus by a plea on 2 January 1915 from the beleaguered Russian Commander in Chief Grand Duke Nicholas for 'a demonstration of some sort against Turkey' to relieve pressure on his armies. The widest ranging proposal came from First Sea Lord Fisher who proposed on 3 January attacks on the Turks using British and Indian troops with Greek and Bulgarian support, and attacks on Austria together with the Russians and Serbs.[4]

---

1   Palmer, *Gardeners*, p.23 quoting Hankey, *The Supreme Command* (London: Allen and Unwin, 1961), Chapter 23.
2   William Robertson, *Soldiers and Statesmen* (London: Cassell, 1926), pp.83–85.
3   Larcher, *Grande Guerre*, p.45.
4   Laffin, *Gallipoli*, p.21.

On 5 January at a War Council meeting Lord Kitchener, Secretary of State for War, said that 'The Dardanelles seemed to be the most suitable objective as an attack here could be made in cooperation with the fleet.' A successful campaign here would 're-establish communications with Russia, draw in Greece, and perhaps Bulgaria and Romania, and release wheat and shipping now tied up in the Black Sea.'[5]

All this led to the critical meeting of the War Council of 13 January 1915 at which Churchill, First Lord of the Admiralty, presented a plan he had received from Admiral Carden, British naval commander in the Mediterranean. Carden, while admitting that it would not be easy to overcome Ottoman defences, sketched out a four-stage programme for forcing the Dardanelles with naval force alone. Unsurprisingly the War Council approved the plan, and Churchill was authorised to 'prepare for a naval expedition in February to bombard and take the Gallipoli peninsula, with Constantinople as its objective'.[6]

The potential benefits of the plan were unquestionable. The presence of a massive Anglo-French fleet before Constantinople, the Dardanelles forts having been destroyed by naval guns, would, the War Council reasoned, lead to the surrender of Turkish forces in Europe and the neutralisation of Turkish forces in the Middle East. It would encourage Greece, Bulgaria and Romania to enter the war and strengthen the Allied cause with a further one and a half million troops. It would give the Allies complete control of the Black Sea, and permanently cut communications between the Central Powers and Turkey. Churchill had little difficulty in bringing the French Navy Minister Augagneur on side. And President Poincaré, having been warned by his friend the *académicien* Pierre Loti of the dangers posed by mines and onshore batteries, simply replied that the British Navy would look after all that.[7]

The Salonica alternative was therefore very much put on the back-burner at this point, both by the British and the French, despite the fact that the French had also examined the possibility of invading Austro-Hungary and southern Europe through Serbia from a base in Salonica.

On 1 January 1915 the French General Gallieni, Commander of the French Second Army, proposed to Prime Minister Viviani that the Allies should attack Constantinople from Salonica and then press up the Danube towards Austro-Hungary with the support of the Balkan nations.[8]

The most complete French proposal however was that of General Franchet d'Espèrey, who as Commander of the French Fifth Army had been one of the major architects of the Allied victory at the First Battle of the Marne in September 1914. Franchet d'Espèrey had visited the Balkans before the war and when approached by his Chief of Staff Colonel de Lardemelle with a suggestion that the Central Powers could be attacked through the Balkans, saw the sense of the concept, and on 4 October mentioned it to President Poincaré. The President asked for a full proposal, which was then prepared by de Lardemelle, with corrections and additions from his General, and submitted to the French Government in November.

Franchet d'Espèrey's plan was interesting in a number of ways. Only French forces would be used, to ensure unity of command and also because 'French troops were at that time the best for a war of movement'. The force would consist of 5 Corps, or about 185,000 men. They would be transported to Serbia via Salonica and other Aegean ports and use both the Vardar valley and the Monastir road to advance north. (This was just after the Serbs had defeated the Austro-Hungarians in the Third Balkan War. From the Greek frontier to Belgrade the rail-link to Belgrade was still totally under Serbian control). The plan presupposed the military participation of Serbia and also of Romania (still neutral at that time), with the support 'if possible' of Bulgaria and Greece – at least

---

5 Gilbert, *First World War*, p.124.
6 Rogan, *Fall of the Ottomans*, p.132.
7 Max Schiavon, *Le Front d'Orient* (Paris:Tallandier, 2014), p.44.
8 Babac, *Serbian Army*, p.70.

as far as freedom of communications was concerned. The offensive would be made by the French and Romanians against Hungary from the south and south east, while the Serbs protected their northern and western frontiers. Although this was to be a French initiative 'the agreement of the Allies would be required', and 'naval support from the British could not be avoided'.[9]

Lloyd George's proposal was to be rejected, amongst other reasons, because the British War Office said it would take six months to set up. Franchet d'Espèrey's plan on the other hand projected being ready to go onto the offensive on this new Hungarian Front within two months, and anyway by spring 1915. The speed with which the French Army of the East was subsequently to get into Serbia in November 1915 suggests that two months from embarkation in France to arrival on the Danube via Salonica could well have been possible given full control of the Serbian and Greek roads and railways.

But by the time Franchet d'Espèrey's plan was submitted the First Battle of the Marne was distant history and the war had taken new and negative directions. Joffre could not contemplate releasing a single division, let alone five Corps, from the struggle on the Western Front, and the proposal for a new front in the Balkans was mothballed.

One of the greater ironies of the First World War is that in 1918, after three years of confrontation on the Macedonian Front, and a vast commitment in terms of men and materials, General Franchet d'Espèrey himself was appointed commander of the 'Allied Armies of the East', made a major breakthrough into occupied Serbia across the Moglena mountains, liberated Belgrade, and could well have pushed on across the Danube into central Europe if he had been given the go-ahead.

The reasons for the failure of the Dardanelles Campaign have been thoroughly examined by historians over the past hundred years – timing, planning, execution, underestimation of enemy preparations and commitment, misconceived landing sites, uncoordinated and incompetent management and leadership. Overlying and contributing to all of these causal factors was the extraordinary geography of the area.

Rome had been built on seven small hills surrounded by flat countryside with a narrow and scarcely navigable river connecting it to the sea. Its position as *Caput Mundi* was a historical accident, and after his arrival in Rome in 313 Constantine the Great determined to move the capital of the Empire to a more suitable position.[10] Protected on one side by the Bosphorus and on the other by the Dardanelles with the site itself on a promontory surrounded on three sides by water it is difficult to imagine that he could have found a more strategically placed position for his new city. History proved him right. While Rome fell in 476, Constantinople held out for almost another 1000 years.

At one point opposite Chanak (today's Canakkale) the straits between the Asian and European shores narrow to 1.6 km – a mile. Leander, Lord Byron and countless others have swum across.[11] In March 1915 the massive Allied fleet never even reached the Narrows, the mines in the water covered by guns onshore forcing it to retreat with three battleships sunk and three more crippled. In due course, as Kitchener had foreseen, troops had to be put ashore. Joffre was against the use of French troops, but the French were unwilling to allow their allies carte-blanche in the Levant and finally contributed almost a third of all Allied forces committed to the campaign. The first landings were on 25 April 1915. Before the final withdrawal at the end of the year almost half a million Allied soldiers had been employed, with casualties of over 250,000, of which 90,000 evacuated for sickness.[12]

---

9   Larcher, *Grande Guerre*, pp.40–44 and Annexe 3 p.268 Extract of General Franchet d'Espèrey's Project of end 1914.
10   Norwich, *The Early Centuries* pp.326–328.
11   George, Lord Byron, *Don Juan* (London: Thomas Davidson, 1819), Canto II Stanza 105.
12   Laffin, *Gallipoli*, p.222.

The tragedy of Gallipoli forms no direct part of a book about the Macedonian Campaign, except that one of the main consequences of this, one of the most unsuccessful major military campaigns in the history of the British Empire, was that it not only delayed but also discouraged Allied deployment in other Mediterranean theatres.

The student of the Macedonian Campaign cannot help but speculate how the outcome of the war might have changed had even half the troops committed to the Dardanelles been sent instead to Salonica in April 1915. At this stage Serbia was still intact, as was the railway from the Aegean to Belgrade. With the prospect of a major Allied thrust from the south into the Austro-Hungarian heartlands, the Italians may have joined in sooner and further fragmented the Habsburg forces. Greek equivocation may have ended two years earlier. Above all, with a strong Allied presence in Serbia and Macedonia, Bulgaria would have thought long and hard before joining the Central Powers.

From the opening of hostilities in 1914 the Allies had realised the importance of Bulgaria in any future Balkan calculations. Besides disposing of an army of over half a million men, many battle-hardened after the recent Balkan Wars, Bulgaria occupied a position of inestimable strategic importance, lying as she did between Serbia and the Black Sea, and with the capacity of threatening – or supporting – the neutral powers of Romania to her north and Greece to her south.[13] Squaring the Bulgarian circle however – satisfying her territorial demands without discountenancing Serbia and Greece – was proving beyond the art of the possible upon which diplomacy is supposedly based. Nevertheless, from as early as August and September 1914 efforts were made.

By the end of 1914 the Allies were asking of Bulgaria no more than guaranteed neutrality against Serbia, Greece and Romania in exchange for territorial concessions which could not be honoured until the end of the war, and which anyway were not accepted. On 2 February Bulgaria secured a large loan from Germany. Contacts with the Allies continued in 1915 with the aim of securing Bulgarian support against Turkey as the Dardanelles Campaign gathered pace. On 8 May Bulgaria stated her conditions which included (as might have been expected) much of Serbian Macedonia and Greek Thrace including the port of Kavalla. This was more or less a return to the 'greater Bulgaria' of the Treaty of San Stefano. It would not have escaped the memories of the Bulgarians that it was above all the British who had refused to sanction San Stefano at the 1878 Congress of Berlin. Obviously this could never be achieved without the agreement of Greece and Serbia, which certainly would not be given.

Indeed it had long been obvious to Serbia and Greece, Bulgaria's traditional enemies who had recently humiliated her in the Second Balkan War, that Bulgaria would inevitably side with the Central Powers, but the Allies refused to listen. Greece's Foreign Minister from 1913, Coromilos, spoke for both countries, and Romania:

> We know beyond a shadow of doubt that Bulgaria is pledged up to the hilt to the Central powers. She has obtained from them a loan of 250 million francs in gold, she has come to terms with Turkey, who the Allies expect her to attack, in exchange for a cession of territory. She is preparing night and day for war. We send despatch after despatch to London, Paris and St Petersburg. The Romanian and Serbian governments do the same, but nothing we can say has the slightest effect. The Allies inform us that Bulgaria is the most loyal, honest, and upright country in the world … we know that the contrary is the case, but MM Sazonoff, Delcassé and Grey turn a deaf ear to all we say. It can only end in disaster.

---

13   Richard C. Hall, *Balkan Breakthrough* (Indiana: Indiana University Press, 2019), p.41. Quoting Bulgarian sources Hall gives Bulgarian Army strength in September 1915 as just over 530,000.

Venizelos was equally dumbfounded by the Allied position:

> We are completely at a loss to understand the aberration of the Allies. They drag on negotiations with our worst enemy when even a child could see that they are being fooled by the wily Bulgarian premier, who is acting under orders from Berlin and Vienna.[14]

Coromilos and Venizelos may or may not have known – they probably did – that the terms of the German loan had already virtually reduced Bulgaria to the status of a German protectorate with control over arms procurement, railways and coal-mines.[15]

Nevertheless the Allied governments continued with their negotiations, offering watered-down versions of the Bulgarian demand, which would not meet her requirements, and would certainly not be accepted by Bulgaria's neighbours. But Bulgaria was already in substantive military discussions with the Central Powers.[16]

While these protracted negotiations were taking place, the risk of their failure and the consequent vulnerability of Serbia to a three-pronged attack from Austro-Hungary, Germany and Bulgaria were not lost sight of. Lloyd George had not given up on his project and in February 1915, even before the Dardanelles decision, it was agreed that Britain and France would both send a division to Salonica, followed by a brigade from Russia, conditional on Greek participation.[17] Once again however Venizelos could not persuade the king to honour the Treaty of Military Support with Serbia, and on 6 March was forced to resign.

The potential Salonica expedition was dropped for the time being, as attention was turned to the Dardanelles Campaign. It was not to be revived until September.

Just as the assault on Constantinople through the Dardanelles could well have succeeded had it been made three months earlier, so the proposals of Franchet d'Espérey and Lloyd George might well have worked had the Salonica initiative been launched in February.

The decision finally to send troops to Salonica was taken for two reasons. Firstly, as had been considered inevitable by the Greeks and the Serbs, if not by the Allies, months previously, Bulgaria mobilised on 23 September, and in accordance with a timetable pre-agreed with the Central Powers declared war on Serbia on 13 October.[18] Britain and France declared war on Bulgaria on 15 and 16 October respectively.

Serbia was now totally exposed and, prompted by Venizelos, the Allies were finally forced to accept that they would have to send troops to help her. A contributory reason, at least for the nature and timing of the intervention in Serbia, was that Joffre was under political pressure to find a new job for General Maurice Sarrail.

Sarrail, destined to play a dominant role in the story of the Macedonian Campaign until the end of 1917, was something of an outlier on the French military spectrum. Born in 1856, he graduated brilliantly from St Cyr in 1877 and then spent six years with the army in North Africa before returning to France in 1883 for two years at the *Ecole Supérieure de Guerre*. His army career then followed a standard pattern, although, unlike most future French First World War generals, it did not include any active campaigning in the colonial wars of the period.

---

14 Gordon Gordon-Smith, *From Serbia to Jugoslavia* (New York and London: G.P. Putnam's, 2020), pp.17–18.
15 Glenny, *Balkans*, p.338.
16 Larcher, *Grande Guerre*, p.63.
17 Palmer, *Gardeners*, p.27.
18 Randal Gray with Christopher Argyle, *Chronicle of the First World War* (Oxford: Facts on File, 1990), Vol. 1, p.151.

From the outset, however, his political leanings were at odds with those of the typical French army officer, and his radical socialism brought him to the attention of the leaders of left wing parties in Government or on the fringe of Government at the time. From 1901 to 1904 as Commandant of the *Ecole Militaire Infanterie* at Saint-Maixent he had the opportunity to share his convictions with men from the ranks aspiring to officer status. From 1907, backed by his political sponsors, and in particular Joseph Caillaux, he became Director of Infantry at the War Office. Caillaux, head of the *Parti Radical*, became Prime Minister from 1911 to 1912, and arranged in 1911 for his protégé to be promoted to general, and given the command of 12th Infantry Division, leap-frogging the role of brigade commander. Of his exact contemporaries, Franchet d'Espèrey only became General a year later, while Petain and Nivelle started the War as Colonels.

In April 1914 he was given the Command of the 8th Army Corps, and as a result of his performance in the First Battle of the Marne in August 1914 was promoted to the head of the Third Army Group. This was his high water mark in active soldiering on the Western Front. On 22 July 1915 Joffre was obliged to relieve him of his post after a commission of enquiry headed by his boss, General Dubail, head of Army Group East, found that the bloody setbacks incurred by the Third Army in the first part of 1915 were directly the result of Sarrail's poor management, tactical errors, and defective planning.[19] Sarrail had a different interpretation, writing after the war *dans le haut commandement tous les généraux qui n'étaient pas anti-républicains furent peu à peu presque complètement éliminés*' (in the high command all generals who were not anti-republican were little by little completely removed).[20]

But Sarrail was so well connected politically that he was allowed to argue the case against his dismissal with two Cabinet Ministers and with Prime Minister Viviani himself. These persuaded Joffre to find a suitable role for him, and, perhaps wanting to get him out of France, Joffre offered him a command in the Dardanelles theatre.[21] This was a remarkable reversal of roles; had war not broken out, Sarrail would have replaced Joffre as Chief of Staff in August 1914.[22]

Previously in May 1915 the same de Lardemelle (now a Brigadier General) who had worked with Franchet d'Espèrey on his Salonica project had come up with another scheme; to land a sizeable (French) force on the Asian shore of the Dardanelles and advance on Constantinople from that direction. The French, particularly the generals on the spot, thought that the idea had possibilities, and on 8 August Sarrail was offered the post of Commander of this force.

His political clout was still such that he was able to insist firstly that he should be Commander of an Army, not a Corps, and secondly that the command would be independent, and not subordinate to the British Commander General Hamilton, conditions which he lays out clearly in the first two pages of his memoirs.[23] The Army of the East (*l'Armée de l'Orient*), shortly to become the Allied Army of the East (*l'Armée Alliée de l'Orient*) therefore has its origins in these rather inelegant manoeuvrings.

Gritting his teeth, Joffre had offered Sarrail four divisions for this enterprise. Sarrail asked for eight, with staffs and services.[24]

As late as 11 September 1915 the Allied leaders at a conference in Calais had seemed prepared to go ahead with this plan of 4–8 divisions under General Sarrail, landing on the Asian side of the Dardanelles and operating separately from the other Allied forces.

---

19   Palmer, *Gardeners*, p.30.
20   Maurice Sarrail, *Mon Commandement en Orient* (Paris: Flammarion, 1920) edition with annotations by Rémy Porte (Soteca, 2012), p.29
21   Schiavon, *Front d'Orient*, p.99.
22   Gilbert, *First World War*, p.158.
23   Sarrail/Porte, *Mon Commandement*, p.31
24   Schiavon, *Front d'Orient*, p.126.

News of the Bulgarian mobilisation on 23 September overrode all of this, even though, until the last minute, the Allies tried to swallow the line put out by the Bulgarian Government that the mobilisation was designed solely to protect the neutrality of the country. The mind-set behind this blank refusal to face the facts is well summed up by Slavko Grujić of the Serbian Foreign Ministry:

> The great mistake of the Entente powers was to consider that there could only be two alternatives; either that Bulgaria would side with the Entente, or that she would continue to remain neutral. The third alternative, which is what actually happened, and the certainty of which we the Serbians, knowing well our neighbour and her designs, were constantly pointing out, was considered unbelievable.[25]

Apart from all other diplomatic or territorial considerations, the Allies failed utterly to understand the depth of Bulgaria's hatred for Serbia following the humiliations of the Second Balkan War. 'The purpose of my life' said Tsar Ferdinand of Bulgaria just before the invasion of Serbia in October 'is the destruction of Serbia.'[26]

The plan to send Sarrail with a newly created Army of the East to the Dardanelles was dropped. With regard to the 4–8 divisions, Joffre breathed a sigh of relief; for the moment most of them remained where they were. Sarrail was redirected to Salonica, and for the moment his Army of the East consisted of one division withdrawn from the Dardanelles, the French 156th Division under General Bailloud, to be followed shortly by two further French divisions. The British 10th Division under General Mahon, also to be sent from the Dardanelles to Salonica, did not come under his control.

On news of the Bulgarian mobilisation Venizelos, newly returned to power in August 1915 with a big majority, yet again pressed the king to honour the Serbo–Greek Treaty. Venizelos is reported to have told his king that as he was the representative of a sovereign people, the decision rested with him, to which the king replied 'As long as it is a question of internal affairs I must bow to the people's will, but in foreign affairs I must decide … for I feel responsible to God.'[27] He then put forward the argument that since Serbia could not provide 150,000 men to fight Bulgaria – because she also had to face the German and Austro-Hungarian armies – Greece was exonerated from her commitments. King Constantine's point was not totally invalid; the Serbo–Greek Treaty was essentially a Balkan affair, centred on a mutual defense of their Macedonian territories; Greek support to Serbia in protecting her northern borders against major-power forces was not really envisaged.[28]

Nevertheless at this same meeting of 23 September between Venizelos and Constantine the decision was taken to mobilise the 180,000 strong Greek Army.[29] The king however remained adamant that this was to ensure the security of national frontiers, not to support Serbia. Venizelos, whose reading of the pact with Serbia was wider than that of his King, had already called in the Ministers of Britain, France and Russia the previous day to explain his difficulties and to ask the Allies to provide the 150,000 men instead.[30]

---

25 Slavko Grujić, forward to Gordon-Smith, p.xii. It was to Grujić who as Secretary General in the Serbian Foreign Office that the Austrian ultimatum of July 1914 had been physically delivered.
26 Glenny, *Balkans*, p.333 quoting Stephen Constant, *Foxy Ferdinand, Tsar of Bulgaria* (London: Olympic,1979), p.290.
27 Palmer, *Gardeners*, p.34.
28 Larcher, *Grande Guerre*, Annexe 2, p.263–268
29 Falls, *Macedonia Vol. 1*, p.38.
30 The figure of 150,000 remains puzzling. According to the Serbo-Greek military convention of June 1913, Greece was supposed to contribute 90,000 men and Serbia 150,000. If Venizelos was trying

Belatedly at a conference in Calais on 5 October 1915 between the British and French Ministers of War and of the Marine agreement was reached to meet this commitment of 150,000 men, France with two more divisions (57th and 122nd) and Britain with four more divisions (22nd, 26th, 27th and 28th).[31] This would bring the British commitment to 85,000 men, the French to 65,000. (The two new French divisions arrived in time to take part together with the two ex-Dardanelles divisions already on the ground in the Allied advance into Serbia. The four new British divisions who started arriving in Salonica on 11 November did not, with the exception of a few days' intervention by a brigade of 22nd Division).

But on the same day, 5 October, caught between the king, whose General Staff had told him that military intervention would be 'political suicide' and an ill-considered speech by Foreign Secretary Grey in the Commons of 28 September in which he again spoke of 'warm feelings' towards Bulgaria, Venizelos again resigned.[32] He was not to return to power as prime Minister of Greece until after the abdication of Constantine in June 1917, but remained active in opposition in Athens until leaving to form a breakaway Government in Salonica in September 1916.

The stated objective of the Allied Army of the East was to support the Serbs. But even at this point, even before an Allied boot had been placed on the quay at Salonica, divergences were apparent in the view of the Allies on the purpose of the mission, British objectives being more angled towards Turkey and the Middle East, and those of the French more directed towards central Europe and linking up with the Russians. The British also – particularly the War Office – continued to think, throughout the campaign, that theirs was only a holding operation until the Greeks finally came in.

---

    to persuade the Allies to take up the Greek shortfall, the number should have been 90,000, at least initially.
31 Larcher, *Grande Guerre*, p.40.
32 Falls, *Macedonia Vol. I*, p.40.

7

1915
The Defeat of Serbia

(Map 2)

In her war with Austro-Hungary in 1914 Serbia had lost 170,000 of 450,000 combatants. During the first half of 1915 a typhus epidemic which had been imported by Austrian troops at Valjevo during the 1914 campaign claimed many more. Despite Red Cross aid from Britain, France and Russia, and the intervention of the Scottish Women's Ambulance and several other volunteer medical organisations, some of which remained with the Serbian Army throughout the war, 35,000 soldiers and countless civilians died, before it was brought under control.[1]

Between July 1914 and October 1915, 40 percent of the Serbian male population was mobilised into the army. The effects of warfare, fever, and lack of manpower had resulted in a critical lack of food for men and animals. Russia, Serbia's closest ally and main sponsor provided what assistance she could up the Danube to Prahovo.[2]

The Allies may or may not have realised that in early 1915 through the depredations of war and sickness the Serbian army was down to half the size it had been in July 1914, was desperately under-equipped with everything from guns to bridge-making materials and was dependent on imported food from Russia. Nevertheless, the Allies continued to pressurise Serbia into attacking 'lightly defended' Croatia in order to draw Austrian forces from other fronts. The Allies made this request three times, the last in the form of a letter from the Tsar, and Serbia refused to move. Part of the reason was certainly lack of manpower and guns. But in part the reason was the – not entirely misplaced – Serbian neurosis that while they were away the Allies would come to some agreement with Bulgaria involving Macedonia.[3]

Luigi Villari, Italy's liaison officer with the other Allied forces throughout the Campaign whose viewpoint on this issue was not entirely unbiased, points out that when the Italians finally entered the war the Austrians were able to withdraw 5 of their 6 divisions on the Sava to face the Italian attack on the Isonzo.[4]

Allied advice to the Serbs on the construction of defensive lines while they were not engaged militarily in the first part of 1915 was more apposite but went unheeded. This could have made some difference, or gained some time, when the blow finally fell. After their triumphs of the previous year, they may have overestimated their position. But by the time they invaded again in October 1915 the Austrians had been through twelve months of battle-hardening experience, were quite

---

1 Gordon-Smith, *From Serbia*, p.12–13.
2 Babac, *Serbian Army*, p.70.
3 Falls, *Macedonia Vol. 1*, p.22.
4 Luigi Villari, *The Macedonian Campaign* (London: Fisher Unwin, 1922. Reprinted by Forgotten Books 2015), p.17.

a different proposition from Potiorek's untried army, and were of course supported by a German army of equal size.

During the spring and summer the Allies continued to seek an accommodation with Bulgaria even after the loan from Germany on 2 June. On 2 August however the British Foreign Office was informed by their Minister in Sofia that a secret military mission had left for Berlin to agree the terms of a convention with the Central Powers.[5] The convention, detailing the parts each would play in the invasion of Serbia was signed by Austro-Hungary, Germany and Bulgaria on 6 August. Bulgarian mobilisation began on 23 September. As already noted, for the benefit of the British Foreign Office they called it 'Armed Neutrality.'

And as already seen, even at this point the Allies continued to prevaricate and seek an agreement with Bulgaria. But the boat had already sailed, and neither Austro-Hungary nor Germany would have let it return to port at this stage. The Austro-Hungarians, besides needing to secure their southern flank, had an enormous account to settle with Serbia. Von Falkenhayn set out the German case for invading Serbia with enormous clarity:

> If we succeed in eliminating Serbia as a serious factor in this war … and of this we have no doubt … the threat to the Austro-Hungarian flank and with it the whole of the South Slav danger would disappear. The establishment of communications with Turkey would ensure the safety of the Dardanelles and the final isolation of Russia from her Entente partners. It also gives prospects of new possibilities for Turkish operations in Asia. The adhesion of Bulgaria to the Central Powers and the successes soon to be obtained in Serbia as a result cannot fail to have an effect on the attitude of Romania. Sources of supply for foodstuffs and the importation of raw materials like copper would be rendered available.[6]

The logic is impeccable. One might only ask why it took the Central Powers a whole year after the reverse of late 1914 before attacking Serbia again. Probably the reasons are to be found not on the German but on the Austro-Hungarian side. Archduke Eugen who had taken over from Potiorok reported that with casualties of over 200,000 his Balkan Army needed a major overhaul before it could take to the field again. Then in March Austro-Hungarian forces had suffered a major setback at Przemysl, with 100,000 of their troops being taken prisoner and the loss of 900 guns. Thirdly, Italy's entry into the war in May had given them a major new enemy on their doorstep.

That the Allies made no greater attempts during this year-long breathing space to reinforce the Serbs with guns and armoured boats and all the military materials they lacked, followed by a robust and timely intervention through Salonica, can only be taken as thinking as confused as von Falkenhayn's was to the point. Apart from all other considerations, the Allied troops in the Dardanelles were in deep trouble – and as von Falkenhayn saw only too clearly, total control of the Berlin-Constantinople railway could only result in yet more guns and shells being despatched from Germany to be fired at them.

Faced with the arrival of combined Austrian and German armies from the north and the now-certainty of a Bulgarian attack from the east Serbia's initial plan, simple, daring, its inherent risks outweighed only by the gravity of the situation, was to launch a pre-emptive strike on Bulgaria while she was still mobilising. Bulgaria's capital, while not quite so exposed as the Serbian one, was only fifty kilometres from the Serbian border. Between Niš and Sofia the country is generally flat, with a direct route provided by the Nišava river. Having neutralised Bulgaria, Serbia would then

---

5 Falls, *Macedonia Vol. 1*, p.28.
6 Erich von Falkenhayn. *General Headquarters 1914–1916 and its Critical Decisions* (London: Hutchinson 1919), p.161.

turn its attention to its enemies on her northern front – a sort of Balkan Schlieffen plan. Joffre was in favour of the idea, and told the French Government so on 26 September.[7]

But although the Serbians, backed up by neutral Romanian intelligence, had provided official proof of Bulgaria's convention with Austria, with even the planned date for Bulgaria's entry into the war, Kitchener and Grey were against it.[8] They still clung to the hope, long gone by this time, of a negotiated peace with Bulgaria, and felt that the imminent arrival of Allied troops in Salonica would have a 'calming effect.' Grey in a speech to Parliament said that an attack on a neutral country could not be permitted, that Bulgaria had given a satisfactory reason for mobilising, that her intentions were not hostile, and that he hoped for an early resolution of differences in the Balkans.[9] The Russians with their historical attachment to Bulgaria were equally deceived. Foreign Minister Sazonov declared that a premature attack by Serbia would be both a crime and a blunder and continued direct discussions with Bulgaria right up to the opening of hostilities.[10]

Having been reprimanded by the Entente, Serbian Prime Minister Pašić then ordered the Serbian Army to withdraw to five kilometres from the Bulgarian frontier giving up among others the defensive position on the Sveti Nikola Planina.[11]

Even the unemotional Official Historian of the Macedonian Campaign Cyril Falls allows himself to comment here that 'Kitchener and Grey bore a grave responsibility' for this decision. For William Robertson, shortly to be appointed CIGS, the issue was less one of moral proprieties, than of military realities. 'The opportunity of falling on Bulgaria before she was ready was thus lost … but the result would probably have been much the same … she could not have achieved anything decisive against the large forces which were eventually sent against her.'[12] He was right, of course, except that such a pre-emptive attack may have allowed greater opportunities for a link-up with the small Allied force coming up from Salonica.

Grey did go to the length at this point of wagging his finger at the Bulgarians and telling them that if they attacked Serbia, 'Britain would help Serbia without reserve and without qualification.'

Serbia was forced to make the best of her predicament. Across the Sava, to the west of Belgrade, she was faced by the Austrian Third Army (eight divisions under General Koevess). Across the Danube to the east of Belgrade the German Eleventh Army (a further eight divisions), withdrawn from Russia under General von Gallwitz was formed up. The folly of the hapless Potiorek in trying to invade over the mountains from Bosnia was not to be repeated, except for one Austrian division detailed to invade Serbia's ally Montenegro from across the Drina. Opposite Niš on the Serbian north-east frontier was the Bulgarian First Army (four Bulgarian divisions which were twice the size of normal divisions) under General Bogadiev. All of these forces came under the direct command of Field Marshal von Mackensen.[13]

South of the Bulgarian First Army and facing Macedonia was the Bulgarian Second Army (two Bulgarian Divisions to be joined by three more) under the independent command of General Todorov.

Against these forces Serbia mustered twelve divisions; facing the Austro-Hungarian forces to the north, the First Army under General Mišić on the left, and the Third Army under General Jurišić-Sturm on the right. Below and to the east of these, to face the Bulgarian armies, were the

---

7   Larcher, *Grande Guerre*, p.70.
8   Arthur James Mann, *The Salonica Front* (London: A.C. Black, 1920), p.45.
9   V.J. Seligman, *The Salonica Sideshow* (London: Allen and Unwin, 1919. Reprinted by Forgotten Books, 2015), p.209.
10 Larcher, *Grande Guerre*, p.74.
11 Gordon-Smith, *From Serbia*, p.19.
12 Robertson, *Soldiers and Statesmen*, p.89.
13 Falls, *Macedonia Vol. 1*, pp.30–31.

Timok Group and the Second Army under General Stepanović. A scratch force of recruits and irregulars faced the Bulgarian forces across the Macedonian frontier.

From the outset, therefore, the Serbs were facing impossible odds, twelve of their divisions against sixteen Austro–German divisions and six, soon to be nine, double-sized Bulgarian divisions. From the outset they were outnumbered two to one, and in addition, as von Falkenhayn noted 'The Serbs can hardly be expected to withstand the effects of our heavy artillery and trench mortar batteries.'[14]

The Central Powers' offensive against Serbia began on 5 October 1915 with a massive bombardment, 300,000 shells and bombs from 170 heavy guns and 420 Heavy Mortars.[15] (Ironically, it was on this same day that the first Allied forces arrived in Salonica). By 9 October both the Austro-Hungarian and German forces had crossed their rivers, and Belgrade had been taken. On the same day the Austrian division in Bosnia invaded Montenegro and met with little resistance. Now, certain of an imminent Bulgarian attack from the east, the Serbian Government decided to evacuate Niš and move to Kragujevac, the Headquarters of the Army.[16]

The German forces, faced with stiff Serbian opposition, paused to reform, then advanced southwards on 18 October. By 25 October they had advanced twenty-five kilometres. The Serbs blew up their arsenals in Kragujevac and retreated south. Bulgaria had finally declared war on 13 October. Serbian resistance was heavy, and it was 29 October before the Bulgarian army forced the Kadi Bogos pass. But on 5 November Niš fell to the Bulgarian First Army. Von Falkenhayn's main objective had been achieved. At Niš, the railway divided, east to Sofia and Constantinople, and south to Salonica. Moreover the Danube was now in friendly or neutral (Romania) hands on both banks from Vienna to the Black Sea. The Berlin–Constantinople railway was officially reopened on 15 January 1916 by the Kaiser in person.

The Bulgarian Second Army, facing less opposition, had advanced more rapidly, and reached the Vardar on 17 October where they cut the railway bridge at Vrania and with it communications between Niš and Salonica.[17] By 19 October they had taken Kumanovo, on 22 October they took Skopje and on 24 October, Veles.

Meanwhile the French forces under Sarrail which had belatedly been sent up from Salonica to support the Serbs had not got much further than Udovo, over 100 kilometres south of Skopje. Already therefore a wedge had been driven between the French and the retreating Serbs. The story of the French (subsequently Anglo-French) Expedition into Serbia is given in Chapter 9 below.

The Serbian army continued to be forced southwards. After the fall of Niš the Serbian Second and Third Armies re-formed at Kruševac from where they retreated southwards through narrow mountain gorges to Kuršumilja and then to Mitrovica. Here they re-joined forces with the First Army which had come down the Ibar valley from Kraljevo.[18] The Serbian Government, together with all the foreign legations attached to it, had accompanied the First Army, having establishing itself, following the evacuation of Kragujevac, firstly at Kraljevo, then Raška, then Mitrovica.[19] With the army and the government the population of the towns threatened by Austro-German advance poured like a flood, inevitably hindering the progress of the Army.

The combined force continued to Priština and arrived on 15 November. At this point the Army had food and forage for 14 days. The vast number of civilians who had followed the Army had run out of food some time ago.

---

14   Falkenhayn, *German Headquarters*, p.161.
15   Gilbert, *First World War*, p.204.
16   Schiavon, *Front d'Orient*, p.133.
17   Villari, *Macedonian Campaign*, p.23.
18   Gordon-Smith, *From Serbia*, p.98.
19   L.F. Waring, *Serbia* (London: Butterworth, 1918), p.238.

It was here at the Kosovo Polje on the Field of the Blackbirds 526 years earlier that the Serbian Army had finally succumbed to the Ottomans. They had only regained it from the Turks two years before. Now, pressed from the north and from the east by overwhelming forces, Putnik decided against one glorious last battle, or even a feigned retreat followed by a fierce attack as on the Kolubara the previous year. Instead he led his forces further southwards in the hope of breaking out into Macedonia and joining up with the Allies. But at this time the small Allied force under General Sarrail was itself heavily engaged against the Bulgarian Second Army around Gradsko, still well south of Skopje, and would get no further. Nevertheless part of the Serbian High Command, and above all Mišić, having heard that von Falkenhayn was withdrawing most of the German forces from Serbia, wanted to throw the combined Serbian Army against the Bulgarians to their south, force the Kačanik pass and retake Skopje.[20]

Other counsels prevailed; Putnik and the Serbian Government decided to retreat to Prizren. To the rear two Serb divisions held the enemy up in a desperate battle at the Kačanik pass, and gained a little time, but on 19 November reports arrived that the Bulgarian army had arrived at Tetovo, virtually closing the circle around the Serbian Army, the Serbian Government, and countless civilians.[21] On 19 November the Austrians reached Raška, by 23 November they were at Mitrovica. Two days later the Germans were in Priština and the Bulgarians at Lipljan, coming up from Skopje. Despite the Serbian forces defending the access routes, the combined enemy forces would have been in Prizren within a matter of days.

Surrounded on three sides and backed up against the Albanian border there were now only two courses of action available to the Serbian Government and Army. To surrender, or to break out over the Albanian mountains to the Adriatic coast. They chose the latter. It was a momentous decision.

On 23 November Prime Minister Pašić told the foreign legations that his staff could no longer guarantee their safety, and advised them to make their way through Dakovica, Peć and Montenegro to the Adriatic coast.[22]

The next day the Serbian Government, King Peter and the Prince Regent set out across the mountains. Then on 25 November Putnik ordered the army to do the same. Voivode Putnik's last order to them was 'convince your troops that this retreat is a national necessity. Our salvation will come when our allies carry all before them in the final victory.'[23] Being by this time too infirm to walk or ride the 68-year old Serbian Commander in Chief was carried over the mountains in a sedan chair, and resigned as head of the Serbian Army once the retreat had been completed.[24]

There was no meaningful pursuit. The Bulgarians had achieved their objective, and von Falkenhayn probably thought that any Serbian forces who made it to the coast would be dealt with by the Austrians.

* * *

Unsurprisingly the accounts of the Serbian exodus over the mountains of Montenegro and Albania are imprecise. It is probable that around 170,000 Serbian soldiers set off on the journey. The number of civilians who accompanied them is unknown and could have been anything from twenty to forty thousand. On top of this there were twenty-four thousand Austrian prisoners of war.

---

20 André Ducasse, *Balkans 1914/18* (Paris: Robert Lafont, 1964), p.126. Mišić may have been misinformed about this. Falkenhayn p.185 only talks about withdrawing half the German forces from the area of battle for logistical reasons at this point.
21 Gordon-Smith, *From Serbia*, pp.116–137.
22 Waring, *Serbia*, p.239.
23 Gray and Argyle, *Chronicle Vol. 1*, p.162.
24 Sadly, Putnik, one of the greatest military leaders of his time, did not live to see the 'final victory' he had predicted, dying in Nice on 17 May 1917.

Three main routes were taken to the coast, two of them leading to the port of San Giovanni de Medua (today Shengjin) south of Scutari (today Shkoder). The main route was via Dakovica, Peć, Rožaj, Berane and Podgorica to Scutari. The second was from Prizren, to the Albanian border at Kukes, then along the valley of the Drin to Puka and on to Scutari. This was the shortest route, but probably the most mountainous. It was the one taken by Putnik and the Headquarters staff, and by Gordon-Smith who had been accompanying the Serbian Army since the fall of Niš, and who covers the campaign and retreat in fine detail. The third route parted company with the second at Kukes, then went south along mountain tracks to Debar. The probable aim of the troops who went this way was to reach Monastir from Debar, but by the time they got there the Bulgarians had already taken Monastir, and they either continued south to Elbassan and then Tirana, or north west to San Giovanni.[25]

All three routes involved mountain passes of over 1,800 metres. It was winter and bitterly cold. There was deep snow. Finding food in such a barren and inhospitable land for such a large body of people was an impossibility. Stragglers and civilians were subject to attacks by Albanian brigands who stripped them of all they had. 'People who shared the retreat tell a confused story of cold, hunger, Albanian attacks, paths covered with the carcasses of horses and dying men … over the hills ran a black line through the snow, the uprooting of a country's population … the exodus of a nation rather than the retreat of an army.'[26] In Montenegro they were joined by other refugees, pushed out of Bosnia by the Austrians. The Montenegrin Army was in turn defeated by the Austrians at the battle of Cetinje on 11 January 1916.[27]

For those who survived, the crossing from Serbia to the coast took two or three weeks. Nobody will ever know how many died on the way. Reports suggest about twenty thousand Serbian soldiers and as many civilians.[28] Even those who arrived at San Giovanni found there was no food; the Austrians had sunk all the ships in the harbour on 6 December. On news of the Serbian withdrawal the British and the French had sent missions to Scutari, both arriving on 24 November. With the Italians these missions coordinated food supplies and then ferries and transport down the coast to the larger and safer ports of Durazzo and Valona.[29] It is believed that around 180,000 people survived the crossing, of whom around 150,000 Serbian troops. Many died on or after arrival. Ten thousand sick and wounded were transported to Bizerta in Tunisia of whom some were later to return to active service. About 5,000 Serbian soldiers reached the Salonica front directly, either with the French of Sarrail's expeditionary force, or by retreating south ahead of the Bulgarian second army through Monastir.[30]

The Serbian Army HQ would have preferred to remain in Albania to re-form and re-equip rather than be transported to Italy, which was a possible solution put forward by the Allies. But this would, yet again, have put their weakened forces in danger of Austrian and Bulgarian advances who within a few weeks overran most of northern Albania.[31] The de facto leader of central Albania, Essad Pasha, was willing to help but had no forces to speak of, while the Italians declared that they could not envisage any further deployment of troops in Albania.

On 17 December the decision was taken to transport the Serbian Army to Corfu, which had been 'borrowed' under protest by the French from Greece. To transport the Serbian army from the Albanian mainland to Corfu, as well as the civilian survivors and the POWs to their various

---

25   Gordon-Smith, *From Serbia*, pp.139–169.
26   Waring, *Serbia*, p.240.
27   Gray and Argyle, *Chronicle Vol. 1*, p.164.
28   Gilbert, *First World War*, p.209.
29   Falls, *Macedonia Vol. 1*, p.35.
30   Gordon-Smith, *From Serbia*, p.240.
31   Gordon-Smith, *From Serbia*, p.190.

destinations, 1,159 voyages were made by 45 Italian, 25 French and 10 British vessels transporting 145,000 surviving Serbian troops to Corfu as well as 10,000 horses. Starting on 12 January 1916 and finishing on 9 February this was until Dunkirk the largest sea evacuation ever undertaken.[32]

Apart from the humanitarian aspects, the management, lodging and feeding the evacuees, whose numbers more than doubled the population of Corfu was a major challenge, efficiently conducted almost entirely by the French. It was also mainly the French who took on the subsequent task of working with Serbian Staffs in the reconstruction of their shattered Army.

Meanwhile the Austro-Hungarian army continued to advance. On 21 January they arrived at Scutari, and the following day the Bulgarian army reached Berat. A week later the Austrian fleet reached San Giovanni da Medua, but by 6 February had been driven back by allied destroyers to Kotor. Despite rear-guard action by the Serbs and the Italian Savona Brigade, the Austrian land forces continued to advance and on 27 February they took Durazzo. The Italians then built an entrenched camp around Valona, to be the base for their XVI Corps for the rest of the war. By March XVI Corps consisted of around 100,000 men in four divisions.[33]

During the period of the evacuation a further 5,000 Serbian soldiers died. Off Corfu the small island of Vido was used as a quarantine camp, and was known as the island of death; the Serbian Government bought land here after the war to set up a memorial to those who had died there.[34] The civilians who had survived the journey were mainly taken to be re-settled in Italy. The surviving Austrian prisoners were interned on the Island of Sardinia.[35]

The Serbian Army had been beaten, but not annihilated. One seemingly impossible escape route had been left to it and had been taken for want of any other. On Corfu 120,000 of them recovered sufficiently to be re-formed into six divisions. Between early April and end May 1916 they were shipped around the Greek mainland in Allied ships to Salonica. A little over two years later by breaking through the Bulgarian defences at Dobropolje east of Monastir they played the key role in liberating their country from the invaders, forcing the Bulgarian capitulation, and contributing to the collapse of the Central Powers in southern Europe.

In his post-campaign analysis von Falkenhayn had noted with satisfaction that 'only a few miserable remnants of the Serbian Army crossed into the Albanian mountains, losing the whole of their artillery.'[36] It was a reasonable assumption, but he was wrong.[37]

In terms of the numbers of soldiers who left their homeland with the intention of fighting their way back again, and in terms of the elapsed time between departure and triumphant return, the history of warfare perhaps contains no parallels.

---

32 Gilbert, *First World War*, p.209.
33 *Armies Françaises de La Grande Guerre Tome VIII Vol. 2* (Paris : Imprimerie Nationale, 1923–1934), Annexe 790.
34 G. Ward Price, *The Story of the Salonica Army* (New York: Clode, 1918), p.126.
35 Villari, *Macedonian Campaign*, p.87.
36 Falkenhayn, *German Headquarters*, p.185.
37 He was wrong about the guns too. The Serbs managed to take with them 81 guns, 179 Machine guns, and 55,000 rifles, as well as several thousand horses. Gray and Argyle, Vol I, p.168.

8

1915
The Allies Arrive in Salonica

The clarity of Allied thinking on Balkan risks and opportunities had been muddied from May 1915 by the developments and setbacks in the Dardanelles. Hurriedly but belatedly the spotlight returned to the Balkans when Bulgaria's hostile intentions became clear in September, but even now the reactions of France and Britain were significantly at variance. France wanted to send troops to Serbia to fight alongside the Serbs. The British unwillingly agreed to send troops to Salonica, but mainly to put pressure on Greece to honour her Serbian commitments. This dichotomy of approach was evident even after the landing of troops; the French under Sarrail advanced immediately into Serbia. The British under Mahon for three weeks were instructed to go no further than the Greek border.

As has been seen the Army of the East had its origins in the Calais Conference of 11 September 1915. At that point the destination of the force was the Dardanelles, but it had been decided to delay its despatch until the outcome of the planned offensive on the Western Front of 25 September was known. Two days before this date however the Bulgarian mobilisation had called for a major change in direction. On the same day Venizelos had had his negative meeting with the king and had called on the Allies to provide 150,000 men. Foreign Secretary Grey, perhaps fully aware neither of the various motivations for the Greek mobilisation of 23 September, nor of the enormous divergences of viewpoint between the king and his prime minister, had asked 'what number of troops will be required at Salonica to induce Greece to give her full support to Serbia if Bulgaria attacks?'[1] At a War Council meeting on 24 September Kitchener confirmed British thinking by stressing that the role of any British troops sent to Salonica would be to support Greece in helping Serbia.

Both Grey and Kitchener must have been puzzled the following day to receive a message from the British Minister in Athens to the effect that the king didn't want any Allied troops 'yet', but that Venizelos did, although in the interests of form he would formally protest on behalf of the Greek Government when they arrived.

Kitchener's support of the whole Salonica project was to remain ambivalent until his tour of the Mediterranean in November. Although the Dardanelles campaign had not been his in its origins, he had taken it over entirely once it became a land battle. His investment in terms of men, materials and personal commitment was enormous. He was still hoping right up to the beginning of November that it would succeed.[2]

The French response to the request of Venizelos was clear from the outset:

---

1   Falls, *Macedonia Vol. 1*, p.39.
2   Falls, *Macedonia Vol. 1*, p.45.

Le gouvernement français, voulant mettre la Grèce en mesure de remplir ses obligations de son traité avec la Serbie, est prêt pour sa part de fournir les troupes demandées. (The French Government, wishing to put Greece in a position to fulfil the obligations of her treaty with Serbia, is ready, for her part, to furnish the troops required).[3]

Joffre, although rightly and understandably continuing to insist that '*le théâtre principale de la guerre est la France*' (the main theatre of the War is France) nevertheless accepted without hesitation that '*il est évident que l'Entente a le devoir impérieux de ne pas laisser écraser la Serbie*' (it is evident that the Entente has an absolute duty not to allow Serbia to be crushed)[4] and on 24 September instructed General Bailloud to prepare for the dispatch of two divisions from the Dardanelles to Salonica.[5] Initially the British had planned also to send two divisions (10th and 11th), but after further talks and the input of the Allied commander of the Dardanelles army, General Hamilton, it was decided to send one each.[6]

An advance party of British and French officers was sent to prepare for their arrival, the story of whose reception in Salonica on 1 October is described below. On the very day of their arrival however and following Grey's ill-considered speech in the House of Commons of 28 September, Venizelos called the Allied ministers to his office to tell them that no troops were to land unless he received assurances that the forces being sent would not be used to force Greece and Serbia to make concessions to Bulgaria. The French 156th Division, which was already on the way, was turned back, and the ships to carry the British 10th Division were held in port. The next day Venizelos was suitably assured, and the ships sailed again.

Then, on 5 October 1915, four events of great significance took place. Firstly, the Central Powers opened their attack on Serbia. Secondly, Allied troops started to arrive in Salonica. Thirdly, the key meeting at Calais took place at which Britain and France committed to raise their collective presence in Salonica to 150,000 men. And finally, Venizelos, the man at whose behest the whole project had been set up, threw in the towel and resigned as head of the Greek Government.

As the writer of the Official History of the Macedonian Campaign put it:

> Here then was a situation which would have been ludicrous had it been less tragic. Britain was sending troops only to help Greece fulfil her obligations; and now it was almost certain that Greece did not intend to fulfil them ... it now appeared that these troops could hope for no more than neutrality and might have to face hostility from the Greek forces. To crown it all it was probable that the landing had in any case been made too late to save Serbia.[7]

The Central Powers must also have been puzzled by these goings-on. Von Falkenhayn's initial comment was that the Allied landings made in Salonica without the consent of the Greeks 'involved a serious breach of international law.' The soldier in him could not then resist mounting an assault from the high ground (moral in this case) by claiming that this action 'deprived the Entente even of ostensible justification for any further outcry against the march through Belgium as an act of aggression.'[8] Although Venizelos had asked the Allies for 150,000 men to enable him

---

3   Armées Françaises, *Tome VIII Vol. 1*, p.145.
4   Larcher, *Grande Guerre*, p.76. quoting *Armées Françaises Tome VIII Vol. 1*, Annexe 101.
5   Schiavon, *Front d'Orient*, p.124.
6   Of the 15 Allied divisions engaged in the Gallipoli campaign, only two were finally transferred to Salonica, the British 10 Division, and the French 156 Division. Elements of 17 Colonial Division also served in the Gallipoli campaign, were transferred to Mudros and then to Salonica in early 1916 where the Division was completed with the arrival of another brigade from France.
7   Falls, *Macedonia Vol. 1*, p.41.
8   Falkenhayn, *German Headquarters*, p.179.

to support Serbia, Greece was still formerly neutral, and this is how von Falkenhayn saw it. (And as to Belgium, in 'crossing' the neutral country the Germans had killed over 5,000 Belgian civilians and destroyed 15,000–20,000 buildings, and, later, deported over 60,000 Belgians to Germany as slave labour.[9] The Allies did nothing like this to the people of Greek Macedonia). Further, *L'Armée de l'Orient payait les droits de douane pour tout homme et tout matériel débarqués*. (The Allies paid customs duties for every man and all material disembarked in Salonica).[10] Certainly, the Germans did nothing of the sort in Belgium.

Otherwise, the potential arrival of 150,000 Allied troops in Salonica seems to have left von Falkenhayn largely unconcerned. For him 'the Serbian operation was substantially a subsidiary one, and the employment in that inhospitable country of even a single German soldier more than necessary could only be justified by some advantage of far-reaching importance.'[11] If the Allies tried to mount a full-scale Balkan operation, 'the Central Powers would limit themselves to digging in and preserving what they had won.' Further, he reasoned, 'the lie of the land was extraordinarily favourable to defence. If the Allies had failed to achieve any success in the Vosges, the Carpathians or the Isonzo, the same result could confidently be expected here.'[12]

When Kitchener heard of Venizelos' resignation he ordered General Mahon, Commander-designate of the British forces in Salonica to remain at Mudros on the island of Lemnos. Two days later the order was rescinded, but, other than 22nd Division which had entrained for Marseille on 27 September, the extra divisions earmarked for Salonica remained in France.

During the two weeks since Bulgarian mobilisation on 23 September to the watershed date of 5 October much had happened. The French had switched much of their attention from the Straits to the Balkans. Following on from the commitments made at Calais Joffre had identified the other two divisions promised by the French to take their total contribution to the agreed 65,000 and arranged for their transport to Salonica.[13] The British however remained unconvinced, and after what they saw as Greek backtracking now waited for two weeks to take stock of the situation, even playing with the idea of diverting two of the divisions intended for Salonica to invade southern Turkey through Iskenderun.[14]

On 29 October, concerned by the apparent inaction on the part of their allies, the French sent Joffre to London to ask again for British support in the war against the Central Powers in Serbia. Three complete French divisions had not only arrived in Salonica, but they were already in Serbia engaging the Bulgarian Second Army. The British had only one division and it was still in Greece. Another was arriving. Couldn't these at least support the French by holding the railway line up as far as Krivolak? And where were the other promised divisions?[15] Not a man naturally given to drama, let alone blackmail, Joffre told his allies that his very position as Commander in Chief and even the 'cordiality of the Entente' depended on receiving a positive answer. He was given his assurances, confirmed in the form of an unenthusiastic note dated 30 October, and conditional on

---

9 Watson, *Ring of Steel*, p.127 and p.387.
10 Larcher, *Grande Guerre*, p.100, quoting Sarrail *Mon Commandement en Orient* p.55.
11 Echoing the dictum of Bismarck, Reichstag, 1876, which surely must have been known to him '*Der ganzen Balkan ist nicht die gesunden Knochen eines einsigen pommerschen Grenadiers wert.*' 'The whole Balkans are not worth the healthy bones of a single one of our Pomeranian grenadiers.'
12 Falkenhayn, *German Headquarters*, pp.180–191.
13 Schiavon, *Front d'Orient*, p.128.
14 The idea re-surfaced in the form of a ruse in April 1916 when 22 Battalion, the Rifle Brigade were sent to Cyprus to prepare dummy camps and airfields to try to convince the Turks that an attack on Iskenderun was being prepared. Although the troops were not supposed to know what they were doing there, Signaller Bailey noted in his diary 'I think it's all bluff.' It is not known whether the Turks were taken in any more than he was.
15 Falls, *Macedonia Vol. I*, p.44 and p.62.

contact with the Serbian army being made. If it were not, the whole force would be withdrawn. It was at this point that the War Council decided that Kitchener should go to the Mediterranean to make an on-the-ground assessment.

A further allied conference was held in Paris on 17 November, but by that time Kitchener was in Salonica. Four days earlier he had been in the Dardanelles to confer with his generals and see the situation for himself. What he heard and saw confirmed that this disastrous campaign should be brought to an end, and the troops withdrawn.

As a follow-on of this decision, orders were finally given for the four extra divisions identified back on 5 October to leave for Salonica, the Iskenderun idea also having been dropped. When he arrived in Salonica himself however, he found a most disquieting situation. All the French and half the British troops so far arrived in Salonica had left Greece and were engaging the Bulgarian Army in Serbia. Venizelos' more moderate successor Alexandros Zaimis had been replaced in Athens by the hardline Stephanos Skouloudis.

The mood of the Greek government was hardening. To quote Larcher; *le roi Constantin évoluait de la neutralité bienveillante vers un hostilité manifeste*. (King Constantine was moving from a state of friendly neutrality to one of an obvious hostility).[16]

By the end of October it would have been clear to Constantine, or if it were not Baron Schenk, the German Minister in Athens, would have filled him in, that the Serbian Army was being overwhelmed by the combined forces of the Central Powers. These were moving inexorably down through Serbia, and would soon be on his doorstep, having pushed the small Anglo-French expeditionary force before them. The King was being nothing less than realistic when he told Guillemin, the French Minister in Athens on 29 October: *Pourquoi je ne l'avouerais pas? Oui, je redoute entrer en conflit avec l'Allemagne et Autriche qui ne ferait qu'une bouchée de la Grèce* (Why not admit it? I dread coming into conflict with Germany and Austria who would swallow up Greece in no time). As October moved into November the pro-German faction in Athens had become dominant. German officers were arriving to speak to the Army. The Germanophile press was even floating the idea of an agreement between Germany, Austria, Bulgaria and Greece to share out Serbia between them.[17]

On 10 November Skouloudis stated that if the Allied forces returned to Greece they would be disarmed by the Greek Army. The British Government immediately imposed economic and commercial sanctions and prepared naval demonstrations with the French. The British Minister Sir Francis Elliot told Skouloudis that if a 'single soldier were touched with a view to disarmament, there would be serious consequences.' Backed with troops on the ground, the stoppage of supplies and a naval stranglehold, this threat was immensely more meaningful than Grey's wagging of the finger against Bulgaria in September.

Not for the last time in this war Allied ships circled around Athens. On 20 November Kitchener had a meeting with the king, following which the British and French Ambassadors presented Constantine with a series of gunship-backed demands – the removal of Greek troops from Salonica, control of the railways to the Greek frontier, the right to build fortifications around Salonica and of the Allied navies to search merchant ships.[18] This particular round of brinkmanship was brought to an end on 28 November with the Greek acceptance of these demands 'within the limits imposed by the independence of Greece, the maintenance of her neutrality, and the requirements of her mobilised army.'[19]

On 4 December another Allied conference was held in Calais. By this time the Serbian Army had been soundly defeated and was struggling across the Albanian mountains to the sea, and the

---

16   Larcher, *Grande Guerre*, p.84.
17   Armées Françaises, *Tome VIII Vol. 1*, pp.379 and 381.
18   Falls, *Macedonia Vol. 1*, p.48.
19   Armées Françaises, *Tome VIII Vol. 1*, p.388.

French expeditionary force into Serbia was also in retreat. The case for remaining in Salonica as agreed with Joffre on 29 October having been removed, and despite the fact that two of the four 'new' British divisions had already arrived in Salonica and the other two were not far away, the French were told by the British that they wanted to withdraw all their troops from this theatre.

On 9 December however France countered with full-scale coalition support. In addition to themselves, Russia, Serbia and Italy all insisted on the maintenance of an Allied front in Macedonia, to which in due course they would all contribute. Britain backed down – the fact that the final evacuation from the Dardanelles had begun the previous day was perhaps not irrelevant to this change of mind – and although the argument for withdrawing some or all troops from Salonica resurfaced again and again over the next three years, the birth of the British Salonica Force really dates from 9 December 1915. Five days later approval was given for the five divisions now present to be divided into two Corps, the XII (General Maitland Wilson) and the XVI (General George Milne) with full Corps headquarters staffs.[20] In August 1917 10th Division was transferred to Palestine, but the four other divisions remained in Macedonia for the remainder of the war.

* * *

The first components of the Allied Army of the East, the French 156th Division and the British 10th Division, which had arrived in Salonica on 5 October had been preceded by an advance party of two French and seven British officers on 1 October. Their reception was less than enthusiastic.

H. Collinson Owen, editor of the *Balkan News*, was given a full account by one of the British officers involved who had been told that preparations should be made for the possible arrival of five divisions. The Salonica Consul General, who was supposed to help, was away on leave, and his deputy knew nothing about it. Unlike the French officers the British remained in uniform, and two of them were temporarily arrested for looking at military facilities. (This was referred to as a *contretemps dû à une maladresse anglaise* in the French sources)[21] Next day the British Minister in Athens told them that their arrival was unexpected and was causing a lot of problems, and that they should go away again. Their position was regularised in the evening, but their mission was largely unsuccessful since 'We found ourselves blocked at every turn by a solid phalanx of Greek obstructionists.'[22]

The Advance party was to achieve little in the way of accommodation, much of which had been taken up by the Greek Army. When the troops started to arrive on 5 October the British set up a camp three miles out of town at Lembet on the Seres road, and the French at Zeitenlik, the site of today's massive Allied military cemetery on the outskirts of Salonica.

The 'obstructionism' became a way of life for the Greek authorities in Salonica, and above all for the Greek Army mobilising in Greek Macedonia. Sarrail devotes the whole of a chapter to the problems he and the Allies faced during the early months in gaining access to railways, roads, vehicles, animal transport, telegraph centres and hospitals, with 'obstructionism' verging at times on sabotage. No space could be found for camps to be established, all available rooms in the town needed for offices had been requisitioned by the Greek Army, and a totally insufficient area of the port allocated to the Allies.[23]

20　Alan Wakefield and Simon Moody, *Under the Devil's Eye* (Stroud: Sutton Publishing, 2004. Republished by Pen and Sword Military, 2011), p.47.
21　Schiavon, *Front d'Orient*, p.125.
22　H. Collinson Owen, *Salonica and After* (London: Hodder and Stoughton, 1919), pp.14–15.
23　Sarrail/Porte, *Mon Commandement*, pp.87-95. The minutes of the long and circular negotiations he had with the Greeks throughout December, are given in his annexes 14 and 15, pp.384–395.

Of the five British divisions now committed to the Salonica Front, 10th Division was the first to arrive, short of transport, much equipment and artillery. They were followed by 22nd and 26th Divisions in bits and pieces from November onwards, followed by 28th Division in December; 27th Division did not arrive until January 1916. The reception accorded to 26th Division as recounted by Captain Owen Rutter in his poem *Tiadatha* was no more enthusiastic than that accorded to the advanced party:

> *Nobody seemed pleased to see them*
> *No one worried much about them*
> *And the folk of Salonica*
> *Did not come to bid them welcome*
> *Did not hang out flags of welcome*
> *Did not cry 'Tis well O brothers*
> *That ye come so far to see us.*[24]

R.H. Davis, an American War Correspondent who had arrived in Salonica shortly after the Allies, describes in colourful detail the confusion and chaos in and around Salonica, a city of 120,000 inhabitants, whose services and facilities were totally unable to cope with the arrival of the Allied forces of 150,000 men – on top of the 120,000 mobilised Greek soldiers assigned to Greek Macedonia who inevitably used Salonica as their base.[25]

When the British Army Ordnance Services set about unloading and stocking all the stores and equipment arriving with the troops, they found that all the wharf space and depot facilities had been commandeered by the Greek Army. Undermanned themselves 'not enough officers or men, not enough room, not enough labour and even not enough stationery to write things down' recounts Major Darwin, temporary Ordnance officer. An initial depot was set up, found too small, then another, also too small, then, on the advice of a General making a flying visit from Egypt, a third on a bare hillside served by a road which was destined after the winter rains to degenerate into a river. He continued:

> The inconvenience of having three depots linked by no telephone and one abominable road needs no emphasizing. Moreover there was the inherent difficulty of troops and their equipment being landed simultaneously. This may be illustrated by one example out of many. A ship called the *Stork* contained a cargo of tentage, the actual tents easily accessible, the poles at the very bottom of the hold. The tents were landed but then the Stork had to put out into the harbour again to make way for the disembarkation of troops. And so long did she have to wait that in one division the troops had to cut down trees to make their own poles.

It took around three months before the Ordnance Services were set up on a sound footing, but throughout the whole campaign the length of the Front covered by the BSF and the limited and often primitive access routes made their work particularly demanding.[26]

---

24 Owen Rutter, *Tiadatha* (London: T. Fisher Unwin, 1920), p.47. Note the accent on the third syllable of Salonìca.
25 Richard Harding Davis, *With the French in France and Salonica* (London: Duckworth and Co., 1916), p.150.
26 Arthur Forbes, *A History of the Army Ordnance Services Volume 3* (London: the Medici Society, 1929), pp.236–40.

General Sir Bryan Mahon the designated commander of the British Salonica Force had arrived on 8 October.[27] A senior career soldier, his finest hour had been in May 1900 when as a colonel he had led the force of 2,000 men who relieved Mafeking.

His command in the Dardanelles however had been conspicuously unsuccessful, and he was being moved to another command for much the same reason as Sarrail, although probably all similarity between the two men ends here.[28]

Sarrail himself first heard from unofficial sources that he was to go to Salonica and not to the Dardanelles on 24 September. His appointment was formalised on 3 October. He reached Salonica on 12 October.[29] He later wrote that he arrived *sans aucun renseignement, sans aucune orientation officielle, ne connaissant rien du pays, rien des événements qui viennent de se dérouler depuis le commencement de la guerre* (without any information, without any official guidance, knowing nothing of the country nor of what had happened since the beginning of the war).[30] This was probably something of an exaggeration.

But he got moving very quickly once he was there. In terms of the men and means available, and the deplorable delay in embarking on the mission into Serbia – which had nothing to do with him – he made an admirable fist of it. Although limited in its scale, and unsuccessful in its outcome, it was possibly in military terms the best achievement of his whole command in Macedonia.

---

27 Palmer, *Gardners*, p.15.
28 *The Irish Times* on 22 October 2014 in a full and interesting article on the part played by Irish troops in the First World War berates Mahon for refusing to commute the death sentence erroneously handed down by a court martial on Patrick Downey, a 19 year old volunteer, while he himself had been guilty of desertion in face of the (Turkish) enemy in August 1915. 'On that occasion' relates the *Times* 'in a fit of pique…he abandoned his 10th Division at Suvla Bay and took himself off to a distant island… his action contributed to the decimation of the 7th Dublin Fusiliers.' Laffin p.173 corroborates this report. When General de Lisle was made corps commander over his head Mahon left the battlefield while his troops were still fighting, an action, according to Laffin, 'tantamount to desertion under fire.' He also reports a note from Asquith to Kitchener of 24 August in which the Prime Minister expresses the view that the 'Generals and staff engaged in the Suvla business ought to be court martialled and dismissed from the army.'
29 Schiavon, *Front d'Orient*, p.130.
30 Schiavon, *Front d'Orient*, p.131 quoting the *Revue de Paris* November–December 1919 p.685.

9

1915
The Allied Expedition to Serbia, October–December

(Map 3)

Even before Sarrail arrived in Salonica General Bailloud had started to take his 156th Division – only two days after it had arrived – up the Vardar railway into Serbia. He was recalled by the French General Staff who told him to wait for Sarrail and also for 57th Division.[1] On 15 October, only three days after his own arrival in Salonica, Sarrail reached Strumica Station with one brigade of 156th Division and adequate artillery. Here he made contact with seven battalions of the Serbian 'Macedonian Army', the scratch force Putnik had put together to face up to the Bulgarian Second Army.

When Sarrail got there, these battalions were instructed to turn north to Veles, their headquarters.[2] By 20 October the other two brigades of 156th Division had arrived and fanned out on the east side of the Vardar. One brigade of 57th Division arrived in support by 16 October with the rest of the Division between 20 and 23 October. On 21 October a short engagement was fought between elements of 156th Division and Bulgarian forces from their Second Army at Rabrovo. This encounter has symbolic weight in that it was the first of the whole Macedonian Campaign, and practical value in that the Bulgarians were prevented from destroying the Strumica rail bridge. It was also, as pointed out by Martin Gilbert, the opening of the First World War's eighth front.[3]

The French advanced up the gorge from Udovo to the appropriately named Demi Kapu – the Gates of Iron – at its northern end. The railway at that time crossed the river twice on this stretch, which is the narrowest of the whole Vardar valley. It was crucial for any further advance that these bridges remained intact, and that the gorge remained in their hands. Sarrail then pushed elements of 156th Division on to Krivolak which they reached on 27 October. Here they found that although the road to Veles via Stip was free of enemy troops, the road bridge over the Vardar had been destroyed during the Balkan conflicts of 1912-13 and had not been repaired.[4] Dispersal of troops and artillery onto the east side of the river was very much hampered by the lack of this bridge, and by the time two flying bridges had been completed by French and British engineers on 9 November much of the impetus had been lost.

---

1   Larcher, *Grande Guerre*, p.82.
2   Palmer, *Gardeners*, p.40.
3   Gilbert, *First World War*, p.205. The other Fronts were the Western and Eastern, the Dardanelles and Mesopotamia, the Serbian, Caucasus and Italian. Fighting was also taking place in East Africa, West Africa and Persia.
4   Sarrail/Porte, *Mon Commandement*, p.49.

Map 3. Anglo–French Campaign October–December 1915.

The Bulgarians had taken Skopje on 22 October and Veles on 24 October – at that time however with relatively modest forces.[5] With difficulty and the use of ferries the French set up a defensive position on the high ground at Karahodjali to cover the Veles road, and a sharp engagement here on 3 November resulted in 3,000 Bulgarian casualties.[6]

The French 122nd Division started arriving in Salonica on 1 November and was immediately sent up to support 57th Division. A further defensive position was set up at Vosartsi to defend the road bridge over the Crna, the last before its confluence with the Vardar, giving the French control over the wedge of land between the Vardar and the Crna.

On 31 October Marshal Putnik contacted Sarrail to say that he was aiming to force his way through the Kačanik pass and re-take Skopje, and to ask for French support by moving up from the south through Veles.

---

5   Larcher, *Grande Guerre*, p.84
6   Manuel Lon, *Bulgaria en la Guerra 1915 – 18* (Madrid; Talleres del Deposito de la Guerra, 1960), p.64. quoted by Falls, *Macedonia Vol.2*, p.57.

In response Sarrail evolved a two-step plan. Between Lake Doiran and the Vardar, 156th Division to be supported by the British 10th Division would press north towards Strumica and east to take the heights of the Belasitsa Planina with the aim of drawing the Bulgarian troops to the east of the Vardar and to Strumica itself.[7]

On the other side of the Vardar, 57th and 122nd Divisions, while conserving their gains and protecting their lines, would push west towards the Babuna River to take the Bulgarians in the flank as they pursued the Serbian 'Macedonian' battalions south of Veles. Given the difficulty of the terrain between the Crna and the Prilep–Veles road however, General Leblois proposed a frontal attack on Veles from the south, and in the meantime took control of Gradsko station and occupied the villages of Kruševica and Kamendol to the west of the Crna.

Command of this, the second part of Sarrail's plan, then passed to General de Lardemelle who aimed instead to take the heights of Ćićevo and the monastery of Arkangel and trap the Bulgarians between this crest and the Prilep road. But the Bulgarians had called off their pursuit of the Serbian battalions and now turned on the French. A confused battle ensued from 10 to 12 November during which the French gained then lost Ćićevo, then lost Gradsko station and Kruševitsa. The Bulgarians who were opposing the French with three brigades called off the action on 13 November and dug in, waiting for two more brigades to arrive. When they did the French lost Vosartsi on 20 November, and de Lardemelle decided to pull all troops back over the Crna. This may have been the correct military response to the situation, but Sarrail didn't think so and the decision was taken without Sarrail's agreement. He was relieved of his command on the spot. *J'avais été toujours hostile à relever un officier général qui n'avait pas réussi. Je ne pouvais pas, par contre, tolérer l'insuffisance doublée de l'indiscipline* (I have always been against sacking an officer because he didn't succeed. But I couldn't accept indiscipline as well as incompetence).[8] De Lardemelle was sent back to France and makes no further appearance in these pages.

By this time Sarrail had been informed by the General Staff in Paris that Serbian resistance was virtually at an end, and that the noises coming out of Greece were worrying if not threatening. Sarrail's proposal to have the newly arrived British divisions sent to Monastir, and then to link up with him and the retreating detachments of the Serbian 'Macedonian Army' at Prilep – which was a good one – was turned down for both these reasons. Instead he was invited to retire, in his own time and on his own terms. Sarrail was unwilling to do this until all hope of linking up with Putnik had gone.[9] By 22 November it had; the Serbs had failed to break through to Skopje and were themselves on the point of retreating towards the mountains of Albania.

Until 26 October, when the French already had two divisions in the field and had reached Krivolak, General Mahon had not even been given permission to cross the Serbian border. If the British were continuing to labour the point that their participation in the battle to save Serbia was dependent on the Greeks also joining in, the point was becoming increasingly sterile. The British may have thought that they had been misled in committing troops to Salonica in the first place, but the troops were there, on the ground, and the Serbs desperately wanted their help. And when finally Mahon got the go-ahead to move into Serbia his instructions from Kitchener were 'not to fail the French' rather than help to drive a new enemy out of an Allied country. What Mahon thought of all this, if anything, is unknown, he left no memoirs. He sent a detachment of engineers to help the French with bridging the Vardar at Krivolak, a task completed on 9 November, and set about joining up with the French 156th Division north-east of Lake Doiran.

---

7   Strumica was then in Bulgaria. After the war this pocket of Bulgarian territory was acquired by Serbia and has remained on the 'Yugoslav' side ever since. Today it forms part of the Republic of North Macedonia.
8   Sarrail/Porte, *Mon Commandement*, pp.75–76.
9   Larcher, *Grande Guerre*, p.90.

Due to the claims, real or bogus, by the Greek Army on the use of the railways – they were after all still mobilizing, and 120,000 of the 180,000 men had been assigned to Macedonia – 10th Division was unable to use the Doiran railway to reach its assigned area. They had instead to take the Vardar railway, detrain at Gevgeli and proceed as best they could cross-country for thirty kilometres to Causli. Here on 2 November three battalions of 30th Brigade relieved three French battalions, but it was 10 November before all three brigades of 10th Division were able to take up their section of the line south of Kosturino and Ormanli with the French to their left, and from this date their contribution could be little more than one of supporting the French in their retreat. By this time also General Mahon had passed the divisional command to General Nicol, his own presence being required in Salonica to oversee the setting up of central staffs to handle an army of five divisions, and to prepare for their arrival, not perhaps concerning his own head too much with what they were coming for.[10]

Having suffered badly in the Dardanelles, 10th Division was physically and numerically very much under-strength. Some topping up had been received from men invalided out of France, but battalion sizes were now not much more than 500. At the end of November the Allied forces in Serbia were hit with a vicious two-day blizzard with temperatures down to -22 degrees.[11] From 10th Division 1,500 men had to be evacuated back to Salonica. Brigadier Nicol asked for reinforcements – the whole of 22nd Division was now ashore – but Mahon only sent him a pioneer battalion.

By the beginning of December all Serbian resistance had ceased, and the Bulgarian Second Army was able to turn its undivided attention to the Anglo-French forces. It had ten brigades in the field. Since each Bulgarian brigade comprised eight battalions, this force was the equivalent of eighty battalions – close on seven British or French divisions. Four of these brigades were on the Crna and three on the Vardar. Their objective was to destroy or severely disrupt the French forces in retreat. The other three brigades faced the French 156th and British 10th Divisions on a line from Gradec to Ormanli at the foot of the Belasitsa mountains. The mission of these two Allied divisions was to help cover the retreat of the French 122nd and 57th Divisions, and to prevent the three Bulgarian brigades from joining in the pursuit.

The French retreat from the Crna and down the Vardar was a masterpiece of its kind. It was conducted by General Leblois on a programme drawn up by Sarrail and his staff. The decision to return to Salonica had finally been taken on 22 November when all hopes of joining up with the Serbian army had been given up. Every step was pre-planned, including, critically, the timing for the displacement and dispatch of guns and stores. These went, together with divisional transport, as they had come, almost entirely on the one-track railway line down the Vardar. The men – including 156th Division there were then upward of 50,000 French troops in Serbia – had in the main to march, and for much of the way along the same narrow route. Two holding positions were set up at Demi Kapu and Gradec, defended by artillery. The programme was set in motion on 3 December. By 7 December 122nd Division held the Demi Kapu position while 57th Division passed through, to hold in their turn the Gradec position. Two more holding positions were then set up, at Mirovca and Gevgeli, and the French forces and their equipment thus worked their way in echelon down the Vardar railway to the Greek border. The Bulgarians were successfully held at bay, the French destroying the rail bridges behind them.[12] Both divisions were then to press on to the Greek frontier, to be followed on 14 December by the two Anglo-French divisions holding the Gradec–Ormanli line A further holding point had been set up in Greek territory north west of Lake Arjan in the event that the Bulgarian army pursued the Allies into Greece.

---

10   Falls, *Macedonia Vol.1* p.56.
11   Jean Saison, *D'Alsace à la Cerna* (Paris: Plon, 1918), pp.121–123 quoted by Schiavon p.154.
12   Sarrail/Porte, *Mon Commandement*, pp.79–86.

On 6 December these two divisions came under heavy attack. The British were defending an L shaped sector, with 30th Brigade facing forward towards Kosturino and 31st Brigade below them and to their right dropping down towards Tatarli. The battle flowed back and forth for three days, with frequent fog creating problems of coordination. Bulgarian skill at seizing dominant hills from which they could direct enfilade fire, to be perfected on the Doiran heights over the next two years, was already apparent. As 30th Brigade fell back 31st Brigade risked encirclement.

On 7 December Mahon came to see for himself and called for 65th Brigade of 22nd Division to be sent up from Salonica. With it arrived the commander of 22nd Division, General Gordon. With his obsession for the due respect of seniority, Mahon now gave Gordon command over Nicol and all British troops in Serbia, adding an unnecessary (and uninformed) extra link to a chain of command already complicated by the fact that for operational purposes two of 10th Division's brigades now answered to General Bailloud.[13] A generally ordered withdrawal was hampered partly through poor messaging, but mainly because the only road into Greece became clogged with the numbers of units passing through, and as a result of Sarrail's (laudable) insistence that nothing would be left behind.

By 12 December all Allied forces were back on Greek territory. The whole expedition into Serbia, the lion's share of which had been borne by the French, had been undertaken at the cost of nearly 6,200 casualties, of which nearly 5,000 were on the French side. Of the 1,200 British casualties just over half were suffered by 30th Brigade who had borne the brunt of the Bulgarian attacks on 6 and 7 December. Bulgarian sources suggest that their losses may have been greater.[14]

Although individual brigades of 10th Division were to be engaged in September 1916 against Bulgarian positions in the Struma Valley, the Kosturino action was the only one in which the whole of 10th division was engaged while on the Macedonian Front. There is a memorial to the Division and to 'all Irishmen who gave their lives in the Great War' at Rabrovo just south of Kosturino.[15]

Sarrail had been informed through the French General Staff's Intelligence Service that the Bulgarian Army would not pursue the Allied forces into Greece, and although he took the defensive precautions available to him in the situation, this proved to be the case.

This may be seen as one of the turning points in the story of the Macedonian Front. In addition to the four double-size divisions of the Bulgarian Second Army, the four double-sized divisions of the Bulgarian First Army were now free of any encumbrances (Monastir had been taken on 4 December, effectively completing the Bulgarian conquest of Serbian Macedonia). The Austrians still had six divisions in the theatre. These fourteen divisions were fully operational, having been in the field for almost two months. Moreover, they could have entered Greek Macedonia from several directions including Monastir and the Struma Valley, as well as down the Vardar.

On the Allied side the four divisions who had been campaigning in Serbia were withdrawing with some order into Greece, but ill-equipped to fight a rearguard action against a determined enemy, and incapable of throwing up sufficient defences in time to withstand such an attack. In Salonica 22nd and 26th Divisions had been ashore long enough to start preparing some sort of defences around the town and manning them but were severely lacking in artillery. As for 28th Division, disembarkation in Salonica was held up until 9 December while the British decided whether or not to withdraw from Salonica entirely (what would have happened to them had the Bulgarians swept down to Salonica pushing the Anglo-French expeditionary force before them is unclear, as is the attitude of the Greek army in such an eventuality). The final British Division, the 27th commanded by General Milne, was not to arrive in Salonica until January.[16]

---

13   Falls, *Macedonia Vol. 1*, p.73.
14   Falls, *Macedonia Vol. 1*, p.82.
15   *The Long Long Trail*, 10th (Irish) Division and *The Irish Times*, 23 April 2015.
16   Falls, *Macedonia Vol.1*, pp.85–86.

The decision to halt the Bulgarian forces on the Greek border was von Falkenhayn's. 'At the request of the German GHQ' he observed, 'the Bulgarian Second Army in their pursuit did not cross the Greek border'. He explained his reasons with his usual clarity:

- Rapidly pushing in more troops than were already in the sector would have been difficult, the distances were long and communications in Serbia and Macedonia rudimentary
- There would be problems with lines of supply to these troops, also because of the destruction by the Allies of the rail bridges
- Rapid progress could not be expected against the 'prepared positions' around Salonica (he was overestimating these)
- Entry of the Bulgarians into Greek territory would have forced the Greek government to take action against them
- The Allies could bring in reinforcements from the Dardanelles
- Bulgarian occupation of Greek Macedonia would have necessitated much support from Germany, who apart from submarine bases in the Peloponnese would not be getting much for it
- Further, the Austrians had designs on Salonica, and Germany didn't want to get involved in territorial arguments between her allies.[17]

For the moment therefore von Falkenhayn limited Central Powers intervention in Salonica to air attacks.

But perhaps the key reason was that the Bulgarians themselves were not particularly enthusiastic. They had come to war to acquire northern Macedonia from Serbia. Now that they had achieved this they were prepared to dig in along the border to prevent the Allies coming over and taking it away from them, confidently waiting for the end of the war when it would finally be attributed to them in permanence. The moment passed. Within a matter of weeks the strength of Allied defences and the growth in size of the Allied Army of the East was such as to reduce the chances for success of any invasion by the Central Powers to virtually nil.

As for the Anglo-French expedition to Serbia in late 1915, the objective of joining up with the Serbs to present a united Allied front to the Central Powers was not met. Much credit should be given to Sarrail and his generals however for getting three divisions a hundred and fifty kilometres up the Vardar valley within three weeks of the first arrival in Salonica. They were due perhaps even more credit for getting them safely back together with almost all of their transport and equipment, particularly in view of the massive and increasing enemy forces facing them. As Memeix observed *'Echapper à l'ennemi est quelquefois plus difficile que le battre.'* (To escape from the enemy is sometimes more difficult than beating him).[18] Clemenceau, with all the freedom of expression allowed to one well outside the circles of Government was far more cutting: *Je crois que jamais dans le monde un pareil exemple d'incohérence ait été donné.* (I don't think there has ever in the world been a greater example of incoherence).[19]

Three years were to pass before the Allied Army got so far again. As it was to be another three years before the BSF re-visited the Bulgarian border at Kosturino.

Unquestionably the whole history of the war in the Balkans would have changed had this Allied expedition been made even two months earlier. Delayed as it was, however, there are grounds for believing that by engaging the Bulgarian Second Army at this moment, the Allies had at least prevented the Serbian Army from being encircled and annihilated.

---

17 Falkenhayn, *German Headquarters*, pp.185ff
18 Gabriel Mermeix, *Le Commandement Unique Vol. 2* (Paris: Société d'Editions Littéraires, 1920).
19 Clemenceau, *L'Homme Enchaîné* 9 décembre 1915.

10

1916
Consolidation and Reinforcement

(Map 4)

To Generals Sarrail and Mahon the fortification of Salonica now seemed imperative but following the departure of Venizelos there was much Greek resistance. On 9 December 1915 they had a joint meeting with the King's envoy Lieutenant Colonel Pallis and presented a number of demands to him. Two days later they heard that the Greek Government had agreed to move its V Corps out of the area proposed for the defensive enceinte and promised that neither these troops nor those remaining in Salonica – which the Government undertook to reduce by 50 percent – would actively oppose its construction.[1] They would not however allow the allies to take control of the forts controlling the entrance to the Gulf of Salonica at Kara Burun or to take over the running of the railways.

For the first three months of 1916 no attempt was made to fortify or permanently occupy the territory between Salonica and the Serbian–Bulgarian border, although elements of the three French divisions, 156th, 57th and 122th used for the Serbian winter campaign remained in place with a watching brief. Much of the Allied manpower however could now be concentrated on fortification work to protect Salonica and its surrounds from any enemy attack. At the same time and subsequently the Allies set in train massive road improvement programmes, but while local labour was used for these, only Allied troops worked on the construction of the defensive fortifications to prevent infiltration by enemy agents.[2]

The line along which the fortified entrenchment would run was established as early as 14 December 1915, and work began soon after. The first objective was a defensive line from Tumba at the western end of Lake Langaza, through Avatli, Balcha and Dautli to Naresh on the 'Constantinople' railway line, then across to the Vardar at Kara Oghlu. The section from Tumba to Dautli was to be the responsibility of the British Salonica Force (BSF). The line along the whole of this sector followed a natural ridge with excellent vision over flatter ground to the north of any approaching enemy. Mahon with the luxury of five divisions at his disposal, allocated his sector from right to left respectively to 26th, 28th and 22nd Divisions, with 27th Division working to their rear on supply routes.[3] Tiadatha of 26th Division had his word to say on this exercise:

> *Guards, fatigues and working parties*
> *Roads to make and hills to dig on*
> *All the livelong day the Dudshires*
> *Spent in digging up the Balkans.*[4]

---

1 Wakefield, *Under the Devil's Eye*, p.34.
2 Palmer, *Gardeners*, p.52.
3 Falls, *Macedonia Vol. 1*, p.90.
4 Rutter, *Tiadatha*, p.51.

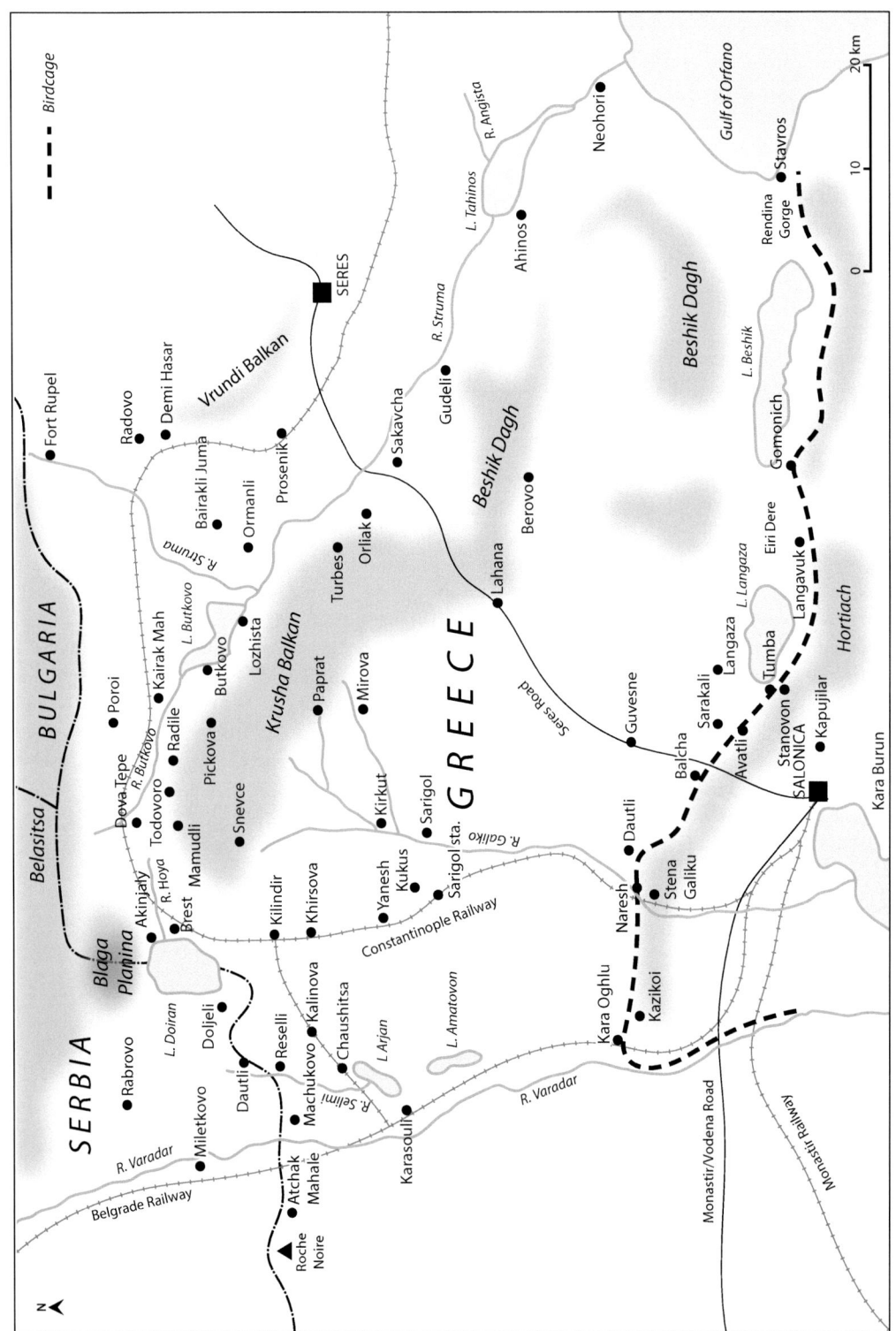

Map 4. From Vardar to Struma and Entrenched camp.

After recuperating from their ordeals in Serbia, 10th Division was set to work on the slopes of Mt. Hortiach to the east of the city, another natural bastion protecting Salonica from the sea.[5]

The French were to continue the defensive line westwards from Dautli through Naresh, across to Kara Oghlu, then down the left bank of the Vardar, following it to the point where the river was crossed by the Monastir road and beyond which the ground became too marshy for military operations. Sarrail recognised that the weak point of the entrenched camp fortifications was along the Vardar and the railway which ran beside it, over which the enemy could mount artillery attacks from high ground on the west bank. Some very low-draught boats equipped with machine guns were built to patrol the Vardar, and fortifications extended to the other side of the river.[6] The French sector between Naresh and the Vardar was flatter ground than that to be worked on by the British, and called for more conventional and continuous trench systems. Sarrail in a letter to his generals in December 1915 asked for:

> *une organisation telle que lorsque l'ennemi se présentera il suffira d'avoir en première ligne la moitié, ou, au plus deux tiers de l'effectif, afin de permettre la relève des unités.* (a defensive structure such that when the enemy attacks, only half, or at the most two-thirds of our personnel will be required to man it, to allow for a proper rotation of relief forces).[7]

Work on the fortified entrenchment proceeded so well that as early as 4 January General Mahon was able to turn his mind to the stretch between the Gulf of Rendina and Lake Langaza.[8] Here also nature had provided a fairly continuous series of ridges to the south of the two lakes, offering excellent positions for the siting of trenches, gun emplacement and forts. The drawback here was the absolute lack of roads, and until this deficiency was addressed troops working on this section were shipped all around the Kalkidiki peninsula to the port of Stavros in the Gulf of Orfano, approaching the problem from the other end. Artillery and transport for this sector however had to make its way cross-country as well as it could.[9]

Between Stavros and Lake Beshik is the ten kilometre-long Rendina Gorge along which two armed motor boats were laboriously hauled on a specially constructed pontoon. One was launched on Lake Beshik on 10 January, and the other on Lake Langaza a few days later.[10]

General Mahon realised early on that the tendency of veterans of the Western Front to dig continuous trenches was inappropriate in this mountainous terrain, and his instruction was to build a series of defensive strong points connected by communication trenches which if necessary could be held against attack. In front of the main defensive line was a series of lower defences to prevent the enemy from creeping up along the numerous river valleys which ran down from the hills. In front of these was a 10 metre-broad wire entanglement. The whole was defended by 30 heavy batteries.[11]

It was mid-winter and wind, cold and snow were major disincentives. But Mahon, as well as having a good eye for the lie of the land, was also a good project manager, personally very involved in the work as it progressed. On 21 December he issued a set of good-sense guidelines called 'Notes on Digging (to reach all officers)'. These were obviously the result of personal observation; for example 'A definite task should be allocated to each unit so that if any individual is asked what

---

5   Collinson Owen, *Salonica*, p.176.
6   Sarrail/Porte, *Mon Commandement*, p.100.
7   Quoted by Schiavon p.178.
8   Wakefield, *Under the Devil's Eye*, p.31.
9   Wakefield, *Under the Devil's Eye*, p.38.
10   Palmer, *Gardeners*, p.52.
11   Villari, *Macedonian Campaign*, p.30.

his job is he will not be as at present at a loss to explain'. Young officers were told to 'roll up their sleeves and take a turn', and 'plenty of space should be given so that men do not interfere with each other's movements'.[12] Caesar, the greatest digging general of antiquity, would have approved wholeheartedly.

One of the side effects of 'digging up the Balkans' was bringing to light sites and artefacts from Macedonia's rich classical past. The French, in true Napoleonic tradition, set up an archaeological service which by the end of the war had identified more than seventy proto-historic sites. British soldiers unearthed artefacts while digging trenches and were ordered to report them. In true Elginesque tradition, a lot of these found their way to the British museum.[13]

By early January both generals felt that the defences were already good enough to withstand an enemy attack. None came, but the perfection of the 'Birdcage' as it came to be known (on account of the immense amount of barbed-wire deployed) continued for another three months. By April 1915 Salonica was probably the best defended town in any theatre of the war, with the Allied base at Mudros on the island of Lemnos providing cover on its seaward side to complement the 'Birdcage' on its landward side. The base at Mudros had been set up to serve the Dardanelles campaign but remained in being for the rest of the war to provide military and logistic support to the British forces in Macedonia.

Inevitably while the allies were digging in around Salonica, the Bulgarian army was digging in along the hills which constituted the border between Greece to the south and Bulgaria and Serbia to the north. While the Salonica defences were never put to the test, the Bulgarian ones were, and heavy allied losses testify to the completeness with which they, too, had done their work.

When it became clear that the risk of an attack on Salonica had passed, and that the Allies had the numbers and equipment to adopt a more offensive stance, further fortifications and entrenchments were constructed along the hills facing these Bulgarian positions, and here once again the Allies found that nature had provided them with ideal terrain. From the Gulf of Rendina all the way around to Lake Doiran runs a ridge of hills, the Beshik Dagh running into the Krusha ridge.[14] These positions also had to be strengthened and defended but provided an immense disincentive to any Bulgarian advance into Greek Macedonia, and during the whole war no attempt was made to test either the extended defensive line, or the entrenched camp around Salonica.[15]

In addition to the 'Birdcage', the British and French Generals, now with considerable manpower at their disposal and with no military operations currently in the offing, occupied themselves with improving (or building) roads, laying down new single-track rail lines (decauvilles) to facilitate movement, and significantly expanding the handling capacity of Salonica harbour.

When the Allies had arrived in Salonica there were essentially only three roads leading out of the city, one to Monastir, one towards Doiran and one to Seres. The first two were backed up by railways, but the Seres road was not. Throughout the war it was virtually the sole supply and transport route between Salonica and the BSF XVI Corps on the Struma Front. On the arrival of the British forces in Salonica it was little more than a track for horse-drawn traffic. Moreover it was horribly congested. Malcolm Burr, working as an officer in charge of local labour units, describes the scene on the first few kilometres of the Seres road at the beginning of 1915 'The confusion was fantastic. Lorries by the hundred, snorting, rattling, boiling, puffing, motors hooting, officers

---

12   Wakefield, *Under the Devil's Eye*, p.36.
13   Mazower, *City of Ghosts*, p.319.
14   Falls, *Macedonia Vol. 1*, p.90.
15   After the Second Battle of Doiran in September 1918 General Nerezov, Commander of the Bulgarian First Army wanted to make a lightning attack on Salonica knowing Salonica was only lightly defended but was dissuaded by the Germans. See Chapter 31.

gesticulating, despatch riders crashing, Greek carts crawling, all on a road far too narrow, the surface honeycombed with potholes of grey slime.'[16]

The road rose more or less regularly for half its 70 kilometre length, then plunged downhill to the Struma valley. Even today's motorway requires wide hairpin bends to make this 600 metre descent. Work to upgrade this road using local labour during the whole of 1916 proved quite inadequate when the winter rains came down, and the BSF was to spend three years constantly rebuilding and resurfacing this vital road link. From August 1916 when the town of Seres was taken by the Bulgarians, the last 20 kilometres of the road from the Struma eastwards became disputed territory. But it remained 'the Seres Road' for the rest of the Campaign. There is probably no account, memoir or history of the British Salonica Force which fails to stress the critical importance of the Seres Road and the difficulty of keeping it in operation.

In June 1917 a branch railway helped with the first 24 kilometres to Guvesne, but extending it any further in this tortuous territory proved beyond the wit and competence of the Army's engineers. The remaining 46 kilometres required constant attention, and units of the ASC spent the whole period of the campaign building, upgrading and maintaining an essential transport link between Salonica and an entire army corps.[17]

During the war 480 km of metalled roads and 280 km of secondary roads were built,[18] and during the winter of 1915–1916 alone the Allies put down 200 km of decauvilles and roads. The French were as concerned and motivated as the British:

> *C'était la conclusion que n'importe quelle opération de guerre imposait dans les Balkans: tous les problèmes s'y ramenaient à la construction de routes et à l'augmentation du trafic par voie ferrée.* (This was a reality facing all military operations in the Balkans, all problems came back to the construction of roads and to increasing the capacity of railways).[19]

Moreover, wells were dug and canals cut for the transport of fresh water.

In January 1916 the issue of overall command of the Allied forces in Salonica was addressed. Now that the War Office had tacitly accepted that the British and French forces were there to stay – at least for the moment – it became obvious, also in light of the experience of the Serbian campaign, that the relationships between the two forces should be defined more precisely. On 11 January Mahon was informed by General Robertson, Chief of the Imperial Staff, that from now on he would 'comply with the instructions of General Sarrail regarding military operations for the defence of the town and harbour of Salonica'. The reasons given for ' the two Governments recognising the necessity for placing their forces under General Sarrail' were the 'military situation and the special interests of France in the Salonica affair'.

Mahon was told that he would continue to report to the Commander-in-Chief, Mediterranean Expeditionary Force 'as regards administration' but was authorised to report directly to the War Office with regard to 'information of the enemy, the progress of events, and questions of administrative detail'. But 'all questions of principle should be forwarded through Commander in Chief, Mediterranean Expeditionary Force.'[20] It is to be hoped that Mahon understood all this. In practice it must have involved him copying both Egypt and London on all correspondence. The use of the word 'affair' sums up perfectly Robertson's barely disguised distaste for the whole Macedonian enterprise.

---

16   Malcolm Burr, *Slouch Hat* (Woking: George Allen and Unwin, 1935), p.111.
17   Seligman, *Salonica Sideshow*, p.16ff.
18   Collinson Owen, *Salonica*, p.181.
19   Larcher, *Grande Guerre*, p.109.
20   Falls, *Macedonia Vol. 1*, p.103 Letter from CIGS to General Mahon, 10 January 1916.

Sir William Robertson had been appointed CIGS on 23 December 1915, very shortly after the Anglo-French expedition into Serbia had got back to Greece. He had previously been Chief of Staff to Sir John French, Commander of the BEF, but was no stranger to the Balkan theatre. In the early 1900s when he had worked in military intelligence the Balkans were part of his remit. He had visited the area in 1906 and come to the conclusion that 'of all the countries in Europe none was defensively stronger, and therefore none less favourable to the offensive than the Balkan Peninsula.'

It can safely be said that of all the political and military leaders in France and Britain during this period, none was so permanently, adamantly, against the Macedonian Campaign as Robertson. Hindsight in no way modified his distaste for the whole business; the first paragraph of his chapter on Salonica in his 1926 book 'Soldiers and Statesmen' reads ' Of all the problems which brought soldiers and statesmen into conference during the years 1915-17 the Salonica Campaign was at once the most persistent, exasperating and unfruitful,' a view which he develops and illustrates over the next 60 pages.[21]

In operational terms, his instruction to Mahon recognised Sarrail as Allied commander within the territory enclosed by the Birdcage, while the two governments would continue to decide on the use of their troops for any offensive action outside it. It was, however, a small step forward. At this time the British contingent at five divisions was greater than the French at three. But the French were stronger in artillery, cavalry and aircraft, and a further French Division, 17th Colonial, was on the way.

After Mahon had been replaced by Milne these instructions were later to be updated in a joint note to Milne and Sarrail on 27 July 1916 from their respective General Staffs prior to the planned Allied offensive to support Romania's entry into the war.[22]

Many of Sarrail's later actions and decisions, and particularly his handling of the 1917 campaign, have been heavily criticised. The high-handedness of his dealings with the Greek Government may also be questioned, but in early 1916 he took three decisions which, from a military point of view, were quite understandable, even if his handling of both matters was poorly coordinated with Mahon.

In the first place it had become obvious that all the movements and dispositions of the Allied forces in Salonica were being passed on to the enemy's intelligence services almost in real time. 'In Salonica the wharfs were as free to anyone as a park bench … spies swarmed. For every landing party they formed a committee of welcome. Of every man, gun, horse brought ashore they kept a tally. The clearing houses for the spies were the consulates of Turkey, Bulgaria, Austria and Germany.'[23]

Up to the end of 1915 each of the four enemy nations had indeed maintained consulates in Salonica. Their presence, particularly that of the Bulgarians, was obviously intolerable.

Mahon, who had been collecting details of these activities and lists of agents had pressed Sarrail to act as soon as the Expeditionary Force returned from Serbia. But nothing happened until 30 December when Sarrail received a report that a German bombing raid had been routed following signals from one of the hostile consulates. He decided to act immediately, rounded up 20 Austrians, 17 Turks, 12 Bulgarians and 5 German diplomats and their wives and had them shipped off to France. When Greek Army and Police representatives complained about this blatant infringement of Greek sovereignty, Sarrail told them that in face of the undeniable aggression and belligerency of the foreign missions he had been forced to arrest them, and in doing so '*j'avais mis les Grecs*

---

21 Robertson, *Soldiers and Statesmen*, pp.83 and 88.
22 See Chapter 11
23 Davis, *With the French*, pp.137–140.

devant un fait accompli qui simplifierait leur tâche. Ils ont compris et souriaient.' (I'd placed the Greeks in a situation of fait accompli, thereby simplifying things for them. They understood and smiled).[24]

Having informed Mahon only twenty minutes before raiding the consulates, Mahon hurriedly put together a token force to join the French, but was not best pleased, also because many of the agents on his books escaped.[25] After this Mahon felt constrained to inform his leaders that although 'good relations with the French are in no way impaired, I hope that in future Sarrail will keep me as frankly informed of his intentions as I always endeavour to keep him informed of mine.' The language of the Greek Government was less measured as they protested angrily at this flagrant abuse of international law in a neutral country.

Secondly, Sarrail ordered on 13 January the destruction of bridges at Kilinder and Khirsova over the railway south of Doiran to forestall any sudden enemy attack from this direction. Less than 60 km separated Salonica from the Bulgarian lines east of Lake Doiran, and command of the railway would have been key had they decided to attack while the entrenched camp around Salonica was still incomplete. More significantly – and more far-sightedly – he sent a task force to destroy the much bigger bridge carrying the 'Constantinople' railway over the Struma at Demi Hasar.[26]

Thirdly, outraged at the sinking of a British troop carrier just outside Salonica harbour on 22 January 1916 by enemy shipping (all the men and most of the mules were able to land safely) the French finally decided that the Kara Burun forts and batteries at the entrance to the Gulf of Salonica would have to be taken over by the Allies. When Sarrail and Mahon had previously asked to take over the forts at their meeting with Lieutenant Colonel Pallis on 9 December, the King, while refusing, had committed never to turn the guns on the Allies 'whatever happened', to reduce the garrison by half, and to discontinue the current programme of upgrading the armaments. By mid-January however photos provided by an Allied surveillance balloon showed that this work was still going on, and there was no sign of a reduction in the garrison.[27]

In December Admiral Gaucher, commander of the French fleet in the Eastern Mediterranean, received orders from the French Admiralty to take the forts with their batteries by force. The French government prevaricated for a while, then agreed. Admiral Gaucher asked Sarrail to provide land support. He was only too pleased to provide it, and on 28 January moved a force composed of infantry, artillery and cavalry and comprising 2,500 men to a position to the east of the forts, where they quietly camped for the night. At the same time two French battalions and two British battalions were moved to the south of Salonica to prevent any Greek forces arriving from the city and impeding the attack on the forts. The commander of the main fort, faced with a battalion of Zouaves, a number of mountain guns and a screen of cavalry quickly accepted the inevitable. A smaller fort to the south held out longer until threatened with a naval bombardment. The members of the Greek garrisons were shipped back to Salonica the same day.[28]

The small battery on the other side of the entrance to the bay near the mouth of the Vardar was then taken.

In terms of clarity of planning and efficiency of execution this cutting-out expedition was a complete success. Not a shot had been fired, the Greek troops in Salonica had not been alerted. The only problem was that Mahon had been cut out as well, having only been informed of the operation less than 12 hours before the French went in.[29] He hurriedly sent a brigade from 10th Division who were closest to the action as back up if required. They were not, and the regimental record

---

24 Sarrail/Porte, *Mon Commandement*, p.108.
25 Falls, *Macedonia Vol.1*, p.99.
26 Sarrail/Porte, *Mon Commandement*, pp.132–133.
27 Ward Price, *Salonica Army*, p.102.
28 Sarrail/Porte, *Mon Commandement*, pp.136–137.
29 Falls, *Macedonia Vol. 1*, p.100.

suggests they had no idea why they were being sent nor why, a day later they were sent back to their fortification work on Mt. Hortiach.

Sarrail was aware that Mahon was totally against taking the forts by force, and maybe forgot to consult him for this reason. Despite all this, and despite the wooliness of their operational interface, the relationships between Sarrail and Mahon seem to have been excellent. In his Memoirs Sarrail often verges on the vituperative, making his tribute to Mahon all the more compelling:

> *J'ai eu pendant la campagne de nombreux collaborateurs français; j'aurais souhaité que tous aient le même sentiment de camaraderie, de devoir, et de connaissances militaires qu'avait le Général Mahon.* (During the Campaign I had many French collaborators; I could have wished that all these had the same spirit of friendship, sense of duty, and depth of military knowledge as General Mahon).[30]

Mahon was however unquestionably right that all three of these actions, particularly the blowing up of the bridges and the taking of the Kara Burun forts were certain to harden Greek opinion, and particularly that of the army, against the Allies.

Although von Falkenhayn had stopped the Bulgarians at the Greek frontier after their occupation of Serbia, he was not averse to reminding the Allies as they settled into Salonica that he had not forgotten them. On 31 January 1916, three days as it happened after Sarrail's taking of the Kara Burun forts, a Zeppelin flying from Timisoara in Hungary appeared over Salonica and dropped fire bombs on the city causing minor mayhem and three million francs of damage at the *Banque de Salonique*. The LZ85 made another successful attack in March. As the Germans had no doubt calculated, the unpredictable visits of this enormous black aerial monster caused as much fear among the townspeople as actual damage, and it was with great relief when on its third appearance on 5 May it was shot down by the guns of HMS *Agamemnon* and the shells of a British torpedo ship.[31]

In February, with the affronts to Greek neutrality represented by the affair of the consuls, the destruction of the bridges and the capture of the forts of Kara Burun of very recent memory, Sarrail was asked by his government to visit King Constantine in Athens. The meeting took place on 23 February:

> *Entrevue avec le roi très courtoise. Avons parlés de généralités militaires, puis de Salonique. M'a longuement parlé de neutralité…. Lui ai dit que jamais il n'y avait eu pression pour l'en faire sortir. Avons parlé de Demi Hasar et Kara Burun. Lui ai donné explications détaillées et basées sur nécessités militaires. N'ai pas eu de réponse.* (Very courteous meeting with the king. We spoke about general military matters, then about Salonica. He spent a long time talking to me about neutrality. I told him we'd never put pressure on him to abandon it. We spoke about Demir Hasar and Kara Burun. I gave him detailed explanations based on the military necessity. He didn't reply).

He also had a meeting with the hard-line Prime Minister Skouloudis; '*m'a paru aussi fourbe que amiable.*' (He seemed more cunning than agreeable).

He reported that the Prime Minister and staff officers were clearly pro-German. He also met the moderate Zaimis who was to play such an important role in the abdication crisis the following year who he found '*franc et courtois*' (open and courteous) and with Venizelos, who was still hoping

---

30 Sarrail/Porte, *Mon Commandement*, p.56
31 H.A. Jones, *The War in the Air being the Part Played during the Great War by the RAF Vol 5*. (Oxford: Clarendon Press, 1935), p.336.

to join the Allied camp, but warned that the Greek Army would need a lot of re-building before it could be used.[32]

* * *

Meantime on the Western Front pressure was building around the French armies at Verdun. Although aware that the Allied forces in Salonica were in no position to launch a sustained offensive Joffre wrote to Sarrail on 28 January – the very day, as it happened, of the storming of the forts at Kara Burun – asking him to mount a strong demonstration against the Bulgarians in order to draw enemy forces away from France. Sarrail accordingly detached two Divisions from their entrenchment activities and sent them up to the border in readiness.

Unsurprisingly and for the same reasons in reverse von Falkenhayn was at the same time giving orders for an assault on the Allied positions in Salonica. But things had moved on since the Allied retreat from Serbia six weeks previously. The Allies had virtually doubled their forces and, although the work was not yet complete, thrown up considerable fortifications around the city. The Belgrade railway was now choked up with traffic to and from Turkey and Bulgaria. On top of this, many of the bridges on the railroad from Niš to Salonica had been destroyed during the French retreat and subsequently. Above all, momentum had been lost.

Plans were made, but for all these reasons, mainly the logistical ones, the German operation was called off in March. Von Falkenhayn's retrospective take on its abandonment was:

> The enemy had meanwhile so strengthened himself that very great resources would have had to be thrown into the scale ... From the point of view of the war as a whole it was more advantageous that between 200,000–300,000 men were being chained to that distant region than to drive them into the French theatre of war.
>
> The German-Bulgarian (defensive) positions were favoured in a quite unusual way by the nature of the country, and in accordance with the circumstances were fortified with exceptional strength, and that the chance of the Allies breaking though these defences was 'outside the bounds of possibility.[33]

It should be noted that the Austrians were working to a rather different agenda from the Germans with respect to the Balkans. Chief of Staff Conrad von Hoetzendorf had been strongly in favour of the pursuit of the Anglo-French forces to Salonica in November 1915, had promoted and supported the newly planned offensive in January, and was bitterly disappointed when it was called off in March. His Director of Military Intelligence Oberst Maximilian Ronge wrote in his memoirs 'Against Conrad's wishes the planned offensive against Salonica was delayed and then definitely abandoned in March 1916. This was one of the greatest mistakes made in the entire war.'[34]

Regular contacts and conferences at staff and government level continued between the French and the British, but the differences between them on the purpose and future of the Salonica forces remained as wide as ever. Repington's description of the Allied conference in Paris of 27 March 1916 as recounted to him by General Robertson suggests that the lack of understanding ran at two levels:[35]

---

32   Sarrail/Porte, *Mon Commandement*, pp.138–139 Sarrail's telegram to the War Ministry following his visit to Athens.
33   Falkenhayn, *German Headquarters*, p.257.
34   Schiavon, *Front d'Orient*, p.172.
35   Charles à Court Repington had left the army as a Lieutenant Colonel in 1902, and from 1904 to 1918 was the Times War Correspondent. The close professional and social relationships between certain

The great struggle was to try to make the French send the Salonica troops to France. He (Robertson) tried his best and was supported by Asquith and Kitchener. They found the French quite immovable. Joffre got angry, or pretended to be, and thumped the table. He (Robertson) complained that our ministers did not take the lead in these debates. None of them, except Kitchener, could speak French properly. Asquith and the others spoke in English. There was a very good translator discovered by Lloyd George. He apparently let them speak for a quarter of an hour, and then gave the speech in English. He (Robertson, who had studied French and was a qualified translator) said the translation was often better than the original.[36]

Despite misunderstandings and disquiet at General Staff level, efforts were made to preserve cordial relationships on the ground. Having completed the 'birdcage' to their satisfaction and weathered the possibility of an enemy offensive in March, Sarrail paid a courtesy visit to the BSF on 12 April, during which Mahon decorated him with the KCMG.

* * *

The Allied forces in Salonica were about to be very significantly strengthened. By the beginning of April 1916 the Serbs, now restored, rebuilt and reconstituted into six divisions each of around twenty thousand men, were raring to leave Corfu. The six divisions retained their traditional names which were to resound throughout the campaign, and particularly at its dénouement: Danube, Drina, Sumadija, Timok, Morava and Vardar.[37] The six divisions were divided into three armies.[38] The commander in chief was Prince Alexander, who moved with his troops to set up a headquarters in Salonica. In mid-March he visited Joffre in France, partly to study the latest military techniques on the Western Front, but also to ask that his Serbian army should not be put under the orders of Sarrail. A compromise similar to that agreed for the British Army was in due course worked out. Other Serbian officers in due course also took part in fact-finding missions to France.[39]

His father, King Peter I who had survived the exodus, but was in very poor health remained on the island of Corfu, as did the Serbian Government in exile. Following the resignation of the venerable and venerated Voivode Putnik, General Bojović had taken over as Chief of Staff, and the three Army commanders were Generals Mišić, Stepanović and Jurišić-Sturm.

On 3 April a request was put to the Greek Government to allow their old allies to use the Greek railways to pass across Greece from the Adriatic to the Aegean.[40] They refused. Sarrail's provocations notwithstanding, this was undeserved, although it is worth noting that the Athens–Salonica railway was not completed until the end of 1916.[41] Even had the Greeks allowed the Serbs the use of their railways across to the Aegean the Serbian army would then either have had to march through Thessaly or be shipped to Salonica from a port in 'Old Greece.' Use of the Corinth Canal which would have avoided the circuit of the Peloponnese was ruled out due to its having insufficient draught for the transport ships.[42]

---

    journalists and the military and political leaders of the day – Ward Price is another – today seem extraordinary.
36 Charles à Court Repington, *The First World War 1914-18* (London: Constable, 1920), p.162.
37 Vardar was re-named Yugoslav in April 1918 following the influx of POWs taken by Russia from Austria, who were largely Croat, Slovene and Bosnian. See Chapter 29.
38 Falls, *Macedonia Vol.1*, p.120. Falls notes that the historic division of the Serbian force into three 'Armies' was retained, although now each 'Army' was about the size of a small corps.
39 Schiavon, *Front d'Orient*, p.165.
40 Gray and Argyle, *Chronicle Vol. 1*, p.196.
41 Palmer, *Gardeners*, p.141.
42 Falls, *Macedonia Vol.1*, p.120.

At considerable risk from enemy submarines the whole Serbian force was shipped all the way around the Peloponnese and up the western Aegean to Salonica in Allied ships between 11 April and 31 May 1916. Under cover of great secrecy the convoys took a single route, patrolled in permanence by Allied fighting ships. Miraculously not a ship was lost, the whole force comprising 112,000 troops – plus 8,500 horses – arrived intact.[43]

It was then equipped with another 12,500 horses and the arms and equipment needed for mountain warfare mainly by the French, who also by the end of 1916 helped the Serbs to develop an air arm.[44] In Salonica they were joined by another 8,000 Serbs who had already made their own way there, either with the retreating Allied force, or through Monastir following the retreat of the Serbian army in 1915. The Serbian General Staffs arrived on 16 May. A further 1700 'Yugoslavs' who had arrived, essentially Bosnians ex- Montenegro, were absorbed into the French army.[45]

---

43 Armées Françaises, *Tome VIII Vol. 1*, p.477.
44 Babac, *Serbian Army*, p.114.
45 Armées Françaises, *Tome VIII Vol. 1*, pp.476, 478.

11

1916
Tensions between the Allies and Pressure on Greece

(Maps 4 & 6)

During March and the first half of April 1916, before the arrival of the Serbian forces, Sarrail decided to move out of the entrenched camp with all four of his French divisions. His aim was to begin the preparation of advanced defensive positions on an arc from the Struma to the Vardar, and to deny strategic forward positions to the enemy. Mahon was asked to move some of his troops in support. By 16 April the Allies were covering the sector from the Struma to Butkovo (17th Colonial Division), the Krusha Range and parts of the Butkovo valley (57th Division), Kirkut to Kilindir south of Lake Doiran (British 22nd Division), and the area between the two railways, and down the Vardar to Lake Arjan (156th and 122nd Divisions). The Greek army had in the main withdrawn from this sector. Its IV Corps was deployed east of the Struma to the Bulgarian border on the river Mesta, and its III Corps spread out from Salonica to Florina.[1]

By the end of May 1916 with the arrival of the Serbs completed, the Allied Army of the East would comprise fifteen divisions – six Serb, five British and four French - or around 300,000 men. This, in the view of Joffre, would be sufficient to mount an offensive campaign. In a letter to Robertson of 24 April he spelled out the potential benefits of such a campaign in descending order. At best it would encourage Romania and as a result probably Greece to join the Allied camp, from which enormous advantages would be derived. If this didn't happen, important inroads could be made into territory held by the enemy, above all given his battle weariness. At the very least the offensive would hold back enemy forces from being switched to other fronts.[2]

Joffre had been working on the issue of an offensive with Sarrail since March. Sarrail had at first been reticent. The Serbs at the time had not arrived. His equipment and transport, he told Joffre, needed completing. To face up to 270,000 enemy forces he needed a total of 21 divisions. The British were not being cooperative.[3] In some of this he was quite right; the Official Historian devotes a page to the issue, and clearly finds it difficult on this occasion to maintain his editorial neutrality.[4]

In May however Sarrail finally presented a plan, based on the 21 divisions which he didn't have. (The Russian Brigades and the Italian 35 Division were not to arrive until August, and even these would take the total to effectively 17 divisions.)

The Serbs were to go for Monastir, the Crna bend and the mountain passes between the Crna and the Vardar. The British were to hold down the enemy between Lake Doiran and the Vardar

---

1   Falls, *Macedonia Vol. 1*, pp.113–114
2   Larcher, *Grande Guerre*, p.129. Joffre's letter to Robertson of 25 April.
3   Schiavon, *Front d'Orient*, pp.189–190.
4   Falls, *Macedonia Vol. 1*, p.121.

and on the lower Struma. Four French Divisions were to move above Lake Doiran from the east and attack enemy positions on the Blaga Planina and the Belasitsa range.[5] (This was an element dropped from the final plan for 1916. It was not resurrected until September 1918 when the British with the Greek Cretan Division tried it. It failed, but for reasons which may not have applied in 1916.) In support of these plans Sarrail set up a new French base at Florina, south of Monastir, on 10 May, and occupied the Greek fortress at Dova Tepe facing the Belasitsa mountains a week later.[6]

On 3 May Robertson made a non-committal reply to Joffre's of 24 April. In the meantime Joffre had carried on with his planning, and on 14 May wrote to Robertson again, this time with specific requests for British support including two more divisions, mountain artillery, cavalry, and transport. Despite the fact that he had given Mahon in April some assurances of this nature when units of the BSF started moving out of the entrenched camp, Robertson did not want to be led by Joffre into deeper involvement in a campaign he had been against from the first.

In his view, he told Joffre on 17 May, the Romanians were not coming, the Greeks were unprepared and unequipped, the Serbs were untried, the Bulgarians would fight tooth and nail, the British forces in Salonica lacked field and mountain artillery and mules, and these shortcomings could not be made up in the short term, British shipping was stretched to the limit, and, well, the best thing to do would be send most of the British units to France and leave a small detachment to guard Salonica.[7]

One thing the British General Staff had already realised however, was that with such momentum building up on the French side they needed a stronger man on the ground to face up to Sarrail. Finding an appropriate assignment for General Mahon in Egypt, Major General George Milne, Commander of XVI Corps in Salonica since the beginning of the year, was promoted to his post.

Milne was a 49-year-old Scotsman who had been commissioned in the Royal Artillery in 1885. Just as Mahon had distinguished himself as a young officer at the relief of Mafeking, so Milne had come to Kitchener's attention at the battle of Khartoum in 1898 as the artillery officer who had landed a direct hit on the tomb of the Mahdi.[8] Milne's appointment was probably piloted by Robertson. The two men had served together in India, 1885-95, had attended Staff College at Camberley at the same time 1898-99, and had served together in the Boer War. From 1903–1906 Milne had worked under Robertson in Military Intelligence, including, as it happened, work on Turkey and the Balkans.[9] Despite this, or perhaps because of it, Milne did not receive his new appointment with any enthusiasm. He was very aware that General H.M. Wilson, commander of XII Corps was senior to him. He noted in his diary on 5 May, the day he received his promotion 'I hate the whole thing. Wilson is the senior. I spend an unhappy evening ... the difficulties ahead are great.'[10] His successor as Commander of XVI Corps was General Briggs, previously commanding 28th Division. Both Wilson and Briggs gave him loyal support for the rest of the Campaign.

However, Milne brought a number of qualities to the job. Firstly, on top of all his colonial service, he had already experienced the very different sort of war on the Western Front. Secondly, an artillery background was indispensable on the Macedonian Front. Thirdly he and his CIGS had a good working relationship, even if their views often diverged. He had a reputation of a strong disciplinarian. Also, at the time of his appointment he had already been in Salonica for almost six

---

5 Falls, *Macedonia Vol. 1*, pp.123–124.
6 Gray and Argyle, *Chronicle Vol. 1*, p.206.
7 Palmer, *Gardeners*, p.63.
8 Palmer, *Gardeners,* p.65.
9 Graham Nicol, *Uncle George, Field Marshal Lord Milne of Salonica* (London: Reedminster Publications, 1976), p.51. There is a superb photo of Robertson and Milne together in South Africa following p.182.
10 Nicol, *Uncle George*, p.88.

months, long enough to understand how things worked there; an external appointment would have faced a steep and lengthy learning curve.

Luigi Villari who as Italian liaison officer had many contacts with him reported that 'he was a man of uncommon intelligence, with extremely shrewd powers of observation and insight, and, unlike Sarrail, he was exclusively a soldier and did not take any interest in political matters.' He disliked Salonica as a hot-bed of personal and political intrigue and established his advanced HQ at Guvesne (about 20 km up the Seres Road) where he could be in touch with both his Corps.[11] Jean-José Frappa, a journalist accredited by the French government to the *Armée de l'Orient* described him as '*grand, vigoureux, énergique, buté, sachant à merveille éluder les questions délicates avec une politesse remplie de dignité.*' (tall, strong, energetic, obstinate, with a wonderful ability to avoid answering questions of a sensitive nature in a polite and dignified way.)[12]

Sarrail's take on the matter in his memoirs was somewhat different. In his view Mahon had been sacked for being '*trop francophile, trop ententiste*' (too pro-French, too pro-Entente). *Il était remplacé,*' he goes on, '*par le Général Milne, ami personnel du Général Robertson, et par suite opposé à tout ce qui touchait à l'expédition de Salonique.* (He was replaced by General Milne, a personal friend of General Robertson and therefore opposed to anything connected with the Salonica campaign.)[13]

General Milne took over from General Mahon on 9 May 1916. He was promoted to Lieutenant-General in January 1917 and remained in command of the BSF until the end of the war. During the first weeks of his command he moved 28th Division north to the new advanced line in support of 22nd Division and the two French divisions covering the sector from the Doiran railroad to lake Arjan, leaving his other three divisions to cover the line of the entrenched camp, to engage in road making, and to act as strategic reserve for the two advanced divisions.

The day after his new appointment Milne had his first official meeting with Sarrail, followed by several others over the next few weeks. He sent his early thoughts on the Commander of the Allied Army of the East to Robertson:

> A strong man with big ideas and outlook with great brain power, but of a conceited, excitable, impetuous and unscrupulous nature, is resentful of control and opposition which lead him to be impatient with those who do not agree with him ... He drives and does not lead, or make allowances for the different mentality of the nations with which he has to deal ... Possibly a good strategist but not a great tactician ... Inclined to descend into detail and control inferior formations possibly due to the lack of a Corps Commander beneath him ... His mental calibre is far and away above his Staff ... He is surrounded by several persons of no standing who do not influence him for good.[14]

This was perceptive but it did not auger well for a collaboration which was to last for nearly 18 months.

Twice during May General Milne was reminded by his General Staff that he was not to engage British troops in any offensive action. In two meetings in early June both his appointment and instructions were tested as Sarrail put further pressure on Milne, telling him finally that he would go ahead with or without British participation. The offensive Sarrail had in mind, a reduced variant of the 21 division plan proposed to Joffre in early May, was one whereby the French would attack between Lake Doiran and the Rupel defile, the Serbs would attack in the direction of Monastir and the Crna basin, and the British would conduct a limited offensive/holding operation between

---
11 Villari, *Macedonian Campaign*, p.70.
12 Jean José Frappa, *Souvenirs d'un Officier de Liaison en Orient* (Paris: Flammarion, 1921), p.171.
13 Sarrail/Porte, *Mon Commandement*, p.126.
14 Nicol, *Uncle George*, p.88.

Lake Doiran and the Vardar. Milne was unimpressed, Robertson even less so, and the British Government and central Staff put a veto on the whole proposal.[15]

Following this however Sarrail did agree to a proposal from Milne that a dedicated sector of the Front should be allocated to the British. In this way the potentially demoralising situation of French units advancing through static British positions could be avoided, and the British would be able to hold their allocated sector against enemy attack while remaining within the rules defined by the General Staff.

This proposal was agreed on 6 June 1916 and the British forces now took over total responsibility for the Struma Front with three divisions, and the sector from the south west of Lake Butkovo to Sarigol on the Galico river with the other two.[16] These dispositions involving movement in the height of the summer, were completed by 27 June 1916. The BSF were to hold this heavily malarial area, shortly to include most of the Butkovo and Doiran Fronts, virtually in exclusivity until late 1918 when part of the lower section was handed over to the Greeks.

At this point the BSF's total lack of aircraft became even more critical. Even for air reconnaissance Milne was having to borrow sea planes from the Naval Air Service. The enemy on the other hand was well equipped in the air and from June 1916 had airfields at Drama, Xanthe, Udovo and Cestova. To defend the long line he had taken over Milne now asked for two aerial squadrons and following the visit of a senior RFC officer on 1 July who discovered that the French had 160 planes to cover the Franco–Serbian sectors, the two squadrons materialised, No.17 Squadron in July and No.47 Squadron in August, together with a balloon section. The planes however were inferior to those of the Germans, who did not follow a policy of sending dated models to secondary theatres. Critically, during 1916–1917 the German planes were put out of reach because they could fly higher. General Trenchard, at that time commander of the RFC in France found that the BE 12 fighters with which the BSF Squadrons were equipped 'incapable of useful work against hostile fighters.' Despite this, the record of the BSF pilots was generally good, making up to some extent material inadequacies with good planning and clever tactics.[17]

Exactly a month earlier an event occurred which had added extra focus to the importance of the Struma Front. On 26 May 1916, a force of Bulgarians and Germans advanced into Greek territory down the Struma valley to the strategically positioned Fort Rupel. The garrison opened fire, and the invaders retired. In the afternoon however the garrison received orders from the Greek Government to cede the fort to the invading force. The Greek commander of the fort was also told not to telegraph the news to Salonica. A Bulgarian division then advanced unopposed, despite the presence of a Greek Division in Seres, for ten kilometres into Greek territory and established defensive positions in villages at its southern end.[18] This decision of the Greek Government seemed as inexplicable as their earlier decision to disallow the transport of their Serbian allies across Greece, but it was later discovered that the cession of Fort Rupel was the result of negotiations which had been going on for some time; it was not, in any way, a panic decision on the spur of the moment. Two massive loans to the Government of Skouloudis from Germany in March and April could perhaps have had something to do with it.[19]

The Bulgarians remained entrenched in the Struma valley for the rest of the war, and the British forces there were to fight many actions against them. Strategically it was an obvious and essential action for the Bulgarians to take, and this no doubt is how it was presented to the Greek Government. The road through the Rupel pass and along the Struma was by far the shortest and

---

15 Nicol, *Uncle George*, p.92.
16 Falls, *Macedonia Vol. 1*, p.125.
17 Jones, *War in the Air*, p.337.
18 Palmer, *Gardeners*, p.66.
19 Falls, *Macedonia Vol. 1*, p.120.

most direct route from Greece to Sofia, and still is. The distance is about 140 km, for half of which the Struma river forms a natural valley before debouching into a plain for the last 70 km to the Bulgarian capital. The Bulgarian invasion into Greece through the Rupel pass was, initially, a defensive move.

But this was a game-changing event, causing dismay in Greece – it was only three years since they had fought these very same Bulgarians over this very same territory. The Venizelist cause was given an enormous shot in the arm. Sarrail, taken completely off guard, was furious. At that moment it was certainly conceivable that the Bulgarians would now proceed with the annexation of the whole of eastern Macedonia up to their border on the river Mesta, and few of Sarrail's forces were anywhere near. British and French military staffs and Governments were for once united in their sense of outrage and their determination to take immediate action against the Greek Government.

Venizelos had resigned on 5 October 1915 as a result of irreconcilable differences with King Constantine over Greek war aims, and particularly over the king's refusal to recognise Greece's commitment to support the Serbs. He and his Liberal Party had then boycotted elections which had been called in November, and from that time the pro-German Skouloudis had governed without an opposition.

Since the departure of Venizelos relations between the Allies and the Greeks had gone rapidly downhill. Firstly there had been the government-backed obstructions to the Allied landings and their establishment in Salonica, then as the Allies prepared to move north to support the Serbs (actually at the behest of the Greeks) the selective denial of the railways, then the threats that on their return the Allied forces would be disarmed and interned by the recently mobilised Greek army, then the refusal to let the reconstructed Serbian army cross Greece to get to Salonica. But the Rupel incident was the most blatant contravention, as the Allied governments saw it, of the Greek government's declared policy of neutrality.

On 9 June a joint note was presented, on behalf of their governments, by the Ministers of Britain, France and Russia (the so-called 'tutelary powers', basing their tutelary rights on the Convention of London 1832) to the Greek Government.[20] It demanded the demobilisation of the Greek army, the removal of the pro-German government of Skouloudis, new elections to be held, and, (strangely reminiscent of the demands made on Serbia by Austria in July 1914) the chastisement of police officials who had insulted the Allied legations, and the reining in of 'foreigners endeavouring to ensnare Greek public opinion', (this last referring to Baron Schenk, the director of German propaganda in Athens who had a deep purse). These were not toothless requests. They were backed up by a blockade of Greek ports by the Allied navies, and the preparation of a naval demonstration against Athens.

King Constantine gave in to all these demands. On 22 June Zaimis once again replaced Skouloudis, the demobilisation order went out and was completed by the end of July. The Allies consequently lifted their blockade, except that of Kavalla which was now more easily accessible to the Bulgarian army.[21]

This was power politics. In northern Greece the Allies greatly outnumbered the Greek forces and had vastly superior weaponry. The Allied navies were omnipotent in the Aegean and the seas around Greece. On this occasion all passed off without physical confrontation. Worse was to come in 1917.

But Sarrail had got in first. As the man on the spot he had been invested by the French government on 1 June with the authority to take any steps he thought necessary to ensure the safety of the

---

20 Villari, *Macedonian Campaign*, p.35
21 Falls, *Macedonia Vol. 1* pp.131–132.

Allied forces in Macedonia.[22] Never a man given to long drawn-out decisions, he acted immediately within two days of receiving the go-ahead, and less than a week after the Rupel incident, by calling a State of Emergency in Salonica. It was unfortunate, but almost certainly fortuitous, that the date chosen, 3 June, happened to coincide with a celebration to honour the King's name day, which was cancelled. French troops took over the main government buildings.[23] Milne, fearing that the anti-German fervour stirred up among the Greeks by the Rupel incident would be lost with the effective declaration of martial law in Salonica, counselled caution but was overruled. In the interests of Allied solidarity he placed units of British military police under the orders of the French to support the enforcement of Sarrail's policy.[24]

The practical result of Sarrail's action was that he finally took control of the press, the post office, and above all of the railways in and out of Salonica. Technically therefore Salonica was now an 'occupied city'. Its inhabitants however had probably never been better off or better defended.

Up to now use of the Greek railway system had depended entirely on the caprices of Greek railway officials, who also charged outrageous prices. These railways consisted of three main lines out of Salonica, respectively to Constantinople, Monastir and Skopje. Any sort of regular services to these final destinations was of course interrupted during the war where they ran through enemy territory. The Constantinople line effectively ended at Demi Hasar where the allies had blown it up to prevent Bulgarian incursions into the Struma valley, and from the end of 1915 the Skopje line stopped at the Greek–Serbian border. The line to Monastir however remained open for most of the time.

Together with an ever increasing number of single track decauvilles constructed during the course of the war these were railway lines of crucial importance for the transport of men and materials within Greek Macedonia and along the very extended allied front.[25] Taking control of the railways was one of Sarrail's most significant achievements during his period of command and was of enormous importance in the direction of the Allied war effort.

---

22 Armées Françaises, *Tome VIII Vol 1*, p.491.
23 Mazower, *City of Ghosts*, p.308.
24 Palmer, *Gardeners*, p.67.
25 Villari, *Macedonian Campaign*, p.221 gives a good list of all the railways and major decauvilles used and built by the Allies during the Campaign.

12

1916
Defeat of Romania

(Map 5)

By the end of 1915 the only remaining non-belligerent nations in central and southern Europe were Greece and Romania. Despite the almost total control exercised by the Allies over her northern territories and the seas around her, Greece persisted in her neutrality. Since the collapse of the Dardanelles campaign and the increasing unlikelihood of Greece's territorial ambitions in Asia Minor being realised, her neutrality had tended more and more towards Germany.

Romania's territorial ambitions however mainly centred on lands within the Austro-Hungarian Empire, giving the Allies hope that sooner or later she would fall into their camp; unlike Bulgaria, Romania would not be seeking territorial gains at the expense of Allied nations.

Romania had been a result of the 1878 Treaty of Berlin, where the borders assigned to her had been those of the Ottoman province of the time. These excluded Transylvania and the Banat, both lost by the Ottomans following the Battle of Vienna in 1683, and which after various incarnations had been incorporated into the Kingdom of Hungary in 1867. Bukovina was also excluded, having been annexed by the Austrians in 1770. On historic and ethnic grounds Romania laid claim to all three territories, of which Transylvania was the largest and much the most important. A complete Romanian wish-list would have included Bessarabia with its significant Romanian population, but this was part of the Russian Empire. Transylvania was always the key object.

For the Allies, Romania's entry into the war at their side would have brought numerous advantages besides her army of half a million men. Access by the Central Powers to the Black Sea, particularly along the Danube, would be seriously impeded. The effectiveness of Turkey as an ally of the Central Powers would be much diminished. Romania's corn and foodstuffs would be valuable for the Alliesbut denying them to the already heavily blockaded Central Powers would have been equally valuable. Romania's oil-fields, based on Ploesti, sixty kilometres north of Bucharest, were the biggest in Europe at the time.

For all these reasons but particularly denying her natural resources and her strategic position to their enemies Romania would equally have been a valuable acquisition by the Central Powers, and the Germans tried to push Austro-Hungary into an act of self-amputation, but Emperor Franz-Josef (unsurprisingly) would have nothing of it.[1]

In the summer of 1916 the Allies were gaining the upper hand on all fronts; in France the Germans had failed to take Verdun. The Italians had repulsed the Trentino offensive by the Austrians and had won the sixth Battle of the Isonzo. In Salonica the Allies were building a force which would soon be big enough to attack Bulgaria from the south. But above all the Russians

---

1   Schiavon, *Front d'Orient*, p.202.

Map 5. The Romanian Campaign August–December 1916.

under Brusilov during June and early July had secured a crushing victory over the Austrians on a wide front north and south of the Dneister,[2] and taken 400,000 prisoners.[3]

At the beginning of July of his total 167 divisions, von Falkenhayn only had seven in reserve for eventual allocation to other fronts.[4] The Austrians were so stretched by their operations against Italy and Russia that they would only have been able to muster five divisions at that time against a Romanian attack. Transylvania itself, according to von Hindenburg who was shortly to take over from von Falkenhayn as Chief of Staff, was only defended by 'customs officers and policemen.'

In that summer of 1916 Joffre saw the adhesion of Romania as the key to closing the war,[5] and when Romania did finally declare for the Allies and marched into Transylvania the German Kaiser is reported to have said 'the war is lost', rather prematurely as it happened.[6]

Apart from her territorial ambitions, Romania's economy was suffering badly from the closure of the Dardanelles through which in normal times 80% of her trade passed.[7]

Romania had opened discussions with the Allies as early as January 1916, principally in search of arms and equipment. The French were willing to provide these, but the logistics were complicated. Supplies would have to be delivered to southern Russia and then shipped by rail to Romania. From the beginning of July, planes, guns and other equipment to the value of 30 million francs were despatched, but then held up due to Russian rail blockages. Sadly, for fear of awakening the suspicions of the Central Powers, the Romanians turned down the offer of a French military mission of the sort which had been so successful in the reconstruction of the Serbian army.

On 4 July 1916 Ion Bratianu, Romania's War Minister as well as Prime Minister made his conditions known for joining the Allies. Romania should continue to receive arms and material at the rate of 300 tonnes a day, Allied offensives on all fronts should continue, and above all the Russians should continue their presence and pressure in Bukovina and Galicia. And finally that the Allies should guarantee against attack from Bulgaria from the south.[8]

The time, if ever, was ripe for action, but another six weeks were now lost in discussion. The French wanted to knock Bulgaria out of the war through concurrent attacks from the south by the whole of the Allied Army of the East and from the north by a Romanian force of 300,000 men. Under this scenario the Russians would take care of the Austro-Hungarian armies on Romania's eastern flank. However the Russians whose Brusilov offensive was faltering wanted to be involved as little as possible, and if so with an independent command. The Romanians wanted to invade and occupy Transylvania while retaining a position of neutrality vis a vis Bulgaria.[9] The British would participate in an Allied offensive against Romania, but only if Romania declared war on Bulgaria, and made a simultaneous attack from the north.

A provisional agreement was reached on 23 July but was not ratified. Following a further month of bi-lateral talks trying to reconcile the various positions, a final agreement was reached on 17 August. Under this Romania committed to declare war no later than 28 August and to commence offensive operations against Austro-Hungary on the same day. This action would be 'generally directed' through Transylvania on Budapest 'so far as the military situation south of the Danube permits'. At least a week before this the Allied Army of the East would open a 'definite offensive'

---

2   Anthony Livesey, *The Viking Atlas of World War 1* (London: Viking, 1994), p.98.
3   Schiavon, *Front d'Orient*, p.189. Some of these prisoners were from unwilling Slav minorities in the Austrian Army and were subsequently released by the Russians to serve in the Allied Army of the East in Macedonia.
4   Falkenhayn, *German Headquarters*, p.199.
5   Larcher, *Grande Guerre*, p.139.
6   Gilbert, *First World War*, p.282.
7   Glenny, *Balkans*, p.339.
8   Larcher, *Grande Guerre*, p.138.
9   Larcher, *Grande Guerre*, p.141.

(*offensive affirmée*) against Bulgaria from her positions on the Serbo–Bulgarian border. Russian involvement was to be limited to sending three divisions into the Dobrujah to 'cooperate with Romania against the Bulgarian army'.[10]

On paper this agreement essentially gave Romania carte blanche to achieve her Transylvanian ambitions while the Allies helped to guard her back against Bulgaria and the Austrians. In reality the possibility of Sarrail's force joining hands with the Romanians south of the Danube was remote and became even more improbable following a two-pronged pre-emptive Bulgarian attack on the Allied Army of the East on 17 August. Moreover, the Russian contingent would only be brought into action if the Bulgarians invaded the Dobrujah.[11]

As agreed, Romania declared war on 27 August, but only on Austro-Hungary. Within hours Romanian forces were crossing the frontier passes into Transylvania.

Germany declared war on Romania the next day. Turkey joined in on 30 August, and Bulgaria on 1 September. It may well have been that following side discussions with the wily Bulgarian premier, Radoslavoff, the Romanians had received indications that in exchange for territorial adjustments – probably in the inevitable Dobrujah – the Bulgarians would not enter the fray. It took four days for them to be disillusioned; in fact the Bulgarians were as primed and ready as they had been against Serbia in September 1915.[12]

The six week delay had given the Central powers an invaluable breathing space. The intelligence services of Conrad von Hoetzendorf were probably aware of the military discussions between the Allies and Romania of 23 July and were certainly reporting to him as early as 2 August of pre-mobilisation steps being taken by the Romanian army. This was time enough for him to put together an emergency force of 25,000 troops and 23 artillery batteries.

On 29 July and again on 4 August the Chiefs of Staff of the four Central Powers had met to review their strategy. Von Falkenhayn was aware that if the Romanians concentrated all their efforts on Bulgaria in a joint action with the Allies in Salonica, Bulgaria could be forced out of the war with far-reaching if not terminal effects on the Central Powers' war effort. If they decided to commit most of their forces to striking through Transylvania, von Falkenhayn thought they could be contained. He expected and planned for the latter, and he was proved right.[13]

Over the next three weeks the Central Powers made admirable use of their railways, and within a few days of the Romanian declaration were rapidly gathering together a force capable of withstanding a Romanian assault on Hungary. To hold the Danube a joint army group of Bulgarian, German and Turkish forces was set up under General von Mackensen.

On 27 August, the day she declared war, Romania had at her disposition 20 divisions. Another seven divisions were due to come into line within a few days. Of the 20 divisions the Romanian High Command decided to keep eight for the moment to guard against a Bulgarian attack, and to send twelve across the Carpathian passes into Hungarian Transylvania. Rather than mounting a single and direct attack towards Budapest across the Hungarian plain, the advance was on a wide front, all the way from the Tolgyes Pass in the north to the Vulcan Pass in the south, a distance of 250 kilometres. By 9 September they were held at Hermannstadt (now Sibiu), and two divisions were sent back to support their fourth army now in action against the Bulgarians.

By 6 September the Austro-Hungarians and Germans between them had put 13 divisions into the field. Von Falkenhayn who had been replaced as German Chief of Staff by von Hindenburg following his reverse at Verdun had been put in charge of the Ninth Army facing the Romanian

---

10 Falls, *Macedonia Vol.1*, pp.138–139.
11 Les Armées Françaises, *Tome VIII Vol 2*, Annexe 1.457 The Russo–Romanian military agreement.
12 Lazar Marcovic, *Serbia and Europe 1914–1920* (London: George Allen and Unwin, 1920), p.237.
13 Falkenhayn, *German Headquarters*, p.279.

thrust into Transylvania. By mid-September a further four divisions had been added, still not much more than half of those facing them, but better armed and trained than their adversaries.[14]

Meanwhile the Bulgarians under General Toshev, the eastern wing of von Mackensen's army group, had moved across the flat country of the southern Dobrujah and secured a notable victory against the Romanians at Bazargic (now Dobrici) on 4 September, taking 28,000 prisoners. This was only four days after Bulgaria had declared war; their troops must have been at a high level of readiness. In Transylvania the Romanians decided to hold their positions until the Bulgarian advance in the Dubrujah had been stemmed. By 20 September a mixed force of 12 Romanian and three Russian divisions faced the Bulgarians, who decided to dig in.

The Romanian armies in Transylvania tried to continue their advance, but new Austro–German units continued to arrive, and when two Romanian divisions were encircled and obliged to return to Romania, the Romanian High Command asked Joffre to intercede with the Russians for support. Joffre advised concentrating all efforts on the Bulgarian army until Russian reinforcements arrived. On 29 September von Falkenhayn secured a victory against the retreating Romanian army at Hermannstadt, and by 9 October all Romanian troops were back in Romania, digging in at their frontiers, and waiting for the Russians. Russia was supposedly sending three army corps via Moldavia, but once again railroad blockages were retarding them.

On 11 November von Falkenhayn forced the Vulcan pass and secured a victory on Romanian territory against the Romanian First Army at Targu Jui, about 50 km north of Turnu Severin. A Romanian counter-attack was unsuccessful. On 25 November General Mackensen with his Austro-Hungarian and Bulgarian troops made a surprise crossing of the Danube at Sistova, drove a wedge between the retreating Romanian troops and defeating them at Tirgovistea less than 50 kilometres from Bucharest. The Central Powers took Bucharest on 5 December, and by 6 December had taken the Ploesti oil-fields (although these were partially put out of action for six months by a team of British engineers/saboteurs). The remaining Romanian forces made their way to Moldavia, which, with Russian help, they held. The Romanian court and government were set up in restricted circumstance in Iasi and remained there for the rest of the war.[15]

Not much more than three months had passed between Romania's declaration of war and her defeat. She had lost two thirds of her territory, suffered 230,000 casualties of which 50,000 fatal, and 140,000 of her troops were taken prisoner. Cyril Falls in his Official History of the Macedonian Campaign concluded that 'The Romanian campaign of 1916 was, on the victors' side, the most brilliant in the annals of the World War, and into the bargain conducted by the War's two ablest commanders.'[16]

Against this however it is worth noting that as a result of declaring for the Allies, once in August 1916 and again in November 1918, Romania was awarded at the end of the war more territory proportionate to her size than any other of the Allied nations. This included, not only the coveted Transylvania, Bukovina and much of the Banat, but also the Maramures from Austria and the Cristana region from Hungary. She also took, but subsequently lost to the Soviet Union, Bessarabia, today's Moldova.

* * *

It has seemed logical to cover the whole Romanian Campaign in one chapter despite the fact that its time-frame overlaps that of the main Macedonian Campaign, and despite the fact that preparations for an Allied offensive, to which the narrative now returns, are made under the presumption of a successful joint action with Romania.

---

14 Falls, *Macedonia Vol. 1*, p.198.
15 Schiavon, *Front d'Orient*, pp.210–212.
16 Falls, *Macedonia Vol. 1*, p.200.

13

1916
The Bulgarians Strike First

(Maps 4 & 6)

In his admirable account of the ever-shifting positions and viewpoints of the British and French High Commands on the purpose and future of their forces in Macedonia, Commandant Larcher notes that the French were ready to mount offensive actions to provoke the adherence of the Greeks and Romanians to the Allied cause. He continued, *L'adhésion de la Grèce et la Romanie était désirable aussi à l'Angleterre mais comme condition préalable et non comme conséquence des opérations dans les Balkans* (The English would also have liked to see Greece and Romania joining the Allies, but as a prerequisite, not as the result of military actions in the Balkans).[1]

On 17 May Robertson had written to Joffre with his habitual clarity that he was against Joffre's proposed summer offensive in the Balkans for a range of reasons including the unlikelihood of Romania entering the war in the near future.

Less than two months later he had been proved wrong. Romania was proposing to join the Allies, and, moreover, on her own assessment of her chances, and not as a 'consequence of Allied operations'.

The BSF had been brought into being in 1915, in theory at least, to help the Greeks support the Serbs. By the end of 1915 this justification for the British presence in Salonica no longer existed. Now however a new justification for the presence of Allied forces in Salonica had presented itself.

As previously highlighted by Mahon and then Milne to Robertson, the BSF was lacking in pack transport and wheeled transport as well as artillery, and at projected rates of supply would not be fully ready for mountain warfare until September.[2] But the British General Staffs now recognised that the Allies had to work together to exploit the opportunity presented by Romania entering the war, and a necessary first step was a clearer definition of the Allied lines of command. A more precise statement of operational terms of reference between the French and British forces was now necessary, and particularly the working relationship between Milne and Sarrail.

These were discussed and agreed at an Allied conference in Paris on 23 July, and were sent by Joffre to Sarrail, and by Robertson to Milne on 25 July. Although an honest attempt had been made to reconcile the ambitions and sensitivities of the two sides, the agreed text still left considerable scope for interpretation, and stopped well short of defining a unified command structure.

Firstly, the objectives of the offensive and subsequent operation were to be 'settled by agreement between the British and French High Commands'. In executing these agreements Milne was to

---

1   Larcher, *Grande Guerre*, p.124.
2   Falls, *Macedonia Vol. 1*, p.140.

Map 6. Monastir and Kaymakcalan 1916.

give Sarrail 'support and cooperation proportionate to the numbers and equipment of the forces under his orders.'

Sarrail was to consult Milne on the use he proposed to make of the British forces but was to have 'latitude as Commander in Chief to decide on the missions, the objectives to be gained, the zones of action, and the dates on which every operation is to commence.'[3]

This was, at least, a more flexible set of rules than those given to Mahon on 11 January but fell well short of the degree of overall command given to Sarrail by the other members of the Allied Army of the East.

The Serbs, conscious that they wouldn't have been there at all without the efforts of the French, effectively put themselves under the direct command of Sarrail. The formula was *le Général Sarrail, commandant en chef des troupes alliées à Salonique, exercera ce commandement au nom du Prince Régent Alexandre* (General Sarrail, supreme commander of the allied troops in Salonica, exercises this command over the Serbian army in the name of Prince Alexander).[4]

The Russian Brigades which arrived on 1 August and which lacked any of their own services were initially attached to the French Army and then in part to the Serbian Army.

The Italian 35th Division which arrived two weeks later accepted an operational formula similar to that of the BSF, but without some of the pre-conditions.[5]

Now that the Allied Army of the East had expanded to include units from five separate nations, Joffre decided that Sarrail could no longer manage the dual role of Commander the Allied Army of the East and Commander of the French Army of the East. Someone needed to be appointed to report to him in the latter role and fulfil the same functions as the heads of the Serbian, British, Russian and Italian contingents. Sarrail wanted General Leblois to be appointed to this post, but Joffre gave him a shortlist of three other candidates. General Sarrail selected General Cordonnier over General Berthelot, and interestingly, over General Guillaumat, the man who in 1917 was to replace him.[6] Cordonnier took up his appointment on 11 August. On quizzing his leaders in London, Milne was told that this appointment didn't affect him. He was told 'Joffre probably made this change so that Sarrail could exercise a better control over French, Serbs, Russians and Italians.'[7] Joffre himself would probably added 'and British', at least within the terms of the 27 July agreement.

The telegrams which Joffre and Robertson had sent to Sarrail and Milne on 27 July had also included a statement of the mission of the Allied Army of the East with respect to supporting Romania:

> Firstly in order to cover Romanian mobilisation and actions against Austro-Hungary the Allied Army would open an offensive against Bulgaria (probably on 1 August) with a view to containing the maximum number of Bulgarian troops.
>
> Afterwards, when Romania had begun her operations south of the Danube the Allied Army would combine its actions with the Russo-Romanian army, and then 'direct all their efforts to destroying enemy forces.[8]

In light of the terms of the final agreement reached with Romania on 17 August, this 'Afterwards' was largely wishful thinking. No Russian 'army' was expected, only three divisions under

---

3   Falls, *Macedonia Vol. 1*, Annexe to Chapter 7 p.150. Telegram from Robertson to Milne of 25 July 1916.
4   Armées Françaises, *Tome VIII Vol. 2*, Annexe 1 451.
5   Larcher, *Grande Guerre*, p.142.
6   Schiavon, *Front d'Orient*, p.199.
7   Falls, *Macedonia Vol. 1*, p.151 Telegram from Robertson to Milne 11 August 1916.
8   Armées Françaises, *Tome VIII Vol. 2*, Annexe 1 392.

independent command, and the Romanians were not even intending to declare war on Bulgaria. Yet the subsequent Allied offensive was predicated on the 'Afterwards' as much as on the 'Firstly'.

* * *

Already in March Joffre had been in favour of an offensive action undertaken by the 15 Allied divisions then available or in arrival. On 24 April he had written to Robertson to this effect. In May Sarrail had put together a wide-ranging proposal based on 21 divisions, which he didn't have.[9] Joffre had presented this plan with its underlying extra requirements to Robertson in mid-May and Robertson had roundly rejected it, as well as a watered down version of the same plan proposed by Sarrail to Milne later in the month.

But by July Romania's entry into the war had become a certainty, and Robertson had agreed to the participation of the BSF in an Allied offensive in accordance with the mission statement agreed at the Paris Conference of 23 July, and with a 'probable' start date of 1 August.

Sarrail's plan in May based on the hypothetical 21 divisions had seen the Allies stretched out from the lower Struma in the east to Lake Prespa in the west, and had involved two major thrusts into enemy territory, by the Serbs through Monastir and by the French north-east of Lake Doiran. To support these, two strong demonstrations were to be made by the British through the Doiran–Vardar gap, and by the French cavalry and Zouave units up the Struma valley.[10] This was probably too much to attempt over such a vast front, and Joffre himself had been in favour of concentrating forces on one major push.

Anyway, the 21 divisions had never materialised, and on 1 August Sarrail would have (or would shortly have) the equivalent of 17 divisions from five nations, with a ration strength of 369,000 and a fighting strength of 250,000 supported by 259 artillery batteries and 13 air squadrons.[11]

Sarrail had to adjust his plan on this basis by reducing the size of the front proposed for the offensive, cutting out the Struma valley element and extending no further than Florina to the west.[12] The Serbs, after a month of reorganization, training and recuperation at their base at Mikra in the Vasilika Valley south of Salonica, began moving to the front on 17 July. They were to take over a sector, until now held very lightly by French forces, from Kupa to Florina; their First Army from Kupa to Strupino, and their Second and Third Armies from here to Florina.

French 122nd Division with the Russian Brigade were to cover the sector from Kupa across the Vardar to Chaushitsa north of Lake Arjan. From here the BSF XII Corps would secure defences as far as Kilinder, linking up with the French 17th and 57th divisions spread along the railway line to Lake Butkovo. The French 156th Division was to be held as a general reserve on the Vardar at the level of Lake Amatovon.

The BSF XVI Corps would patrol the Struma from Lake Butkovo to the sea, while on the east bank of the Struma four French brigades were positioned to execute the original plan of a strong demonstration up the Struma Valley.

Effectively, as a result of not having the 21 divisions he had planned for in May, Sarrail was shortening his front and planning his major assault sixty kilometres east of Monastir rather than through Monastir itself. The main attack was to be made by the Serbs through the 800 metre high pass in the Moglena mountains to Huma,[13] from where a road ran to the Vardar. Subsidiary attacks

---

9   See Chapter 10.
10 Falls, *Macedonia Vol. 1*, p.123.
11 Armées Françaises, *Tome VIII Vol. 1*, p.581.
12 Armées Françaises, *Tome VIII Vol. 1*, p.499
13 See Map 10.

would be made east of the Vardar.¹⁴ The proposed attack to the north-east of Lake Doiran, a major feature of the '21 division' plan of May had been dropped.

By 3 August all of these pieces were in place except for the Serbian First Army, hampered by transport problems, but a further three weeks were to pass before Romania finally declared war and invaded Hungary.

Significantly, and ominously, before the Serbs had taken up their allocated positions the Bulgarian army decided to test the waters on 5 August with a push down from Monastir into Greece. They took two Greek villages, Negochani and Rahmanli just over the Greek border and waited to see what the Allied response would be. Still waiting for the Romanian declaration before unleashing his main offensive, Sarrail limited himself to minor actions on the Doiran and Struma fronts.

To the south of Lake Doiran between 10 and 17 August the French 17th Colonial Division took Hill 227 and the Tortue Hill, while BSF 22 Division took Kidney Hill and Horseshoe Hill, 'at the point of bayonet in the face of stubborn opposition'.¹⁵ These were strategically useful positions and enabled the Allied line to be straightened and a line of advanced posts to be established on the line Doljeli to Reselli.¹⁶ The Petit Couronné was to elude the Allies until 1918. Some minor actions were taken by the French 57th Division in the Belasitsa valley, and the French brigades over the Struma conducted armed reconnaissances.¹⁷

Then, satisfied with the results of their exploratory probe of 5 August, and on 17 August, the very day that Romania finally committed herself, the Bulgarians pounced.

* * *

Certainly aware that the Allies were holding back in expectation of the Romanian declaration, and equally aware that it had not yet been made, Bulgarian forces made determined and successful pre-emptive strikes down both of their flanks. On their right, western, flank Bulgarian forces on 17 August advanced rapidly down both sides of the Kenali Valley and captured Florina station. The following morning 18,000 Bulgarian troops poured down through the gap and within a few days had taken Florina and Banitsa and reached Lake Ostrovo.¹⁸

On the same day, on their left flank, the Bulgarian Second Army came down through the Rupel Pass. Part of their force made towards Demi Hasar, part advanced over the Vrundi Balkan to Seres. A third incursion was made over the Mesta river towards Kavalla. The Greek IV Corps in Seres following instructions from Athens made no opposition, except for parts of the 6th Division under Colonel Christodoulon, who defended the fort of Phea Petra before falling back on Kavalla. Moving southwards and westwards the Bulgarian forces occupied Seres on 25 August. They began digging in on the left bank of the Struma and pushed on towards the coast. When they reached Kavalla the Greek commander handed over the forts of the town. Of the 9,500 Greek troops in the area, only the force of Colonel Christodoulon, 1,500 men with their batteries, elected to be moved by Allied ships to Salonica. The remainder were interned in Gorlitz in Germany for the rest of the war.¹⁹

The Bulgarians then completed the take-over of all of eastern Greek Macedonia up to their own frontier along the Mesta River. The Bulgarian forces used for this offensive and the occupation of

---

14 Sarrail/Porte, *Mon Commandement*, p.428ff
15 See Map 9.
16 George Milne, *Despatch of 6 December 1916* (London: HMSO Gazette, 1916), Paragraph 3.
17 Sarrail/Porte, *Mon Commandement*, p.179.
18 Palmer, *Gardeners*, p.76.
19 Gordon-Smith, *From Serbia*, p.282.

eastern Macedonia were a complete Division (the 7th) and three or four brigades from other divisions, in total the equivalent of four Allied divisions.[20]

As it turned out this well-coordinated east-west Bulgarian advance was by far their greatest and furthest offensive action of the whole war. The moves were if not directed then certainly approved by von Falkenhayn, still for a few more days in the driving seat. The demobilisation of the Greek army – which the Allies had demanded to clear their backs – von Falkenhayn had seen as an opportunity to be seized by the Central Powers; if the Bulgarian army now invaded Greece there could be no risk of a clash with the Greek army. And there was always a chance that the King, faced with such a *fait accompli* might finally declare where his interests and his instincts lay.[21]

It is possible that the German High Command had even greater hopes from this pincer movement. Despite the pressing need for troops to face the perceived Romanian threat, two precious German divisions had been found to support the Bulgarian attack.[22] If the thrust down from Monastir had succeeded in piercing Allied defences, and had then swung left to join up with Bulgarian Second Army advancing across the Struma, would they have been able to encircle the Allied forces and lay siege to Salonica? Some commentators have suggested that this might have been the German intention.[23] However, as long as the Allies controlled the road and rail routes from Vodena to Salonica, the risk was small. Also, the Bulgarians, having occupied eastern Macedonia had achieved their equivalent of Transylvania, and had small motivation to go much further.

Inevitably the situation soon turned sour within the territories occupied by the Bulgarians, particularly in eastern Macedonia and even more so when part of the garrisoning of this newly conquered area was passed over to the Turks, which began as early as 11 September with the Turkish 50th Division taking over the sector from Drama to the sea. Those units of the Greek (now peacetime) army in Macedonia now viewed the 'occupation' by the Allies in a different light. The declaration of a separatist Provisional Government by Venizelos would probably have happened anyway, but the Bulgarian occupation of Greek eastern Macedonia gave it greater weight and immediacy.[24]

At the time however the two pronged pre-emptive strike was a brilliant move on the part of the Bulgarians and their German mentors. At a stroke they had consolidated their position in eastern Macedonia and had rendered the option of an Allied attack up the Rupel valley for the rest of the war much more problematic. In the west they had totally disrupted the Serbian build-up and had forced Sarrail to turn his attention to Monastir, the approaches to which the Bulgarians were now able to fortify and as a result inflict very significant casualties on the French and the Serbs over the next two months.

The Allies had been taken badly by surprise. On their left flank the Serbian Danube division, outnumbered two to one, had been forced to retreat deep into Greek territory, finally falling back on Ekshisu and Sorovic. A line was established on the Malareka Ridge where on 22 August they repulsed a succession of five Bulgarian attacks. A brigade of French 156th Division was sent from Verria to support them.[25] Meanwhile Serbian reinforcements were rushed in to the north of Lake Ostrovo, setting up their guns on the ridge north of Ostrovo station, and then advancing through the Gornicevo defile.[26] The Serbian Third Army, supported by the Vardar Division and the French

---

20   Milne, *Despatch of 1916*, Para 5.
21   Larcher, *Grande Guerre*, p.150.
22   Palmer, *Gardeners*, p.75.
23   Ducasse, *Balkans*, p.150, Villari, *Macedonian Campaign*, p.43, Larcher, *Grande Guerre*, p.151.
24   Larcher, *Grande Guerre*, p.154.
25   Villari, *Macedonian Campaign*, p.43.
26   Ducasse, *Balkans*, p.151.

had stopped the advance, but the Bulgarian front line as a result of this surprise action had extended forward by over 20 kilometres including Florina and the Malka Nidje ridge.[27]

The Bulgarian thrust into eastern Macedonia on the other hand had involved no confrontation with Allied lines or positions. Since moving out of the entrenched camp some patrolling and reconnaissance work across the Struma had taken place but no permanent Allied presence had been established. This was, purely, a Bulgarian invasion of a part of Greek territory to satisfy Bulgarian territorial ambitions as well as to deny it to the Allies. At the time of the invasion only the French detachment and three squadrons of the British 7th Mounted Brigade were across the river. Faced with overwhelming odds these withdrew, but not before sustaining casualties of over 300.

The unexpected Bulgarian attacks of 17 August had several consequences. Firstly (as they had intended), they had forced the Allies to delay their planned offensive to support Romania's entry into the war; in fact the new Allied offensive would not start until 12 September instead of the planned date of 1 August in line with the final Romanian timing. Secondly, Sarrail was obliged to change his game plan yet again. Thirdly, the Serbian Army had had its first taste of battle since 1915. Lessons had been learnt and changes made including the replacement of the veteran Commander of the Serbian Third Army, General Jurišić Sturm with General Vasić.[28]

As for Sarrail, events had forced him to recognise that although he had shortened his front westwards, the enemy had not, and in addition to their 8th Division based between Monastir and Sović, of which he was aware, they also had the equivalent of another division to its right, of which he had not been aware.[29] But as per usual he reacted quickly, and on 20 August called a conference of all Allied commanders.

---

27 Villari, *Macedonian Campaign*, p.44.
28 Jurišić-Sturm's military career went back, amazingly, to the 1870 Franco-Prussian War. He was born in 1848 and was only one year younger than Voivode Putnik who retired at the end of the Albanian retreat.
29 Falls, *Macedonia Vol. 1*, p.149.

14

1916
The Allies Re-enter Serbia

(Map 6)

Most of Sarrail's carefully worked plans of July were now obsolete. An offensive based on a Serbian advance to the Vardar over the Huma pass supported by subsidiary Anglo-French attacks up the Vardar valley was no longer sustainable with the enemy already in Florina and on Lake Ostrovo. And with the Bulgarian Second Army already pouring down the Struma valley and on their way to Kavalla the concept of a strong demonstration at the mouth of the Rupel Pass had been completely overtaken by events.

Sarrail was now obliged to accept battle on the enemy's terms, and this involved a major shift westwards of his operations. He now had to address himself to regaining the land lost south of the Greek border, recapturing Florina and advancing on Monastir. This was to be the mission of the French army with the Russian Brigade. The Serbs were now to turn the enemy's flanks by taking and holding Mount Kaymakcalan and advancing over the Malka Nidje ridge to the Crna bend. The Allied armies would then press on to the Vardar along the Prilep road and Babuna pass and/or the Crna valley. There were to be no subsidiary thrusts up the Vardar valley. The line of the Struma had to be reinforced against eventual Bulgarian attacks towards Salonica and demonstrative attacks on this and the Butkovo front were to be made only in the interests of defence and of tying down the enemy forces.

All this called for a fundamental realignment of his forces, and above all bringing almost all of the French Army of the East, now commanded by General Cordonnier, to the far left of his line, beyond the Serbs.[1] From Verria, south of Vodena, 156th Division was brought out of reserve. The Zouaves were brought back from the Struma. The Russian Brigade and part of 122nd Division were brought across from the east bank of the Vardar where they were replaced by the British 22nd Division. The French 57th Division was removed from the Butkovo front, which was then taken over by the newly arrived Italian 35th Division. The Italians were subsequently to extend their line almost to Lake Doiran, relieving parts of French 17th Colonial Division also for service across the Vardar.[2]

The earlier move of the Serbs from their base south of Salonica to their new positions from Kupa to Florina, begun on 17 July, had been a pre-planned move benefitting from the full backing of Allied transport and services. Yet it had been barely completed before the Bulgarian attack on Florina a month later. In view of this the logistical difficulties of completing an unplanned move of virtually all French and Russian units from their current positions to the extreme left of the

---

1 Larcher, *Grande Guerre*, p.164.
2 Villari, *Macedonian Campaign*, p.44.

Allied line between 20 August and 12 September, Sarrail's chosen date for the counter-attack, can be imagined.

Bringing the French 156th across from their base in Verria was the easiest part of the problem. But the 57th and 17th Colonial divisions, the Russian Brigade and parts of 122nd Division, with all their arms and services would have to be brought down from the distant Butkovo and Doiran fronts, and the Zouaves from even further, distances of 150–170 kilometres, much of which would have to be marched. Cordonnier would inevitably receive these units piecemeal, tired and short of equipment.

Sarrail nevertheless remained upbeat and on 5 September issued a heady order of the day:

> *Les armées alliées vont prendre l'offensive à l'ouest du Vardar dans le but de rejeter les forces ennemies au-delà de la Crna. Cette offensive sera menée par l'armée serbe ainsi que par une armée franco-russe commandée par le Général Cordonnier* (The Allied armies will go on the offensive to the west of the Vardar with the aim of throwing enemy forces back across the Crna. This offensive will be led by the Serbian army, as well as a Franco–Russian force commanded by General Cordonnier).[3]

The new offensive commenced on 12 September. Due to the delay in the Romanian declaration and the subsequent Bulgarian attack, this was nearly six weeks later than Sarrail had planned.

It started well, with the Serbs taking the town of Ostrovo and the Malka Nidge ridge on 13 September. By 17 September they had forced the Gornicevo pass and completed all preparatory work to moving up the slopes of Kaymakcalan.

Kaymakcalan, which has two summits both over 2500 metres connected by a ridge of 1,500 metres, was to become the pivot on which the whole Macedonian Campaign turned. For the purposes of the current Allied offensive, however, its possession was seen as essential to protect and cover any Allied advance up the Crna valley towards Monastir and beyond. The mission was assigned to the Serbian Third Army, General Vasić, supported by elements of the French 17th Colonial. Six batteries of mountain artillery were manhandled up the mountainside to support this attack. They gained, then lost, 'Fort Boris' three ranges of trenches on the upper slopes, with casualties of 900, but on 30 September after a day of vicious hand to hand fighting the Bulgarians were put to flight.[4] The battle of Kaymakcalan may have been the fiercest of the many battles the Serbs were to fight during the course of the war, but it was certainly also the most important; it was from these imposing heights, dominating the Bulgarian positions on the Moglena, that the artillery cover for the final breakthrough in September 1918 was to be provided.

On 13 September the French 156th Division, coming in from below Lake Ostrovo, moved forward from Rudnik to Banitsa. The Russians branched off along the Mala Reka towards Neretska, and 57th Division moved up the left flank and on 19 September reached the Col of Pisoderi. Before retreating from Ekshisu however the Bulgarians had blown up the viaduct on the railway from Salonica to Monastir. This was a considerable loss to the Allies, restricting the passage of supplies and troops on their advance first to Florina, then to Monastir.[5] It was not repaired until 17 November.

Cordonnier advanced slowly against light opposition and took Florina on 17 September, four days after Sarrail had planned, the delay due to the time needed to consolidate the incoming French forces. But four days was little compared with the two months it was now going to take before the Allies finally reached Monastir. The first task which faced Cordonnier and his Franco–Russian

---

3   Armées Françaises, *Tome VIII Vol. 2*, p.27.
4   Ducasse, *Balkans*, p.151.
5   Schiavon, *Front d'Orient*, p.217– 18.

forces was to clear the Bulgarian defences around Florina, and above all the dominantly positioned St Mark's Monastery hill. This had to be neutralised before any further advance, and it took until 2 October.[6] At this point the Allies had regained the line they had held before the Bulgarian attack of 17 August, and the Serbs had gone beyond it, but it had taken six weeks.[7]

Even before the monastery hill had been taken, Cordonnier had reconnoitred the land north of Florina as far as Kenali. Here he found three state-of-the-art defensive lines, one behind the other, complete with trenches, dugouts, gun emplacements and machine gun posts. They ran from the foothills west of Kenali, below Kenali itself, then along the northern bank of the River Brod until they reached the ridges above the town of Brod itself.[8] The Bulgarians and their German advisors had been working on these since January, methodically, undisturbed by enemy action, just as the Allies had worked on the Salonica entrenchments during the same period. Cordonnier reported all this to Sarrail.

At the best of times Sarrail had little patience, and it was fast running out. While Cordonnier was only conscious of the strength of the enemy positions before him, Sarrail was also conscious of the days ticking away in his programme to meet his assigned objective of supporting the supposed Russo–Romanian army moving south. Convinced that Cordonnier was overestimating Bulgarian strength he ordered a joint attack, Serbs to the right, French and Russians to the left on 3 October.[9]

The attack went ahead, the Serbian Third Army reached the Crna through Petalino, Cordonnier's forces were repulsed on the left. On 5 October Cordonnier made an aerial reconnaissance and saw a way of turning the Bulgarian defences by advancing westward through the foothills of the Baba range south of Monastir.[10]

Sarrail would have none of it and ordered another attack on the Kenali defences on 6 October. Again, no progress was made and many casualties incurred. Meanwhile the Serbs were on the Crna, and to the north of Kaymakcalan had even mounted an unsuccessful attack on the high plateau of Dobropolje.[11]

Some reinforcements were rushed to the French, and on 14 October Cordonnier was ordered to make another frontal attack. Before this there had been a face-to-face showdown between Sarrail and Cordonnier, the former having come up from his base in Salonica. The Serbs, Sarrail told Cordonnier, were over the Crna and were meeting all their objectives while the French were hesitating in front of Kenali. Cordonnier replied, *vous verrez le chiffre de nos morts ce soir, vous verrez si l'infanterie a fait son devoir* (You will see from the number of our dead this evening that the infantry has done its duty).[12]

The day's casualties were 1,500 French and 600 Russians.[13] Cordonnier had had enough and ordered for 20 October not another attack but an armed reconnaissance of the route he had identified from his aerial survey. *Il s'agit d'un combat d'étude, non d'une attaque* (This is a reconnaissance,

---

6   Palmer, *Gardeners*, pp.81–82.
7   Larcher, *Grande Guerre*, p.164.
8   Schiavon, *Front d'Orient*, p.128.
9   Schiavon, *Front d'Orient*, p.219.
10 Falls, *Macedonia Vol. 1*, p.187.
11 Schiavon, *Front d'Orient*, p.219.
12 Schiavon, *Front d'Orient*, p.220.
13 By the end of October French casualties killed and wounded were over 4,000. During the whole Macedonian Campaign the French soldiers who were killed in what is now the Republic of Macedonia are all interred in an enormous, sombre, poorly tended and unsigned military cemetery just east of Monastir, now Bitola. There are 6,000 individual graves and a further 7,000 to 10,000 interred in two ossuaries. 8,000 French soldiers died in Greece, many of them of illnesses. They are buried in the main Allied Cemetery at Zeitenlik on the Lembet road in Salonica, countless unrelenting lines of crosses, even for the non-Christian colonial soldiers.

not an attack).[14] For Sarrail this was the last straw. He wrote to Joffre asking permission to replace Cordonnier with Leblois, and within a few days Cordonnier was back in France.[15]

* * *

On 27 October while this was going on Milne wrote an intriguing letter to Robertson in which he recounted that Sarrail had been 'nearly recalled in disgrace' some time ago, and that Cordonnier had in fact been sent to replace him. Sarrail had certainly won that one. Milne goes on to muse that 'should Sarrail now be able to discredit Joffre by showing that the latter had not properly supported him with men and reinforcements, he may hope to step into his shoes.' If so, Milne further surmises, Sarrail would make the east a main, if not the main, theatre of war, so satisfying 'his following in France because they wish so far as possible to save their country and their army from further loss … Sarrail is a clever politician but a shocking strategist.' In support of this rather startling train of thought, Milne sent a telegram on the same date stating that 'Briand (the French Premier) is greatly under the influence of Sarrail who is doing all he can for French interests in the near east after the war … I gather that he sent in his resignation of this command unless reinforcements were sent …'[16]

* * *

On 20 October therefore the Allied centre was still held up in front of the Kenali defences.

But on the Allied right both the First and Third Serbian Armies had been making steady progress. On 6 October elements of the Third Army (Vasić) reached the Crna at Skocevir. By 24 October it had cleared remaining enemy forces from the Starkov Stob hills to the south of the Crna and reached the confluence of the Crna and the Strosvica. On 4 November battle was joined with the Bulgarian forces south of Polog. On 9 November with strong artillery support, both Serb and French, the Serbs took Polog at bayonet point, and then the heavily defended summit of Mount Chuke, taking 600 captives and a number of guns. By 11 November the Serbian Third Army was in control of the eastern sector of the Crna bend up to Iven.

The Serbian First Army (Mišić) had crossed the Crna at Brod on 11 October. On 17 October they took Volisedo and released the cavalry in a charge on Baldenci which was taken on 19 October with 1,000 prisoners including many Germans and a large number of guns. Torrential rain then intervened, halting operations, and allowing the Germans to bring up more troops. On 29 October the Serbs destroyed the bridge at Bukri to prevent the enemy from crossing the Crna. On 13 November supported by a regiment of Zouaves they had reached Jarasok.[17]

On the Allied left the Russians and French 57th Division were approaching Monastir through the hills to its south, an outflanking operation remarkably similar to the one which Cordonnier had been proposing. In this they were supported by the Italian Cagliari Brigade, brought down from the Butkovo front.

---

14 Ducasse, *Balkans*, p.153.
15 Cordonnier of course has a different point of view. In 1930 he published 350 pages of memoirs entitled '*Ai-je trahi Sarrail?*' His version is that he resigned but had no chance to put his views until he got back to France. Leblois' appointment was an interim one. In January 1917 General Grossetti was sent out to take up the role of Commandant of the French *Armée de l'Orient*. He got on well with Sarrail but had to be replaced at the end of the year due to an illness which was shortly to prove fatal. As it happened he left the scene almost on the same day as his boss.
16 Nicol, *Uncle George*, p.106. Milne had previously informed Robertson, who probably knew anyway, that Sarrail's son-in-law was Briand's secretary.
17 Gordon-Smith, *From Serbia*, pp.314–325.

During October a third Italian brigade had arrived in Salonica to join the other two brigades which had arrived in August. Each Italian brigade was composed of six battalions: two brigades were therefore the equivalent of a British or French division. Composed now of three brigades, the Italian 35th Division, together with its mountain batteries, machine gun companies, cavalry squadron, engineers, transport and services amounted to nearly 50,000 men.[18] On the arrival of this third brigade, Sarrail had asked for one, Cagliari, to be sent to the Monastir front. The other two remained for the moment on defensive duties between the British XVI and XII corps.

Due to poor organization and transport delays the move of the Italian Cagliari brigade took three weeks.[19] It did, however, arrive in time to contribute to the taking of Veluščina on 19 November and Bratindol two days later thereafter establishing a presence in the Crna bend which was to be its location for the rest of the campaign.[20]

Action against the Kenali lines recommenced on 10 November, and after four days' fierce fighting the Bulgarians decided to abandon the position in view of the risk of encirclement by the French–Russian–Italian forces on their right, and the continuing Serbian onslaught on their left.

On 19 November the Allies finally arrived in Monastir, although the Bulgarians continued to hold strategic positions to the north of the city, including the infamous Hill 1248 only four kilometres away, and would continue to hold them for another year.[21] Monastir was subjected to sporadic shelling. One casualty was General Pettiti, Commander of the Italian 35th Division, wounded by shrapnel a few days after the Allied entry to the town.[22]

The weather had now broken, Allied supply lines were at full stretch, and casualties had been unaccountably high. Sarrail would have liked to press on towards Prilep, but it was not on, particularly with the uncertain Greek situation to his rear.[23] The Serbs continued to press northwards for a few more days and took but later lost Hill 1050 in the centre of the Crna bend. They also had lost a lot of men and had been actively campaigning now for more than two months. Joffre officially called an end to operations for the year on 11 December.

The taking of Monastir was unquestionably an achievement, even if Sarrail's claim that it was the first French victory since the Marne could be subjected to objective analysis. It was a mere twenty kilometres into Serbia, still 300 kilometres from Sofia and even further from the Danube, but, as a city of 50,000 inhabitants it was a good base. It was also, theoretically, an ideal jumping-off point for a further offensive in 1917. Unfortunately the Bulgarians had applied a scorched earth policy as they withdrew, and the people of the town needed to be fed as well as the soldiers.[24]

However, other than to make certain inroads into Bulgarian resources and resolve, and to cause the Germans to commit some of their valuable forces to a theatre in which they had no interest, Sarrail's 1916 offensive had not met its stated objectives: within a few days of the Allied Army of the East taking Monastir, the Central Powers took Bucharest.

---

18 Villari, *Macedonian Campaign*, p.46.
19 Falls, *Macedonia Vol. 1*, p.186. Falls who is normally reticent about the other members of the Allied forces on the Macedonian Front notes that Colonel Maynard, liaison officer between the War Office and the BSF considered that the main reason for the slow progress was incompetence at the HQ of the *Armée de l'Orient*. 'It is doubtful whether the French without the transport lent by the British would have moved at all.' See the rather more guarded comments made by Milne at the same time.
20 Villari, *Macedonian Campaign*, p.47.
21 Schiavon, *Front d'Orient*, p.227.
22 Another casualty, this one fatal, in March 1917, was Mrs Catherine Harley, sister of Field Marshal French who had directed a Scottish Women's nursing centre in Salonica (and had been decorated for it by General Sarrail on the same day as he himself received the KMCG), and subsequently a hospital centre for the Serbs in Monastir. There is a handsome memorial to her in the Serbian section of the Allied Military cemetery in Salonica.
23 See Chapter 16.
24 Schiavon, *Front d'Orient*, p.228.

Sarrail had not been responsible for the delay in Romania's declaration of war. Had he been able to launch his planned offensive on 1 August (the 'probable' date agreed by both high commands) he may well have forestalled the Bulgarian surprise attacks of 17 August, retained the initiative, and indeed provided material support for the Romanian campaign, assuming – a big assumption – that all the necessary troop dispositions had been completed in time. Nevertheless, despite his uneven performance, the unease caused by the Cordonnier affair, and the heavy criticism dealt out by some of the Allied commanders, the history books would show that Monastir had been taken under his leadership, and he kept his job on the back of it.

15

1916
Autumn Campaigns on the Vardar and Struma Fronts

(Maps 4 & 7)

Meanwhile on the Struma Front the withdrawal across the river of the French task force and of the British 7th Mounted Brigade on 19 August had enabled the Bulgarians to consolidate a hold on the left bank of the river, particularly along the Constantinople railway and the villages south of Seres. Following the Allied Commanders' crisis conference of 20 August, and the decision by Sarrail to move most of his French divisions across to the Monastir front, a significant re-structuring of Allied forces on the Struma, Butkovo and Doiran–Vardar fronts had been necessary.

By the end of August a re-distribution of forces from the Gulf of Orfano all the way around to the Vardar at Machukovo was more or less in place. The Struma Front from the mouth of the river at Neohori to Butkovo was now fully assigned to BSF's XVI Corps, except for a stretch from Ahinos to Gedeli, still held for the moment by the French detachment. Two brigades of 27th Division were left to guard the Salonica entrenched camp.

From Lake Butkovo covering the entire Butkovo front up to the east of Lake Doiran were two brigades of the Italian 35th Division. South of Lake Doiran parts of the French 17th Colonial Division retained a small sector until their departure on 10 November. This was then transferred to BSF's XII Corps who from that point held the whole of the crucial sector from Doiran to Vardar, facing the strongest enemy defences on the whole Macedonian Front.[1]

While all these changes were being made a small unit from 27th Division nipped across the Struma over its last bridge at Neohori and blew up two rail bridges where the Constantinople railway crossed the Angista river, and the next day destroyed two road bridges over the river.[2]

Then, to support Sarrail's offensive of 12 September, Milne decided to mount a major attack on enemy positions at Machukovo by 22nd Division, and at the same time ordered General Briggs, Commander of XVI Corps to conduct a series of extensive raids on enemy positions across the Struma.

Machukovo was a village just inside the Greek border two kilometres east of the Vardar. Behind Machukovo was a bulge in the enemy line. In the centre of the bulge was a hill which the French who had previously held this sector had named the Piton des Mitrailleuses. To the right of this ran a ridge which they had called the Dorsale, and behind was another hill, the Dome, beyond which the land fell away slightly. On these hills, and to the right and left of them the enemy had been perfecting sturdy and integrated defensive lines for the best part of six months. The lines were

---

1 Falls, *Macedonia Vol. 1*, pp.160–161.
2 Milne, *Despatch of 1916*, Paragraph 5

1916 Autumn Campaigns on the Vardar and Struma Fronts

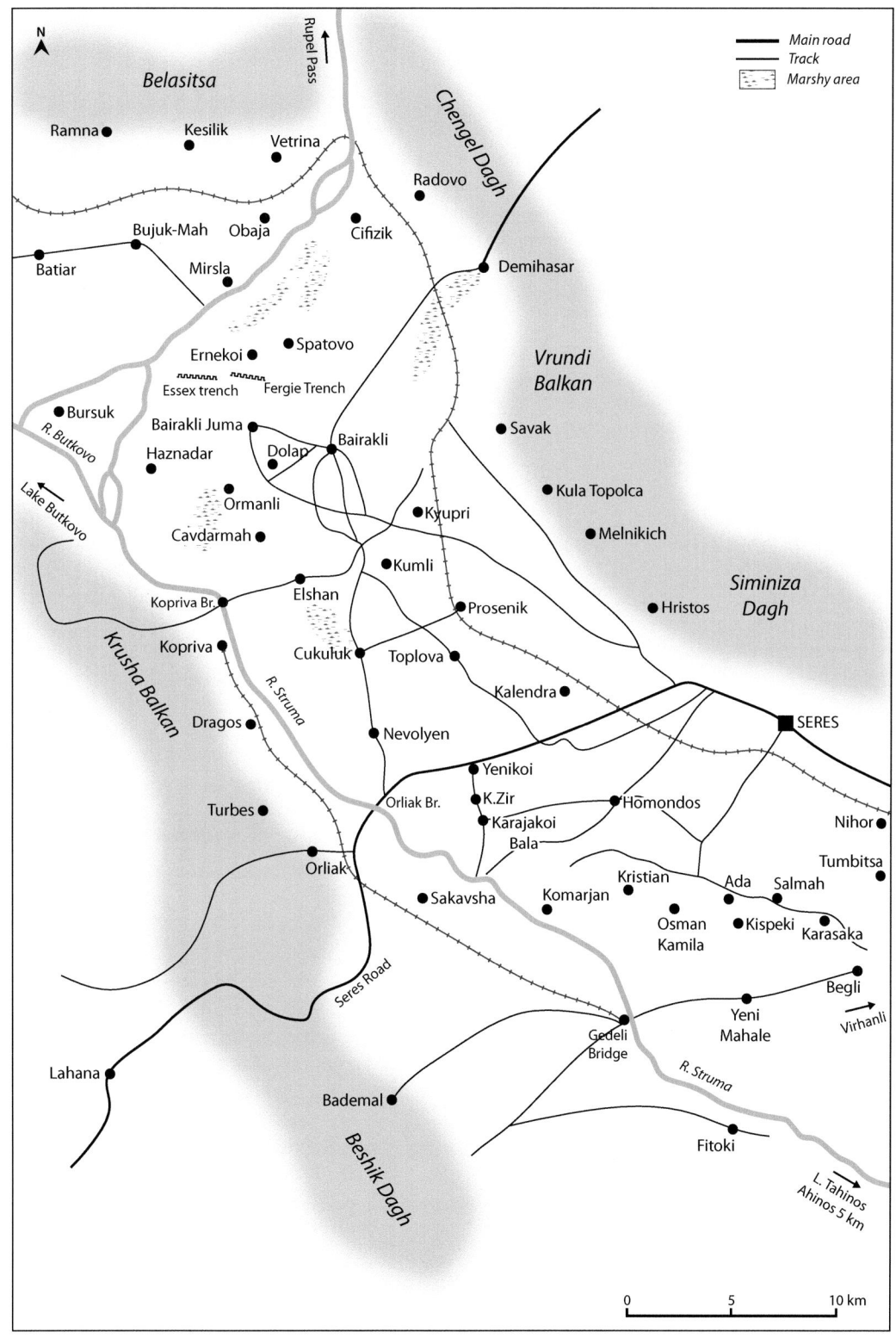

Map 7. The Struma Front.

manned by the German 59th and 146th brigades. Milne's objectives were to take and hold the Piton and the Dorsale.

An artillery barrage opened on 12 September and was intensified on 13 September with French heavy guns from across the Vardar joining in. The infantry attack was launched at 0200 on the morning of 14 September by units from 22nd Division. The Piton and the Dorsale were both taken but were then subjected to a withering artillery attack from three sides, coupled with murderous machine gun enfilade fire from the Dome. The Germans counter-attacked at 1400. The Dorsale was lost. The Piton was lost, then regained, then lost again. The action was called off at 1630, the retreat was well covered by the gunners, but casualties of almost 600 represented fifty percent of those units directly engaged.[3]

With all the sad resignation of hindsight the Campaign's Official Historian recorded that:

> The enterprise had been well-planned, well led and gallantly executed. The artillery had done its wire-cutting work thoroughly, though it had had little effect on the dug-outs constructed by the Germans. After this experience it would have been over-sanguine to expect that any large operation on this heavily fortified front could be carried out without heavy losses.[4]

Particularly, he might have added, with many units undermanned and weakened with illness. This set-back at Machukovo was a smaller-scale forerunner of the slaughter at Doiran during 1917-18.

Since the establishment of the Macedonian Front it had been obvious to both sides that there were three main routes out of Greece into Serbia and Bulgaria. One, the widest but the most distant, was through Monastir where the French were having major difficulties in piercing enemy defences in essentially flat country around Kenali, and, despite having nearly ten divisions to throw at the problem would advance no further than 30 kilometres into enemy territory during the current offensive.

The second was up the Rupel Pass into Bulgaria itself. The Bulgarian attack of 17 August had essentially closed off this route unless excessive force were applied – far greater anyway than anything the BSF XVI Corps in its current strength could muster.

The third and most direct route was between Lake Doiran and the Vardar which, once breached, would offer the invader both the Vardar valley to Skopje and Belgrade, and the Strumica valley to Bulgaria.

It was not surprising that the Germans had paid particular attention to the construction of a line of fortifications along this 15 kilometre stretch from the lake to the river of unparalleled strength and sophistication. This work, started in late 1915, had been carried on by the Bulgarians over the following sixteen months untroubled by any serious Allied interference. Facing the Allies on this sector was the crack Bulgarian 9th Division (Plevna), one Brigade of their 2nd Division, and two thirds of the German 101st Division.[5]

The attack on the Piton and the Dorsale had shown that attacking these defences with anything short of unlimited firepower and expendably large follow-up forces was as unproductive in military terms as it was tragically wasteful in human terms.

Nevertheless, General Wilson, Commander of XII Corps, persisted with nightly patrols, raids, shelling, and local in-depth attacks on selected parts of this enemy line, including three separate brigade-strength raids with artillery support between 18 and 22 October. On one of these Private H.W.Lewis, three times wounded in the fighting, became the first of only two members of the BSF

---

3   Charles Packer, *Return to Salonica* (London: Cassell, 1964), pp.38–41.
4   Falls, *Macedonia Vol. 1*, p.169.
5   Milne, *Despatch of 1916*, Paragraph 7

to win the Victoria Cross during the whole campaign on the Macedonian Front.[6] Raids and probes were continued by XII Corps right up to end December, by which time all activity on the Monastir Front had been discontinued.

These actions inflicted some damage and casualties and obliged the enemy to stay alert and remain at his post, which was the main objective. But casualties mounted up also on the British side. Success was much more likely on the BSF's other front, the Struma, where the flat country did not so easily favour the construction of defensive positions, and anyway the Bulgarians had not yet had much time to dig themselves in.

The Machukovo action by 22nd Division had been timed to support Sarrail's general offensive date of 12 September. Milne had asked General Briggs, Commander of XVI Corps, to mount concurrent actions on the Struma Front with the same intention.

On 10 September large scale raids were launched on the villages of Karajakoi Bala, Karajakoi Zir, Yenikoi and Nevolyen across the Struma. The advance was repulsed by heavy fire and although the village of Nevolyen was taken, it was then lost to a strong Bulgarian counter attack. The British forces were surprised by the unexpectedly fast reaction of the enemy. Lessons were learned and over 250 casualties sustained.[7]

A week later on 17 September on the Butkovo Front four companies from the Italian 35 Division who were holding advanced positions in the Belasitsa Valley were attacked by an overwhelming Bulgarian force. Casualties of 180 including prisoners were incurred while withdrawing.[8]

After the unpropitious start against the Bulgarian forces over the Struma in September, General Briggs aimed at something much more substantial in October. The ensuing campaign of carefully programmed attacks, gains and consolidations following one after the other with methodical precision until the enemy had been pushed back from the Struma to ever more distant holding positions was of copybook standards, and among the BSF's most complete military achievements during their whole time on the Macedonian Front.

Briggs' first objective was to succeed where he had failed earlier in September by taking and holding the villages of Karajakoi Bala, Karajakoi Zir and Yenikoi, and securing a major bridgehead over the Orliak Bridge on the Seres road. In support Milne sent up three 6-inch howitzer batteries from HQ Heavy Artillery Group to complement the artillery of 27th Division which was positioned on the right bank of the Struma between Orliak and Sakavsha. The attack was to be spear-headed by 81st Brigade of 27th Division while 82nd Brigade would be held in reserve.[9] The scourge of malaria had reduced some BSF battalions on the Struma Front to as little as 250 men.[10] Some consolidation had taken place, and 29th Brigade of 10th Division now had only two battalions. These were to advance on the flanks of 81st Brigade.

The engineers of 10th Division threw three bridges across the river downstream from the Orliak bridge one of which capable of carrying gun carriages. The Struma here ran in two swift flowing channels of 50 metres each.[11] Again, Caesar would have approved.

The attack was launched at 0545 on 30 September and following artillery support Karajakoi Bala was taken at 0750. Wiring parties were rushed up, and troops from reserve to help in reversing the Bulgarian trenches. By mid-afternoon after neutralising enemy firing positions Karajakoi Zir

---

6 Packer, *Return to Salonika*, p.41. Charles Packer, who was there at the time as part of 99 Brigade RFA, notes drily that this operation which resulted in 35 casualties was set up primarily 'to establish whether the German 59 Regiment was still on this front.'
7 Falls, *Macedonia Vol. 1*, pp.163–165.
8 Villari, *Macedonian Campaign*, p.39
9 Wakefield, *Under the Devil's Eye*, p.99.
10 In the summer of 1916 from 10th Division there were over six thousand admissions to hospital for malaria – a third of their manpower. The 28th division suffered almost as badly.
11 Wakefield, *Under the Devil's Eye*, p.99.

was also taken. Supplies to consolidate the position had already arrived at Karajakai Bala and were brought up immediately. Bulgarian counter-attacks during the night and the following morning and afternoon were all repulsed.[12]

General Briggs now set about widening his bridge-head and Yekinoi was taken after a lightning early morning attack on 3 October. The work of re-trenching and wiring for which the equipment had followed closely behind the attackers was again addressed. A major enemy counter-attack, infantry and artillery, was launched in the morning. Their infantry, advancing in open formation across the plain were cut down with heavy casualties and eventually retired.[13] On 5 October Nevolyen was taken and immediately secured.

Intelligence following reconnaissance by 7th Mounted Brigade showed that the Bulgarians in this sector had withdrawn up to the railway line. British losses from this action to date were nearly 1,250 of whom 159 killed and 51 missing, divided almost equally between 27th and 10th Division. Given the headcount shortfalls in most units, this was a heavy level of casualty. Bulgarian casualties were greater than this with at least 1,375 killed and 340 taken prisoner.[14]

General Briggs' next objective was Bairakli Juma, a much larger village 15 kilometres north of Nevolyen, and only ten kilometres south of the entrance to of the Rupel valley, and for this 28th Division was to be brought into action.

From the air and from ground patrols it appeared that Bairakli Juma had become the key point in a new line of Bulgarian defences on the Upper Struma. On 11 October an armed reconnaissance met with very heavy resistance and resulted in 98 casualties. The Bulgarians were clearly present in numbers and were determined to hold this position.[15]

Plans for the main attack on Bairakli Juma were made accordingly. On 26 October the villages of Cukuluk, Elshan, Ormanli and Haznadar were all taken with little opposition. A new artillery bridge was built across the river north of Kopriva bridge. Once again divisional artillery was reinforced by the 6-inch howitzer batteries from the Heavy Artillery Group.[16] At dawn on 31 October after a short artillery burst a fast and determined attack by two brigades from 28th Division was launched from north of Ormanli on Bairakli Juma and Dolap.

The Bulgarian defenders, taken totally by surprise, were quickly driven out, and subsequent forceful counter-attacks from Spatovo and Bairakli were halted by British artillery. Once again, immediately the positions had been taken, support units rushed up with the materials for their fortification. Casualties suffered during the taking of Bairakli Juma and Dolap were considerably less than those suffered during the earlier 'armed reconnaissance' and over 400 prisoners were taken.[17]

All three divisions now took part in pushing the XVI Corps' forward line right up to the Constantinople railway line, and of fortifying the villages of Prosenik, Topolova, Kalendra, Homondos and Osman Kamila.[18] The Bulgarian back had been broken. It was clear that they would now establish their line further back.

By the end of October the British front line had been pushed forward at least five kilometres on a front of twenty kilometres across the Struma. All three divisions of XVI Corps had been brought into play and were now holding their new positions, 28th Division to the north, 10th Division in

---

12 Falls, *Macedonia Vol. 1*, pp.178–180.
13 Wakefield, *Under the Devil's Eye*, p.108.
14 Falls, *Macedonia Vol. 1*, p.184.
15 Wakefield, *Under the Devil's Eye*, pp.110–111.
16 George Milne, *Despatch of 1917* (London: HMSO Gazette, 2017), Paragraph 5
17 Wakefield, *Under the Devil's Eye*, p.111.
18 Wakefield, *Under the Devil's Eye*, p.113. Alan Wakefield gives superb plans of the defenses built around the villages of Nevolyen and Topolova on p.112.

the centre, and 27th Division to the south. Patrolling had been thorough, tactics had been impeccable, and the speed of follow up by reserves and support services would have served as a classroom model for General Franchet d'Espèrey's offensives of 1918.

While these events were unfolding, the French detachment had continued to hold the line on the Struma below the Seres road. And almost unperceived, Macedonian Front history was being made with three battalions of Greek Nationalist troops operating under its orders. On 10 November the French detachment was withdrawn by Sarrail to join all the other French formations on the Monastir Front. The Greek battalions remained and were put under the orders of 27th Division until the end of the year when Sarrail ordered them back to Salonica. In his annual report Milne commented 'I much regret the severance of the cordial relations which had been established with this gallant group', but as it turned out, this was only the beginning of his work with the Greek forces during the rest of the Campaign.[19]

XVI Corps continued operations until the end of the year. These however were severely hampered by incessant rain which made movement difficult in the Struma Valley, turning previously dry or innocuous streams into un-fordable torrents, and above all playing havoc with the Seres road along which 90 percent of all stores and provisions for the Corps had to pass. Battalion-strength raids made on enemy positions along their new line including Ernekoi and Kyupri achieved their limited objectives, but major 'surprise' attacks on Tumbitsa Farm and Virhanli to remove and replace enemy positions above Lake Tahinos were unsuccessful.

All these actions on both BSF Fronts were set in motion above all to dissuade the enemy from moving troops from the east to the west side of the Vardar to face the greater threat of the Franco–Serbian force advancing on Monastir and perhaps even further. There was, however, an inevitable seepage. At the beginning of August there had been five Bulgarian divisions (each of 24 battalions) east of the Vardar, and two German brigades. By the end of September the Bulgarians had moved five of their brigades across to the Monastir front, and the Germans half a brigade.[20] In October however some of this shortfall had been made up when the Turkish 50th Division came into line on the lower Struma.

It has to be remembered that it was not only the Bulgarians and Germans who were transferring forces across the Vardar; during the same period Sarrail had also moved most of his remaining three French divisions across to the Monastir front, receiving in their place only the Italian Division.

The Campaigns of 1916 were now over on all Allied Fronts, Monastir, Moglena, Vardar-Doiran, Butkovo and Struma. Allied casualties sustained over the year were just short of 50,000, of which more than half (28,000) were Serbian. France accounted for 14,000, the Russians and Italians about 2,000, and the British just over 5,000. Enemy losses were calculated to be around 60,000 of which 52,000 Bulgarian and 8,000 German.[21]

In October Sarrail had called the Cagliari Brigade across to the Monastir Front. On 26 November he visited the wounded General Pettiti in hospital and told him he now wanted the remaining two Italian brigades on the other side of the Vardar, firstly against a perceived Greek Royalist threat from Thessaly, and then against a possible counter-attack by new German troops on the Allied lines around Monastir. The continuing rain, the mud, the consequent state of the roads and the tracks, and above all the poor organisation, about which Villari is particularly scathing, resulted in a journey of several weeks before the Italians could take up their new sector. This, agreed between Pettiti and Sarrail, was to be the western part of the Crna bend from Novak to Makavo.[22] The

---

19 Milne, *Despatch of 1917*, p.2.
20 Falls, *Macedonia Vol. 1*, pp.149 and 173
21 Martin Marix-Evans, *Forgotten Battlefields of the First World War, Salonica* (Stroud: Sutton Publishing, 2003), p.216.
22 See Map 6.

Italian 35th Division, with all three brigades now united, was to hold this sector almost until the end of the war.[23]

The French detachment having already gone, the departure of the Italians from the Butkovo front finally left the BSF with total responsibility for the whole Allied Front from the mouth of the Struma, up to Lake Butkovo, across to Lake Doiran then down to the Vardar. As General Milne noted in his annual Despatch to the War Office, this represented a distance of 90 miles, or 140 km.[24] The BSF were to hold this long sector virtually in exclusivity until the last months of the war with a maximum of six divisions.

---

23   Villari, *Macedonian Campaign*, pp.50–52.
24   Milne, *Despatch of 1917*, Para 1.

Serbian troops defending a hilltop from the Bulgarians before withdrawing to Prizren, October 1915. (*Illustrated War News*)

Voivode Radomir Putnik. Chief of Staff of the Serbian Army during the three Balkan Wars and the tripartite invasion of Serbia in 1915. Ill health forced his retirement following the retreat through Albania.

The exodus of the Serbian Army and countless civilians through Albania to the Adriatic in November–December 1915. (IWM)

The Serbian central staffs crossing the Drin river during the retreat through Albania, the sick Voivode Putnik being carried in a sedan chair. (MCM)

The landing of French forces in Corfu. 'The Entente have notified Greece that in order to save the Serbian Army from starvation, they have been transferred to Corfu.' (*The Sphere*)

Sacks of flour to provision Serbian bakeries during the reconstitution of the Serbian Army on Corfu, January 1916. (MCM/Opérateur H)

Arrival of French troops in Salonica, October 1915.

General Maurice Sarrail, Commander of the French Army of the East and subsequently of the Allied Army of the East from October 1915 – December 1917. (*Illustrated War News*)

Members of the French 122nd Division retreating down the Vardar valley towards Demi Kapu at the end of the 1915 Anglo–French expedition to Serbia. (MCM/Opérateur K)

The Vardar passing through the Demi Kapu (Iron Gates) gorge. (Author)

A leisurely moment in the trenches. The Balkan News was published every day from November 1915 to May 1919. It contained news wired from Britain, but also much home-grown material, and served as a link between the members of the BSF spread out over an increasingly extensive front. (NAM)

General Sir Bryan Mahon, Commander of the British Salonica Force from October 1915 to May 1916. (*Illustrated War News*)

French troops returning from the Anglo–French expedition to Serbia passing members of the recently mobilised Greek Army, December 1915. (*The Sphere*)

General Sarrail and staff inspecting part of the 'Birdcage' fortifications around Salonica, December 1915. (MCM)

The destruction of the railway bridge across the Struma at Demi Hasar ordered by General Sarrail, January 1916. (SCS)

Road building by British engineers using stones gathered by local labour. (*The Sphere*)

General George Milne, Commander of the British Salonica Force from May 1916 to the end of the Campaign. (SCS)

Zeppelin LZ85 shot down on 5 May 1916 by the guns of HMS *Agamemnon*.

'Digging up Macedonia' inevitably brought many ancient artefacts to light. The French set up an archeological service which identified more than 70 historical sites. (*The Sphere*)

The Serbian Drina Division embarking for Salonica from Corfu, April 1916. (MCM/Opérateur H)

Arrival of Serbian troops in Salonica. Around 120,000 men were shipped, without loss, around Greece from Corfu to Salonica between 11 April and 31 May 1916. (MCM/Opérateur K)

General von Falkenhayn on his way to the front during the Romanian campaign, accompanied by his Chief of Staff and an Austrian officer. (IWM)

The Ekshisu railway viaduct destroyed by the Bulgarians during their pre-emptive strike through Florina, August 1916. (SCS)

Serbian forces manning trenches before the Battle of Kaymakcalan, September 1916. (NAM)

Between 4 and 11 November 1916 the Serbian 3rd Army routed Bulgarian forces in the Mount Chuke area north of the Crna bend, capturing 36 guns and 600 prisoners. (*The Sphere*)

The bend of the Crna, a quiet river to have seen so much action. At the time of the Campaign its flood plain gave it a much greater width. (Author)

French troops entering Monastir 19 November 1916. (SCS)

Eleutherios Venizelos and the formation of his Provisional Government in Salonica, October 1916. On his right, Admiral Koundouriotis, on his left General Danglis. (MCM/Opérateur T)

British engineers constructing a bridge over the Struma. (SCS)

BSF gunners with 6-inch Howitzer on the Doiran Front. (NAM)

16

1916
Allied Interventions in Greece

In June 1916, following the Rupel incident the Allies had wrung gunboat-backed concessions from the Greeks, including de-mobilisation and a change of government. Simultaneously in Salonica Sarrail had declared a state of emergency and taken control of the railways. But matters did not stop here. Rupel was not just an opportunist foray by the Bulgarians into Greece, it was one step in a long-standing German programme to secure the adherence of the Greek Government to their cause. Unsurprisingly this programme bore strong resemblances to their earlier and successful campaign to bring Turkey onside – money, a show of military strength, and above all personal contacts, promises, and propaganda work on the ground. And in Greece they also had the advantage of dealing with a pro-German head of state with wide-ranging powers and a strong following.

As early as February 1916 when Sarrail's expeditionary force had been pushed back into Salonica by the Bulgarians of Mackensen's Eleventh Army, an agreement had been reached by the Germans with the Greek Government – headed by Skouloudis at the time – that the Greek Army would not offer resistance to invading troops if commanded or accompanied by German officers. On 23 May Skouloudis was reminded of this agreement, and consequently no resistance was given when the Bulgarians advanced on Fort Rupel four days later.[1]

In light of these understandings, the subsequent Allied demand for the de-mobilisation of the Greek Army was seen by von Falkenhayn as an advantage rather than the contrary when planning the Bulgarian two-pronged attack of 17 August. Here again, the Greeks were reassured by von Falkenhayn that their sovereignty would not be affected; their allies the Bulgarians would simply establish garrisons in those parts of Greece which, with the Greek Government's connivance, they had taken over. King Constantine if he needed to, and he probably did, could pretend to himself that he was simply respecting his declared policy of 'even-handed neutrality' by offering to the Central Powers the same sort of access to Greek territory already allowed to the Allies.

If the Bulgarians had ever signed up to von Falkenhayn's 'protective garrisons' concept they soon forgot about it, overrunning eastern Macedonia as victors, arming the Turkish and Bulgarian populations and committing atrocities against the Greeks.[2] Some 8,000 of the surrendering Greek troops were rounded up and sent to Germany, whether or not as formal prisoners of war being, from their point of view, irrelevant. Whatever von Falkenhayn's long term game plan, all this worked against it. Public opinion in the whole of Greece moved against the Germans, and in Macedonia the Allies came to be regarded as protectors rather than intruders. As Larcher observed, *L'antithèse était en effet frappante entre les exactions des Bulgares en Thrace et la correction des Alliés en Macédoine* (The contrast between the abuses perpetrated by the Bulgarians in Thrace compared with the correct behaviour of the Allies in Macedonia was indeed striking).[3]

---

1 Larcher, *Grande Guerre*, p.147.
2 Palmer, *Gardeners*, p.94.
3 Larcher, *Grande Guerre*, p.154.

Just before the end of August 1916 however von Falkenhayn had been relieved of his duties and replaced by the dynamic Hindenburg-Ludendorff duo, but the events he had set in motion continued to run their confused and unedifying course for another nine months.

On 30 August as a fast and first reaction to the Bulgarian invasion of eastern Macedonia a group of liberals and patriots in Salonica formed a Committee of Public Safety. This soon received backing from part of the Greek military including the artillery regiment, the police and the gendarmerie. The next day there were clashes between this new movement and the royalist Greek garrison in the city and three people were killed. Sarrail sent in French troops to separate the two parties. Some of the royalist soldiers joined the 'revolutionary' movement, the rest were temporarily interned before being sent back to Athens where their officers were warmly congratulated by the King.[4]

Although the members of the Committee of Public Safety were openly Venizelist, calling on his name during their demonstrations, the man himself remained in Athens developing and nurturing his supporter base.[5] He had to agree however with Prime Minister Zaimis that in view of the situation in Macedonia the general election due at that time would have to be put off.

Events gathered pace. On 24 August the British Minister in Athens Sir Francis Elliot informed his government that he had received indications that, supported by his Prime Minister and Head of Staff, King Constantine was considering declaring for the Allies. The possibility that this was true should not be ruled out. Stanley Casson, intelligence officer with the BSF whose intimate knowledge of Athenian affairs went back many years, rated Sir Francis highly 'As British Minister of long standing, doyen of the Diplomatic Corps, he knew not only Greece but Constantine like a book. He knew exactly where the Royal Family was wrong, and exactly how far they were right. A man of immaculate impartiality …'[6]

A meeting between Elliot and the King was scheduled for 1 September. Sadly the results of Elliot's patient diplomacy were never put to the test; the French Ministry of Marine, no doubt supported by Sarrail, was setting up what amounted to a military showdown with the Athens government. On the day planned for Elliot's meeting with the King, an enormous French squadron of over 70 ships including ten battleships under the command of Admiral Dartige du Fournet assembled off Piraeus and in the Bay of Salamis.[7]

The British having not been consulted were once more faced with a French *fait accompli*. But not wanting to rattle the French government at the height of the Battle of the Somme, they again opted for low-key solidarity and added some ships of the Royal Navy to the venture.

The declared purpose of this overwhelming French naval force, with belated and reluctant British support, was to seize some Austrian and German merchant ships sheltering in Greek waters, and to present a note to the Greek Government demanding control of all posts and telecommunications in Athens (with or without wires), the expulsion from Greece of all 'enemy agents of corruption and espionage' and the arrest of their accomplices.[8]

Promoted by Sarrail, and certainly not without foundation, the French belief was that these agents were reporting all the movements of Sarrail's forces during this critical period, opening up the possibility of the German and Bulgarian armies breaking though the gap which they had opened up in western Macedonia and joining up with Greek royalist forces in Thessaly.

The size of the naval force assembled to achieve this must have seemed excessive even at the time. True, Sarrail had wished to send troops with the naval force – a brigade – but is unclear what such

---

4   Falls, *Macedonia Vol. 1*, pp.209, 215.
5   Palmer, *Gardeners*, p.95.
6   Stanley Casson, *Steady Drummer* (London: G. Bell and Sons, 1935, Reprinted by Naval and Military Press, 2010), p.122.
7   Palmer, *Gardeners*, p.96.
8   Falls, *Macedonia Vol. 1*, p.214.

a small body of troops could have achieved. Anyway this was one element of the French plan over which the British managed to place a veto.⁹

A side effect of this sorry episode was that Asquith and Grey not only had to suffer the indignity of being out-manoeuvred by the French, but also the wrath of their King. In one of his rare interventions in the management of the war, George V addressed a letter to Asquith on 4 September to the effect that:

> I cannot help feeling that in this Greek issue we have allowed France too much to dictate the policy, and that as a republic she may be somewhat intolerant of, if not anxious to abolish, the monarchy in Greece. But this is *not* the policy of my government.

After a few lines saying that the Russian Tsar agreed with him, his Majesty moved on to the recent confrontation between revolutionary and royalist troops in Salonica:

> I cannot refrain from expressing my astonishment and regret at General Sarrail's arbitrary conduct towards those troops who, loyal to their king and Government, refused to join the Revolutionary movement in Salonica. Could not a protest of some kind be sent to the French Government against General Sarrail's proceedings? Public opinion in Greece, as well as the opinion of the King, is obviously changing, and if the Allies would treat her kindly and not, if I may say so, in a bullying spirit, she will in all probability join them.¹⁰

King George may well have been right in his judgment of the intentions and motives of his fellow monarch, but the story so far contained few examples of Constantine's good faith. And while the French would not have had sight of this royal protest, they continued to consider the British 'soft' approach to the Greek Government to be partly the result of their ally's monarchical reflexes. For example (Gauvain, *l'Affaire Grecque*):

> *Les monarchies de l'Entente ne renonçaient pas à considérer le Gouvernement Grec de la Défense Nationale comme insurrectionnel, alors qu'il défendait la constitution hellénique contre le souverain autocratique et exprimait le sentiment populaire de son pays.* (The monarchies within the Entente could not refrain from considering the Greek Nationalist Government as insurrectional, whereas in fact it defended the Greek constitution against an autocratic sovereign and represented the views of the people).¹¹

This was wildly off the mark, as events proved. But the sentiment expressed here by Gauvain no doubt encapsulated the point of view of French political and military leaders of the time, and historians and commentators since.

The Allied fleet remained in front of Athens. The Greek Government agreed as usual to the demands of the Allied note about the corrupt agents, but as usual showed no urgency in implementing this agreement. Then on 20 September they sent a note to the British and French governments spelling out their terms for abandoning their 'neutrality' and joining the Allied side in the war. Under this the Greek army would be mobilized, would be financed and equipped by the Allies, and would fight alongside the Allies if 'a disparity in force strengths required their intervention', whatever that meant. The note was conspicuously more precise in detailing the political pay-off expected from joining the Allies:

---

9   Falls, *Macedonia Vol. 1*, p.212.
10 Harold Nicholson, *King George V* (London: Doubleday, 1952), p.281.
11 Larcher, *Grande Guerre*, p.179 quoting Auguste Gauvain, *l'Affaire Grecque* (Paris: Bossard, 1918).

In becoming an ally of the Entente Powers Greece counts upon gaining all the advantages which may flow from that alliance, as well during the course of the struggle as at the time of the settlement of peace ... at the peace, the Allies having in view the situation in northern Epirus, and the promises given at various times in Thrace and on the coast of Asia Minor, will be good enough to render all their help towards the possible realization of her national aspirations.[12]

It is worth recalling that Romania had just entered the war on the Allied side, in theory totally altering the balance of power in the Balkans. Greece's proposal of 20 September probably had as much to do with this as with an enormous Allied fleet on her doorstep.

The views of King George V on the Greek note are not recorded, but the British War Committee gave it short shrift, Lord Hardinge, Permanent Under Secretary of State at the Foreign Office dismissing it as 'a brazen-faced proposal.'

Despite the formation, more or less in his name, of the 'Committee of Public Safety' in Salonica on 1 September, and despite pressure from the French, Venizelos continued to bide his time in Athens. There had been numerous developments, military and political, during September, and he wanted to be on the spot as the situation unfolded, apply pressure where he could, and seize any opportunity which presented itself. There were still real possibilities, he must have thought, that with the entry of Romania into the war, the Bulgarians being pushed back on both flanks by the Allies, the national uproar over the Bulgarian occupation of eastern Macedonia and the Allied fleet omnipotent in Greek waters, that the King would finally see the writing on the wall, change sides, and call on Venizelos to form a government. This would have been so immensely preferable to splitting the country by setting up a break-away administration in Salonica, and as long as the slimmest chance remained of it happening, Venizelos preferred to stay where he was.

On 16 September however the pragmatic Zaimis resigned, apparently on realising that, once again, the King was only feigning collaboration with the Allies, and that his basic instincts and preferences remained unchanged.

At this point Venizelos finally decided that there was to be no regime change in Athens as long as Constantine remained on the throne, and on 25 September he left with Admiral Koundouriotis and General Danglis, not for Salonica but for Crete which was both his birthplace and his power base. On 9 October he arrived in Salonica to set up a 'Provisional Government' in direct opposition to that in Athens.[13]

He brought with him the whole-hearted support of Crete and the islands and set out immediately with the intention of raising three divisions to fight with the Allies. Even before he arrived in Salonica his adherents in the Committee of Public Safety had started raising forces – three battalions were already serving with the French detachment on the Struma Front in September.[14] As the days passed volunteers from other parts of Greece arrived in Salonica to join these nascent nationalist forces; on 29 October a Greek volunteer transport ship was torpedoed on its way from Athens to Salonica, fortunately without loss of life.[15] The credibility of Venizelos' Provisional Government depended on it being seen firstly as a national rather than simply a Macedonian movement, and secondly as an independent component of the Allied coalition and not as its puppet.

In due course Venizelos' Provisional Government formally declared war on Bulgaria and Germany for violating Greek territory,[16] but it was not until 19 December that the Provisional

---

12 Falls, *Macedonia Vol. 1*, p.215.
13 Gordon-Smith, *From Serbia*, p.288.
14 Chapter 15 above. They were transferred to the BSF in November
15 Gray and Argyle, *Chronicle Vol 1*, p.259
16 Larcher, *Grande Guerre*, p.180.

Government was recognized by Britain and France.[17] The British (in total contradiction to the views of M. Gauvain above) would have done so on 24 October had the French agreed.[18]

Meanwhile Admiral Dartige du Fournet's enormous fleet remained in front of Athens, suggesting that the French Government, or the French Ministry of the Marine acting on its own initiative – but no doubt in concert with Sarrail – had further ideas for its deployment. Indeed, on 9 October Dartige du Fournet received orders from the French Minister of the Marine to take control of the Greek fleet and the Greek railways. He duly instructed the Greek navy to surrender all their vessels and shore batteries by 11 October. They had no option. Marines were sent into Athens to take control of the railways.[19]

That these actions were taken two days after Venizelos arrived in Salonica and set up his Provisional Government appears to have been completely fortuitous, although Athenian reaction to these two events – and particularly that of the 'League of Reserve Officers' – against Venizelist institutions and sympathizers can be imagined.

The justification for this seizure of the Greek fleet given by the French was 'for the protection of the Allied fleet and in consequence of the build-up of troops and munitions near Larissa.' Subsequently the French Ministry of the Marine added as a supplementary reason that since the French fleet had arrived off Piraeus the Greeks had replaced their normal naval crews with 'hostile personnel' who would have been able to release torpedoes against the French ships.[20] Certainly the provocation had been given to incite the Greeks to stiffen their defences but being sandwiched between the Allied fleet and the shore, any such attack would have been an act of self-immolation. Nevertheless, breach blocks were removed from the Greek ships' guns, and munitions confiscated.

The idea that the Allied fleet needed protection from the Greek fleet was patently absurd. The build-up of royalist troops in Thessaly was a greater possible threat. But the immobilisation of the Greek fleet was unlikely to prevent troop movements in the centre of Greece, except as a bargaining chip.

An itinerant French Deputy called Bénazet now appeared on the scene. He somehow secured an interview with King Constantine during which he thought he had reached agreement for the withdrawal of two Greek army corps from Thessaly to the Peloponnese, and the handing over of a number of mountain batteries to the Allies to 'compensate' them for the ones taken over by the Bulgarians in Kavalla.[21]

Even in this period of extreme diplomatic fluidity it is astonishing that the French allowed an uninformed bystander this degree of latitude – and equally astonishing that they had given Admiral Dartige du Fournet *carte blanche* in negotiating with the Greek Government on behalf of the Allies. He duly picked up the wrong end of the stick passed to him by Bénazet and wrote to the Greek Government confirming what he thought had been agreed and drawing up a long list of munitions which he thought they should hand over to him. Three days later to his astonishment he received a reply from them refusing almost all he had asked for.

He wrote back that if the materials were not made available to him by 1 December he would send a force of marines into Athens to take what they found. He then had a meeting with the King to go over this letter. The King recognized that he was faced with force majeure but promised Dartige du Fournet that if he really had to send troops into Athens, he would order the Greek Army not to fire on them.[22]

---

17 Palmer, *Gardeners*, p.106.
18 Falls, *Macedonia Vol. 1*, p.221.
19 Palmer, *Gardeners*, p.102.
20 Falls, *Macedonia Vol. 1*, p.218.
21 Palmer, *Gardeners*, pp.102–103.
22 Palmer, *Gardeners*, p.104.

On 1 December 3,000 marines, British and French, advanced into central Athens to take up positions on the central hills of the Greek capital, and at an arsenal and munitions depot. At 1100 shots were fired and fighting broke out. Dartige du Fournet, who was holed up in the Zappeion buildings ordered his ships to fire at the Stadium, a kilometre east of the Parthenon, from whence the Greeks were firing at the Zappeion. At 1145 negotiations were opened with the King, who offered 6 mountain batteries if the French Admiral would take his marines away. But fighting broke out again in the afternoon, resulting in over 200 Allied casualties, 21 of them British.[23]

This pointless action achieved nothing but a promised transfer of six mountain batteries (which in fact were never delivered) at the cost not only of the marine casualties,[24] but of days of bloody account-settling in the city and untold damage to the Venizelist cause. It also contributed significantly to delaying for many more months the final resolution of the Greek problem. Dartige du Fournet was only with difficulty dissuaded by the French Minister to Greece from turning his guns onto the city. He was then relieved of his command and returned to France to write his memoirs.

Unsurprisingly, these events served to strengthen royalist sentiment in 'old' Greece, and troops loyal to the King began to assemble in Thessaly. The extent of the threat these forces posed, even at the time, was obscured by Sarrail's now obsessive desire to bring down King Constantine. It is true that during the final gruelling weeks of the Monastir campaign a large part of the Allied Army was too far away to immediately resist a determined attack from the rear, and Salonica itself would have been particularly vulnerable. This was no doubt the theory advanced by Sarrail to the French war office. The reality was that the Greek forces were far too small to represent any sort of serious military threat, and above all they lacked the necessary artillery.

The real danger was the risk of civil war between nationalist and royalist forces. A clash indeed took place near Katerini on 4 November compelling Sarrail to define a neutral zone in northern Thessaly.[25] As Stanley Casson noted, the zone ran along the southern slopes of Mount Olympus as if the gods were to descend and take sides between the forces of Constantine and those of Venizelos as they would have done in Homeric times.[26]

The neutral zone was policed initially by units from the newly-arrived 16th Colonial Division and part of the also newly-arrived British 60th Division, and by the end of 1916 Sarrail had three divisions on stand-by to resist attacks from Greek royalist divisions out of Thessaly should they ever materialise.

None of this could have been foreseen by Joffre when he had called for an offensive based on 15 divisions back in May, but like his great adversary von Falkenhayn he too was now out of the picture. In early December he had been replaced by Nivelle, perhaps the most flawed supreme commander from either side during the war, but who spoke fluent English and was much admired by Lloyd George. Larcher spoke with hindsight, but his valedictory assessment of Joffre is no less valid for that:

> *Le Général Joffre quitta ses hautes fonctions le 13 décembre. Avec lui disparaissait un des grands inspirateurs de la campagne de 1916. La direction de la guerre, déjà si précaire, perdait encore de sa netteté.* (General Joffre gave up the supreme command on 13 December. With his departure one of the major leaders of the 1916 campaign was lost. The conduct of the war, already in a precarious state, became even more confused).[27]

---

23   Falls, *Macedonia Vol. 1*, p.224.
24   Sarrail/Porte, *Mon Commandement*, p.285.
25   Gray and Argyle, *Chronicle Vol. 1*, p.261.
26   Casson, *Steady Drummer*, p.151.
27   Larcher, *Grande Guerre*, p.176.

A few days before the departure of Joffre, Asquith had been replaced by Lloyd George as British Prime Minister. After eleven years Sir Edward Grey left the Foreign Office and was replaced by Balfour. A crisis within the French Government had been avoided, but ministerial changes had been made. Whilst all these changes were underway with their effects rippling in all directions, it is not surprising that the eye was taken off the ball and that decisions were taken with regard to the Greek situation which should not have been taken, and by people who should not have been taking them.

17

1916-17
Stocktaking and Perplexity

With the Greek Tragedy being played out in the background, the Allies embarked on a series of 'where do we go from here in Macedonia?' meetings. The first was an Anglo- French conference in Boulogne on 20 October 1916, attended by both Prime Ministers, both Ministers of War, Haig, Joffre and other political and military leaders.[1]

At this point the battle for Monastir was still very much ongoing. The Serbs had taken Kaymakcalan and were advancing into the Crna bend, but the French, despite the sacking of Cordonnier three days earlier, were still held up before the enemy defences at Kenali.

On the other side of the Vardar two brigades of the Italian 35th Division were holding the enemy on the Butkovo Front, while the British XII Corps, after their unsuccessful action at Machukovo, were mounting small attacks and raids on the enemy defences between Lake Doiran and the river. On the Struma Front XVI Corps was making considerable gains and was only a few days short of consolidating a new line from Bairakli Juma all the way down to Begli.

All of these actions offensive and defensive had been set in motion with the aim of squeezing the Bulgarian armies between the Allied Army of the East and a Russo–Romanian force moving southwards to meet it.

But on the date of the Boulogne conference, the Romanians far from crossing the Danube to invade Bulgaria from the north, were themselves being squeezed by the armies of von Falkenhayn to the west, and Mackensen to the south. They had withdrawn all their forces from Transylvania and within two days would lose Constanza as they retreated further into Dobrujah, while the small force committed to the campaign by the Russians was bottled up in Dobrujah with them.[2]

In an attempt to resolve the perplexities of this situation – and also those of the political situation in Greece – two rather conflicting decisions were taken at the meeting in Boulogne. Firstly to increase the size of the Allied Army of the East to 23 divisions.[3] Secondly to task their Chiefs of Staff, together with those of their Russian and Italian allies, to define how many divisions would be required for the prosecution of the current campaign and to link up with the Romanians and the Russians in a major attack on Bulgaria.[4]

At the same meeting and above all as a result of Lloyd George's *bonne volonté envers la Romanie, pour porter secours à une alliée en détresse* (good will towards Romania, to give support to an ally in distress) and without waiting for their staffs to report back, both the British and the French agreed to send two more divisions to Salonica. Italy would be asked to do the same.

After a delay of nearly a month the Chiefs of Staff duly met on 17 November at Chantilly. Despite the fact that by this time the Romanian campaign was coming to an ignominious end, and

---

1   Falls, *Macedonia Vol. 1*, p.210.
2   Gray and Argyle, *Chronicle Vol. 1*, p.256.
3   Larcher, *Grande Guerre*, p.169.
4   Robertson, *Soldiers and Statesman*, p.130.

within two weeks the Germans would take Bucharest, the delegates had no difficulty in coming up with a fine-sounding Mission Statement; *La mise hors de combat de la Bulgarie par action combinée des Russo–Romains et des Armées d'Orient*, (Putting Bulgaria out of the war through the joint action of the Russo–Romanian armies and the Allied Army of the East), and also in confirming the need to expand the Allied Army of the Orient to 23 divisions.[5]

However, General Cadorna would only commit to increasing Italy's forces in Macedonia if the Russians agreed to a very significant expansion of their forces in Romania, and the Russians would only commit to this if the Allied Army of the East was increased to 30 divisions. In this debate, with the Romanian army by now virtually encircled, and with the Brusilov Offensive long past its high water mark, Cadorna's may have been the most realistic assessment of the situation.[6]

The practical outcome of the Chantilly conference was that neither the Russians nor the Italians added to their forces on the Macedonian Front, the French agreed to send two more divisions, 11th Colonial and 16th Colonial, the British one more division, the 60th, and even this against the will of Robertson.[7] This anyway and finally would bring the British and French to parity at six divisions apiece, and the Allied total to 20 divisions, not including the Venizelist divisions in formation.[8]

In addition to the extra division Milne was promised the 8th Mounted Brigade, four batteries of heavy artillery, two battalions of un-mounted yeomanry, and top up drafts of 20,000 men to replace losses in action and through sickness. Which was not nothing.[9]

The Greek situation however continued to cause grave concern. No commentator has yet presented a credible analysis of the objectives and motivations of King Constantine during this period. It is clear however that Romania's entry into the war at the end of August 1916 must have mightily affected his thinking. As has been seen he made conciliatory gestures towards the Allies on 24 August and again on 20 September. A Russo–Romanian attack from the north combined with an Allied offensive from the south to force Bulgaria out of the war must have seemed a very distinct possibility. Even a probability. Over the next couple of months it became obvious that this was not going to happen, and that, on the contrary, the Central Powers would be significantly strengthened by their occupation of Romania – with the opportunity also of releasing the forces they had put together for the Romanian campaign for use elsewhere.

At this point it is probable that Constantine's reading of the political entrails once more coincided with his personal preferences. And if he believed that the Allies had gone too far with their naval menaces, and their armed attack on Athens to secure a small amount of military material, he would have been right. Normal diplomatic activity, he may have reasoned, would resume; he would be asked to make commitments which he would not fulfil, or fulfil very slowly.

There was no way however that Sarrail was going to leave it this way, and he continued to turn the screw.

His conviction that a large Greek royalist army was assembling in Thessaly in order to attack him from the rear, and quite possibly in coordination with a Bulgarian thrust from the north was probably bordering on the fanciful. But it continued to dominate much of his strategic thinking, and he was successfully transferring his preoccupation to the French high command and Government. On 2 December, the day after the Battle of Athens, he secured their go-ahead to prepare for a military confrontation with the Greek royalist forces. By mid-December he would have three

---

5   Larcher, *Grande Guerre*, p.169.
6   Larcher, *Grande Guerre*, p.170.
7   60 Division was only to remain in Macedonia for six months before being transferred to Palestine in June 1917.
8   In early 1917 the French added another two divisions, taking their total to eight.
9   Falls, *Macedonia Vol. 1*, p.202.

divisions ready to advance into Thessaly, and one to advance on Athens.[10] At the same time the naval blockade was extended to all Greek ports with the aim of preventing, or at least controlling, all goods coming into Greece.

With the French determined on a military solution to the Greek problem, another Allied conference was essential. It was held in London on 27 December and took place under new auspices. Lloyd George had replaced Asquith as Prime Minister on 7 December. Balfour had replaced Grey as Foreign Secretary. In France Briand remained as Prime Minister, but following major political upheavals in the French parliament, had been obliged to make major changes within his government. Ribot came forward again, this time as Finance Minister, and Lyautey took over at the War Office, coinciding with the replacement of Joffre by Nivelle as French Commander in Chief.

It was Ribot, together with Thomas, Minister of Munitions, who represented the French government at the London Conference.[11] The French position was that the Allied Army of the East should be increased to 29 divisions in order to enable Sarrail, as they saw it, to be able to face off both to the Bulgarians and the Greeks.

On the British side Robertson '*l'adversaire irreducible de l'aventure Balkanique*' chose to call what he felt was the French bluff by proposing that the Allies should 'select and prepare a defensive line to the rear of the present one' but that ' any of the recently won ground, including Monastir, need not be abandoned until the need for that step arose'.

The French representatives argued that if Monastir was relinquished after all the sacrifices made by the French and the Serbs to take it, the Serbs might well seek terms with Bulgaria, and the French government would almost certainly fall.[12]

After three days of discussion the British persuaded the French not to allow Sarrail to march on Greece, but that an ultimatum should be sent to the Greek government to the effect that the Greek army with all its arms should be removed to the Peloponnese. This move would be monitored by an Allied Control Commission headed by the French General Camboue.

Apart from this the London conference broke up with no clear agreement on Sarrail's request for reinforcements, or (it was the same question) the future shape and purpose of the Allied Army of the East. Instead it was decided – the idea was Lloyd George's – to meet at the beginning of January in Rome with the Italians to agree joint actions on both the Italian and the Macedonian fronts.[13] This could also with great profit have been extended to a meeting of all the nations involved in the Macedonian conflict. As it was, Russia was only represented at Ambassadorial level, Serbia, Romania and the Greek nationalist government not at all.

Both Sarrail and Milne, however, were invited. From 1 January Milne had finally been given the substantive rank of Lieutenant General.[14] As for Sarrail, his position had been much strengthened following the departure of Joffre in that he now reported directly to the French War Ministry.

Since Italy's interests coincided (but for different reasons – suspicions of Serbian and of Venizelist ambitions in Albania and elsewhere) with those of Britain, no extra troops were voted to Sarrail. Of concrete value was the Italian agreement to collaborate with the French in completing the road from Florina to Santi Quaranta on the Albanian coast, south of Valona. However limited the contacts between the Italian XVI Corps in Albania and the Allied Army of the East, this could surely be of value in disrupting any Austrian attempts to force their way down into Greece.

---

10   Larcher, *Grande Guerre*, p.183.
11   Robertson, *Soldiers and Statesmen*, p.134.
12   Robertson, *Soldiers and Statesmen*, p.135.
13   Palmer, *Gardeners*, p.109.
14   *London Gazette*, 29 Dec 1916. Up to this point his rank of Temporary Lieutenant General had been the same as his two corps Commanders, Wilson and Briggs. It was not until June 1918 that Milne was given the temporary rank of General, a rank which did not become substantive until May 1920.

The meeting was also of value in raising the profile of Milne in the eyes of the Allied governments, including his own. Sarrail also gave a very good account of himself. Lloyd George later wrote 'I was not prepared for the attractive and magnetic personality to whom I was introduced at the Rome conference.'[15] To Robertson's relief this excellent impression did not extend to Lloyd George's promising either extra divisions or to 'turning his head for a fortnight while Sarrail dealt with the Greek royalists'.

It was however agreed to enhance Sarrail's position as Allied Commander in Chief. Henceforth the 'commander of each of the Allied forces should comply with the orders of the Commander in Chief with respect to military operations, subject to the right of direct communications with and reference to his own government.'[16]

On 25 January Sarrail proposed taking over the port of Volos, 200 kilometres south of Salonica, to ease congestion in Salonica and establish an Allied presence on the coast of Thessaly. To ensure communications, this would also have involved taking Thessaly. The British Government (with Milne's input) firmly turned down the idea for both political and logistical reasons.[17]

The risks attendant upon military intervention by the Allies in 'Old Greece' anyway were considerable. Robertson defines them with his usual clarity:

> In the opinion of the British Central Staff the high-handed course advocated was unwise, since it was essential that we should not embroil ourselves in complicated matters unconnected with the main object in view, and therefore should not for choice enter upon a new campaign in Thessaly in addition to the one in which we were already engaged in Macedonia. It had to be remembered too, that internal disturbances might be more troublesome than a Greek declaration of war. Our diplomatic and military representatives on the ground were unanimous in reporting that the hostile invasion of Greek territory by Entente forces and the deposition of the king would inevitably lead to civil war, and thereby necessitate the occupation and subjugation of the whole country.[18]

But, in fact, how great was this Greek threat to which Sarrail and through him the French government attached such importance? In December 1916 Milne thought that there were between 20,000 and 30,000 Greek servicemen and reservists concentrated in central Thessaly, with about 100 guns, plus around 6,000 men and 50 guns in Epirus.[19]

General Philips, the British representative on the Allied Control Commission gave Milne a regular assessment of the number of Greek soldiers and guns passing through from Thessaly to the Peloponnese in line with the Allied ultimatum. He and Milne were generally satisfied. Général Camboue however, wanting to provide Sarrail with the information his boss wanted, complained that Philips' figures were higher than his, and that they should be cleared with him first. An instruction which he ignored. Milne wrote to Robertson on 27 January 'the Greeks are trying to carry out the terms of the agreement, but the French refuse to believe that they can do anything right.'[20]

On the ground it fell to Stanley Casson and a French captain to inspect and count the Greek forces present and negotiate with the Greek General in charge of the Larissa garrison for the agreed number of troops and guns to be sent by rail to Athens, where they were then counted through to Corinth. As the troops left the station, he reports, they would fire their rifles into the

---

15   Palmer, *Gardeners*, p.111.
16   Larcher, *Grande Guerre*, p.189.
17   Nicol, *Uncle George*, p.122.
18   Robertson, *Soldiers and Statesmen*, p.139.
19   Falls, *Macedonia Vol. 1*, p.226.
20   Nicol, *Uncle George*, p.121.

air and shout 'Long live Constantine'. In due course Casson acquired a motor bike and drove round Thessaly looking for the groups of armed brigands and *franc-tireurs* reported by the French intelligence network as forming throughout the province and found none.[21]

Whatever the degree of danger posed by the Greek royalist forces to the Allied Army, however, neither the French nor the British seem to have been in any doubt that King Constantine was in touch with Germany. Commandant Larcher reports that the Allies had known this for a long time and had proof of it.[22] Robertson, not by nature a conspiracy theorist, has no hesitation in asserting that 'the king was in constant correspondence with Berlin, and still hoped that an offensive by the Central Powers would solve the problem for him by driving the Entente forces out of Salonica to the sea.'[23]

On 19 January Milne reported to London that wireless communication was being carried out between the Greeks and the Germans, by means of a station in Larissa.[24] In the Official History of the campaign written fifteen years after the event Cyril Falls confirms this:

> We now know from the Greek White Book that several messages passed between the Kaiser and the Greek royal family in December and January, including on the one hand demands that 'Tino' should attack the left wing of the Allies, and on the other questions as to whether a German attack was in preparation, and if it was, when it would begin.[25]

While all this was going on Sarrail managed nevertheless to finish January on a bellicose note by occupying the Mount Athos peninsula, which he said had become a '*foyer d'intrigues germanophiles*'. No one seems to have objected, except perhaps the monks.[26]

* * *

Prior to the 17 November meeting the British General Staffs had thought to seek the views of the man-on-the-spot, and to ask for his assessment of the forces required in Macedonia. Milne responded with an extensive report on 30 October containing proposals and a direction of strategic thinking quite at variance with that of Sarrail.

In the first place, Milne's priority concern related not to the conduct of the Allied Army's military operations, but to 'back-office' organisational issues. Operations on a front of 300 km held by forces from five nations, and suffering from totally inadequate lateral transport links, required a depth of planning and a quality of administrative support which he clearly felt had been lacking in the preparations for the current offensive. The situation cried out for the creation of a competent central staff at Allied Army level. Couched in the neutral terms of a military report, this was a damning criticism of Sarrail's management.

For a major break-through to meet up with the supposed Russo–Romanian armies and force Bulgaria out of the war he considered that 29 divisions would be necessary, the most anyway that the port of Salonica could handle. (It is interesting that when the final break-through was achieved in September 1918, General d'Espèrey, the then Commander of the Allied Army of the East had twenty-eight divisions at his disposal, although of course by this time both the Russians and the Romanians were out of the picture).

---

21 Casson, *Steady Drummer*, pp.167–172.
22 Larcher, *Grande Guerre*, p.183.
23 Robertson, *Soldiers and Statesmen*, p.133.
24 Nicol, *Uncle George*, p.121.
25 Falls, *Macedonia Vol. 1*, p.227.
26 Armées Françaises, *Tome VIII Vol. 2*, p.403.

For the present, however, Milne's ongoing contacts with Robertson would have made him fully aware that a Macedonian force of 29 divisions was out of the question, so he focussed his thinking on a total of 20 divisions plus the three Venizelist divisions being formed under newly established Provisional Government. It is in his proposed use of these 23 divisions that Milne's ideas move in a very different direction.

Firstly, the Italian 35th Division would be supported by part of the reinforced French forces in pushing the Bulgarians back into the Belasitsa mountains and enabling the re-opening of the Doiran to Demi Hazar railway. Secondly, the Serbs with the rest of the French and the Russians would pursue their current offensive through Monastir.

Thirdly, the BSF supported by the three planned Greek divisions would open a 'second front' on the Allied right flank, clear the enemy out of eastern Macedonia up to the River Mesta, force the Rupel pass, and link up with the Franco–Serbian force in the Strumica valley, turning the entire Bulgarian defensive line from the Belasitsa mountains to Doiran and the Vardar. This he felt would be possible when the promised BSF reinforcements had arrived and the Greek divisions had been equipped and trained.[27] This was a totally new approach in that Sarrail's entire offensive strategy (and that of Guillaumat and Franchet d'Espèrey after him) was concentrated on the Allied left flank while simply holding the line on the right flank.

There was a great deal to be said for Milne's proposal. Firstly using the Greek nationalist forces to take the lead in liberating eastern Macedonia was an excellent – if obvious – idea and was likely to attract thousands of new recruits to Venizelos' army to avenge the scandalous cession of this territory by the Royalist Greek Government. Secondly, the route up the Struma was the most direct to Sofia; Sarrail's current offensive was aimed at territory occupied by Bulgaria, not at Bulgaria itself. Thirdly, the Central Powers were well placed in terms of rail, road and river communications to bring swift aid to their allies in Serbian Macedonia – as was frequently proved – but southern Bulgaria was far from their railheads and supply depots. Fourthly, Milne wanted to get his troops out of the malarial Struma and Butkovo valleys and allow them to fight their battles fit and at full establishment: he already knew that another summer on the Struma would reduce his forces in number and strength by many tens of thousands.

Finally, and perhaps most importantly, the current extremely successful operations against the Bulgarians in the Struma valley were proving that it could be done, and done here, where enemy forces were less concentrated, less favoured by nature in their defensive positions, and less or not at all thickened by German forces. It is also of interest that independently of Lloyd George, but in concert with his thinking, Milne's concept would bring the BSF closer to Turkey and the east, where British interests were always greater than in the central Balkans.

This then, is another of the might-have-beens of the Macedonian Front. Had Milne been properly supplied with transport and artillery for the forces he had, and had he been provided with the means to arm, equip and train three new Greek divisions, the opening of another Macedonian Front may indeed have squeezed the Bulgarians out of the war earlier, without any help from the Russians or Romanians. The BSF might have been returned more or less to independent command and thousands of lives may not have been wasted to malaria and the Doiran defences. But British General Staffs continued to look on the Macedonian venture as a liability rather than an opportunity.

Milne was convinced at the time, however, and remained convinced throughout the campaign, that even a set of determined local offensives could 'at any moment cause a break-up of the Bulgarian Army'. In other words, however strong their defences, they would be vulnerable once these defences were pierced and they were brought to battle behind them. Sadly he was never given the chance to test this belief until the very end.

---

27 Falls, *Macedonia Vol. 1*, pp.203–205.

18

1917
The Italians in Albania

(Map 8)

If the Allies during the winter conferences had finally concluded that military intervention in Old Greece would be a big mistake, the Central Powers had come to the same conclusion. Their victory in Romania had secured all sorts of benefits and opened up all sorts of possibilities including extending their line eastwards.

But it had also thrown up new conflicts of interest between them. Both Bulgaria and Turkey laid claim to the Dobrujah. Now that both banks of the Danube were in their hands, the issue of the respective shipping rights to be accorded to each of the Central Powers became an issue, as did the share of Romanian spoils.

A conference was held in Kreuznach in May 1917 to address these issues and also to agree a post-war order following victory by the Central Powers. Despite the fact that – unlike the Entente – the Central Powers alliance was totally dominated by one of its members, the Kreuznach protocol seeks to achieve a compromise between all of its members, with the ambitions of Bulgaria given special attention. Of particular interest is the total lack of any reference to Greece, except that she should receive, presumably from Italy, 'southern Albania', and that Salonica should become a Freeport, whatever that meant.[1]

It was clear, not only from the conclusions of this convention, but also from Germany's management of the Macedonian Front from 1915 onwards, that it was seen purely as a defensive operation. To support Bulgaria in the invasion of Old Greece would have done nothing to further Germany's war aims and would have added enormous extra complications to any post-war settlement. Better by far for von Falkenhayn and his successors to carry on encouraging King Constantine in his stance of disruptive neutrality towards the Allies, to continue to assist their Bulgarian allies in constructing impregnable defences on the Greek border, and to be able to provide a stiffening of German troops at short notice to the Bulgarians in the event of an Allied attack.

* * *

The Treaty of Berlin in 1878 had left Albania under Ottoman control. At the London Convention of 1913 following the Second Balkan War, the Great Powers had decided to establish Albania as an independent country, and not allow it to be shared out between Serbia and Greece who had occupied parts of it during the war. A provisional government set up by the Albanians in 1912 was ignored by the Great Powers who, such was the habit of the times, instead imposed a European

---

1 Larcher, *Grande Guerre*, Annexe 12 p.276. Convention of Kreuznach, 17–18 May 1917.

Map 8. Albania 1915 – 1918.

king. Prince Wilhelm of Wied lasted for six months, his writ running not much further than Durazzo, and from the moment of his departure any semblance of a central Albanian government ceased to exist.

Following the defeat of Serbia in 1915 most of the north of Albania fell under Austrian control. Italy, who in the 'Secret' Treaty of London of April 1915 had identified Albania as one of its conditions/objectives had begun building up a military presence in Valona in November 1915.[2] By March 1916 this had become a Corps of around 100,000 men in four divisions. For unconnected reasons therefore, while Anglo-French forces were building defences around Salonica in early 1916, their Italian allies were doing the same on the other side of the peninsula. During 1916 the Italians extended their control down the coast to Santi Quaranta and moved inland to occupy Tepelen, Chimara, Agirocastro, Premeti and Lescovici.[3]

Throughout the war there was very little military collaboration between General Ferrero's XVI Corps and the Allied Army of the East in Macedonia, but the Italian presence in Albania unquestionably added value to the Allied war effort. Firstly, a large part of the Serbian evacuation from the Albanian coast to Corfu was handled by the Italian navy.[4] Secondly, by controlling both sides of the narrow Otranto straits the allies could monitor Austrian entry and exit to the Adriatic. Thirdly XVI Corps' presence in Valona and control over much of the Albanian hinterland stood in the way of any physical or military link-up through Albania or down the Adriatic coast between the Central Powers and the as-yet uncommitted Kingdom of Greece – certainly a matter of some comfort to Sarrail.

After a series of purely Anglo–French meetings in late 1916, the Rome conference of January 1917 had served to widen the scope of the discussions and allowed the Italians to better familiarise their allies with the contribution being made by XVI Corps to Allied interests. The Anglo–French participants at the conference were probably under no illusion that the Italians were not in Albania just for the duration of the war – they intended to stay. Roads, bridges and aqueducts were being built far beyond the requirements of troop movements. The road along and through the rugged cliffs and ravines between Valona and Santi Quaranta was a masterpiece of Italian engineering and is still in use. Hospitals and schools were being set up for the local populations, and Italian was being taught. Urban councils were set up, agricultural training was provided, mines were being opened.[5]

It cannot have come as a surprise when on June 3 1917 General Ferrero proclaimed the 'unity and independence of Albania under Italian protection' even though they were at the time controlling less than a quarter of the country. Before the Italians had established and fortified their positions at Valona and along the line of the Voyussa, the Austrians had followed the retreating Serbs down the Albanian coast, taken Durazzo and occupied much of northern Albania. For most of the war the Italians looked down from their Corps HQ on the Mala Kastra ridge about ten kilometres north of Valona onto units of the Austrian XIX Corps five kilometres below them on the coastal plain. This Austrian military presence extended from the Adriatic coast to Lake Ohrid, beyond which it faced the Allied Army of the East.[6]

The stand-off between Ferrero's force and the Austrians lasted for over two years. During this time the Italians only engaged in one serious offensive, and this in July 1918. They reached Durazzo and were driven back. It was only after the Bulgarian capitulation in September 1918 that they

---

2   Thompson, *White War*, p.31.
3   Mann, *Salonica Front*, p.40.
4   Villari, *Macedonian Campaign*, p.86.
5   Mann, *Salonica Front*, p.41.
6   Villari, *Macedonian Campaign*, p.120, Mann, *Salonica Front*, p.41.

drove north again, taking Berat on 1 October, and Elbassan on 7 October. On 14 October they finally dislodged the Austrians from Durazzo and entered Tirana the next day.[7]

As has been seen, one of the decisions of the Rome Conference was that the French and Italians should collaborate in the construction of a road from Florina to Santi Quaranta. This was more of a warm political statement than the go-ahead for a major civil engineering project. The road between Florina and Koritsa was already in place, although the infamously difficult Col de Pisoderi about half way along made contact between Koritsa and Sarrail's main force slow and unpredictable, particularly in winter. Sarrail had secured Koritsa in November 1916 and had installed a structure of local government controlled by a garrison of 1,000 men.[8] Then, in view of Koritsa's strategic importance as a crossroads between Serbia, Albania and Greece, Sarrail sent the newly arrived 76th Division there in January 1917 to clear and secure a bigger cordon sanitaire around the town.

From the other direction, the stretch between Santi Quaranta and Ersek had already been completed by the Italians. The remaining task was to connect Koritsa and Ersek, fifty kilometres of no-man's land infested by Albanian bandits and an eventual gap through which Bulgarian or Austrian units could slip into Greece. Ferrero and Sarrail agreed to advance each from their ends on 17 February 1917, but the French jumped the gun and were already in Ersek within two days. They had encountered very little opposition while clearing and fortifying the key points between the two towns, the most important of which was the Col de Tiafra about half way down.[9] A small squabble then took place between Sarrail and Ferrero over who should hold Ersek, which Ferrero won.[10] Sarrail had managed to cool the warm political intention, but, despite this, the new link was to prove useful as the fastest land and sea route between Macedonia and the outside world – particularly for Italian 35th Division leave parties but also for other components of the Allied Army – until the simpler, if longer, route through Itea and the Gulf of Corinth became available later in the year.[11]

About half way between Koritsa and Santi Quaranta a branch road ran off from Lescovici, along the south bank of the Voyussa, to Valona. The closing of the Koritsa – Ersek gap had thus also served to provide a direct link between the HQ of the Italian XVI Corps with that of the Allied Army in Salonica. Although patchy in parts, an Allied front of over 400 kilometres now ran from the Adriatic to the far side of the Kalkidiki peninsula on the Aegean.

On 30 September 1917 Sarrail went to visit Ferrero in Valona to suggest that a more coordinated military approach could be adopted between their two forces. He was exquisitely received – *notre entrevue fût des plus courtoises* – but it was very clear to Sarrail that the Commander of XVI Corps was working to a completely different job description, was little concerned with the present, but was 'hypnotised by post-war political objectives'.[12]

There was never, throughout the whole period of the Macedonian Campaign, any command relationship between the Italian 35th Division and the Italian XVI Corps; both reported separately to the Italian Chiefs of Staff, but 35th Division via the operational command of the Commander in Chief of the Allied Army of the East.

---

7   Gray and Argyle, *Chronicle Vol. 2*, p.228.
8   Schiavon, *Front d'Orient*, p.256.
9   Armées Françaises, *Tome VIII Vol 2*, p.411.
10   Villari, *Macedonian Campaign*, p.121.
11   See Chapter 24.
12   Sarrail/Porte, *Mon Commandement*, p.330.

19

1917
Preparations for a Spring Offensive

(Maps 4 & 9)

The prospects for 1917 on the Macedonian Front were not propitious. The Greek problem was unresolved. Shipping losses in the Mediterranean were reaching unsustainable levels. French and British views on the purpose and future of the Macedonian Campaign had never been more at variance. Although the French continued to deploy new divisions into the theatre, both the French and the British – and therefore the Serbs, the Russians and the Greeks who depended upon them in this respect – were significantly short of heavy and mountain artillery. Unknown to the rest of the Alliance, very serious trouble was brewing in the Serbian army. On top of this the 1916–1917 winter weather was atrocious even by Macedonian standards, rain, floods and late snow hindering the movement of men and supplies and preventing meaningful military action.

The overall Allied position was equally grim. Germany introduced unrestrained submarine warfare from 1 February. The February Revolution in Petrograd set in train a series of events, via the Tsar's abdication in March, which would lead to the military disintegration and withdrawal of one of the Entente's founder members by the end of the year. Continuing political turmoil in France saw the replacement of Briand as Prime Minister and Lyautey as War Minister by Ribot and Painlevé in March. The failure of the Nivelle offensive and subsequent mutinies was still in the future.

Despite the shortage of artillery however, the force under Sarrail's command for the 1917 campaign season was considerably stronger than the one which had been available to him for the 1916 counter-offensive.

In mid-1916 the strength of the Allied Army of the East had been 15 Divisions. The addition in July of two Russian Brigades (at six battalions to a brigade, the equivalent of a division), and in August of the Italian 35th Division (three brigades also of six battalions each) brought the total to 17.[1] The Chantilly conference of 17 November had added two more divisions from France, and one more from Britain. This brought the Allied total to 20.

In view of the perceived threat from the Royalist Greek army to the Allied Army's rear, France then sent at the beginning of 1917 two more divisions (30th and 76th), serving to make up a shortfall in the establishment of the total Allied army of around 30,000 men.[2]

---

1   Mann, *Salonica Front*, p.37. While the Russian Brigades arrived without artillery, the Italian 35 Division was, and remained, fully equipped with mountain artillery, cavalry, trench mortars and all auxiliary services.
2   Falls, *Macedonia Vol. 1*, p.255, Gray and Argyle *Chronicle Vol. 2*, p.8.

1917 Preparations for a Spring Offensive 125

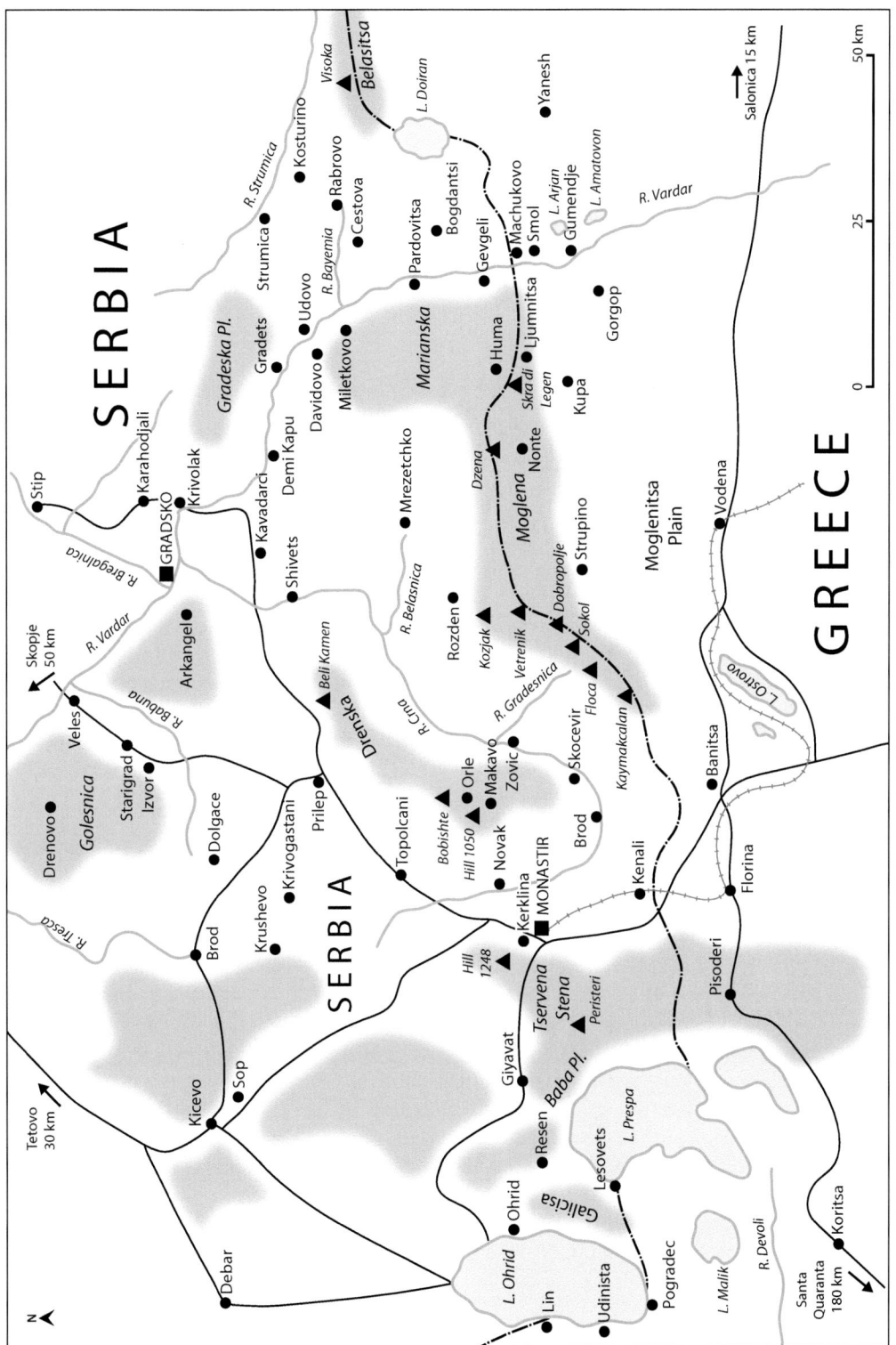

Map 9. Macedonian Theatre West of the Vardar.

By the end of March 1917 therefore, the Allied Army of the East had amassed 22 divisions – eight French, six British, six Serbian, one Italian and one Russian, not counting the Venizelist units now in line or in formation.

French, Serb and Russian forces had entered Monastir on 19 November 1916. Campaigning north of Monastir and within the upper Crna bend continued until mid-December, by which time cold, floods, snow, the depletion of Allied forces, general exhaustion and the impossibility of maintaining lines of supply, had led to a formal instruction by the French War Office to discontinue operations for the year.

No one had expected the advance on Monastir to have taken so long, least of all Sarrail whose original ambitions – and instructions – were aimed at Prilep and the Vardar. No one had expected the Bulgarian defensive positions to be so strong. No one had anticipated the degree of support which the Germans would provide to their allies, or the speed with which it would arrive.[3] Eighteen crack German battalions were committed to the war theatre and had suffered enormous casualties in holding up the Allied advance.

On the Allied side, casualties of 50,000 in the campaigning year were serious numbers in a secondary theatre for a single – if extended – campaign, and it is unsurprising that the French and Serbs would never have accepted a voluntary withdrawal from the positions they had won to 'lines further back'. Moreover, occupation of Monastir and the Crna bend was of critical importance for the launch of forward probes and actions in 1917, and a key factor to the success of the final push into Serbia in 1918.

The discussions during the winter conferences had flowed back and forth, and each took from them what he could. Sarrail's take was that the Allied commanders now reported to him. Fortified with this, he started to prepare a plan for an offensive involving all elements of the Allied Army of the East and covering virtually the whole of its long front.

On 8 February he wrote to his War Minister giving an account of the current distribution of the now eight French divisions under his command and outlining other factors which impacted on the planning and success of an offensive in the spring. The need to allow the Serbian Army time for rest and restructuring after their heavy involvement in the 1916 campaign had led to the need to add 11th Colonial Division to the four *anciennes divisions* (156th, 57th, 122nd and 17th Colonial) holding the present front line.

An advance by Austrian troops down between Lakes Prespa and Ohrid, and the related necessity of completing the road between Florina and Santi Quaranta, had obliged him on 20 January to send the newly arrived 76th Division to Koritsa. Further to the south, below Lake Ostrovo 16th Colonial Division was positioned to intervene in Old Greece if required. The last of his eight French divisions, the 30th, had only just arrived and was very incomplete. This was his only reserve.

He remained very preoccupied about the Greek situation and would have liked to see this matter settled before embarking on any operations against the Bulgarians. Finally, he reminded the Minister, he was short of both heavy artillery and mountain artillery.

The plan he sketched out on 8 February went little further than describing the main thrust of the attack. One Serbian Army was to cross the Moglena in the Dobropolje–Vetrenik area, the other would move east from the Crna bend.[4] They would meet up on the Marianska plateau, then advance up to Demi Kapu and Gradsko. The British were to make artillery demonstrations from the Krusha Balkan hills to the Vardar, but to make a concentrated attack on the Struma Front and take the town of Seres. The following day, 9 February, he sent another message saying that the ultimate objective was Sofia, with the British moving up the Struma valley, while the other Allied

---

3   Ward-Price, *Salonica Army*, p.253 makes an instructive point. 'In case of need the enemy can rush a whole division and its equipment to the Balkan Front in six days, it would take us six weeks.'
4   The three Serbian Armies were merged into two in early 1917, for reasons described in Chapter 22.

contingents would close in on Bulgaria via Stip and Kumanovo.[5] The plan was subsequently fleshed out, and the roles of the other parts of the Allied Army clarified. It was approved by War Minister Lyautey on 21 February.[6]

The overall objectives of the two Serbian Armies remained unchanged. Two French divisions, the Italians and the Russians would push northward up the Crna bend towards Prilep. Three French divisions would move up from Monastir and from positions between the Ohrid and Prespa Lakes, neutralise enemy positions north of Monastir and join the Crna bend group. One French division with Venizelist units would hold the line eastwards from the Serbian positions to the Vardar. One BSF division would neutralise enemy units south of the Belasitsa range and move towards Demi Hasar while two others would be used for the attack on Seres.[7] The Thessaly protection force was to remain in place.

This was an exceedingly ambitious programme. For success it required full commitment from all Sarrail's commanders, no residual worries about 'royalists to the rear', a supremacy in field and mountain artillery, the numerical advantage required for an attacking rather defending force, excellent communications, thorough staff work, good weather and an element of surprise. It became evident in due course that it had none of these.

Above all the success of the operation depended on the vital 'x' factor, the Serbian Army fit, motivated and keen to advance. It was soon to transpire that for a host of reasons later to be explored, the 'x' factor on this occasion was completely missing.

Furthermore, the conference season was not yet over, another was held in Calais on 26 February. Although all parties present at this conference agreed that action must be mounted on all the Allied war fronts to support the forthcoming Nivelle offensive in Champagne and Artois, the British delegates managed to exclude the Macedonian front from this worthy objective. The form of words which emerged was:

> As the co-operation of the Russo–Romanian forces against Bulgaria is not yet possible, the conference agrees to confirm the decision of the Rome conference and decides that for the present the decisive defeat of the Bulgarian army is not a practical objective, and that the mission of the Allied forces in Salonica is to keep on their front the enemy now there, and to take the advantage of striking the enemy if opportunity offers.[8]

Therefore, one could strike the enemy, but not with the hope or intention of defeating him.

The French preferred the 'striking' bit, and on 9 March Lyautey was writing to Sarrail to the effect that:

> *Vous gardez toute liberté pour prendre initiative des opérations dès que vous jugerez l'occasion favorable.* (When you consider the situation favourable you remain free to take any operational initiatives you think necessary). He continued *il n'y a pas moins avantage à ce que les armées alliées de l'orient attaquent au moment de l'offensive générale* (it would be advantageous if the Allied Army of the East made their attack at the moment of the general offensive) and then, for the elimination of all doubt, *tenez-vous donc prêt à déclencher votre offensive vers le 15 avril* (you should therefore get ready to launch your initiative on 15 April).[9]

---

5 Sarrail/Porte, *Mon Commandement*, Annexes 84 and 85, pp.464–465, Telegrams from Sarrail to War Minister of 8 and 9 February 1917.
6 Palmer, *Gardeners*, p.115.
7 Palmer, *Gardeners*, p.114. Larcher, *Grande Guerre*, p.195.
8 Robertson, *Soldiers and Statesmen*, p.136.
9 Sarrail/Porte, *Mon Commandement*, Annexe 89 p.468. Telegram from War Minister to Sarrail of 9 March.

The bit between his teeth and armed with not only an official instruction but also required timing from his boss, Sarrail proceeded with his dispositions, amongst which was briefing Milne on the role envisaged for the BSF. Milne, whose reading of the Calais instruction was somewhat different, asked for clarification from Robertson, was told somewhat gnomically that it was up to him and Sarrail to act in accordance 'with the policy given'.

In accordance with the 'policy given', therefore, Milne confirmed his support for Sarrail's plan, but rejected the Seres–Struma part of it as beyond his logistical reach. He told Sarrail that until the railway to Demi Hasar was made available for Allied use, the supply lines to his forces on the Struma Front were totally dependent on the use of the Seres road, large stretches of which had suffered major deterioration after the 1916–1917 winter. But above all, attacking Seres, or even liberating eastern Macedonia, had no strategic connection with the rest of Sarrail's plan.

He told Sarrail, that while he would continue to remain active on the Struma front, he would concentrate his heaviest forces against the Bulgarian positions to the east of Lake Doiran.[10] This change of plan was reported to Lyautey on 19 February without any particular comment ; *Sur front Britannique l'action principal sera vers Petit et Grand Couronné, zone Lac Doiran, où Général Milne escompte pouvoir faire quelque chose, et action secondaire vers Seres* (On the British front the main attack will be on the Petit and Grand Couronné where General Milne reckons he can achieve something, with a lesser action towards Seres).[11]

By the time he came to write his memoirs however, *j'étais forcé d'accepter pour qu'il veuille bien faire quelque chose*. (I was forced to accept it in order to get him to do anything at all).[12] Theirs was never a happy relationship.

* * *

Sarrail planned to launch the main offensive in April, but first of all was anxious to secure the left flank of his front above and below Koritsa, between Lakes Prespa and Ohrid, and above all to the north and west of Monastir. Here the enemy was strongly entrenched along the crest and slopes of the Tservena Stena massif, and to the north of the Monastir–Resen road on and around the notorious Hill 1248.

General Grossetti, who had arrived in January to replace the unfortunate Cordonnier as Commander of the *Armée Française de l'Orient* (AFO), therefore prepared two series of operations, one in the Koritsa region, the other to push the Bulgarians back from their positions near Monastir.[13]

In Koritsa since January 76th Division was already assuring an Allied presence at the extreme left of its front. In February 1917, in addition to collaborating with the Italian XVI Corps in completing the Koritsa–Ersek road, it was now charged with extending and occupying a larger area around Koritsa to the north and west, to assure safe passage along the road to Florina, and to put the town out of gunfire range from the hills to the east. The aim was to give Koritsa and the Ersek road at least 25 kilometres of secured and patrolled breathing space. Enemy resistance (mainly Austrian) during this cleansing operation was minimal, and when the exercise was concluded on 18 February, casualties had been limited to 34 of which five killed.[14]

---

10   Nicol, *Uncle George*, p.126.
11   Sarrail/Porte, *Mon Commandement*, Annexe 86 p.466. Telegram from Sarrail to War Minister of 19 February.
12   Sarrail/Porte, *Mon Commandement*, p.299.
13   Armées Françaises, *Tome VIII Vol. 2*, p.406.
14   Armées Françaises, *Tome VIII Vol. 2*, p.412.

For the second phase of Gossetti's plan a pincer movement was envisaged, with 76th Division moving up between Lakes Prespa and Ohrid to combine with 156th and 57th Divisions in an attack on Mount Peristeri and the Tservena Stena range with the ultimate aim of taking Hill 1248. The reason for mounting a major three division operation was given in Grossetti's order of 3 February:

> *Les observatoires que l'ennemi a installés possèdent les vues sur toute la plaine de Monastir et sur les contreforts sud du massif 1248. Un succès important en ce point dégagerait immédiatement la plaine et permettrait un déploiement rationnel de l'artillerie des alliés.* (The enemy's observation points give them views over the whole plain of Monastir and on the southern foothills of the 1248 massif. Removal of them would immediately free up our use of the plain and enable us to deploy our artillery in a rational manner).[15]

On 11 March 76th Division set out from Leskovets, aiming to arrive at the Giyavat pass by 13 March. However the lie of the land between the Galicisa hills and Lake Prespa overwhelmingly favoured the defending forces, which although comprising not much more than three battalions with minimal artillery were able to hold up the French advance for five days. At this point the weather intervened with waist-deep snow and the lakeside road flooding. By 18 March they had got no further than four kilometres from Leskovets. Sarrail called a halt on 19 March and was particularly scathing in his comments about the Divisional Commander:

> *Le Général de Vassart ne savait rien de la guerre de montagne, rien de l'utilisation de l'artillerie de montagne ... et que, pour lui, l'infanterie ne devait être employé qu'au compte-goutte* (General de Vassart knew nothing about mountain warfare, nothing about the use of mountain artillery ... and for him the infantry should only be used a drop at a time).[16]

Commandant Larcher's more generous interpretation of the reasons for this setback were the snow and the unexpectedly tenacious defence of '*les villes saintes de la vieille Bulgarie*' by the Bulgarians.[17] Bulgarian attachment to Ohrid was indeed to play a significant role in delaying the retreat of the enemy's LXII Corps in September 1918,[18] but on this occasion the majority of the 'tenacious defenders' were in fact German and Austrian.

For its attack on the Tservena, half of 156th Division was directed at Mount Peristeri (2,541 metres), and the other half on the northern part of the massif. For Mount Persteri it had been recognised from the outset that *il sera enlevé de suite, ou il ne sera pas du tout* (It had to be taken immediately or not at all). Surprise was essential and there was to be no artillery preparation. The attack was launched on 13 March. The Bulgarians were unsurprised, and the numerous machine-gun posts on the crest prevented the attackers from getting closer than 200–300 metres from their lines. The same storm encountered by 76th Division broke on 16 March and operations were suspended.

Greater success was achieved by the units of 156th Division attacking the northern part of the Tservena Stena. By 15 March the first and second lines of Bulgarian defences had been taken. But the enemy was quick to call up reinforcements and on 25 March counter-attacked with flame throwers, and the attacking force was hard put to hold and consolidate the positions they had won.

---

15   Armées Françaises, *Tome VIII Vol. 2*, p.414. Reporting Order from Grossetti to Divisional Commanders of 3 February.
16   Sarrail/Porte, *Mon Commandement*, p.280.
17   Larcher, *Grande Guerre*, p.196.
18   See Chapter 35 below

The operation was called off on 28 March. The Bulgarian lines had been pushed back 500 metres over a front of a kilometre.[19]

The task of 57th Division was to neutralise enemy positions on Hill 1248, its surrounding foothills and the spur which stretched north of it. The attack was launched on 16 March. With Monastir within firing range, and the whole of the Monastir plain spread out beneath them, this was a prime site for the Bulgarian forces and was strongly defended. On 17 March a brigade strength attack occupied the Monastery of Kerklina and adjoining trenches. On 18 March the summit of 1248 was reached then lost to a strong German counter-attack on 20 March. But other gains representing an advance of the Allied line of 700 to 2,000 metres over a front of five kilometres were made and consolidated, reducing the effectiveness of the Hill as an artillery position and observation post until it was finally taken in September 1918.[20]

The casualties incurred by the three divisions over seventeen days were 3,932 of which 1,027 killed or missing. On the plus side over 2,200 prisoners had been taken. But for an operation designed solely as a preparatory forerunner to the main offensive, the casualty list was a long one. In his memoirs Sarrail allocates it twelve lines.[21] Larcher's summary of the final outcome was even more curt; *Monastir non dégagé resta bombardé.*' (Monastir remained unrelieved and subject to bombardment).[22]

Meanwhile east of the Vardar the BSF was undertaking a series of raids aimed at surprising and disrupting the enemy as well as attempting to mislead him as to where the main weight of the forthcoming offensive was to fall. On 5 January a brigade-strength attack was made on the village of Akinjali to the northeast of Lake Doiran. The village was taken with a three-pronged attack, but most of the defending forces escaped. Further such raids were made in February on the villages of Palmis and Brest with minimal casualties and prisoners taken, followed by a major attack on Peroi station which was taken and held for twenty hours. Later in February another brigade-strength raid was made on the 'Piton des Mitrailleuses' on the far left of the British line, scene of the action of Machukovo in June 1916. Enemy trenches were occupied and prisoners taken before withdrawal.

On the Struma lightly held front line positions at Karakaska, Kispeki and Ada were held against enemy incursions, and the villages of Kyupri and Kumli were raided.[23]

But while the forthcoming Allied offensive called for supportive action on the Struma front, the BSF's major effort was not to be made here, but between Lake Doiran and the Vardar. Any ground gained in this sector prior to the general assault would be invaluable. A determined attempt was made on 10 February to take the Petit Couronné hill but was driven back with over 150 casualties and no illusions of the magnitude of the task ahead. Further to the west a month later 26th Division advanced unopposed across ground unoccupied by the enemy further to the west, establishing a new line about a kilometre closer to the Doiran defences and entrenching it.[24]

* * *

Although it must have been obvious to the German General Staff in Skopje that Sarrail would be preparing a major offensive in 1917, no significant ground attacks were made by the enemy in the first months of 1917 except an attempt to consolidate their already strong position east of Monastir.

---

19   Armées Françaises, *Tome VIII Vol. 2*, pp.432–435.
20   Armées Françaises, *Tome VIII Vol. 2*, pp.435–439.
21   Sarrail/Porte, *Mon Commandement*, pp.280–281.
22   Larcher, *Grande Guerre*, p.196.
23   Falls, *Macedonia Vol. 1*, pp.264–265.
24   Milne, *Despatch of 1917*, p.2.

Hill 1050, which dominates the central part of the Crna bend had been taken by the Serbs as a last gasp effort in December 1916, then lost. Always known as such, although it was in fact higher than this, Hill 1050 complemented Hill 1248 in giving the Germano–Bulgarian forces a high degree of control over the Monastir plain. Before any Allied move towards Prilep could be contemplated, enemy positions on Hill 1050, together with its western extension the Piton Brulé and its eastern extension the Piton Rocheux, would need to be neutralised. For the enemy any strengthening of this position would be of enormous value. Most of the enemy troops allocated to Hill 1050 were German, even after all but a few German battalions had been removed from the Macedonian theatre. Interconnected lines of fire from the three peaks covered much of the Allied line from south of Zovik to north of Novak right across the Crna bend, a distance of 25 kilometres.

From December 1916 the western 15 kilometres of this line including those facing Hill 1050 and its surrounding positions had been assigned by Sarrail to the Italian 35th Division. The Germano–Bulgarian forces held the summits, but the Italian front line on the southern slopes of the hills was in places less than 30 metres from the enemy lines. During their twenty months of presence on this sector, 35th Division perfected three lines of defence, digging in total around 100 kilometres of trenches, often two metres deep, and hollowing out over 500 dugout shelters.[25]

On 12 February 1917 the enemy struck. The left of the Italian line was subjected to a tremendous bombardment by artillery, trench mortars and flame-throwers, the first use of this weapon in Macedonia. Six hundred metres of front line trenches were lost. On 27 February the Italians launched a strong counter-attack using 150 guns with the expenditure of 20,000 rounds of ammunition, directed principally on Hill 1050 and Piton Brulé. Infantry follow-up secured almost all the trenches lost in the first attack but failed to take Hill 1050 as a result of lethal crossfire from Piton Rocheux. Italian casualties were 400 over the action. The 74 prisoners taken were all German.[26]

Apart from this, enemy ground forces made no move against the Allied Army in the first part of the year, and up to this point the activities of German and Bulgarian aircraft had been limited and containable. But on 27 February a 'V' formation of 20 German planes, twin-engine bombers with fighter support, appeared out of the blue, and bombed the French airfield at Gorgop, destroying eight planes and damaging four others. Little damage was inflicted on the British airfield at Yanesh on the way back, the pilots of No. 47 Squadron having been forewarned. But the next day they were back and bombed Summerhill Camp, causing casualties of 375, of which 115 killed.[27] One enemy plane was shot down by No.17 Squadron.[28]

The German planes were from the No. 1 Kampfgeschwader Squadron and had been sent from Bucharest following the end of the Romanian Campaign. They came with their own supply railway train and were based at Udovo. The two RFC squadrons responded with sorties against Udovo and Cestova, but the Germans returned in force, bombing Salonica on 4 March and Vertekop on the Franco/Serbian sector on 12 March. The RFC kept up sorties against enemy airfields and dumps, but the superiority of the German planes was obvious, and in addition they were almost untroubled by anti-aircraft fire. On the whole British front there were only 16 anti-aircraft guns.[29]

Milne asked for support from the navy, and a composite RFC/RNAS force was put together which operated with increasing success during March and April, especially when reinforced with Sopwith aircraft from the RNAS, but the discovery on 11 May that the Udovo hangars were empty and that the Kampfsgeschwader Squadron had gone provided much relief.[30]

---

25 Villari, *Macedonian Campaign*, pp.108–115.
26 Villari, *Macedonian Campaign*, pp.122–25.
27 Jones, *War in the Air*, p.43
28 Signaller Bailey, 28 February, counted 20 out and 19 back.
29 Jones, *War in the Air*, pp.345–346.
30 Wakefield, *Under the Devil's Eye*, p.186.

The only other major enemy action prior to the launch of the Allied offensive was a massive artillery barrage opened up by the Bulgarians on 17 March on the whole of the BSF sector between Doiran to the Vardar, and on part of the French sector on the west bank of the river. This included, for the first time in Macedonia, gas shells.[31] The bombardment extended, on a more limited scale, to the Struma, but on neither sector was the bombing followed up with infantry attacks for which such artillery demonstrations were the usual precursor. Both sides relapsed into waiting mode for the next three weeks.

* * *

By the end of February Milne was re-organising his forces for the forthcoming offensive. Unquestionably of the 140 km front under his command, the fifteen kilometre sector from Lake Doiran to the Vardar was the most critical. Here the attack was to be made, and here the enemy forces were at their strongest. He decided that he needed all three divisions of XII Corps to be concentrated here, 60th Division to the left, 26th Division to the right and 22nd Division in the central stretch between Krastali and the Vladaya ravine.

The rest of the long BSF Front, from Lake Doiran to the Aegean at Stavros, remained the responsibility of XVI Corps. A brigade of 28th Division was detached to cover the stretch from Lake Doiran to the old Greek fortress of Dova Tepe, but since the rest of the Corps' three divisions were required for action on the Struma Front, a creative solution to cover the quieter sector between Dova Tepe and Lake Butkovo was found.

The BSF on its establishment had six garrison battalions engaged mainly on lines of communication activities. Four of these were taken to form a new Brigade, the 228th, mobilised on March 15 1917. At the time of their call-up most of these man were working on a mid-line set of defences between Lahana and Lake Arjan.[32]

The garrison battalions consisted mainly of older men, never intended for front-line duties. They had no transport, only long old-fashioned rifles, and no specific training. The confusion attendant upon pulling these battalions together and getting them to the front was such as to justify more than half a page of description in the Official History.[33] Most of the problems had been sorted out by the end of March, by which time the new Brigade had reached its position on the front line.

Otherwise the dispositions of General Briggs' XVI Corps remained largely unchanged, stretching along the new front line gained in the 1916 autumn campaign: 27th Division to the south, 10th Division in the centre, and 28th Division to the north, meeting up with 228th Brigade at Lozhista.

31　Falls, *Macedonia Vol. 1*, p.300.
32　Signaller Bailey Jan 29 1917. 'No signalling now. All on defence work, pick and shovel, wire entanglements, trenches. Very hard work and weather beastly, raining, over boots in mud, and very cold. Get rum allowance sometimes. Very acceptable.'
33　Falls, *Macedonia Vol. 1*, p.298. Signaller Bailey March 15 1917 reports his experience 'Brigade 228 to be mobilized at Kutus. Camp struck at 0700, all had to be carried over the river. C Coy off first on march to Kutus. Arrived at around five, found no tents there, nor anything. Other Coys arrived later. Turns out awful muddle, no food, no blankets, tents arrive after dark, very cold overnight, no greatcoats even; mismanagement'.

20

1917
First Battle of Doiran

(Maps 7 & 10)

In his Despatch of October 1917 Milne reported that although the BSF had completed their preparations well beforehand 'the Commander in Chief for various reasons found it necessary to postpone operations to 26 April.'[1] The British attack was to take place on 24 April, two days before the launch of the main offensive by the French and Serbs to the west of the Vardar.

In early April General Wilson, commander of XII Corps, had presented a three-stage plan of attack aimed at capturing each of the enemy's three lines of defence. Milne found this too ambitious given the nature of the terrain and the known strength of the Bulgarian positions. He also understood, who better, the limitations of his own artillery both in quantity and penetrating power.[2]

Wilson's modified plan was issued on 9 April. This involved taking the enemy's front line of defences north of the Jumeaux ravine and including the Petit Couronné, (26th Division, 78th and 79th Brigades) and also Hill 380, the Mamelon, and the lowest of the enemy-held spurs on Pip Ridge, (22nd Division, 66th Brigade). The Bulgarian fortifications from the lake, through the Petit Couronné, and along the north face of the Jumeaux ravine were continuous, while Hill 380, the Mamelon and Pip 4½ were surrounded by gun emplacements and trenches independent of the main line, and to its south.[3] To the left 60th Division was to hold the line and make a raid, once again, on the Machukovo position with the hope, once again, of confusing the enemy.[4]

Taking the enemy's first line of defence would have been a worthwhile achievement, above all by establishing a line north of the Jumeaux ravine; but retaining it, manning and equipping it in the face of inevitable and incessant artillery pounding from the Bulgarian second line would not have been simple. In the event of a successful outcome to the attack of 24 April, Milne had envisaged a second phase, advancing along the lakeside to Doiran town.[5]

Wilson planned a night attack, partly to cloak the movements of his advancing troop, partly to achieve surprise. There would be little of the latter. All the British positions – and preparations – were highly visible to the Bulgarians entrenched above them, and particularly to their control centre at the top of the Grand Couronné, and these were confirmed by German reconnaissance aircraft. The RFC on the other hand had a more difficult task in registering enemy gun positions

---

1 Milne, *Despatch of 1917*, p.3.
2 Falls, *Macedonia Vol. 1*, p.303.
3 Packer, *Return to Salonica*, p.55.
4 Wakefield, *Under the Devil's Eye*, p.69.
5 Packer, *Return to Salonica*, p.56.

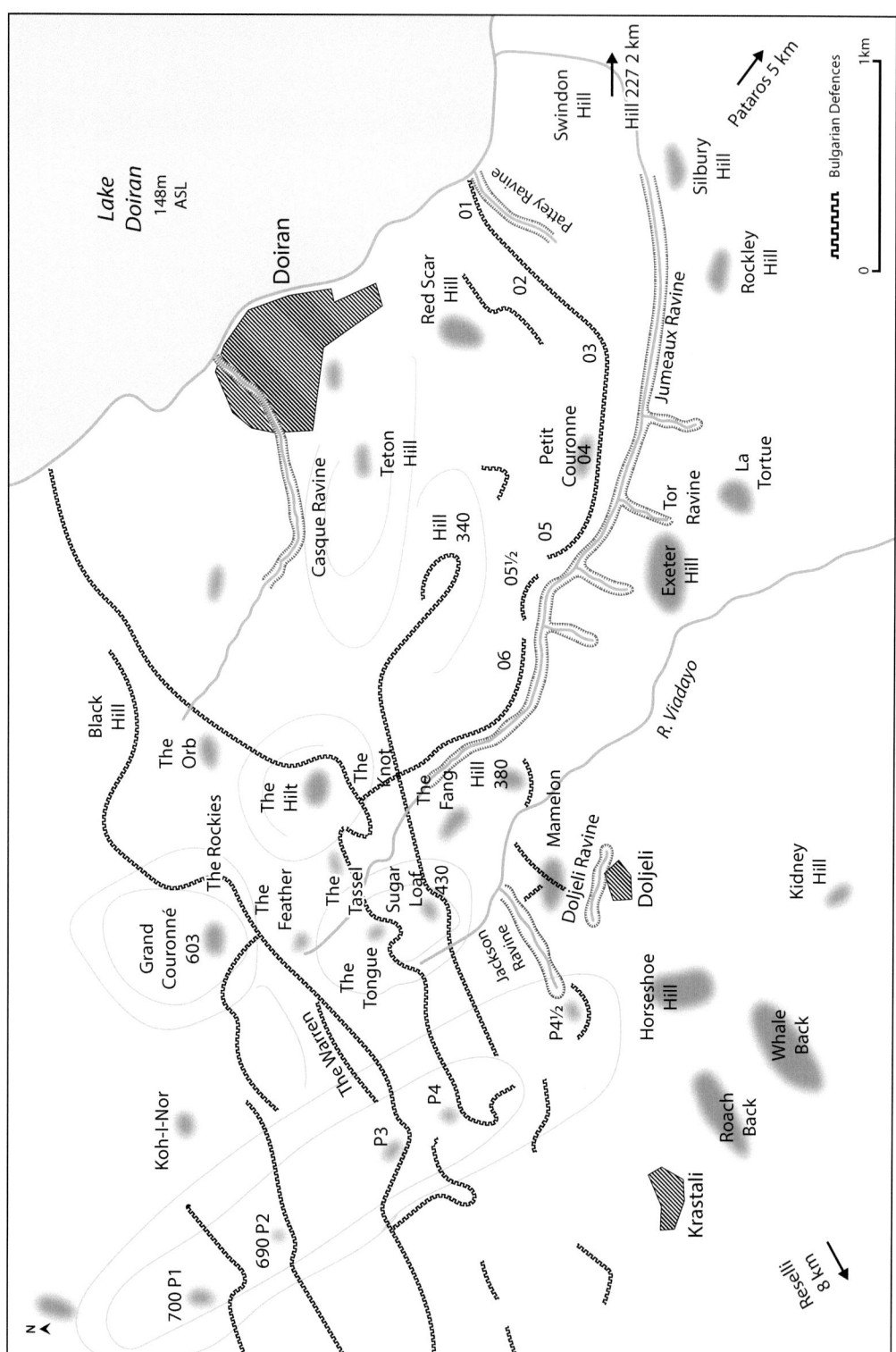

Map 10. Doiran Battlefield April–May 1917, September 1918.

given the broken terrain, and the decision to go for a night attack made the services of spotting and reconnaissance aircraft impossible. Balloons were also used.[6]

Major Nedev in his account of the Bulgarian side of the battle reports that arrivals of trains, movements of lorries and artillery limbers were all monitored and recorded. He further reports that on the morning of 24 April telephone messages containing operational orders were intercepted.[7] Certain now of a night attack the Bulgarians also provided for 33 strong searchlights. These were to play an important role when battle was joined, negating to a significant extent the presumed advantages of a night attack.

The attack was to be preceded by a three day artillery bombardment with the aim of damaging trenches, putting gun emplacements out of action, and cutting wire. Six days' supply of ammunition had been delivered to the batteries and ammunition dumps prior to the three-day bombardment.[8] Milne had asked Wilson not to make the customary intense barrage just prior to the attack in order not to forewarn the enemy.

It appeared however that they had already been forewarned; on the morning of 24 April a prisoner captured by a wire cutting patrol reported that the British attack was expected that night, and that the enemy forces had been strengthened by another brigade and further artillery.[9]

It was too late in the day to unravel all the preparations. Milne decided to go ahead with the attack as planned.

* * *

Bulgarian defensive lines to the west of Lake Doiran culminating with the 'Devil's Eye' of the Grand Couronné and the heavily fortified 'Pip' ridge were unquestionably the strongest in the whole Macedonian theatre.

The reason for the Bulgarians building such extensive defences on these hills was that they are much lower than the almost continuous mountain ranges running along the northern frontiers of Greek Macedonia and have little depth. This was why Milne was concentrating his attack here. Forces breaking through at this point would have instant access to the Vardar and Strumica valleys, but the terrain they would have to cross first was forbidding.

To the west of Lake Doiran a jumble of small hills rose to the higher, rounder hill of the Grand Couronné (603 metres) at the top. The more prominent of the hills were fortified with artillery and machine gun emplacements, and most could be covered with fire from other hills. Three successive lines of trenches had been dug, or where necessary blasted out of the hillside, and reinforced with concrete. These ran along the hills and ridges running all the way from Lake Doiran to Pip Ridge, then on through Machukovo down to the Vardar, and were of course protected by wire.[10]

The lines were not necessarily parallel, but were linked by carefully calculated lines of fire, and each line covered that below it. The third and highest line protected the Grand Couronné fortification and control centre which dominated the hills and all upward approach to them.

Even today, over a hundred years later, the Bulgarian defences are still very visible beneath the undergrowth, with many of their artillery and command positions dug deep beneath the hillside. Today's visitor is struck above all by the steepness of the hills on which the Bulgarian defences had

---

6   Jones, *War in the Air*, p.350. The artist William Wood whose 40 watercolours adorn Arthur Mann's *Salonica Front* was a corporal with the balloon service and made sketches to augment the photographs taken from the balloons.
7   Wakefield, *Under the Devil's Eye*, p.74.
8   Packer, *Return to Salonica*, p.57.
9   Palmer, *Gardeners*, p.119.
10   Falls, *Macedonia Vol. 1*, p.191.

been built. The distance between the British lines and the Grand Couronné was only about three kilometres, but the upwards climb over this short distance was four hundred metres, not counting the ups and downs through the ravines and over the ridges lying between the two positions. Viewed from the top – which the BSF was not able to do until 20 September 1918 – the virtual impossibility of ever overcoming these defences by direct assault becomes very clear.

About five kilometres from Lake Doiran the long, narrow and very steep-sided hill known as Pip Ridge runs north-south, more or less parallel with the lake. At its most northerly point it is 700 metres high. It then gradually descends southwards, punctuated with little peaks, the 'Ps' or 'Pips' of the ridge. The most southerly expression of Pip Ridge is Horseshoe Hill which the BSF had taken in August 1916. The five more northerly Pips however remained in Bulgarian hands and were heavily fortified. The narrowness of the ridge made a frontal attack without carefully calibrated artillery support potentially lethal, an attack up the steep flanks even more so.

Between the hills lay depressions or shallow valleys, and in many places rivers or streams had cut deeper valleys or ravines. These had been fully exploited by the Bulgarians in the design of their defensive system.

The greatest was the Jumeaux Ravine, which ran along beneath the Bulgarian first defensive line for 2.5 kilometres. At its maximum this ravine was 120 metres deep, and any attacker would have to cross it. Although the Bulgarian first line lay some way south of their second line at this point, it effectively benefitted from a second natural line of protection in the Jumeaux Ravine. The problem of the ravine had already been apparent in the attempt on Petit Couronné in March. Now they had to face it again. To add to their difficulties, the wire cutting in front of 26th Division had been less complete than in front of 22nd Division.

* * *

The Bulgarians who knew that an attack was imminent put down a tremendous barrage on the evening of 24 April, carefully targeting the 79th Brigade assembly points. Of the three battalions engaged, the one to the right climbed out of Patty Ravine and were met with unremitting fire and uncut wire. This was Owen Rutter's Battalion, 7/ Wiltshire. Only one company made it to the enemy lines before the whole battalion was forced back. The Regimental historian recorded that 14 out of 15 officers became casualties, together with 300 OR, and this out of a total of 500.[11] The lilting rhythm of *Tiadatha* gives dramatic force to his description of the action:

> *There the dread trench mortar barrage*
> *Swept upon them like a hailstorm,*
> *Storm with stones as big as footballs*
> *Stones alive with death and torture.*
> *Through that blinding storm he led them,*
> *Up the farther side he led them –*
> *All that were not killed or wounded…*
> *Through the broken wire they scrambled*
> *Some men cursing, some men shouting,*
> *Some men muttering little prayers,*
> *Some in grim and deadly silence.*[12]

---

11 Packer, *Return to Salonica*, p.58 quoting 7/ Wiltshire Regiment history.
12 Rutter, *Tiadatha*, Chapter 12.

The other seven battalions of 78th and 79th Brigade were no more successful. Footholds gained by small bodies of troops on the far side of the ravine between positions O3 and O6 were soon lost in face of withering enemy fire frequently guided by searchlight, and the survivors from all units were forced to retire by 0400 hours. Severe casualties were incurred above all in crossing the ravine where enemy shells caused a mayhem of flying rocks and stones as well as steel splinters.[13]

Having no ravines to cross and setting off from positions much closer to the enemy lines, the attacking force of 22nd Division's 66th Brigade succeeded in all its objectives, taking Hill 380, the Mamelon and P4½ by 2200 hours. Specialist units following close behind then secured defensive lines around these positions, incorporating Jackson's ravine. Counter-attacks during the process of consolidation were held off, as were further massive attacks including an artillery barrage over the next 48 hours.[14]

The planned attack above Machukovo by 60th Division had succeeded in piercing the first enemy line but came up against severe mortar gun attacks with the Bulgarians using their searchlights at the second line and were forced to retire. Casualties for this action were minimal, but the casualties for 26th and 22nd Divisions were very high, particularly since only three brigades were involved. Killed or missing were 800, of which 'missing' represented two thirds. The wounded total was 2,363, total casualties therefore 3,163. Of these the great majority, 2,397, were from 26th Division.[15]

Many factors had contributed, the readiness of the enemy, the ferocity of his barrages, confused signals and reporting, and above all the death trap of the Jumeaux Ravine. Charles Packer who was there and may well have become statistic himself is less restrained about the qualities of leadership and the staff-work of 26th Division than is the Official Historian.[16]

A small but useful gain had been made, and then secured, by 66th Brigade, but the over-arching objective of taking the Petit Couronné and establishing a new line north of the Jumeaux Ravine had been a total and costly failure.

Milne's report on the 26th Division's attack in his annual despatch, while heartily commending the 'gallantry and determination by representative battalions of the English county regiments' had to conclude that;

'Owing to the very heavy artillery and trench mortar fire encountered, more especially in the Jumeaux ravine, a deep and difficult obstacle with steep sides which separated the opposing lines, only the leading troops were able to gain a footing, and reinforcements found the greatest difficulty in advancing to their support.'

He could, justifiably, be more upbeat about 22nd Division: 'On the left all objectives were gained, and the enemy's front trenches occupied on a Front of nearly a mile ... During the following days the captured position was consolidated in spite of repeated counter-attacks.'[17]

Meantime, the Allied attack west of the Vardar to which the BSF assault on the Doiran heights was supposed to be a precursor was not taking place.

On 26 April Sarrail informed Milne that due to adverse weather conditions in the mountains he was now planning to open his artillery barrage on 28 April and launch the general offensive shortly afterwards. He asked Milne to order another attack at Doiran to coincide with this. Sarrail then delayed the artillery until 5 May with the general attack to take place on 8 May. Milne instructed Wilson to plan for a second attack on the Doiran defences on 8 May.[18]

---

13 Packer, *Return to Salonica*, p.60, Falls, Macedonia Vol I, p.307.
14 Falls, *Macedonia Vol. 1*, p.312.
15 Falls, *Macedonia Vol. 1*, p.316.
16 Packer, *Return to Salonica*, pp.57–62.
17 Milne, *Despatch of 1917*, p.3.
18 Wakefield, *Under the Devil's Eye*, p.85.

138   The Forgotten Front

A hundred years on it is difficult to understand why Sarrail did not warn Milne earlier of his launch day delays and difficulties – which were probably not simply meteorological. He must have known of them well before 24 April.

To add another element of confusion, the *Armées Françaises dans la Grande Guerre* states with all the authority of the Official History that *Le 13 avril le Commandant en Chef fixait le commencement des attaques au 24 avril pour l'Armée Britannique et 30 pour les autres* (On 13 April the Commander in Chief fixed the date for the commencement of hostilities as 24 April for the British and 30 April for the others).[19]

And why, in the first place, was the British attack to precede the general offensive by two days? Milne himself had wanted a synchronised attack but had bowed to Sarrail's strategy of 'First the British, then the French, then the Serbs.' The answer, or part of the answer, may lie in an ultimatum Sarrail had received from the Serbian High Command in mid-March. One of their three conditions for participating in the 1917 campaign was that their offensive '*ne serait engagée qu'après offensives engagées sur autres fronts*' (would only be launched after the launch of offensive action on other fronts).[20]

In his memoirs Sarrail maintains that it was the British Government who were pressing for an early attack *sous pression des événements en Asie Mineure*' (because of the pressure of events in Asia Minor), and '*d'après le War Office il semblait y avoir urgenc*e (According to the War Office there seemed to be some urgency).[21] The possible explanation for this strange assertion is that a Turkish division based on the lower Struma was reportedly being recalled for operations in Iraq.[22] Even so, it is unlikely that the War Office would have wanted Milne to make an isolated attack which would then have to be repeated two weeks later.

As to the events of 24–25 April, Sarrail dismissed them in a short passage:

Le 22 avril les Anglais commencent la préparation de l'artillerie malgré le temps affreux. Le 25 ils passent à l'attaque infanterie, deux divisions accolées s'engagent dans un conflit de nuit. Le résultat sans être négatif n'était pas un succès. 1,500 yards de tranchées tombent simplement entre les mains des Britanniques. (On 22 April the British started an artillery barrage despite the awful weather. On 25 April they launched a night attack with two infantry divisions side by side. The result was not entirely negative, but not very successful. Just 1500 metres of trenches were taken by the British).

The 'awful weather' is puzzling; British accounts report uniformly good weather, several ear-witness accounts exist of birds singing the following morning. One of these was Captain Rutter in the guise of Tiadatha.[23]

Sarrail continues even more dismissively:

Cette opération ne pouvait du reste avoir aucune influence sur le développement qui devrait être donné à notre action. Les contingents Britanniques n'étaient au fond chargés que d'une diversion pour faciliter l'acte final qui devait se jouer entre Monastir et Huma. (This operation couldn't anyway have had any influence on the development of the overall offensive. Basically the British forces

---

19   Armées Françaises, *Tome VIII Vol. 2*, p.453.
20   Sarrail/Porte, *Mon Commandement*, Annexe 90 p.468. Telegram from Sarrail to War Minister of 20 March.
21   Sarrail/Porte, *Mon Commandement*, p.301.
22   Larcher, *Grand Guerre*, p.195.
23   Rutter, *Tiadatha,* Chap 12 'Very clear it was and starlight/ And a nightingale was singing.'

were only to provide a diversion in support of the main action which was to take place between Monastir and Huma).²⁴

Any soldier or officer engaged in the action may well have asked why 3,163 men had been killed or wounded to provide a '*diversion*' to a main attack that never took place. To these questions must be added another; why did Milne commit to repeating the attack two weeks later?

When Milne consulted Robertson on the matter he was told to use his own judgement.²⁵ (Robertson had given Milne a similar I-wash-my-hands-of-the-whole-business reply to the question of whether he should participate in the spring offensive in the first place). In his memoirs Robertson makes no mention of this, simply reporting that:

> After the British attack had been launched General Milne discovered to his surprise that the French and the Serbs were not ready, partly on account of the weather, but mainly because insufficient time had been allowed for preparation. The attack was therefore a waste of effort and life. On 8 May the British attacked a second time, the other contingents making their main attack on the following day.²⁶

In his own annual report Milne gives no evidence whatsoever of any heart-searching about committing his troops once again to assaulting the best Bulgarian defensive position in Macedonia. 'Finally I received instructions that the 8th May had been selected as the date for the re-commencement of the Allied advance, on which date the Army under my command should again concentrate its main effort in the vicinity of Doiran.'²⁷

There are several explanations for his decision. Firstly, Sarrail was his Commander-in Chief; since the Rome conference Milne came under his orders for all operational matters. Secondly, he believed that the spring offensive (for which Sarrail may have briefed him on the plans, but not on the underlying problems soon to surface) could well succeed in driving the Bulgarians out of the war. He had always believed that once they cracked they would disintegrate.²⁸

Thirdly another inter-governmental meeting was about to take place, and Milne would have had a fair idea of what was on the agenda – the withdrawal of troops to other theatres and restricting the activities of a slimmed-down Allied Army solely to the defence of Salonica and the Greek border – unless of course the upcoming offensive was remarkably successful.

A fourth reason for Milne's decision to renew the attack on 8 May – and probably not the least important – surfaces in his post-battle report to Robertson; 'to allow the French no grounds for saying that we were not fully supporting them. Sarrail had I think begun to realise the difficulties to be overcome, and was looking for a scapegoat... I think the Allies are now assured that the British Army at least did what it could.'²⁹

Milne and Wilson again decided on attacking by night on 8 May. The main responsibility for the attack remained with 26th Division, 77th Brigade having replaced the depleted 79th Brigade. The Petit Couronné inevitably remained the key objective of this second assault on the Doiran defences, with 77th Brigade aiming to roll up the Bulgarian first line from the lake to position O3, meeting

---

24 Sarrail/Porte, *Mon Commandement*, p.301.
25 Falls, *Macedonia Vol I*, p.318.
26 Robertson, *Soldiers and Statesmen*, p.94.
27 Milne, *Despatch of 1917*, p.3.
28 Palmer, *Gardeners*, p.122.
29 Nicol, *Uncle George*, p.128.

up with a battalion of 78th Brigade who would make a direct attack on the hill.[30] Above all, the Jumeaux ravine should be avoided as far as possible.

Meanwhile 22nd Division would make raids and demonstrations over the sector from O6 to Krastali and aim to extend and strengthen the British front. To their left 60th Division would also strive to gain ground to the north, but mainly on ground where the Bulgarians had no permanent presence.

The attack was preceded by two days of artillery bombardment. Of the 60,000 gas shells Milne had requested only 20,000 had arrived in time, and 60 percent of these were defective. This was insufficient to allow any concentration of gas on the hilly and windy hillside, and anyway the Bulgarians were extremely well prepared for gas attacks.[31]

The general attack commenced at 2150 on 8 May. Despite enfilade fire and uncut wire, and hampered by smoke and night mist, some units of 77th Brigade penetrated the enemy trenches in several places, but no critical mass was achieved, and they were driven back before daybreak.

The one battalion of 78th Brigade, accompanied by pioneers and specialists crossed the dreaded ravine so quickly that it was held up by its own supporting barrage. Reinforcements arrived and the joint force took almost all of the Petit Couronné position. But with the enemy still holding positions O3 and O5 on either side of them, they were unable to hold it, and the last remnants were forced to retire by 1150 the following day.[32] The Allies were to get no closer to taking this strategically positioned hill and the defence lines it dominated for over a year.

The culprit this time was not the Jumeaux ravine, but the almost total breakdown in communication. Field telephone was still in an early state of development. Telegraph communication relied on cables, which between static positions could be dug into the ground; for offensive advances the battalion signallers could only run them along the ground during advances, and they often got cut, particularly by enemy artillery.[33] Visual signalling was not possible during the night, which also restricted the effectiveness of forward observation points. The nature of the terrain as well as the smoke of battle made lamp signalling almost totally ineffective. The most reliable communication was word of mouth, but if runners got lost or were killed, there was no way of knowing if the message had got through.

Essentially 22nd and 60th divisions further down the line achieved their objectives with minimal casualties, but they were minor, largely involving the incorporation of unoccupied territory rather than forcing the enemy out of fortified positions. Although eventually useful for future actions, they were of no great tactical value at the time or in the months to come.

Milne put the failure of this second attack, succinctly, down to 'lack of information and delay in using reserves'. He was also heavily out-gunned. In his report to Robertson of 15 May he noted 'the unexpected and numerous artillery barrages of the enemy. Heavy howitzers and trench mortars were plentifully used and ammunition seemed unlimited'.[34] In fact the BSF had nothing bigger than 6-inch howitzers and 60 pounder guns. The Bulgarians, heavily supported by the Germans in this operation, had 8-inch and 6-inch howitzers and heavy trench mortars. Also an overwhelming supply of well-positioned machine guns.

He also noted in his letter to Robertson 'however good the superiority of British troops on the flat, in hill-fighting the superiority was with the enemy.'[35]

---

30 Wakefield, *Under the Devil's Eye*, p.85.
31 Wakefield, *Under the Devil's Eye*, p.86.
32 Falls, *Macedonia Vol I*, p.321.
33 Falls, *Macedonia Vol. 1*, p.323.
34 Nicol, *Uncle George*, p.128.
35 Packer, *Return to Salonica*, p.73.

Casualties for the night were 1,861, 483 killed or missing, 1,478 wounded. Almost all of these were with 26th Division which had incurred 3,888 casualties from ten battalions used over the two attacks.[36] Total casualties for XII Corps for the two attacks 24-25 April and 8-9 May were just over 5,000, almost a quarter of total battle casualties sustained by the BSF during the whole Macedonian Campaign.[37]

* * *

In 1916 the operations of XVI Corps on the Struma Front had been almost entirely successful, giving credence to Milne's contention that his troops were superior 'on the flat.' The Corps' short campaign on the Struma in 1917 was to prove him right again. At Milne's request General Briggs, Commander of XVI Corps had drawn up a plan of action with the aim of occupying as many Bulgarian divisions as possible while the main offensive was unfolding to the west.

Between 12 and 15 May artillery attacks were made along a 40 kilometre line from Tumbitsa to Mirsla. Infantry attacks were then made on the enemy line between Kalendra and Bairakli by 10th Division. The key was Kyupri, which was taken by 29th and 30th Brigades on 15 May and held against strong ground and artillery counter-attacks.

The next objective was to capture and hold a series of enemy defences north of Bairakli Juma known as the Fergie and Essex trenches. This was undertaken by 85th Brigade of 28th Division and was launched from recently dug communication trenches half a kilometre to the south. The assault supported by a lifting artillery barrage was a complete success, and in this one action alone 89 prisoners were taken (four times more than were taken at Doiran during the whole XII Corps attack of 8 May).[38]

In accordance with the procedure perfected in 1916, forward-facing defences were quickly established and wire laid. The division was now well placed to proceed with the fourth and final part of Briggs' plan – capturing and holding Ernekoi and Spatovo, strongly held villages just south of the mouth of the Rupel valley, and within striking distance of Demi Hasar and the site of the destroyed railway bridge over the Struma. Momentum was such that they could well have succeeded, and the advance was already underway on 22 May when at Milne's command, Briggs was told to suspend hostilities. The reason was that the main French–Serbian offensive to which this and indeed the Doiran battles were tributary, had got nowhere and had been called off.[39]

It is possible that Milne, with hindsight, or even at the time, wondered whether he had been right to reject Sarrail's original proposal for the part to be played by the BSF in the spring offensive – to concentrate its forces against the enemy on the Butkovo and Struma fronts rather than battering away at the lowest level of the formidable Doiran defences. He was, as it turned out, at the highest level of his establishment with six divisions, two mounted brigades, full headquarters services and artillery adequate for this purpose, if not for hill warfare. If the BSF had threatened the Rupel valley, the gateway to Bulgaria proper, cleared the Butkovo plain and put the Constantinople railway into operation, all sorts of tables would have turned.

With the enemy threatening Bulgaria would the Plevna division have marched on Salonica? It seems improbable. A key consideration however in all Milne's thinking, and one which certainly played a part in his preference to attack at Doiran, was malaria. At all costs he didn't want his forces engaged on the malarial plains during the summer, even at the cost of giving up what XVI Corps had just won, a point he makes very clearly, in his 1917 despatch:

---

36 Falls, *Macedonia Vol. 1*, p.331.
37 Palmer, *Gardeners*, p.125.
38 Falls, *Macedonia Vol. 1*, p.338.
39 Falls, *Macedonia Vol. 1*, p.338.

As summer was commencing I now had to consider the best ways of maintaining the health and efficiency of the Army during a period when malaria and dysentery are more or less prevalent in the low-lying areas. In view of the experience gained last year, and despite the fact that a considerable amount of anti-malarial work had been carried out in the valleys during the winter, I decided to abandon the forward positions on the right and centre of the line and retire to the foothills on the right bank of the Struma river, and to the south of the Butkova valley. This withdrawal was completed by 14 June, without incident or interference by the enemy.[40]

---

40 Milne, *Despatch of 1917*. Signaller Bailey 7 June reports from the Butkovo Front 'Orders to move back to summer line. Off in morning at day break'. His brigade was moved back to Mahmudli where on 15 June he reports 'Aeroplanes (hostile) busy. Several raids from Bulgars, stand-to ordered.' Perhaps this didn't count as 'interference', just as business as normal.

21

1917
The Failed Offensive

(Map 9)

The centrepiece offensive for 1917 was finally to be launched, after many delays, on 8 May following three days of bombardment. At this point the entire Allied force amounted to 274 battalions. Of these, 72 were those of the BSF, to the east of the Vardar, whose involvement in the offensive has already been covered in Chapter 20 above. Sarrail therefore had at his disposal the equivalent of 202 battalions with which to face the enemy in the main battle theatre on the west side of the Vardar.

The Allied 274 battalions faced 255 on the enemy side. Of these 102 were on the east side of the Vardar, covering the Doiran, Butkovo, and Struma fronts. Sarrail's 202 battalions on the west of the Vardar would therefore be facing 153 Germano–Bulgarian battalions, by no means a decisive majority given the strength of the enemy defences perfected over the last six months.[1]

In early February Sarrail had presented an aggressive and wide-ranging plan for a 1917 spring offensive to Lyautey, Minister of War, telling him that his objective was the Vardar but if all went well *l'objectif final serait Sofia* (the final objective would be Sofia).[2] Lyautey had approved this on 21 February. On 26 February the Allied Conference at Calais had concluded that a decisive defeat of the Bulgarian Army was not possible at that time. But on 9 March Lyautey had given Sarrail clear instructions to go ahead with his plan, with a preferred launch date of 15 April to coincide with the Nivelle offensive.

On 20 March however Lyautey was replaced as Minister of War by Painlevé who, perhaps more realistically, saw the mission of the Allied Army in 1917 as one of retaining on the Macedonian Front *le maximum des forces enemies aux profit des offensives alliées déclenchées sur les fronts principaux* (as many enemy forces as possible in order to support the main Allied offensives elsewhere).[3] This suggested a rather different sort of campaign to the one presented by Sarrail to Lyautey; one of heavy artillery actions, holding operations and regular engagements along the line with no major territorial ambitions.

Sarrail however seems not to have modified his plans in any way. Even in his memoirs, although Sofia is no longer mentioned, he confirms that from the outset the objectives of the 1917 offensive were for the Serbs to push over the Moglena mountains to the Vardar, and for his forces in the Crna bend to break through and advance on Topolcani.[4] In addition, advances between Lake Prespa and the west Crna, between Nonte and the Vardar, and by the BSF at Doiran and on the Struma Front

---

1 Falls, *Macedonia Vol. 1*, p.339.
2 Sarrail/Porte, *Mon Commandement*, Annexe 85 p.465.
3 Armées Françaises, *Tome VIII Vol. 2*, p.445.
4 Sarrail/Porte, *Mon Commandement*, p.299.

were still programmed. In short, concurrent attacks of greater or lesser import were to be made along the whole length of the 300 kilometre Allied front.

In 1918 Franchet d'Espèrey was to recognize at once that the break-through could only be made by attacking one sector of the enemy line with an overwhelming force of troops and artillery while holding firm defensive positions along the rest of the front. Interestingly General Lebouc who at this point was commanding the 'Crna group of Divisions' had suggested such a plan to Sarrail – four French divisions, both Russian Brigades, the Italian 35th Division and the Serbian First Army to break through in the bend of the Crna, allowing the Serbian Second Army to pass through and reach the Vardar.[5] But this was not Sarrail's preferred approach, the idea went no further and Sarrail compensated by making an almost paranoiac attack on Lebouc in his memoirs three years later.[6]

Since the original definition of Sarrail's plan, however, much had taken place which was to have a bearing on its success. First, the pre-requisite cleansing action around Monastir on the Tservena range and Hill 1248 had been largely unsuccessful; advances up the Monastir gap towards Prilep were still as problematic as ever. Second, Sarrail had been presented with an ultimatum by the Serbs on 20 March that this time, they were not going to attack unless the French went first, and unless they were provided with much more heavy artillery.[7] Third, communication with the BSF had more or less broken down following the pointless attack at Doiran on 24 April.

Fourth, the creeping delays in the launch date had sapped morale, created confusion both at staff and operational level, and worsened the already taut relations between the Sarrail and his allied commanders. These delays were certainly in part the result of late snowfalls – particularly critical in the Serbian sector – but also due to defective planning and administration by Sarrail's staffs as observed at first hand by Milne's liaison officer with the French headquarters, Colonel Plunkett.[8]

Then of course there was the Greek situation simmering in the background. During the whole period of the Macedonian Campaign the political and military situation in Greece was never more volatile than in the first months of 1917. To a greater or lesser extent royalist forces were gathering in Thessaly. Rightly or wrongly Sarrail felt the need to protect his back and ensure at least a minimum of cover north of Thessaly.

As the final preparations for the 1917 offensive were made, the forces of Allied Army of the East to the west of the Vardar were distributed as follows:

- Koritsa to Lake Prespa, 76th Division;
- Lake Prespa to Novak on the west Crna, 156th, 57th and 11th Colonial Divisions (essentially the Monastir sector);
- Novak to Hill 1050, Italian 35th Division;
- Hill 1050 to north of Zovik on the east Crna, 16th Colonial, Russian brigade, 17th Colonial
- Zovik to the Kaymakcalan ridge, Serbian First Army;
- Kaymakcalan ridge to Nonte, Serbian Second Army;
- Nonte to the Vardar, 122nd Division and Greek Seres Division.[9]

This left 11th Colonial and 30th divisions in reserve, to the south of the Crna bend and around Lake Ostrovo respectively, less of a *masse de manoeuvre* to reinforce the formations on the front line

---

5 Falls, *Macedonia Vol. 1*, p.344.
6 Sarrail/Porte, *Mon Commandement*, p.306.
7 Sarrail/Porte, *Mon Commandement*, Annexe 90 p.468.
8 Sarrail/Porte, *Mon Commandement*, p.302.
9 Armées Françaises, *Tome VIII Vol. 2*, pp.446–448.

than a first line of defence in the event of negative developments to the south. The Greek nationalist Archipelago and Crete Divisions were in training.

To bring some coherence to the full-frontal offensive about to be launched, the French Official History (perhaps retrospectively) breaks it down into three categories *un secteur d'attaque pricipale, des secteurs d'attaque secondaires, et des secteurs de demonstration*. Or, main attack sector, secondary attack sectors, and demonstration sectors.

The main attack was that of the two Serbian Armies over and round the Moglena to the Vardar. Secondary attacks were to be made by the Italo–Franco–Russian forces in the bend of the Crna, and by the BSF XII Corps at Doiran. The aim of the secondary attackers was to *pousser si possible jusqu'à la rupture des lignes enemies* (push as hard as possible to achieve a break-through in the enemy lines). The remaining divisions or groupings, 122nd and Seres Divisions, 76th Division, the grouping around Monastir, and the BSF XVI Corps on the Struma were to indulge in '*actions énergiques*' with the aim of holding down the enemy units facing them.[10]

The 122nd and Seres Divisions under General Regnault, although only destined under the plan for 'energetic action', occupied a position of strategic importance between the Serbs and the British XII Corps. If their neighbours achieved the planned break-through, Regnault's force would need to advance with them, and move from demonstration to attack mode. A year later, under Franchet d'Espèrey's plan for the 1918 offensive, the same position was to be held by the French First Group of Divisions under General Anselme. On that occasion the break-through was achieved, and Anselme's Divisions combined impeccably with the Serbs and the British in securing the defeat and rout of the Bulgarian forces in this critical sector.[11] This time, however, the break-through did not occur.

For unexplained reasons (perhaps to respond in part to the Serbian 'French-first' condition) 122nd and Seres Divisions were sent into action on 5 October, three days before the launch date for the general offensive, and not benefitting from the three day bombardment to which enemy lines along the rest of the front were subjected. Using their own artillery however, the two divisions successfully pushed the Bulgarian lines back by between 500 and 1,200 metres over a five kilometer front, taking the advanced enemy positions of Ljumnitsa and Hadji Bari Mahala. They then attacked, took, then lost, part of the heavily defended rocky salient of Skra di Legen at the cost of 600 – 700 casualties, but established new lines 800 metres to the south of it. (This was to prove valuable in the successful action against the Skra in May 1918 where Seres Division was also engaged).

The Greeks had performed well in their first major action, probably better than the restrained language of the official report *Les troupes helleniques s'étaient montrées très braves, mais n'étaient pas encore suffisament instruites* (The Greek troops showed themselves to be very brave but are not sufficiently well trained).[12]

Sadly, this small subsidiary action was probably the most successful of the entire 1917 offensive to the west of the Vardar. In Sarrail's telegram to Painlevé of 15 May it was about the only positive thing he had to report.[13]

On the Crna bend front it was found that the three day bombardment had not achieved the desired results and the Allied artillery pounded away for another day, delaying the ground attacks until 9 May. Four divisions were allocated to the sector; to the left up to Hill 1050, the Italian 35th Division. To the right of the Italians, facing the Piton Rocheux, and designated the lead unit in this assault was 16th Colonial, to their right, the Russian brigade, and to the far right 17th Colonial.

---

10   Armées Françaises, *Tome VIII Vol. 2*, pp.452–453.
11   See Chapter 35 below
12   Armées Françaises, *Tome VIII Vol. 2*, p.456.
13   Sarrail/Porte, *Mon Commandement*, p.305.

The first objective was to take and hold the Bobishte ridge, which ran behind Hill 1050 and the two Pitons.[14] They were to advance line abreast over a front of eight kilometres in order not to be subjected to attacks on their flanks; *le seul moyen de diminuer ce grave danger … était de marcher à l'ennemi tous ensemble* (The only way of avoiding this serious danger … was to advance towards the enemy all together).[15]

The attack began at dawn and for the first hour they held their own, with the Russians even reaching Orle two kilometres behind the Bulgarian lines. But they had gone too far too fast and were eventually isolated and cut down by German fire suffering casualties of 1,650. This may well have been the last ever action of the old Imperial Russian army.[16] To the right of the Russians 16th Colonial made very little progress, while 17th Colonial gained some enemy trenches which they then lost.

The Italian 35th Division had been nurturing the lines around Hill 1050 for six months, had fought over it twice and knew it intimately. However despite General Pettiti's proposal for an outflanking manoeuvre the Italians had been instructed by Sarrail to make a frontal attack based on an hour's reconnaissance from a nearby hill. Once again the Italians took the Hill, and once again were blown back by murderous enemy crossfire. No ground was gained and casualties were over 2,600.[17]

The attack was to be renewed the following day, 10 May. Grossetti had defined a narrower front of attack essentially restricted to Hill 1050 and the two 'Pitons' on either side. At 0730 however the commander of 16th Colonial decided his troops were not ready and his artillery was not in place and called the action off. News of the cancellation failed to reach one French and one Italian battalion who had already pushed forward and taken certain enemy trenches. But they were not supported and had to retire, taking heavy losses. From this point the Italians lost any shred of confidence they had ever had in the leadership of Sarrail.[18]

A further attack was ordered for the next day but got nowhere. The attack frontage was reduced again on 12 May with no further success. By this time the Bulgarian 1st Division had been moved into the Monastir area, liberating 19 German battalions for action in the Crna bend. They arrived with an impressive array of artillery. Three days of artillery exchanges followed. On 17 May the Allied forces advanced again, this time with a Brigade of 11th Colonial in support of 16th Colonial. The fresh troops gained a footing on Piton Rocheux but were again driven off. The Bulgarians with a strong admixture of Germans had exploited their strongly fortified defensive positions to the full, and benefitted from superior weaponry at all levels, as the French Official History sadly concluded.[19] Over the eight day period nothing had been gained. It was the same picture on the Monastir Front where on 16 May 57th Division had taken 800 metres of the enemy defensive line on the north slopes of Hill 1248 but had then lost them.

The major assault of the 1917 offensive however was to be made by the Serbian Armies. The plan, simple in definition, was for the Serbian Second Army (Stepanović) to cross the Moglena range at Dobropolje, take Kotka and Sokol, and proceed to the Vardar via Kozjak. The Serbian First Army (Mišić), once Sokol and Dobropolje had been taken, would push through the gap to the east of the Crna and turn right north of the mountain range to join up with the Serbian Second Army at the

---

14 Schiavon, *Front d'Orient*, p.259.
15 Armées Françaises, *Tome VIII Vol. 2*, p.460.
16 Palmer, *Gardeners*, p.126.
17 Villari, *Macedonian Campaign*, p.132.
18 Villari, *Macedonian Campaign*, p.132.
19 Armées Françaises, *Tome VIII Vol. 2*, p.471.

Marianska plateau. For this endeavour, in accordance with the Serbian 'ultimatum', Sarrail had loaned nine heavy batteries to them, five to the Second Army and four to the First Army.[20]

The numerous delays in the launch of the offensive had been due, in the main, to the weather. A long autumn which had favoured the advance on Monastir the previous year had been followed by a late, hard and prolonged winter. The effects which the biting cold and the heavy snowfalls throughout winter had on the movement of men and guns into their final positions were nowhere more severe than on the mountainous sectors held by the Serbs. Despite this, the artillery to support the Serbian attack had mainly been pulled into place by 3 May.

The attack was opened on the night of 8 May, with the Sumadija division of the Serbian Second Army advancing northwards towards its first objective, the Dobropolje.

This fortified steep-sided ridge rising to 1,880 metres was seen by both sides as crucial to Bulgarian defences in the central Moglena mountains. Beyond it lay the descending plateau of Krivatsa, sloping down to the lower Crna and providing the most direct backdoor access to the Vardar and the Bulgarian Army's nerve-centre at Gradsko. General Ribarov of the Bulgarian 3rd Division wrote:

> Once the defences of Dobropolje are taken the succeeding positions will be open for immediate (enemy) advances, and because of the bad roads and the extraordinary terrain over which we must retreat, we cannot take the better part of our artillery with us. After a few days it is doomed to be in the hands of the enemy.[21]

Mišić was to convince Franchet d'Espèrey a year later that the Dobropolje was the key to unlocking the whole Macedonian stalemate. Stepanović may well have understood this in May 1917, but also quickly realised that the forces then available to him were totally inadequate for the job.

Initially the Serbian advance met with some success. By 11 May the southern summit of Kotka had been reached, but despite covering fire from Floka the Serbian Army failed in its assault on the Dobropolje, and by 14 May had only taken two precarious positions on the southern flank of the massif. Parallel attacks on Vetrenik on 17 May were repulsed by determined enemy fire, which also forestalled all attempts on the supposedly lightly held Oblo Tchouka.[22] Almost nothing had been achieved at the cost of 900 casualties.

Above all, Sokol had not been taken. From this heavily fortified mountain the Bulgarian forces dominated the Crna valley and the planned line of advance of the Serbian First Army. In view of this, of the failure of the second Army to reach the Moglena ridge, and of the now obvious lack of any Allied break-through in the Crna bend, Mišić saw no point in committing the First Army. On 21 May, Bojović, the Serbian Chief of Staff called on Sarrail to bring the whole offensive to an end.[23]

Five days earlier Painlevé had telegraphed new guidelines to Sarrail:

> *En raison de situation générale et situation particulière Grèce, opérations offensives contre Germano/Bulgares ne doivent pas être poursuivies au prix de sacrifices hors de proportion avec but à atteindre. Il vous appartient à juger, en conséquence, le moment où ces opérations doivent être arrêtées.* (In view of the general situation and particularly that in Greece, offensive operations against the Germano–Bulgarian forces should not be pursued at a cost disproportionate to the aims to

---

20 Armées Françaises, *Tome VIII Vol. 2*, p.457.
21 Hall, *Balkan Breakthrough*, p.88 quoting from Markov *Golyamata voina I Bulgariata* p.120.
22 Armées Françaises, *Tome VIII Vol. 2*, p.458.
23 Palmer, *Gardeners*, p.129.

be achieved. It is up to you therefore to decide when these operations should be brought to a halt).[24]

Faced with the inevitable Sarrail called a halt to all Allied operations on 23 May. The much-vaunted offensive had petered out within fourteen days. Including those of the BSF 14,000 casualties had been incurred.[25] No statistics survive of enemy casualties, but Falls considered that they must have been much less than Allied casualties. Gains had been microscopic.

In the actions preparatory to the main offensive in February and March, 76th Division had cleared a larger territory around Koritsa, and the enemy had been removed from some of his positions north of Lake Prespa. Slight gains had been made on Hill 1248, but not enough to prevent enemy artillery from continuing to menace Monastir from this position for another sixteen months.

During the full offensive the Serbs had taken the southern summit of Kotka and had established two small positions on southern flanks of Dobropolje. In the Vardar valley, 122nd and Seres divisions had gained some useful ground. But no further progress had been made around Monastir, and the combined attack in the bend of the Crna had achieved nothing. On the Doiran Front 66th Brigade had captured three sets of trenches with their gun emplacements and pushed the British line forward beyond the Jackson Ravine. To the west of the Doiran battlefield a slice of largely unoccupied territory had been taken, essentially reducing the no-man's land gap.

On the Struma front alone BSF's XVI Corps had made significant advances and achieved all its objectives – in fact it was still moving forward when the final whistle was blown. But being so far from the epicentre of Allied operations its gains were of limited strategic value to the success of the overall offensive, and anyway were to be mostly retroceded with the onset of the malarial season.

There had been no break-through, major or secondary. The surface of the enemy front had scarcely been scratched. Had he been given to introspection *l'objectif final serait Sofia* would have haunted Sarrail for the rest of his days. But he was not and dedicates only nine of the 400 pages of his memoirs to what should have been the definitive campaign of his Macedonian command, and most of these carping about *obstruction Britannique*.

He could however claim, and did, that in line with Painlevé's guidelines, the threat of his offensive and the brief offensive itself had tied up enemy troops who could have been switched to other theatres, particularly the Western Front. With regard to the 21 German battalions employed at this time to stiffen the Bulgarian forces he may have been right. No elements of the Bulgarian army however were ever going to be switched to the Western Front, and the withdrawal of some Bulgarian forces from the Dobrujah had little practical value since it led to no offensive action by the Russo–Romanian forces who had been facing them.[26]

If this was a small positive, there were many negatives. Enemy morale, said to be wavering at the end of 1916, was given a tremendous boost. All elements of the Allied army, including the French, had lost confidence in Sarrail's abilities not only as a general and strategist, but also as a manager and leader. The British who had, despite all their underlying reservations as to the value of the Macedonian campaign, given their agreement to this offensive, now announced their intention to withdraw two divisions and two mounted brigades for more useful employment in Palestine.

CIGS Robertson's conclusions were, as ever, brief and to the point:

---

24 Armées Françaises, *Tome VIII Vol. 2*, p.472. Also quoted by Larcher, *Grande Guerre*, p.197. Telegram from War Minister to Sarrail 15 May 1917.
25 Falls, *Macedonia Vol. 1* p.342.
26 Larcher, *Grande Guerre*, p.198.

As in previous offensives, there was never the least prospect of achieving anything in the nature of a decisive success, for in addition to the defects just mentioned (inadequate staff coordination and friction between the armies) the forces possessed neither the resolution, cohesion, nor the numerical superiority required to dislodge the enemy from the naturally strong and well entrenched positions in which he was established.[27]

With all their attention now taken up with the collapse of the Nivelle offensive on the Western Front the French and British Governments and High Commands had anyway little time and inclination to pick over the reasons for the failure of the spring offensive on the Macedonian Front. If they had, they would have wondered what had happened to the Serbs.

---

27   Robertson, *Soldiers and Statesmen*, p.94.

22

1917
Disaffection and Disarray in the Serbian Army

The Serbian Army had been in the field since the First Balkan War in 1912. Over a period of five years they had firstly triumphed over the Ottomans, then over the Bulgarians, only to have some of the territory they had gained re-distributed by the Great Powers. In 1914 in the Third Balkan war they had trounced the Austrians but had taken very heavy losses in the process. In 1915 they had been deplorably let down both by the Allies and by the Greeks who refused to honour a treaty of mutual defence. Following defeat against a three-pronged attack by Germany, Austria and Bulgaria the remnants of the army, about a third of its original size, crossed the Albanian mountains in the winter to the Adriatic coast, where they were picked up by Allied ships and taken to Corfu. Those who survived were then reconstituted by the French into three armies of two divisions each – about 120,000 men – and shipped around the Peloponnese to join the Allies on the Macedonian Front in May 1916.

In September 1916 they played a central role in the battle for Monastir, and in one of the most savage actions of the whole Macedonian Campaign drove the Bulgarians from their mountain stronghold of Kaymakcalan. But at a cost. Serbian casualties during the autumn campaign at 27,337 were twice those of the French at 13,784.[1]

The soldiers of the Serbian army had not seen their homes for many years. They had suffered the trauma of defeat and retreat in 1915. They had seen more than half their numbers killed or maimed in battle, or victims of cholera and typhoid epidemics. The plight of their families under an Austrian occupation in the north and Bulgarian occupation in the south must have been constantly in their minds. They would have learned that in February 1917 conscription had been imposed on their countrymen by the Bulgarian occupiers in the Serbian provinces of Timok, Niš, Uskub and Macedonia; their own people were being forced to support the military effort against them.[2]

They would also have heard of the outcome of the 'Toplica Uprising' in February 1917 in Eastern Serbia south of Niš, undertaken partly as a reaction to the enforced conscription, and partly under the misapprehension that the Allies had reached Skopje. Some 8,000 Serbian irregulars had succeeded in liberating a number of towns before being beaten back by the Bulgarian army with Austrian assistance. Casualties, military and civil, were very significant.[3]

News would also have reached the Serbian Army of the Surdulica massacre, which followed hard on the heels of the failed uprising. In this little remembered Balkan pre-cursor to Srebrenica between 2,000 and 3,000 Serbian men were rounded up by the Bulgarian occupying force, executed and buried in the forests surrounding the town of Surdulica on the Bulgarian border about 100 kilometres south of Niš.[4]

---

1   Larcher, *Grande Guerre*, p.177.
2   Gray and Argyle, *Chronicle Vol. 2*, p.16.
3   Gray and Argyle, *Chronicle Vol. 2*, p.24.
4   Andrei Mitrovic, *Serbia's Great War 1914 – 18* (London: Hurst, 2007), pp.222–223.

These were the major atrocities, but Serbian civilians were subjected to brutal persecutions throughout the war. These are reported in agonizing detail by R.A.Reiss, a Swiss criminologist attached to the Serbian Government during the Campaign. The 130 pages of his distressing account cover massacres, hangings, executions, deportations, the torching of villages committed by the Austrian and Bulgarian occupying forces in forensic detail; times, places, names, numbers, photos.[5] There was also evidence of the forced conscription of Serbians into the Bulgarian army, as well as early attempts at ethnic cleansing.[6]

Unquestionably, word of this would have got through to the Serbian troops, and as they advanced through enemy-held Macedonia to Monastir and the Crna they would have seen evidence at first hand.

From all this it is not difficult to imagine that in May 1917 morale in the Serbian camp was at a very low ebb, coupled with a growing resentment that Sarrail was giving them all the most difficult assignments, something which Sarrail himself confirmed in his memoirs; *Les attaques françaises jouèrent seulement le rôle d'ensemble immobilisateur au profit des Serbes* (The French attacks will only play the role of an immobilising force for the benefit of the Serbs).[7]

There were several other contributive factors. The planning time frame for the offensive had always been short, and the long winter, particularly in the mountains, had made it shorter. No time had been available for training, particularly in the placing and role of artillery. The provision of the extra artillery required for the assault on the Dobropolje had been delayed by the snows, and in view of the need for artillery support for a series of simultaneous attacks along the whole of the Allied front, firepower was inevitably diluted.[8] General Milne, an artilleryman himself, attributed the failure of the whole offensive to the inability of the Allies to obtain and retain superiority of firepower, due also to an unexpected increase in the quantity and strength of the enemy's artillery. Milne, who generally confined his commentary to military matters (and this was in a telegraph to Robertson of 14 May before the Serbs' refusal to move), reported 'Considerable mistrust and friction exists among our Allies.' and in particular citing the unwillingness of the Serbs to bear the brunt of the fighting again.[9]

A more insidious influence was closer to hand. News of the February revolution, of the abdication of the Tsar, and of the arrival of Lenin in St Petersburg in April was widespread among the Russian contingent and revolutionary thought was taking a grip particularly in the Second Brigade which was attached for this exercise to the Serbian Army. Sarrail cites both of these issues as contributing to the 'malaise' in the Serbian ranks, although he himself was presumably responsible for mixing the Russian and Serb forces in the first place. The logic of putting the Slavic language members of the Alliance together may have made operational sense, but in this case was backfiring as the Russians attempted to radicalise the Serbs.

In his memoirs however Sarrail devotes more space to a conspiracy within his own ranks. Remarkably, he accused General Lebouc of plotting against him:

Le Général Lebouc qui commandait dans le boucle de la Cerna s'était imaginé que le commandement de deux divisions ne suffisait pas à ses talents. Il aurait voulu commander en Orient, mais comme

---

5 R.A. Reiss. *The Kingdom of Serbia. Infringements of the rules and laws of war committed by the Austro-Bulgaro- Germans. Letters of a criminologist on the Serbian Macedonian Front* (London: George Allen and Unwin, 1919).
6 Marcovic, *Serbia's Great War*, pp.346–355. Marcovic quotes from Austrian and Bulgarian sources and from Dr Victor Kuhne, *Ceux dont on Ignore le Martyr*, Geneva 1917.
7 Larcher, *Grande Guerre*, p.197 quoting Memoirs of Sarrail p.250.
8 Palmer, *Gardeners*, p.127 reports that two of the guns used to support the Dobropolje attack were two old British naval guns of Boer War vintage.
9 Nicol, *Uncle George*, p.134.

son grade s'y opposait, il avait songé à me faire remplacer officiellement par le Prince Régent, dont il aurait été major-général. (General Lebouc who was in charge of the forces within the bend of the Crna felt that command of two divisions was insufficient for the exercise of his talents. He would have liked to be Commander in Chief, but because his rank was not senior enough, he had conceived the idea of having me officially replaced by the Serbian Prince Regent, to whom he would have been Chief of Staff).[10]

One has to assume that if Sarrail had any real proof of this, Lebouc would have been sent packing with the expedition previously accorded to de Lamardelle and Cordonnier. And if he had no proof of it is curious that he should have brought the matter up years later as another instance of the 'malaise' which had reduced the effect of his offensive.

Curious also in that he passes by what must have been the main reason for the inaction of the Serbs, and therefore the complete failure of the offensive, simply by referring to 'political problems among the Serbs' which he went on 'have nothing to do with me.'

Certainly they were nothing to do with him in that they fell well outside the scope of his duties as Allied Commander in Chief; the problems were, very definitely, internal to the Serbs. But if Sarrail had been watching what was going on and had properly understood the implications, he would either have cancelled his offensive, or structured it in a totally different way with different objectives.

The 'political problems among the Serbs' had deep roots, going back to the beginning of the 19th century, and the so-called First Serbian Uprising against the Ottomans led by the Karadjordjević family and the Second Serbian Uprising led by the Obrenović family. Following the success of the Second Uprising in 1818 the Ottomans agreed to the formation of a semi-autonomous Serbian Principality. For almost the next century the Obrenović family provided the princes and from 1882 the kings of Serbia except for a period from 1842 to 1858 when the Karadjordjević family returned to power.

At the turn of the century the throne was occupied by the 21 year old Alexander Obrenović, an unstable and incompetent monarch with (for the Serbs) entirely unforgivable pro-Austrian sympathies. The travel writer Rebecca West described him as 'a flabby young man with pince-nez and a taste for clumsy experiments in absolutism'.[11] In 1903 a group of young army officers stormed the royal palace and assassinated the hapless Alexander and his equally detested queen, Draga Mašin. The coup had been planned and led by a 26-year-old Captain in the Serbian Army named Dragutin Dimitrijević.

The Karadjordjević returned to the throne in the person of King Peter 1, and the Government passed a motion awarding Dimitrijević the title of 'Saviour of the Nation' and making him Professor of Tactics at the Military Academy.[12]

Dimitrijević who had graduated brilliantly from the Serbian Military Academy was then recruited immediately by the Serbian General Staffs where his talents and instincts drove him into the areas of strategy and intelligence. Politically he was an extreme, militant, Serb nationalist.

Having gained a taste for assassination and regime change he became the driving force in a secret organization called founded in 1911, '*Ujedinjenje ili Smrt*' – better known to posterity as 'The Black

---

10 Sarrail/Porte, *Mon Commandement*, p.306. This may have been a retrospective take on Lebouc's suggested alternative strategy for the 1917 offensive, see Chapter 21 above. The bit about the Prince Regent sounds like a bitter post-retirement embellishment.
11 West, *Black Lamb and Grey Falcon*, Prologue.
12 David Mackenzie, *Apis the Congenial Conspirator* (New York: Boulder, 1989).

Hand' – to project and further his political agenda; and embedded within military intelligence he was well placed to do this. He adopted the code name 'Apis'.[13]

In 1911 he organized an assassination attempt on the aged Austrian Emperor, Franz Josef, but this failed. With world-shattering results however the attempt on Archduke Franz Ferdinand in Sarajevo on 28 June 1914 succeeded, and history has generally assigned responsibility for this to 'Apis' and the Black Hand. In fact, Gavrilo Princip and his collaborators were lone Bosnian operators, only becoming known to the Black Hand when they approached one of its members for arms. The Black Hand then provided the necessary weapons, an element of training and the expertise for smuggling the conspirators and their arms back across the Serbian border into Bosnia.[14]

Ironically Princip's political motivation was pan-slavism, rather at variance to Dimitrijević's drive for a greater Serbia, but from different directions they both thought that the elimination of the Austrian heir to the Imperial throne would suit their purposes. Years after the mayhem which they had unleashed the emerging political solution in the Balkans was closer to the dream of Princip, but by then neither of them were there to see it.

Apis's (short) future career was interwoven with that of Nikola Pašić, the 'Serbian Venizelos', leader of the Radical Party and Prime Minister of Serbia almost without interruption from 1904 to 1918 – and then three times Prime Minister of Yugoslavia. Pašić was not involved in the 1903 assassination but having been imprisoned twice and exiled for six years by the Obrenović dynasty, he must have been pleased, not only for personal reasons, but also because his party regained power at the next election and he became Prime Minister in 1904.

Pašić was at the helm during the so-called 'ten golden years' for Serbia, expanding the economy, removing trade dependence on Austria and opening Serbia to a wider world, particularly France and Britain. Under Pašić Serbia was one of the founders of the Balkan league leading to success in the Balkan wars of 1912-13 and Pašić was the Serbian signatory to the Treaty of Bucharest in 1913.

Apis, also, was involved in his professional capacity with the strategic planning during the Balkan wars. Following the successful incorporation of Northern Macedonia into the Serbian kingdom however, while Pašić wanted normal democratic structures to be implanted, the army, and presumably Apis, wanted the new province to be put under military occupation.

Pašić's diplomatic leanings (he served concurrently as Prime Minister and Foreign Minister for long periods) were pro-Russian and anti-Austrian. But his approach was pragmatic. When Austria annexed Bosnia in 1908 Pašić managed to reign in the understandable anger of his countrymen and held back any cries for military intervention. When an associate of the Black Hand apprised him of the assassination plot in 1914 he attempted to warn the Austrian Government and gave instructions for the conspirators to be stopped at the frontier. But the Black Hand had a wide network of sympathisers, and Princip and his team got through.[15]

Following the assassination it was Pašić who prepared the conciliatory reply to the Austrian ten point ultimatum. Two members of the Black Hand were arrested in Serbia although it is interesting that Dimitrijević was neither named by Austria nor pursued in Serbia.

But despite Pašić's efforts, the Austrians were determined to destroy Serbia. In the Third Balkan War they failed, but the following year the Serbian Army was defeated by the joint Austrian, German and Bulgarian armies and forced to retreat to the Adriatic coast.[16] With them went old King Peter, the Prince Regent Alexander to whom the King in 1914 had devolved all his duties including Commander in Chief of the armed forces, as well as Pašić and the Serbian government ministers.

---

13   Glenny, *The Balkans*, p.299
14   Butcher, *Trigger*, p.255.
15   Butcher, *Trigger*, p.256.
16   Chapter 7 above.

During the war Pašić ran a government in exile on the island of Corfu. As part of the French reconstruction of the Serbians into three Armies each of two divisions, Apis, now Colonel, became chief of intelligence in the Third Army.[17] A man with a towering personality, persuasive strengths in line with the certainty of his convictions, and a post within the military hierarchy ideal for his purposes, he set about converting his fellow officers in the Third Army, many of whom would have been his students in the Military Academy, into supporting his programme. Which was? Quite possibly he was preparing the groundwork for a middle-ranking young officer military take-over, a trend which was to gather force during the mid-twentieth century.

It would not anyway have been difficult for Apis to stir up discontent with the management of the campaign in 1916. And if he had wished, which no doubt he did, to portray the distant government of Pašić as irrelevant, and the Prince Regent Commander and his ageing generals as dupes or collaborators in the Sarrail military regime, then he was well placed to do so.

Somewhere the penny dropped; when a conspiracy or even a conspiratorial tendency gets too widespread word gets out. Colonel Apis was not after all to provide an early 20th century role model for Colonels Nasser and Gaddafi. On 20 December 1916 he was arrested and charged with planning to assassinate the Prince Regent and foment mutiny. With regard to assassination he was known to have form. With regard to mutiny the investigators went on to arrest one in thirty of all the officers in the Serbian army, with a higher incidence in the Third Army. Of these 180 were handed over to the French authorities who sent them to Tunisia for internment during the duration of the war.[18]

With regard to the Third Army Bojović was obliged to dismantle it completely in March 1917. Both its divisions, Drina and Danube, were reconstituted and put with the First Army under Mišić. The Vardar Division was moved from the First Army to the Second Army. In view of the high number of casualties, sickness, and the lack of reinforcements, each of the newly distributed divisions (Drina, Danube, Morava, Sumadija, Timok and Vardar) was then reduced from 12 to 9 battalions.[19]

The erstwhile Commander of the Third Army, General Vasić had only taken over from the veteran General Sturm in August 1916. No involvement in the Apis plotting attached to him. He was sent as Serbia's liaison officer to Italy, and resurfaced after the war as Yugoslav defence minister for a couple of years in the 1920s.[20]

The charge against Apis, as well as planning assassination and fomenting mutiny was that he was conspiring to replace the elected government and the Karadjordjević dynasty with a military junta. The collection of evidence from dozens of witnesses covered the period from December 1916 to March 1917. The Third Army was being wound up at the same time as the final preparations for the Sarrail offensive were being made. Small wonder that for the Serbs it scarcely got off the ground. Evidence of the prevalent confusion was that as late as 2 April, the Allied Army General Staffs didn't know where the Headquarters of Serbia's First Army was situated.[21]

The trial of Apis began on 2 April 1917 and ran through until June. No conclusive evidence was found, particularly of any assassination plot. Nevertheless Apis and two senior collaborators were found guilty and were executed just outside Salonica on 26 June 1917,[22] as it happened almost exactly three action packed years since the murder of the Archduke in Sarajevo in 1914.

---

17 Palmer, *Gardeners*, p.133.
18 Palmer, *Gardeners*, p.134.
19 Falls, *Macedonia Vol. 1*, p.257.
20 M. Bjelajac, *Generals and Admirals of Yugoslavia* (Beograd, 2004), pp.298–299.
21 Palmer, *Gardeners*, p.135.
22 Palmer, *Gardeners*, p.135.

The Pašić government in exile did not fall. The Prince Regent remained Commander in Chief of the Serbian Army. His three key generals, Bojović, Stepanović and Mišić remained in place. But morale in the Serbian army had plumbed new depths and would remain so until the arrival of Guillaumat and until the new 'Yugoslav' recruits arrived in early 1918.

After the end of the war there were two related developments. Firstly, it was put about that the Apis plot was mounted because Pašić was rumoured to be treating with the Austrians. This seems immensely unlikely. Secondly, the evidence on which Apis was condemned was re-examined by the judicial powers of the new Yugoslavia and he was posthumously exonerated of trying to assassinate the Crown Prince.

Apis's ambitions may have been limited to regime change within Serbia and an extension of her ethnic borders. But history can never exonerate him from the part he played in lighting the match which sparked the First World War.

23

1917
Dethronement of Constantine

The Greek War of Independence began with in-house revolts by the Greeks against their Ottoman overlords particularly in Mani and the Peloponnese. Independence only became a reality however following the intervention of France, Britain and Russia whose joint fleet crushed that of the Ottomans at the Battle of Navarino in 1827.

And it was these 'Protecting' or 'Tutelary' powers who at a conference in London in 1832 decided the boundaries of the new state, and its form of government – and who subsequently, on behalf of the Greeks, agreed terms with the Ottomans in Constantinople later that year. The same three powers then made two very handsome loans to the new Kingdom of Greece to help it on its way.

All this occurred more than eighty years before the beginning of the First World War, and much had changed in the meantime; a new royal dynasty, a new constitution, the addition of Thessaly and the Ionian Islands to Greek territory, and then the fruits of the Balkan Wars, Macedonia, Epirus and Crete.

Nevertheless in view of their undisputed role in the creation of the Greek state, and the full weight of their political support throughout the 19th century, the 'Protecting Powers' still felt that they had the right if not duty to intervene in Greek affairs when necessity called. The Protectors' reaction to a King who quite clearly recognized no such right was at first one of surprise at the negative reception they received when they first landed in Salonica. It then passed in stages through dismay when Greece would not give passage to their Serbian allies to pass through the country, to incredulity at the Rupel incident, to deep-seated mistrust as successive agreements with the king were not honoured, and to blind fury when even a naval blockade, the seizure of the fleet and the landing of marines failed to make the King see the errors of his ways.

With the Greek nation split between the royalist government in Athens and the Venizelist nationalists in Salonica, Sarrail's solution would have been to invade Old Greece and force the capitulation of the royalist government. At the Rome conference in January he had tried to get Lloyd George to see it this way. In view of the possible consequences enumerated by Robertson, Lloyd George continued to favour a peaceful solution.[1]

But by mid-1917 matters were coming to a head. With increasing frustration Sarrail noted in his diary information being brought to him of further stratagems being employed by the royalist government to increase its military presence in Thessaly; gendarmes sent to Thessaly were soldiers in disguise, soldiers who had been sent to the Peloponnese were being given 'leave' and then returning to Thessaly. The League of Loyalists (Epistrates), not officially part of the military were being used

---

1   Robertson, *Soldiers and Statesmen*, p.139.

to increase the armed forces on the ground. Sarrail notes also the discovery of caches of arms, and forty food depots sufficient to support 50,000 men.²

Much of this information was based on unverified hearsay and reported to Sarrail with a large dose of telling him what he wanted to hear. When French forces finally advanced into Thessaly at the end of May all the scores of places where arms were supposed to have been hidden were checked out, and nothing was found except a few hunting rifles.³ But Sarrail had certainly become obsessed with the subject, and Robertson was probably more than half-right when he wrote in his memoirs:

> The French were continually pressing for dramatic action and the invasion of Thessaly. Sarrail was always eager to recommend that course of action and seemed to devote at least as much attention to Greek politics as to the defeat of the Bulgarians on his front.

No Frenchman likes to 'se faire avoir' and by May 1917 Sarrail must have felt that the Greek King was not only taking him for a ride, but he had also been doing so since the start, and if he were not forcibly stopped he would continue to do so with impunity.

An Allied conference was held in Savoie on 19 April, before, as it happened, both the first Battle of Doiran and the debacle of the May offensive west of the Vardar. The Greek issue dominated the Salonica agenda, all parties were now agreed that something had to be done. The Italians prudently stepped aside, leaving the two remaining 'Protecting Powers' (Russia was by now more or less out of the picture) to solve the problem – with the condition that the monarchy should be retained in order to dilute the influence (and territorial aspirations) of Venizelos.⁴

The French wanted the Allied army to occupy Thessaly, bread basket of the kingdom, in order to ensure an equitable sharing of the harvest – an excuse as good as any to send a military force down there. The British wanted to wait until the conclusion of the May offensive before moving.⁵

By the time of the next conference, in Paris on 5 May, hard decisions had to be made, not only on the Greek issue, but on the whole future of the Macedonian campaign. In mid-1917 more than at any other time the justification for keeping well over half a million men on the Macedonian Front was seriously open to question.⁶

Caught between a rock and a hard place, a gloomily circular discussion came to the conclusion that on the one hand the Allies had nothing like the amount of shipping required to move 500,000 soldiers and their equipment to other theatres, but on the other hand, in view of submarine depredations they had not the shipping to continue to feed and supply them. Britain anyway was about to withdraw one division (60th) and two mounted brigades for service in Palestine and would shortly be extracting another division (10th) to embark for the same destination.

A conclusion was reached that the only way to reduce the increased exposure to which the remaining Allied forces would be exposed following the British withdrawals would be to fill the gaps with Greek forces. And, however reluctantly, the British also had to accept that this could only be done by removing King Constantine and uniting Greece under one of his sons and a pro-Entente Venizelist government.⁷ The advantages this would also bring in shortening shipping routes and reducing the time and risks inherent in transferring men and materials to Salonica

---

2   Sarrail/Porte, *Mon Commandement*, p.285.
3   Casson, *Steady Drummer*, p.169.
4   Robertson, *Soldiers and Statesmen*, p.138. 'As to Venizelos' he noted 'France supported him, Britain admired him and Italy suspected him.'
5   Larcher, *Grande Guerre*, p.202.
6   Robertson, *Soldiers and Statesmen*, p.140 assessed the ration strength of the Allied Army of the East at that time as 670,000 – 240,000 British, 210,000 French, 120,000 Serbs, 17,000 Russian, 50,000 Italian and 23,000 Venizelist. French figures were similar.
7   Larcher, *Grande Guerre*, p.203.

were also enormous and obvious. While they accepted the logic, however, playing an active part in the final showdown with the King proved a step too far for the British delegation. Bowing to the inevitable they passed full responsibility for the final resolution of the Greek issue to the French, retaining only a consultative role in the identification and nomination of a French High Commissioner charged with implementing the decision.[8]

Just prior to this meeting and its game-changing conclusions, King Constantine played what turned out to be his last card. By replacing the royalist Lambros as prime minister with the pragmatic Zaimos his probable intention was to convince the Allies of a new wish for engagement and reconciliation. It was too late. By now a whole combination of factors was leading to a denouement – the reports of clandestine gatherings in Thessaly, the hard-nosed government of Ribot, the need to shorten shipping routes, the perceived necessity for additional Greek forces to shore up the front with Bulgaria, the Thessalian harvest, the impatience of the Venizelist faction in Salonica, now perhaps turning towards republicanism – to say nothing of Sarrail's fervent desire to achieve a political victory to counterbalance the military one which was eluding him.

In a further exchange of messages between Allied ministers during May, the British continued in their efforts to prevent a military solution being imposed on Greece. Sarrail notes that although the abdication finally became a reality *tout fut mis en œuvre pour l'empêcher par nos alliés les Anglais* (Everything was done by the English allies to stop it happening.)[9] With some justification the British government was afraid of provoking a civil war, and the British High Command was fearful of having to provide yet more troops to this theatre to occupy Greece and hold the two sides apart. This may well have been the advice of the Minister, Sir Francis Eliot; there is no evidence of Milne having, or giving, views on the subject. Politics was not his business.

But in the final conference on the subject held in London on 28 May, the British government finally conceded to the French programme.[10] A French division was to be sent to Thessaly, another to Piraeus, and an infantry brigade to the Corinthian Isthmus. For the sake of form the equivalent of two companies of British troops were to accompany the Thessalian division, and an equal number to be used at either Piraeus or the Isthmus 'in case of necessity'.[11] Another piece that had fallen into place was the agreement of Venizelos to the Allied plan. This was achieved on 7 May with his declaration that his only interest was the unity of Greece, and that he would accept the Crown Prince as King.[12]

The decision having finally been taken to depose the King, events now took place at a bewildering speed. The French, following the agreement of 5 May had nominated Charles Jonnart as 'High Commissioner for Allied purposes in Greece', theoretically representing all three 'Protecting Powers' although at this stage Russia had effectively withdrawn from all such commitments. M. Guillemin, France's long-term minister in Athens (he who had persuaded Admiral Dartige not to bombard central Athens during the crisis of the previous December) would step aside. In order to avoid any cross purposing on the ground, the British also withdrew their veteran minister, Sir Francis Eliot.

Jonnart had served in several French governments since the 1890s, including Foreign Minister in the 1911 government of Briand. He was best known as having been Governor General of Algeria for most of the 1990s, and as a specialist in colonial affairs.[13] Sarrail was to work under his

---

8   Falls, *Macedonia Vol. 1*, p.351.
9   Sarrail/Porte, *Mon Commandement*, p.295.
10 Falls, *Macedonia Vol. 1*, p.352.
11 Larcher, *Grande Guerre*, p.204.
12 Falls, *Macedonia Vol. 1*, p.350.
13 Schiavon, *Front d'Orient*, p.262.

political direction. Since Jonnart was a civilian, there were no considerations of rank to confuse this relationship.

Jonnart arrived in Brindisi on 4 June, took ship for Corfu, and then through the Corinth Canal to Salamis. Here he received news that Zaimis was prepared to remain in office while Jonnart fulfilled his mission.[14] This was of fundamental importance and did more than anything else to secure a smooth transfer of power. Jonnart moved on to Salonica where he met with Sarrail and Rear Admiral Salaun, to agree the timing and nature of military and naval dispositions. Sarrail had already written a long memo to Jonnart on 3 June detailing his plans and dispositions for moving into Old Greece, listing the forces to be used down to battalion and battery level, with timing and destinations.[15] Jonnart must have accepted these plans in their entirety; the programme went ahead just as Sarrail had proposed.

On 9 June Jonnart left Salonica for Piraeus, where on 10 June he met with Zaimis to agree on the distribution of the Thessalian harvest. For the British and French Governments the purpose of the forces being sent to Thessaly, Piraeus and the Isthmus of Corinth was essentially to keep the peace at key points while Jonnart completed his mission. For Sarrail, on the other hand, their function was the invasion and conquest of Old Greece which he had long had in mind.

The division sent to Thessaly had orders to occupy the barracks of the Greek garrison in Larissa, now reduced to the strength of a battalion. The Greek officers were ordered to hand over their swords. For a unit of the crack 'evzone' troops, this was too much and they tried to make their escape. Pursued by the French cavalry they holed up in an old fortress and fire was exchanged. Ten French soldiers and about 50 Greeks were killed. The French cavalry returned with 300 prisoners. According to the Commander of the French force, Sarrail had given orders for any Greeks found firing on French troops to be shot without trial. Sarrail was almost certainly referring to un-uniformed *franc tireurs* with whom he was obsessed. However it was only the intervention of a British consular official and a British naval commander who had been summoned which enabled sanity to be restored to a tense situation.[16] This was on 11 June, the small British force of 500 didn't turn up until five days later. At least the evzones were not accused of trampling on the Thessalian harvest. At the Isthmus the British at the very last minute tried to prevent the landing of troops, but Jonnart went ahead anyway. There was no opposition.[17]

On 11 June Jonnart, on behalf of the 'Protecting Powers' presented Prime Minister Zaimis with the demand that King Constantine should abdicate. The wording of the ultimatum could scarcely have been briefer or clearer:

> Monsieur le Président,
> The Protecting Powers of Greece have decided to reconstitute the unity of the kingdom without prejudice to the Monarchical constitution which they have guaranteed to Greece.
>
> HM King Constantine, having manifestly violated, on his own initiative, the constitution of which France, Great Britain and Russia are the guarantors, I have the honour to declare to your Excellency that the King has forfeited the confidence of the Protecting Powers, and that they consider themselves liberated, where he is concerned, from the obligations resulting from their rights of protection.
>
> My mission is therefore, in order to re-establish constitutional verity, to demand the abdication of HM King Constantine, who will himself nominate, in accord with the Protecting Powers, a successor from among his heirs.

---

14 R. David, *Le Drame Ignoré de l'Armée de l'Orient* (Paris: Plon, 1927), p.214 quoted by Falls, Vol. I p.354.
15 Sarrail/Porte, *Mon Commandement*, pp.293–295.
16 Casson, *Steady Drummer*, pp.174–179. He was present.
17 Larcher, Grande Guerre, p.205.

I am under the obligation of requesting a reply within a period of 24 hours.
Please accept, M. le Président, the assurance of my high consideration
Jonnart[18]

In an equally brief footnote the Protecting Powers, for the elimination of all doubt, declared that they would not accept the Diadoch (Crown Prince) as his successor.

The same evening, 11 June, Zaimis sent word to Jonnart, on board the *Bruix* in Piraeus harbour that the King had accepted the ultimatum, 'mindful only of the interests of Greece.' He had decided to leave the country with the Crown Prince and nominated Prince Alexander as his successor. On 12 June the royal party left Athens, and on 14 June took ship for Italy on their way to Switzerland.[19]

An announcement, no doubt drafted by Zaimis, was made by the new King that he meant to 'follow in the glorious footsteps of his father'. This was a perplexing sentiment in the circumstances; but Zaimis, a public servant of many years' standing probably wanted no one to forget the then Crown Prince Constantine's glorious part in the Balkan wars, the conquest of Macedonia and the incorporation of Salonica into the Greek kingdom.[20]

On 12 June the division sent to Piraeus disembarked and took up positions south of the city. Interestingly this force included, as well as the small British contingent, a Russian battalion. The Russian brigades still formed part of the Allied Army at this point. Including representatives from the third 'Protecting Power' was an imaginative idea, even if in Russia itself at that moment little attention could be given to commitments made nearly a century ago under a now defunct Tsardom.

Not to miss an opportunity to extend her influence on the Adriatic coast, on 8 June and without warning, Italy invaded Epirus and took Ionnina. To Italy's Allies, and above all to Venizelos, Epirus was part of Greece. The Italians promised to leave once the British and French had withdrawn their troops from Old Greece. And so they did, eventually.

On 27 June Venizelos arrived in Athens and was sworn in as Prime Minister by the new king. There were, inevitably, royalist disturbances, and parts of the French Piraeus force and some artillery were brought up into central Athens. The trouble was minimal, some extreme royalist politicians and officers were banished to the islands for the duration of the war.

Two quite separate issues helped the Greek people to accept the alignment with the Entente. One was the lifting of the naval blockade, immediately announced by Jonnart. The other was the entry of the United States into the war on 6 April, which the Greeks, always more open to the outside world than the other Balkan nations, would have seen as proof that they were now on the right side.

The entire process of replacing a hostile government in Athens with a friendly one and reuniting the kingdom had taken less than three weeks. Sarrail, in the end, had played little part, but to a large degree the achievement was his. His memoirs are often grumpy and sometimes vitriolic, but one can sympathise whole-heartedly with his disgust at a High Commissioner suddenly being imposed on him and taking all the credit for an operation which he had been planning and advocating for months but had never been given the authority to implement:

Je n'avais pas l'honneur de diriger l'opération d'assainissement de la Grèce royaliste que j'avais préconisé depuis de longs mois. M. Jonnart arrivait de France pour récolter ce qui avait déjà été semé et

---

18   Falls, *Macedonia Vol. 1*, p.361. quoting R. David, *Le Drame Ignoré*.
19   Schiavon, *Front d'Orient*, p.265.
20   King Constantine when heir apparent and commander of the Greek army had of course been the liberator of Salonica from the Turks in 1912. Despite his abdication this remained a major step in the establishment of Greek nationhood and despite finally losing in his long confrontation with Venizelos, there are still statues of both men in Salonica, one kilometre apart on the Via Egnatia.

moissonné (I wasn't allowed the privilege of putting into operation the programme for clearing up the situation in Old Greece that I had been recommending for months. M. Jonnart arrived from France to gather in that which had already been sown and harvested.)[21]

The nationalist government of Venizelos in Salonica had already declared war on the Central powers in November 1916; indeed the first of the Venizelos nationalist forces to become operational had already been engaged in actions alongside the Allies on both the Struma and the Vardar fronts. One of Venizelos' first actions on becoming Greek Prime Minister was to recall Greece's ambassadors to Germany, Austria, Bulgaria and Turkey and confirm that the declaration of war made by his provisional government now applied for the whole of Greece. While King Constantine had vacillated for three years, Venizelos had never had any doubt about where Greece's best interests would be served. His courage in following his convictions had been rewarded.

Although after his long wait he had been denied the privilege of administering the knockout blow himself, Sarrail must also have been satisfied. His long and bitter confrontation with Constantine had finally been brought to a successful conclusion.

The importance of Constantine to the shape and prosecution of the war in the Balkans can scarcely be overstated. But it might have turned out so differently. Had the Allies in August 1914 and more significantly in March 1915 accepted Constantine's offer of military support against Turkey the Dardanelles Campaign would have taken a different shape; it might even have succeeded. In this case Bulgaria would probably have retained neutrality, or, if not, Allied landings in Salonica would have formed part of a wider strategy of which Greece would have been a part and would not have been seen as an uninvited incursion into her sovereign territory.

Again, had Constantine in 1915 promptly honoured his treaty commitments to support Serbia against the threat of a Bulgarian attack, the southern front would have taken a completely different form. Serbia may not have fallen or might have held out long enough for the Allies to establish a meaningful presence in the theatre rather than arriving after her defeat was certain. Bulgaria might have maintained her stance of Germanophile neutrality for longer, in which light Romania might have declared for the Allies earlier, further reducing the likelihood of Bulgarian intervention and increasing immeasurably the chances for a successful outcome of the Romanian campaign.

Constantine's belief and that of his government that the Greek army was in no condition to mount a major campaign after the Balkan wars and was short of materials can however be given some credence. In addition it should be noted that following the crisis with Venizelos in October 1915, the moment at which, if ever, the Greek army should have been dispatched to support the Serbs, Constantine was so seriously ill that he received the last rites.

Then in 1916 the entry of Romania into the war clearly gave Constantine much food for thought. Had the Allies followed the diplomatic leads and possibilities thrown up at this time rather than a naval blockade and a force majeure fiasco in Athens, it is quite possible that Constantine may have realised that Greece's best interests would be best served by aligning herself with her oldest allies rather than maintaining a neutrality which played into the hands of her greatest traditional enemies.

Instead of which for a period of nearly two years Constantine followed a policy of wavering ambiguity. He was subject unquestionably to powerful influences, the Kaiser his brother-in-law who was constantly on his shoulder, his wife Queen Sophie despite her long estrangement from her brother, royalist sentiment in Athens and the government, his military staffs, many of whom had also trained in Germany. His thinking was further affected by the strength of the German mission in Athens and of Baron Schenk, by suspicions of the British Government (Grey) in their apparent

---

21   Sarrail/Porte, *Mon Commandement*, p.295.

offer of Greek territory to Bulgaria in exchange for Bulgarian goodwill, by assassination attempts rather neurotically believed to have been piloted by the French in 1916, and by the failure of the Dardanelles campaign and any hopes it held of further Greek acquisitions in Asia Minor.

Another consideration to be taken into account was that Greece is not self-supporting in food, particularly cereal. Had he declared for the Central Powers, the Allies, with their overwhelming naval supremacy in the Mediterranean could have prevented the importation of foodstuffs.

Some or all of these factors might, to a greater or lesser degree, have played a part in his decision-making, or lack of it. There is ample cause to believe however that behind all the prevarication was an underlying desire to do what he felt was best for Greece. Some sort of logic emerges from his moves, now to one side, now to the other. And objectively Constantine's analysis of Greece's position and best interests at this time was not mistaken.

Had he declared for the Entente powers and had they lost the war, the Central Powers would have seized all of northern Greece and probably Epirus and Thessaly as well. Any hope of an understanding with Turkey about Greek populations and claims in Asia Minor and the adjacent islands would have been forfeited. Greece would have returned to the pre-war boundaries of Old Greece, heavily under German domination.

Had he opted for the Central Powers and they had lost, the victorious allies would certainly have called for his departure but probably left Greece intact as a bulwark against any future Bulgar or Turkish military expansion. Ironically, following the death of his son King Alexander in 1920, Constantine returned to the throne, only to be expelled again following defeat in the Greco–Turkish war of 1922. He died the following year, once more in exile.

24

1917
Summer of Discontent

For CIGS Robertson, whose belief in the 'Salonica Affair' had always been close to zero, the failure of the Spring Offensive was further proof that his troops were wasted down there, that the cost of maintaining six divisions in Macedonia was quite disproportionate to the results achieved, and that the Allied Army was badly led. On 1 May he had written to the War Cabinet 'it is lamentable to think that at the present time when the French Government hesitates to continue fighting in France because of deficient manpower, they and ourselves have over 400,000 men at Salonika who are unlikely to achieve any useful results, while an absolutely intolerable strain is being put on our naval and shipping resources.'[1]

While in a further report of 29 July 1917 he concludes gloomily 'We cannot use the large army we have there for an offensive, and when we desire to move troops elsewhere for urgent and necessary purposes we are compelled to consider potential dangers arising from the false position in which we are placed.'[2]

The 'false position', he surmised, had only been worsened by the abdication of the King; the Allied Army now had the additional responsibility of defending a friendly power whose contribution to her own defense was likely to be realized slowly, and anyway with the need for much support in training and materials.

And when he finally secured the agreement of Lloyd George to the withdrawal of two divisions, he was disappointed that this was not because Lloyd George had seen the light of day, but because he wanted to achieve glory in yet another peripheral theatre:

> Even the Prime Minister, one of the earliest and most persistent advocates of Balkan enterprises, now began to realise that no benefit, political or other, could be derived from them, and he accordingly ceased to take interest in them. But he was not prepared to use his influence in the Allied councils for the purpose of bringing divisions away if they were afterwards to be sent to the Western Front. His alternative to the threadbare Balkan project was an all-British campaign for the conquest of Palestine, and he told me quite frankly that if he consented to help the General Staff to extricate divisions from Salonica, he expected the General Staff to use the divisions thus set free in furtherance of his Palestine plan. He seemed to regard this proposal as a perfectly fair and proper bargain, but of course it was not a question of bargaining, but of doing the right thing. The right thing was to keep on strengthening the Western Front as the Russian defection became more pronounced.'[3]

---

1 Nigel Birch, *No Sideshow* (University of Buckingham: Niroad Publications, 2018), p.21.
2 Palmer, *Gardeners*, p.148.
3 Robertson, *Soldiers and Statesmen*, p.99.

At a meeting of 25 July of all the Allies *une sorte de parlement de l'Entente sous la forme d'une conférence* (A sort of Entente Parliament in the form of a conference) as Larcher rather sniffily put it:

> *M Lloyd George fut catégorique. L'Angleterre soutenait seule le poids de la guerre contre les Turcs : elle n'avait que 480,000 hommes en Egypte et Irak – était-il juste quelle maintient 190,000 dans les Balkans* (Lloyd George was categorical. Britain was conducting the campaign against the Turks by itself. She only had 480,000 men in Egypt and Iraq – was it right for her to keep 190,000 men in the Balkans?).[4]

The Serbs, Greeks and Romanians who were concerned that they would be left to their own devices protested loudly. No decision was reached. The matter was taken up again in the more manageable setting of an Anglo-French meeting in London on 8 August, where Lloyd George was pressed by the French to promise:

> *à ne pas retirer des nouvelles troupes à moins que des événements imprévus ne survinssent auquel la question serait soumise à la discussions des Alliés; il reconnaissait la nécessité de maintenir la force des armées Alliés à Salonique* (not to remove more troops except in unforeseen circumstances in which case the matter would be referred to the Allies: he recognized the importance of maintaining an armed force in Salonica).[5]

Lloyd George's over-riding objective at this stage of the war was 'Jerusalem before Christmas', but with or without the input of Robertson there may have been other considerations holding him back from removing further divisions from the Macedonian Front. The new Austrian Emperor Karl was reported to be putting out peace feelers.[6] Should Austro-Hungary withdraw from the war, with or without forcible occupation by the Germans, an army available on the Macedonian Front to exploit any power vacuum could prove invaluable. Also, Lloyd George was always conscious that Milne's were the closest British forces to Constantinople.[7]

Back on the ground, after the departure of 60th Division in June, Milne had only 5 divisions to cover his 140 kilometre front, and asked Sarrail for the transfer of French forces across the Vardar to help. Sarrail's excuse for not doing so at that time was that many of his forces were still down in Thessaly and Athens. When in September 10th Division also departed, leaving Milne with only four divisions and, four squadrons of cavalry, Sarrail still refused to move any of the 18 divisions covering 150 kilometres from the Vardar to Lake Prespa across to the British sector,[8] this time without advancing any reason other than (in his memoirs) asking himself '*Qui commande? Le Général ou moi ?*' (Who's in charge, Milne or me?)[9] and telling Painlevé (after having presumably reviewed the disposition of Milne's forces) that by modifying the distribution of his current forces Milne could plug the gaps.[10]

---

4   Alexandre Ribot, *Lettres à un Ami; Souvenir de ma Vie Politique* (Paris: Bossard, 1924), p.338. General Wilson who was present reports that there were 43 nations involved 'including the Portuguese and Siamese, who made passionate speeches'
5   Ribot, *Lettres à un Ami*, p.339.
6   The veteran Emperor Franz Josef had finally died at the age of 86 in November 1916 after a reign of 68 years.
7   Palmer, *Gardeners*, p.147.
8   Nicol, *Uncle George*, p.139 His calculation is ; French sector (with Greeks), 50 km, Serbian sector 55 km, Italian sector 15 km. Beyond Lake Prespa the Russians loosely covered 36 km of mountainous country.
9   Sarrail/Porte, *Mon Commandement*, p.323.
10 Sarrail/Porte, *Mon Commandement*, p.475. Telegrams from Sarrail to War Minister 15 and 20 August 1917.

In a further reply on the issue to the French chiefs of staff (who had obviously been lobbied by their British counterparts) he pointed out that the BSF was only in close contact with the enemy on along 22 kilometres of its long front (the Doiran sector) whereas the rest of the Allied Army (without quoting kilometres) were in closer contact with the enemy. Anyway, he went on, the Russians and Italians were not properly covering their sector and the Greeks were untrained.[11] The pressures of his job were clearly closing in on him.

The 1917 Spring offensive had been called off on 23 May with minimal gains and 14,000 casualties. In June the main military manoeuvre had been the advance of two and a half mixed divisions into Old Greece to support the mission of M. Jonnart, while the remainder of the Allied Army remained on the alert to defend the front against any opportunistic Bulgarian incursion.

By July the 'abdication support' force had returned, duty done. Back on the front however other problems were surfacing, to add to those which had already been present for some time but which had not been addressed.

Following the Apis trial, the weeding out and expulsion of many of his followers, and the re-grouping of the three Armies into two, Serb morale was at its lowest level since the retreat through Albania in 1915. Resentment over the disproportionate casualties they had suffered during the Monastir campaign still rankled, and their numbers were also being reduced by a trickle of desertions.[12] Of all the soldiers serving on the Macedonian Front the Serbs of course were the only ones who could have walked home; and the Bulgarians were quietly passing through messages to encourage them to do so. But the numbers were small. The forthcoming withdrawal of the two British divisions also unsettled the Serbs.

The Russians were in a worse position. Their service on an active front had been continuous for eight months. Following the exploit at Orle in May, General Dietrichs told Sarrail that the 1st Brigade was exhausted and needed six weeks' rest. News of events in Russia however was inevitably seeping through, and revolutionary ideas were beginning to take hold, especially in the 2nd Brigade, who anyway resented being attached to the Serbian army. At the end of May, shortly after the abdication of the Tsar, Dietrichs wrote 'rumours and gossip reaching the trenches from the rear…can only strain the men's nerves still further, worrying them and paralyzing their will'.[13]

At the end of June the situation worsened with many of the men from the Russian battalion which had been sent to Athens refusing to re-embark for Salonica. The French had to use force to oblige them to do so. In July, in an attempt to stem the discontent, the 18,500 men of the two brigades were combined into one division under the command of Dietrichs.

But then, sadly, Dietrichs the one Russian leader of whom everyone, including Sarrail, spoke well, was recalled to Russia and things began to fall apart. The Russians participated in one final and successful action, the assault on Pogradec, but by the end of the year, following the November Russian Revolution, Bolshevism had taken a grip and soviets were being set up within the Russian division. Finally it mutinied and in January the Russians had to be withdrawn and disarmed. Some joined the French Foreign Legion, many became absorbed into the Allied labour forces, and the rest were interned awaiting repatriation.[14]

The French forces were not immune from the general malaise. Some French divisions had been in Macedonia for two years without leave or relief, mostly at the front and frequently engaged in military action. The fatigue which was setting in was fanned by news received from France that the French Chamber of Deputies in its wisdom had declared that all French soldiers had the right to have leave after eighteen months service. On 15 July Sarrail reported to Paris that he had at least

---

11   Sarrail/Porte, *Mon Commandement*, p.334.
12   Palmer, *Gardeners*, p.135.
13   Palmer, *Gardeners*, p.135.
14   Palmer, *Gardeners*, p.137.

20,000 men in this category. Shortly afterwards he was confronted with a mutiny within 57th Division, one of the longest serving French divisions on the Macedonian Front, after leave parties had been turned back through lack of shipping. One battalion, then all of 242nd Brigade mutinied with the risk that 372nd Brigade would follow.[15] Sarrail considered that the officers of the mutineers were also at fault for egging the men on, since they also wanted leave.

What could have become a very serious problem, at least as great within its context as that experienced on the Western Front in May following the failure of the Nivelle offensive, was de-fused with a mixture of firmness and sensitivity by General Grossetti, Commander of the French Army, a genial and competent leader shortly to be withdrawn from Macedonia with a critical health condition. In the end only ninety men had to be disarmed and put under arrest.[16]

Help was at hand. As another welcome spin-off of the re-unification of Greece, the newly completed Salonica to Athens railway became available. Just south of Lamia, a few kilometres from the pass of Thermopylae as it happens, the station of the town of Bralo assumed – and retained – a major significance for the rest of the war. Troops from Salonica de-training here could be taken by road to Itea, a port on the Gulf of Corinth, and then shipped to Taranto. The 24 hour passage hugging the Greek coast up to Corfu was well protected against enemy submarines by the Allied navy, after which the presence of the Italian navy in their ports of Valona and Santi Quaranta added an additional security.

The Salonica–Bralo–Itea–Taranto route was simpler and capable of handling much more traffic than the Salonica–Koritsa–Santi Quaranta–Taranto route which had been opened in February. Although the Santa Quaranta route took three days instead of four, and had a much shorter sea crossing, the road across Albania was more difficult, and much longer – 200 kilometres even from Florina – and there was no rail. It was mostly used by the Italians and by the Serbs for contact with their government in Corfu.[17]

The result of the quantity of long bottled-up leave now being taken was that over a period of months the French divisions became seriously undermanned and were to remain so as a result of a French government decision of April 1917 to allow soldiers taking leave from Macedonia to opt to transfer to the Western Front, and most did, despite the heightened risks.[18] In the August attack to the west of Lake Ohrid, for example, 156th and 157th Divisions had to be combined.

As for the Italians, 35th Division had no problems with leave, having their own route to Italy via Santi Quaranta, and throughout the whole campaign was the one element of the Allied force kept consistently up to establishment and fully equipped with artillery and services. At the end of 1916 Milne had visited them and wrote enviously in his diary 'The division is wonderfully equipped.'[19] Sarrail's problems with the Italians were more personal in origin, and relations had more or less fallen apart after the failure of the May offensive. In a reverse situation to that of Sarrail's attitude to the BSF, the Italians were refusing to extend their line and support the French north of Monastir.[20]

Further, the fall of Constantine and the re-unification of Greece had confused Anglo-French relations with their Italian ally rather than the contrary, and Sarrail was suffering the backlash of this on the ground. Italian and Greek territorial ambitions in southern Albania and northern Epirus overlapped. The Italian 35th Division was now under the command of General Mombelli, like Milne, an artillery officer by upbringing. He was now being encouraged by the Italian High Command via General Ferrero to try to engineer a move for his force from the Crna bend to a

---

15 Sarrail/Porte, *Mon Commandement*, p.319.
16 Palmer, *Gardeners*, p.140.
17 Villari, *Macedonian Campaign*, p.170.
18 Schiavon, *Front d'Orient*, p.279.
19 Nicol, *Uncle George*, p.111.
20 Sarrail/Porte, *Mon Commandement*, p.331.

position between lakes Prespa and Ohrid where, obviously, they would be more in touch with Ferrero's XVI Corps.[21]

As has been seen Sarrail went to visit Ferrero in Valona in September 1917, was received hospitably, but achieved nothing in the way of greater military collaboration.[22]

And as to his latest allies, the Greeks, Sarrail was to find that far from being grateful for all the support and training they were being given they were talking about 'an autonomous Greek army to proceed if necessary to re-occupy Eastern Macedonia.' Further, in order to remain responsible for security in Northern Greece, Sarrail wanted to maintain the State of Emergency he had declared in 1916. The Greeks didn't see it this way.

He also wanted to keep, in accordance with the State of Emergency, a censored press, such as was maintained in the French, British and Serbian papers published for the troops. With a Greece undivided by a border, this was no longer possible, and Athens newspapers were available in Salonica. On top of this the Athenian press was suggesting that Sarrail should be replaced by General Gouraud, a view which was being supported by the Greek Foreign Minister.[23] Furthermore, Sarrail was now finding it impolitic, when assigning sectors of the front, to put the new Greek units next to either the Serbs or the Italians.

All of this was obviously getting under his normally resilient skin; of all the Allies, surely, he must have thought, the Greeks owed him the most. But when he listed these grievances to Painlevé in a message of 8 August, the French Minister of War must have been puzzled, if not dismayed, that the Commander of a force of over half a million men felt it necessary to bother him with them.[24]

The British from their position across the Vardar were less affected by most of the issues which were troubling their allies spread out along the front from the river to Lake Prespa. They lived amongst themselves, and apart from Milne himself, his staffs, liaison officers, specialist operations in Salonica and officers on occasional leave, had little contact with the other components of the Allied Army.[25]

Inevitably leave was also an issue for the British troops, most of whom had been away from home at least since the end of 1915. They also took their share of the Salonica–Bralo–Itea–Taranto convoys, but a large part of the places available had to be taken up with the repatriation of chronic malaria cases. By mid-1918 it transpired that 29,000 men had been more than two and a half years without leave.

One of these was Signaller Bailey. No doubt based on news of the opening up of the Bralo route he put in for leave on 7 August 1917. He was told that lots were being drawn. On 9 August he wrote ' Draw for leave. Blank. Only 6 per company to go.' Six per company equates to about 25 per battalion, or around 2 percent of all fit soldiers. He doesn't mention the subject again until nearly a year later. Again it came to nothing.[26]

---

21 Villari, *Macedonian Campaign*, p.171.
22 Sarrail/Porte, *Mon Commandement*, p.330.
23 General Gouraud was at the time commander of the French Fourth Army on the Western Front. During the Gallipoli campaign he had been commander of the French forces there. His previous experience had been in French North Africa where he had served under Lyautey. After the war he became commander of the French Army of the Levant, and High Commissioner in Syria and Lebanon. The Greek Government did not know this at the time of course, but possibly put his name forward through contacts with Lyautey, now no longer Minister of War.
24 Sarrail/Porte, *Mon Commandement*, p.326
25 In his diary Signaller Bailey makes no reference whatsoever to the other national forces engaged on the Macedonia Front until 27 September 1918 when parts of the Greek Cretan Division passed through his lines. His horizons and contacts were limited to 'Johnny Bulgar'.
26 E Bailey, 17 August 1917, 25 July 1918

Besides malaria and the physical difficulty of regular leave for troops so far from home, the main problem facing the BSF was boredom; weeks and months of watching enemy positions with little movement, but the constant need for vigilance against shelling, enemy patrols and raids by enemy aircraft.

Officers had the occasional relief of trips to Salonica, and all accounts of their time on the Macedonian Front, until the Great Fire, are enlivened by descriptions of the day and night life of Salonica, Flocca's restaurant, the Odeon theatre, the Skating Rink, cafés, cabarets, cinemas and music halls.[27]

In his narrative poem *Tiadatha* Owen Rutter devotes a complete chapter to 'A Day in Salonique', from a morning's shopping to relaxation in the Turkish baths, then tea at Flocca's, more shopping, a visit to the cinema, dinner at Bastasini, then to the theatre at the Tour Blanche.[28]

This option was not however open to the men. Even if they had been allowed passes they could not have afforded the life style enjoyed by officers in Salonica. An infantry captain's pay, for example, was twelve times that of an infantry private and five times that of a sergeant.[29]

Other ranks therefore were kept to the hills and the valleys and even when sent to the hospital town in Kalamaria or the slopes of Mt. Hortiach for malarial or other reasons were not allowed into the town. All other components of the Allied Army followed the same principle of reserving the town of Salonica to officers only. This enabled officers in this multi-national force to meet socially, make contacts and share ideas, and at an informal level gain a better understanding of how the whole piece fitted together. The men had no such contacts.

When not on the front they had to make their own amusements, and all the commentators report up-country dramatic performances, concerts, sing-songs, bands, horse shows, and hunting, and above all sporting events.[30] Behind the XII Corps lines two brick stadiums and one in wood were constructed.[31]

Even Sarrail attended – and only a few days after the resolution of the French mutinies – the 27th Division three day horse show. The enemy allowed football to proceed in full view but sent warning shots if football morphed into training.[32]

An additional distraction was '*The Balkan News*' published every day from November 1915 until May 1919, containing news wired from Britain, but also home-grown humorous articles, cartoons and poetry. As the editor, H. Collinson Owen pointed out, this was not just a link with home but also a point of contact between the members of the BSF, spread out over their very long front.[33] Luigi Villari wrote 'It was purely a paper for the army … well written, bright, full of wholesome cheerfulness, and wholly free from local political tendencies – it never tried to create bad feeling between the Allies'.[34] The expeditionary force canteen and above all the YMCA also contributed much to the well-being of the troops.

All the English language commentators are at pains to stress that morale within the BSF, despite Doiran and despite the mosquito was kept at a good level. During the First World War over 3,000 British soldiers were condemned to death by courts martial, although the sentences were only carried out in 346 cases (overwhelmingly for desertion). But while the BSF accounted for about 8 percent of British forces serving on all fronts, only 3 men, were condemned and executed by

---

27 Collinson Owen, *Salonica*, pp.37–49.
28 Rutter, *Tiadatha*, Chapter 8.
29 The Long Long Trail website < longlongtrail.co.uk> British Army Pay Rates 1914.
30 Signaller Bailey reports taking part in many football matches, a battalion sports day, and, this was a favourite, shooting competitions with prizes.
31 Falls, *Macedonia Vol. 2*, p.9.
32 Seligman, *Salonica Sideshow*, p.197.
33 Collinson Owen, *Salonica*, pp.50–62.
34 Villari, Macedonian Campaign, p.283.

military firing squads.[35] Nonetheless, the second half of 1917 saw much disruption in the British sector, firstly from the withdrawal of 60th and 10th Divisions, and the consequent dilution of coverage along their front, and secondly from another summer's exposure to the attentions of the anopheles mosquito.

---

35 Gordon Corrigan, *Mud, Blood and Poppycock* (London: Cassell, 2003), pp.229–230.

25

1917
Malaria – The Enemy Within

In 1880 Dr. Alphonse Laveran, specialist in military medicine and parasitology discovered the protozoan parasite responsible for malaria. Dr. Lavaren, who was awarded the Nobel Prize for medicine in 1907, remained active in the field until his death in 1922. In his preface to *Malaria in Macedonia* by four French doctors working with the French *Armée de l'Orient*, Laveran points out that malaria had bedevilled military campaigns since antiquity, citing among others 140,000 cases of malaria during the Turco-Russian war of 1878 and over 26,000 as far north as the Dutch island of Walcheren occupied by the British during the Napoleonic wars in 1808.[1]

In Greece malaria had always been endemic as testified by Hippocrates in the Fourth Century BC. Laveran's work was then developed and supplemented by researchers from Austria, Italy, France and Britain over the next 30 years, and by the beginning of the First World War the causes of malaria were thoroughly understood. What was less completely understood were the mosquitoes themselves, their breeding cycle, their range, their climatic preferences. A lot of empirical work was done on this during the Macedonian Campaign and these are issues well covered, with diagrams, by Dr. A. Alport whose lengthy *Malaria and its Treatment* is the result of observation and analysis over two years' work in a BSF hospital and in the field.[2]

There also remained considerable differences of opinion over the treatment of the disease. All authorities unhesitatingly endorse quinine. Alport also experimented with morphine, chamomile, strychnine and magnesium sulphate, but always came back to quinine. There remained open issues however over dosage, frequency, and method of application. It had become common practice throughout the Army to issue 15 grammes of quinine in liquid form twice a week. However, all specialists from Laveran to Sir Ronald Ross, recognized as the greatest British authority on malaria, maintained that quinine was ineffective as preventative medicine. Alport reports 'Quinine prophylaxis has been used extensively in the Salonica area and has turned out to be a complete failure.'[3]

In more restrained language the British Commander in Chief himself had come to the same conclusion. When in 1918 the BSF was stripped of 12 battalions, for the Western Front, the British GHQ in France was horrified by the incidence of malaria in the troops they received and wrote to Milne to ensure that they were given quinine for the journey. Milne wrote back 'possibly it is not understood in France that in the whole of this army malaria is prevalent. Except when suffering from actual attacks troops are better off without quinine, as is shown by our experience here.'[4] He

---

1   Felix Armand - Delille, Paisseau, Abrami and Lemaire, *Malaria in Macedonia* (London: London University Press, 2018), Preface by A. Laveran p xiii
2   Cecil A. Alport, *Malaria and its Treatment in the Line and at the Base* (London: J.Bale, Sons and Daniellsson, 1919)
3   Alport, *Malaria and its Treatment*, p.16
4   Falls, *Macedonia Vol. 2*, p.94.

had come to this conclusion as early as 1916: 'as summer progressed it has gradually come about that every unit in the Army is taking the drug. But the results have been disappointing, and very many men who have contracted malaria have undoubtedly been taking quinine regularly for several months previously.'[5] It had become, he concluded, 'a sort of fetish', but harmless in thin quantities and good for morale.

A more acute debate surrounded the method of administration to patients in hospital and following discharge. Ross held that oral application was just as effective as injection, but that quinine should continue to be taken after an attack to reduce the chance of a relapse.[6]

The first major outbreak of malaria was in the summer of 1916. No one had expected or been prepared for the virulence and extent of the attack. The speed of transmission had been totally underestimated, and the incidence of re-infection largely misunderstood. 'The anopheles mosquito sucks blood from chronic carriers and spreads the disease with rapidity and certainty' was Alport's sad conclusion.

The necessity to move chronic cases out to prevent mosquitoes from passing on the illness from persons already affected was not properly appreciated. Nor was the pattern and significance of relapses. As Collinson Owen put it in hindsight:

> The chief difficulty about dealing with malaria on such a scale is that the patient is subject to frequent relapses. The Salonica Army was full of listless, anaemic, unhappy, sallow men whose lives were a physical burden to them and a material burden to the Army; who circulated backwards and forwards between hospital and convalescent camps, passing only a few occasional days at work with their units, and then being sent away to do the round of hospital and convalescent camp again.'[7]

There was also the issue of variability in the nature of malarial attacks. 'Sometimes a man would have so severe an attack that there was nothing for it but to pack him off to hospital at once. On the other hand there are very many cases where after two or three days the victim will be back at work.'[8]

Between 6 April and 11 November 1916 there were 29,594 cases requiring hospitalisation. By any standards in an Army of five divisions this was an enormous number, indeed it represented nearly a quarter of the BSF total headcount. Hospital facilities were quite inadequate to deal with such numbers, and 20,278 men were sent to Malta for treatment. Of these, only 4,789 were invalided back to the UK, the remainder returned to Salonica under the risk of relapses and infecting their colleagues.[9] In 1917 with the Germans declaring unlimited submarine warfare, hospital ships were no longer safe. An enormous, tented hospital town was constructed at Kalamaria, and then a second one on the slopes of Mt. Hortiach. In 1917 there were 63,000 hospital admissions, almost entirely for malaria.[10]

On 13 October 1917 Milne reported to Robertson that he had 35,000 soldiers either in hospital or in convalescent camps. This was getting on for the equivalent of two divisions.[11] It was only at this point that the Directorate of Army Medical Services saw fit to send Sir Ronald Ross to Salonica to have a look. In his report of 30 December 1917 he recommended that 15,000 chronic cases should be sent home 'and replaced by drafts'. By the end of April 9,000 had gone. The programme gathered

---

5   Nicol, *Uncle George*, p.96.
6   Armand - Delille, *Malaria in Macedonia*, Second Preface by Sir Ronald Ross
7   Collinson Owen, *Salonica*, p.187.
8   Harold Lake, *In Salonica with our Army* (London: Andrew Melrose, 1917-18), p.207.
9   Nicol, *Uncle George*, p.98.
10 Collinson Owen, *Salonica*, p.181.
11 Nicol, *Uncle George*, p.142.

pace, by the end of 1918, including earlier repatriation and the Maltese cases, nearly 35,000 men were evacuated for malarial reasons.[12]

By 1918 the situation had improved, numerically at least: in July 'only' 22,000 men were in hospital or at convalescent camps with malaria. This however represented more than a division, and Milne only had four by this time, and many battalions were down to less than 500 men. Repatriation of the chronic cases however had undoubtedly had some effect on rates of infection.[13]

Although Milne recognized, together with his medical team, that regular shots of quinine did little to keep the disease at bay, the full range of other preventative measures they took was rational and comprehensive.

Among the stores maintained by the Ordnance Services were mosquito nets for two-man bivouacs, and special nets for the circular tents used at base. Nets were tailored for individual hospital beds. Anti-mosquito screens were designed for the doors of huts and buildings. Netting was unquestionably the best way of keeping the mosquito at bay.[14] Regrettably supplies from the UK were below requirements for both 1916 and 1917, and there were cases of nets having to be re-distributed according to perceived need. In June 1917 2,500 nets were taken from 28th Division and given to 27th and 10th Divisions – resulting in a notable spike in infection in 84th Brigade.[15]

Milne was forever on the case; for him 'mosquito netting was as important as the rifle.' It was however also part of his job to balance the constraints of medical necessity with the leisure requirements of his forces, objectives which often conflicted. As Alport dryly comments 'open air theatres in the summer are one of the malaria parasite's most valuable assets.'[16]

Other items held for the troops in the Ordnance stores were veils and gauntlet gloves, particularly for sentries, and shorts with flaps which could be let down and tucked into puttees at nightfall. Swamps were drained by cutting canals in order to transfer stagnant water to lower levels. Where this was not possible they were filled with earth, and where this was not feasible they would be sprayed with paraffin, or better still creosote, which killed off the mosquito larvae. Bushes and reeds where mosquitoes would spend the night were cut down. Away from the front interior walls were whitewashed so that settling mosquitoes could be seen more easily.

Each battalion had its anti-malaria officer and an anti-malaria squad of 21 men whose job was to implant and monitor anti-mosquito measures, down to the level of tent inspections.[17]

Despite all this, the anopheles mosquito continued to hold his own – or her own since it is only the female which passes on the parasite. All the counter-attacks mounted by the members of the BSF in the form of netting, draining, cutting, spraying, quinine treatment in the hospitals, and the repatriation of chronic cases only seemed to serve to keep the levels of infection stable. No mathematical model could predict what would have happened in their absence.

The Army Medical Services Malaria Statistics on the Macedonian Front collated at the end of the war show 167,519 hospital admissions (not much less than the maximum establishment of the BSF – and of course not including cases which were not hospitalised), 787 deaths resulting from malaria and 34,762 evacuations of chronic cases. The deaths represent 0.05 percent of hospital admissions, a low percentage and minimal compared with battle casualties. But the number of men incapacitated or debilitated by the disease 'doing little but circulating between hospitals and convalescent centres with an occasional day of light duty'[18] was immensely more significant. On the

---

12 Falls, *Macedonia Vol. 2*, p.58 and p.351.
13 Nicol, *Uncle George*, p.170.
14 Forbes, *History of Army Ordnance*, p.246
15 Falls, *Macedonia Vol. 2*, p.100.
16 Alport, *Malaria and its Treatment*, p.17.
17 Alport, *Malaria and its Treatment*, p.22.
18 Army Medical Services, *Diseases of the War Vol. 1*, p.282.

British sector of the Macedonian Front it was the mosquito, which was the real enemy, accounting for ten times more casualties than enemy action.[19]

It significant and appropriate that Milne ended his final Despatch from the Macedonian Front with the words 'I cannot finish this report without expressing my high appreciation of the splendid spirit and devotion to the service of their country shown by all ranks in this Army, the majority of whom will return to their homes with their constitutions shattered by a prolonged stay in this malarious and inhospitable country.'[20]

Malaria affected other units in the Allied Army on other sectors, but the Struma and Butkovo valleys where the British were destined to spend three summers were by far the worst. It was discovered that the mosquitoes had a particular fondness for younger soldiers, which perhaps explains why none of the BSF senior officers seems to have come down with the disease.[21] It was also the case that the French colonial forces, as well as the Greeks and the Bulgarians were less prone to malaria.

It was an act of courage on the part of Milne to withdraw from the malarial valleys in June 1917, and again in the summer of 1918, to protect his troops from the height of the malarial season. Facing him, the Bulgarians did the same thing for more or less the same reasons, at one point leaving a message when on patrol 'we see you are wisely going back to the hills. So are we.'[22] Sarrail, perhaps not a frequent visitor to the British base hospitals, placed the summer withdrawal from the malarial valleys on a par with the withdrawal by the British of the two divisions; 'Further to this' he wrote *dès le 1 juin tous les éléments Britanniques, sous prétexte de paludisme, abandonnaient la rive gauche de la Struma* (from 1 June all British forces, under the pretext of paludism, abandoned the left bank of the Struma).[23]

The French Army was also affected by malaria, but this was not a subject featuring at the top of Sarrail's priorities. Furthermore he appears to have been unable to disentangle his vendetta with the Army's health corps from his duty as Commander in Chief for his troops' health. On 7 October 1916 the Army's chief health officer M. Ruotte had reported:

> *Il faut bien dire que le Commandant n'a pas compris les raisons hygiéniques d'établir les campements sur les hauteurs. La direction du service n'a pas eu suffisamment d'authorité …* (It ought to be said that the C-in-C hasn't understood the health reasons for establishing encampments on higher ground. The health service isn't given sufficient authority…)

Not perhaps the best choice of words when dealing with Sarrail, a person with antennae fine-tuned to pick up any hint of insubordination. But when Ruotte went on to cross what Sarrail would have seen as the borderline between specialist advice and operational interference he effectively damned himself and his service in the eyes of his Commandant for the duration:

> *A l'état majeur du Général Sarrail on se laisse trop dominé par l'appréhension – que je dirais un peu trop fébrile – d'une attaque Grecque (en concertant) le maximum d'armés dans le camp retranché qui est une sentine de fièvre.* (General Sarrail's staffs allow themselves to be dominated by the idea

---

19 Palmer, *Gardeners*, p.142.
20 Milne, *Despatch of 1 December 1918* (London: HMSO Gazette, 22 January 1919), p.5.
21 The older members of 228 Brigade also suffered less. Signaller Bailey except for two short bouts lasted the course until October 1918, after the Bulgarian capitulation. Less than 50 years later his grandson picked up malaria in Egypt. There is a family interest in the subject.
22 Nicol, *Uncle George*, p.143.
23 Sarrail/Porte, *Mon Commandement*, p.310.

– which I find rather exaggerated – of an attack by Greece, and thus concentrate many troops in the fever-ridden Salonica plain.)[24]

The wandering Bénazet had already presented the concerns of the health corps to Sarrail in July, causing him to condemn:

> *les stupidités des spécialistes ou mal intentionnés…voulant jouer un rôle de direction au lieu de se contenter de leur recherches au microscopes.* (the stupidities of specialists or people of bad faith who wanted to get involved in the direction of the war rather than stick to their research with the microscope).[25]

On 29 July, the issue having presumably been raised in High Places, Sarrail wrote to Painlevé to tell him that the situation with the troops' health was as satisfactory as could be hoped, but that the professional value of the military health corps was only of value if exercised with good sense and in the knowledge of military necessities. He concluded :

> *Je ne peux pas empêcher l'ennemi de se mettre dans la région à moustiques, et comme je dois soit lui résister, soit l'attaquer, je suis forcé d'avoir des éléments dans la zone à anophèles.* (I can't prevent the enemy from basing himself in a malarial area, and because it's my job to resist him, then to attack him, I am obliged to position troops in zones of the anopheles mosquitoes.)[26]

But the enemy – except in the Struma and Butkovo valleys where both Milne and the Bulgarians took Ruotte's advice and retreated to the '*hauteurs*' in the summer – was dug in on the hills and mountains of southern Serbia and Bulgaria, far from the malarial plains of Salonica and northern Greece.

Sarrail saw the intransigence of King Constantine as a problem capable of a military solution, and so it was, eventually. The insistence of French deputies on leave allowances, however, internal turmoil among the Serbs, the withdrawal of British divisions, disaffection among the Russians as news of the revolution spread, the territorial ambitions of the Italians and, above all, malaria, these were not. But greater foresight and mental flexibility on Sarrail's part, and a more collegiate style of leadership may have helped him to reduce their effects.

An event for which Sarrail bore not even the remotest responsibility was the Great Fire of Salonica which raged from 18 to 21 August 1917. This began in the crowded centre of the old Ottoman town and spread, fanned by the 'Vardar' winds, with remarkable speed right down to the waterfront. Desperate attempts made to evacuate refugees by sea and road were highly successful in that the death toll from the fire was minimal. For the local populations the presence of the Allied armies was a blessing – over a period of hours tens of thousands of people who had been obliged to flee their homes were driven out of town in military lorries or picked up by naval lighters from the quays.[27] Given the scale of the conflagration local fire-fighting equipment was almost valueless, but a couple of British fire engines just landed, and water sprayed by hose from naval craft in the harbor facilitated the rescue process. Allied army units also began dynamiting areas to create space

---

24 Sarrail/Porte, *Mon Commandement*, p.233.
25 Sarrail/Porte, *Mon Commandement*, p.321.
26 Sarrail/Porte, *Mon Commandement*, p.322.
27 Rutter, *Tiadatha*, Chapter 13. Rutter devotes a whole chapter of his narrative poem to the fire and the support given by the Allied forces in getting the people out: the clarity of the reporting suggests that he really was there that night in the guise of his hero.

in front of the fire, to little effect as it turned out, the flames shot across the Via Egnatia almost without pausing.

The dwellings in the old town were not only packed tightly together, they were also almost entirely built of wood. Fires in Salonica were as commonplace as the plague, but there had never been one on this scale. In the Jewish quarter, the epicentre of the disaster, 37 synagogues were burnt down. Many mosques were also burnt, although a number of minarets survived. The fifth century church of St Demetrios, the City's patron Saint, was swept up in the flames.[28] When the fire was finally brought under control between a third and a half of the town had been destroyed, and eighty thousand inhabitants had been made homeless.

By an extraordinary coincidence, Monastir was subjected to an overwhelming bombardment by enemy incendiary bombs at exactly the same time as the Salonica fire, and a third of the town was burnt. Monastir remained within enemy artillery range right up until the final allied breakthrough in September 1918.[29]

For the officers of the Allied Army the disaster of the Salonica fire was compounded by the destruction of all but one of the town's cafés hotels and restaurants including the iconic Flocca's. The French Military HQ was evacuated but not destroyed. Milne's HQ was not in the city, but several of the BSF's facilities were burnt down including the Base Medical store depot where vast supplies of quinine were lost.[30] All Allied forces based in Salonica set about providing tented and then more solid accommodation for the refugees and feeding them; the BSF had three camps operating even before the fire was brought under control on 20 August.[31]

Within five days a committee was formed to determine the future of the city after the fire. A decision was taken for the Government to expropriate the land and build a new, modern, safer Salonica. Venizelos was the prime mover, but the French and British provided the technical and architectural support. Initially the lead architect was Thomas Mawson, who had already been working on urban development in Athens; the project was then taken over by the French archaeologist and architect Ernst Hébrard. In due course a new city rose out of the ashes, perhaps not too fancifully hailed as 'the first great work of European urban planning in the twentieth century.' Venizelos was later to call the fire as 'almost a gift of divine providence' in making all this possible, a view which the crowded populations of Salonica would have found hard to share in August 1917.[32]

---

28 Mazower, *City of Ghosts*, pp.318–321.
29 Schiavon, *Front d'Orient*, p.277.
30 Palmer, *Gardeners*, p.152.
31 Falls, *Macedonia Vol. 2*, p.21.
32 Mazower, *City of Ghosts*, p.324.

26

1917
Allied Actions and Initiatives Summer and Autumn 1917

(Maps 7 & 8)

The withdrawal of British 60th Division from the Doiran front was completed on 6 June. By the end of the month, together with the 7th and 8th Mounted Brigades, it had left for Palestine. In view of Sarrail's refusal to move any other of his forces across the river to plug the gap, the sectors of the front covered by XII Corps' remaining two Divisions, 22nd and 26th, had to be lengthened.

The tactical withdrawal of XVI Corps' three divisions, 10th, 27th and 28th, to their summer quarters in the hills was a more complex exercise, particularly on the Struma Front. All the bridge-heads over the river were to be strongly garrisoned, but apart from this no permanent establishment was to be maintained on the east side of the Struma. Milne's intention was that an intermediate line of villages seized and held during the winter campaign, from Yeni Mahale through Yenikoi and Nevolyen to Ormanli and Haznadar would be regularly patrolled to prevent the Bulgarians from establishing a fixed presence and thereby threatening the line of the river. All equipment which could possibly be of use to the enemy, even to the duck-boards in the trenches, was removed and brought back across the river.

This task took three weeks and was concluded on 12 June. Only some telegraph wires were left for use by the patrols. These were to be conducted daily by the two remaining cavalry regiments and the XVI Corps' cyclists.[1]

Although contact was frequently made with enemy patrols, it soon became clear that the Bulgarians had no intention of occupying the malarial Struma plain in the summer either.

Similar withdrawals were made from the Butkovo valley to the Krusha Balkan ridge. Signaller Bailey of 228th Brigade noted on 7 June 'Orders to move back to the summer line, off in the morning at daybreak.' And on 8 June 'Up all night waiting to move, getting wires in etc, raining in torrents. Mules very obstinate, delayed about an hour, off at last at 0500. What a climb, and what lovely scenery! Reached HQRS at Usemli at about 0830.'[2]

As the summer progressed Milne stepped up patrols but arranged to keep a rotation of six brigades in reserve. In order to keep the men alert and committed when in reserve, divisional commanders were ordered to run programmes of specialist and inter-functional training. In the case of 228th Brigade, who were withdrawn in their turn to Mirova, intensive training in signalling, firing, route marching, hill warfare and cross-discipline lectures went on for over a month before the brigade was called back to the Krusha Balkan hills at the end of August.[3]

---

1   Falls, *Macedonia Vol. 2*, p.5.
2   E Bailey, 7-8 June 1917.
3   E Bailey July 1917

On 26 July the British government had announced its intention to withdraw another division, the 10th, for transfer to Palestine, together with four further artillery batteries. By September they had all gone and Milne, having once again been refused support by Sarrail, was yet again obliged to re-organise his forces. 228th Brigade was brought back into the front line, firstly, as early as August 24 and despite the mosquitoes, on the Butkovo Front. Signaller Bailey's diary entry on this date suggest that resources were being spread very thinly and corners being cut in order to hold the line:

> On the march again in the evening, mostly downhill, destination Kairak Mah, on the plain again facing Johnny Bulgar ... Took over the signal station ... on duty till midnight, at advanced outpost, awfully tired, nothing happening although almost eaten by mosquitoes. Awful place for them, Butkovo Lake not far away. Only supposed to stay at post a week, then move back on top of hill. Food very bad and scarce ... shocking transport, breakfast sometimes at 1100 hours ... Three cases of malaria here, sent down to aid post. Other troops moved back but signallers have to stay. Too bad. Our post looks down on Lozhista, considered third unhealthiest place in the world[4] ... Johnny Bulgar quiet.'

With the overall reduced headcount Milne could only allow five battalions to be held in reserve.[5]

* * *

For many of the reasons described in Chapter 24, the summer and autumn of 1917 saw only limited action by the Allied Army. There had however been considerable movement to the north; in August the reconstituted Romanian army in concert with the Russians had made gains in Bukovina and had resisted Austro-German counter attacks. The Russians soon faded, but the Romanians continued to resist until forced to accept an armistice on 9 December. In support of these developments, and with the continuing objective of holding down as many enemy divisions as possible on the Macedonian Front, Sarrail had been instructed for the closing months of 1917 to *immobiliser l'ennemi par les attaques locales en y consacrant le minimum d'infanterie et le maximum d'artillerie* (to immobilize the enemy through local actions, using as little infantry and as much artillery as possible).[6]

On August 21 the Italian 35th Division made another surprise attack on Hill 1050, but were once more driven back by lethal trench mortar fire.[7] The Serbs, who were picking themselves up after the dark events of earlier in the year, were also contributing to the task of unsettling the Bulgarians by further attacks on their outposts on the Dobropolje. *Je retrouvais dans les contingents Serbes l'appui que j'avais toujours escompté* noted Sarrail approvingly (I found once again in the Serbian contingent the support I had always expected).[8]

On 25 August Milne had sent a long ranging letter to Robertson about the destination of the six to eight Greek divisions now starting to come into line. He is very strongly of the view that they should be sent to the Struma Front, and, with the British forces, re-take Eastern Macedonia. Striking at the Bulgarians in Eastern Macedonia and up the Rupel valley was a plan Milne had put forward previously, and in various forms was to prefer in the future. He may well have been right.[9]

---

4 E Bailey 24 August 1917. An interesting statistic, begging the question which two places were considered unhealthier. We shall never know.
5 Falls, *Macedonia Vol. 2*, p.14.
6 Larcher, *Grande Guerre*, p.209 quoting Telegram of War Ministry to Sarrail of 20 August.
7 Villari, *Macedonian Campaign*, p.182.
8 Sarrail/Porte, *Mon Commandement*, p.324.
9 Nicol, *Uncle George*, p.146.

In the same letter Milne reports on his meeting with the new Greek King. He was mightily unimpressed 'Seems to have no love for his people but respect for his father Constantine. A nominal King and rather a querulous boy.'

On the British side of the Vardar the RFC and the Naval Air Service were particularly active against targets in Eastern Macedonia. Encountering little enemy air opposition almost daily sorties were made against the enemy airfields at Drama, Angista and Porna, Bulgarian depots and dumps, and the HQs of both the First and Second Bulgarian army. RFC's No.17 Squadron also helped the French at Florina, with bombing missions against Topolcani and Prilep. On the Struma Front however the enemy struck back from the ground on 9 August with a pin-point howitzer attack on the forward aerodrome at Orliak destroying three aircraft.[10]

Apart from this the relative success of the combined air forces in the latter part of 1917 brought Milne even more to the conclusion that this arm was being under-exploited. Never afraid of asking, and still undaunted by a series of negative replies, he wrote on 17 September to the War Office 'I would strongly urge that the RFC in this country be reinforced with a strong bomber squadron, containing a suitable proportion of up-to-date flying machines.' To which inevitably Robertson replied that such machines were all required on the Western Front. In the first part of 1918 the RFC did however get four up-to-date fighters for each squadron.[11]

Milne gave orders for a return to the 'winter line' in October. Concurrent with this move he set in motion the construction of a light railway from Sarakli, just north of Salonica, running along the south shores of Lakes Langaza and Beshik to Stavros. At over 60 kilometres this was no mean undertaking and required the cooperation of the War Office in trans-shipping 4,000 Turkish prisoners being held on Cyprus to provide most of the labour. It was finished in May 1918, providing another transport link with XVI Corps, and above all cutting off the time and risk inherent in the old sea-route around the Kalkidiki peninsula.[12]

On the XVI Corps sector Milne's strength had been reduced following the departure of 10th Division and four artillery batteries, as well as the two Mounted Brigades. He therefore decided to occupy a line on the left bank of the Struma only half as far as the one gained during the previous winter. This was more or less equivalent to the area patrolled by the cavalry during the summer, but shorter at both ends running from the Gedeli Bridge through Yeni Mahale, Osman Kamila, Yenikoi, Nevolyen, Cukuluk, Elshan, Bairakli Juma, and Haznadar.[13] To ensure the defensive integrity of this line it was necessary to attack and take the town of Homondos, already subject of an exploratory raid in the summer. Homondos, strategically positioned about half way between the Struma and Seres, was held in strength by the enemy.

In order to achieve surprise the plan of attack was necessarily complex, involving the taking and securing of four intermediate villages followed by the convergence on Homondos of two separate columns, each with artillery, setting out three kilometres apart, both of which had river crossings to make. Two brigades of 27th Division were used. The attack was made during the night of 14 October and was a resounding success; 'a perfect example of a night operation; perhaps the cleverest of the many skillful ones carried out by XVI Corps in the Struma valley'.[14] Over 150 prisoners were taken together with guns and ammunition. Enemy casualties were 79 killed against British 11 killed.

The mood in XVI Corps was justifiably up-beat. General Briggs wrote to Repington on 13 October:

---

10 Jones, *War in the Air*, p.358.
11 Jones, *War in the Air*, p.360.
12 Grey and Argyle, *Chronicle Vol. 2*, p.106, Falls, *Macedonia Vol. 2*, p.34.
13 Milne, *Despatch of 1917*, p.2.
14 Falls, *Macedonia Vol. 2*, p.27.

Had we the troops and the guns you would very soon see the Bulgar fly. He is a clean and honest fighter but has no heart in the war. If he had one real knock I'm sure the troops would not put up another fight. Twice here I have felt that with another fresh division and a regular cavalry brigade I could have kept him on the move.[15]

To the north of 27th Division, elements of 28th Division including 228th Brigade occupied villages in the centre of the Struma valley.[16]

On 25 October two brigades of 27th Division attacked and secured villages to the south east of Homondos, culminating at Salmah. All objectives were achieved, but slightly fewer prisoners were taken.

The battle for air space continued: following the return in October of XVI Corps to the Struma valley much use was made of reconnaissance by balloon. These balloons were fair game for enemy aircraft who could reach the British lines, particularly the German 'ace', Rudolf von Eschwege. The story of how he met his end forms part of BSF folklore; on 11 November he attacked but failed to destroy a balloon manned by an observer who successfully parachuted to safety.[17] He returned the next day and shot down the balloon, wounding the observer who, unable to activate his parachute, fell to the ground and was killed. On 21 November von Eshwege returned to attack another balloon. In the meantime however the Army Ordnance services had developed a retaliatory measure. Captain George Finch, in peacetime a professor of electro-chemistry had arranged for the balloon, manned by a dummy observer, to be packed with explosives. When the German pilot got within range he detonated the explosive charges from the ground blowing von Eschwege and his aircraft out of the sky.[18]

Several British pilots thought that this was not fair play and dropped a note of condolence over enemy lines.[19] This form of fellow-feeling between the pilots of the two sides was evidenced on several occasions by the dropping of notes to inform the other side of the fate of pilots brought down in enemy territory. Following a dog-fight in which Lieutenant Montague's B.E.12 was brought down by a German opponent, for example, a note was dropped on the British side to the effect that 'on 29 October (1917) one of your comrades met with a hero's death in an air fight. He was buried with full military honours, and a memorial stone has been put on his grave' and asking for the airman's name so that this could be put on the stone.[20]

* * *

However, the major Allied action of late 1917, and as it happened the last under Sarrail's leadership, was at the opposite extremity of the Allied front, on the Serbo–Albanian border. As has been

---

15 Repington, *First World War Vol.2*, p.124.
16 Whatever Milne's original intentions in creating a sort of reserve brigade from four garrison battalions, 228th Brigade were now very much on the front line. Signaller Bailey reports on 14 October 'Left Dragos for Cuculuk, our destination on the front line at 1830. Enemy had shelled it previous day. Silent march, absolute silence, had to cross Struma….three hours march, carried packs, had to run telegraph wire at once, difficult, very dark, but got in communication with all posts all right.'
17 E Bailey, Nov 11 - 12
18 Forbes, *History of Army Ordnance*, p.245. Forbes notes that Finch's chemical knowledge also came to the fore in finding a solution to the problem of exhudation in amatol bombshells which was exercising the Ordnance services at the time. Finch later came to prominence in the 1922 Everest Expedition when he pioneered the use of supplementary oxygen for climbing at high altitudes. On this expedition he and Charles Bruce reached an altitude of 8,326 metres, the highest yet achieved.
19 Wakefield, *Under the Devil's Eye*, p.195.
20 Jones, *War in the Air*, p.358.

seen, a road had been completed by the French and Italians from Florina to Santi Quaranta on the Adriatic coast. Along this road Sarrail's writ ran not much further than Koritsa, the rest being jealously guarded by the Italian XVI Corps based in Valona. In Koritsa itself Sarrail had established a sort of small self-governing republic under the loose control of the Allied Army's most westerly military outpost.

Above and below the road the French 76th Division had established in February a cordon sanitaire – rather like the medieval bowshot distance – to prevent enemy infiltration or the depredations of bandits. To the north of Koritsa this extended to the Devoli river. Twenty five kilometres north of the river, on the extreme southern end of Lake Ohrid, was the town of Pogradec, where an Austrian division was based.

Back in the early months of 1916 following the defeat of Serbia and Montenegro the Austrians had moved down into northern Albania. Their main interest was the coast, where they established a firm presence at Durazzo, and as far south as the river Voyussa where they came up against the Italian XVI Corps. Inland Albania was held much more lightly. The only road to cut across the country from Durazzo to Lake Ohrid (the old Via Egnatia) was well guarded, and small garrisons placed in the territory to the west of the lake down to Pogradec. Theoretically these Austrian forces covered the right flank of the Germano–Bulgarian Army on the Macedonian Front and on paper assured control by the Central Powers from Eastern Macedonia to the Adriatic. In practice military contact and collaboration between the two parties was more or less on a par with that obtaining between General Sarrail's force and the Italian XVI Corps.

Denied by the strength of enemy defences along the main front, as well as by the negative attitudes of some of the national components of his Allied Army, Sarrail spotted Pogradec and the disconnected Austrians as an opportunity to regain some of the initiative, create some good news for home consumption, and even, if his forces could work their way up the west side of Lake Ohrid, trouble the Bulgarians with an out-flanking movement. It was, unquestionably, a good idea.

Sarrail's proposal of the plan was presented to the War Ministry on 20 August 1917. In his memoirs however he presents the case for his plan in few words and with unusual restraint:

> … *une véritable action vers le ouest, sur la région de Pogradec au moyen d'une division formée par la fusion des 156ème et 57ème appauvries par les permissions. Il n'était possible de manoeuvrer que sur les ailes et pour plus tard, il pouvait être espéré que nous atteindrions ainsi une région où l'ennemi n'avait pas encore établi des solides fortifications* (a substantial action towards the west, in the region of Pogradec, with a joint division formed from the 156th and the 157th, both weakened as a result of leave programmes. Being only possible to work on the flanks, one could hope perhaps to reach an area where the enemy hadn't yet built up any strong fortifications).[21]

Between Koritsa and Lake Ohrid at that time (since drained and cultivated) was the shallow Lake Malik. General Jacquemot's combined division proceeded in two columns on either side of the lake and on 10 September entered and took Pogradec. Over 400 prisoners were taken, together with considerable quantities of materials and munitions at the cost of 175 French casualties, of which 44 killed.[22] The Austrians were completely taken by surprise. Rémy Porte noted, probably justly, that the ease with which Pogradec had been taken *témoigne surtout de la très faible capacité des unités austro-hongroises engagés au coeur de l'Albanie.* (was above all testimony to the poor quality of Austro-Hungarian forces employed in Albania).[23] This was a situation that could have been exploited.

---

21   Sarrail/Porte, *Mon Commandement*, p.327.
22   Palmer, *Gardeners*, p.156.
23   Sarrail/Porte, *Mon Commandement*, p.327.

Sadly, Sarrail once again fell afoul of the political fears and aspirations of three of his allies. Pogradec was (and still is) on the border between Albania and North Macedonia since the Balkan Wars part of Serbia. Immediately after the taking of Pogradec the Serbian Prime Minister Pašić petitioned Sarrail to station a Serbian regiment there. This, at least, Sarrail was able to refuse.

Italy had made no secret of her intention to take over the whole of Albania after the war. As noted above in Chapter 18, General Ferrero from his HQ in Valona had openly proclaimed on 3 June 1917 the 'unity and independence of Albania under Italian protection,' although at the time about three quarters of the country was nominally under Austrian control. The Greek border was close enough for Venizelos, as ever, to feel the need to monitor Italian pretensions in Epirus.

Sarrail could have foreseen all this, and perhaps he did. His mistake was to attach a unit of Albanian irregulars under Essad Bey to Jacquemont's force. Essad Bey had been around a long time as an unattached war lord and opinion leader. He may have been behind the ejection of the German Prince William of Wied who the Great Powers had tried to foist on Albania before the war. He arrived in Salonica in 1916 and (on the instructions of the French Government of the time) had been set up with his five hundred warriors almost as a government in exile. When he styled himself as 'President of the Albanian Republic' and was gifted a number of Albanian soldiers trained by the Italians, Italian hackles were bound to rise.

The Pogradec campaign was the first time Essad Bey's force had been used, and it turned out to be very effective. Following the capture of Pogradec it was sent on an expedition to the upper Skumbi and came back with over 150 prisoners.[24]

On 19 October, Sarrail ordered Jacquemont to proceed up the west side of the lake, eventually to attack Struga and turn the enemy's flank. He had reached Udinista, about half way up the lake, when Sarrail received instructions from Paris to call a halt to the whole operation. As Sarrail said *'l'Italie avait parlé'*.[25] The Allied front line on Lake Ohrid remained at Udinista for the rest of the war. Nevertheless, Pogradec was something to shout about, and Sarrail did, as he had about Monastir the previous year. Curiously, the French victory parade in 1919 at the end of the war included Pogradec as one of the key campaigns of the war, while Monastir was not mentioned.[26]

---

24 Palmer, *Gardeners*, p.159.
25 Sarrail/Porte, *Mon Commandement*, p.338.
26 Palmer, *Gardeners*, p.156, Falls, *Macedonia Vol 2*, p.283. Incredibly, the only other Macedonian victory mentioned was Skra di Legen. No mention at all of Dobropolje.

27

1917
Recall of Sarrail

The year 1917 had seen the arrival on the Macedonian Front of three new French divisions, 11th Colonial in January, and then 76th and 30th in March.[1] Despite this, due to losses, leave and sickness, as well as the departure of the two British divisions, the headcount of the Allied Army would have been much reduced during the year had it not been for the arrival of the three 'Nationalist' Greek divisions. Following the abdication of Constantine and the re-unification of Greece Venizelos delayed calling the 'Royalist' Army to the colours until he had purged it of remaining pro-Constantine and pro-German elements. He finally called for mobilization in October.[2] In the meantime however two classes of conscripts had been called up at the beginning of August. A French Military commission under General Braquet had been set up to train them.[3]

On other fronts the disaster of the Nivelle offensive had been succeeded on the Western Front with the horrors of Third Ypres/Passchendaele, where casualties alone were equivalent to half the total strength of the Allied Army of the East. Italy had suffered the defeat and ignominy of the Battle of Caporetto and retreat to the Piave. The Russo–Romanian campaign in Bukovina had come to a halt, and with the armistice of Brest-Litovsk the Russians were effectively withdrawing from the war. As a result of this the Central Powers had upwards of fifty divisions to send somewhere else.

Understandably they chose to strengthen their forces on the Western Front rather than descend on Salonica, where they could rely on their Bulgarian allies to uphold the stalemate, which was tying up over 20 Allied divisions to, as they probably thought, little purpose. Indeed, the lull in action in the Balkans, and the unlikelihood of any in the foreseeable future, encouraged the German High Command gradually to order the withdrawal of the twenty or so battalions of German troops on the Macedonian Front to strengthen their planned retaliatory offensive on the Western Front.

Cyril Falls rarely allows himself to enliven his presentation of facts with an analysis of consequences, and such analyses are all the more compelling for their rarity. On this issue he writes 'It appears to have been an error. A German force of which the infantry numbered about 21 battalions had saved Bulgaria in the Autumn and Winter of 1916. The presence of such a force on the Western Front would not win the war; its absence from Macedonia in September 1918 probably contributed a great deal to losing it.'[4]

As the Pogradec action drew to a close, Sarrail finally relented on sending French troops across the Vardar to thicken Allied defences on the Doiran Front following the removal of 60th Division.

---

1   Larcher, *Grande Guerre*, p.295. It is worth noting (Sarrail, *Mon Commandement,* p.334) that the French battalion was composed of three companies, not four as was the case with British, Italian, Russian and Greek battalions.
2   Falls, *Macedonia Vol. 2*, p.31.
3   Gray and Argyle, *Chronicle Vol. 2* p.72.
4   Falls, *Macedonia Vol. 2* p.46.

By 9 November a brigade of 122nd Division had taken over the sector from the Vardar to the Selimli Deresi river, thereby reducing the long BSF line by about five kilometres. *Je faisais ainsi ce que j'avais refusé de faire il y a quelque temps, mais les circonstances avaient changé.*' (Thereby doing what I had refused to do some time before, but the circumstances had changed.)[5]

In fact the circumstances had been changing ever since the debacle of the May offensive. As far back as 6 June the Lloyd George had written to the French Prime Minister asking for Sarrail's immediate replacement.[6] Ribot promised to look at it but pointed out that the height of the abdication crisis was not the right moment.[7] Nothing further came of it at that time. The British voted with their boots and all the other components of the Allied Army expressed their dissatisfaction with Sarrail's leadership in their different ways.

However, while the Allied Army was suffering its Summer of Discontent in Macedonia, Georges Clemenceau was creating political turmoil in France. In his newspaper *L'Homme Enchaîné* he accused Miguel Almereyda, notorious editor of *Bonnet Rouge,* of collaboration with the enemy. Indeed, following the discovery of incriminating evidence in his house Almereyda was arrested, and shortly afterwards committed suicide in the Santé prison. Next, Louis Malvy, Minister of the Interior (one of the ministers Sarrail had approached when relieved of his command of the Third Army in 1915) was found to have been subsidizing and supporting Almereyda. He was removed from office and subsequently imprisoned. As a result of this the Ribot government fell on 12 September, and Painlevé took over as Prime Minister.[8]

Clemenceau then turned his attack on Joseph Caillaux, a prominent member of the Radical Socialist party, (also one of Sarrail's key parliamentary contacts), who also had provided money to Almereyda. The political debate became so heated that on 13 November Painlevé called for a vote of confidence in his government and lost it. President Poincaré then had to bow to the inevitable and call on Clemenceau to form a government. Clemenceau, who also took the title of War Minister, remained in power until 1920.[9]

As the implacable Clemenceau carried on with his investigations it turned out that three of the incriminating documents which had been found in Almereyda's possession – and which Almereyda had probably passed on to the Germans – had come to him via the French Staffs of the Allied Army of the East. One was a report penned by Sarrail and addressed to the Minister of War following the Cordonnier affair in 1916 in which (aiming for reinforcements) he had painted the strength and the resources of the Allied Army in the blackest terms. A Captain Mathieu claimed responsibility for the leaks, all of which would have contained valuable information for the enemy, but even if he had been totally unaware of them, which is almost certain, some suspicion was bound to attach to Sarrail.[10]

As Clemenceau continued to stir the can of worms it was revealed that Caillaux had written dozens of letters to German agents, and, most bizarre of all, had been the author of a memorandum planning a form of coup d'état proposing the recall of Sarrail as commander of the French army under his own leadership.[11] The possibility of Sarrail knowing anything at all about this, assuming that it was not a fabrication in the first place, are so close to zero as to be discounted. But with friends like this, as well as the sourcing of sensitive documents from his own staffs, Sarrail was now so far on the wrong side as to be politically as well as militarily dispensable.

---

5 Sarrail/Porte, *Mon Commandement*, p.336.
6 Lloyd George, *War Memories*, p.189.
7 Ribot, *Lettres à un Ami*, p.322.
8 Ribot's account of these events is given in Letter XXXVII of his *Lettres à un Ami*, p.341.
9 Palmer, *Gardeners*, p.160.
10 Villari, *Macedonian Campaign*, p.189.
11 Palmer, Gardeners, p.162.

Clemenceau had long been a critic of the Macedonian Campaign (the 'Gardeners of Salonica' jibe was his). On 1 December he attended the second session of the new Supreme War Council in Versailles. The British, Italians, Serbs and Greeks all pressed again for Sarrail's recall. The military case was clear enough. The status of international relations required it. And now that Sarrail had been politically marginalized Clemenceau could act.

As for Sarrail, the advantages which his political affiliations had brought had now turned full circle. It was Caillaux who had brought him to prominence, it was now his associations with Caillaux, soon to be given a three year prison sentence, which were a major factor in enabling Clemenceau to engineer his downfall.

On 9 December Sarrail received a telegram from Clemenceau whose words were as few as their meaning was clear:

> *J'ai l'honneur de vous faire connaître que le Gouvernement, se basant sur les considérations de l'ordre général a décidé votre rappel en France et votre remplacement à la tête des armées alliées en orient par le Général Guillaumat* (I have the honour of informing you that, acting in the general interest, the Government has decided on your recall to France and your replacement as head of the Allied Army of the East by General Guillaumat).[12]

Even at this point military and political circles were discussing what posting Sarrail would be given on his return. There was talk of him becoming Military Governor of Paris,[13] but Clemenceau had no such intention and he was simply put on the Reserve List, not returning to any sort of military command until 1924.

Two days earlier Clemenceau had prepared the French Parliament for the announcement, telling them that:

> *Tous nos alliés ont demandé le remplacement de Sarrail. Si nous le maintenons, notre responsabilité serait immense, car une offensive Germano–Bulgare est toujours possible sur Salonique, et ce n'est pas avec des armées désunies, dont les chefs ne veulent pas se reconnaître, qu'on pourrait tenir* (All the Allies have called for Sarrail's recall. If we retain him our responsibility will be immense in that a Germano–Bulgarian offensive in Macedonia is still a possibility, and that such an offensive could not be held off by a disunited allied army whose national commanders cannot work together).[14]

Two days later, on the same day as Clemenceau revealed to Parliament his findings on Caillaux, an official public announcement was made to the effect that 'General Sarrail has had to contend with serious difficulties and has rendered great service,'[15] faint praise, one feels, through gritted teeth.

Ribot's comment back in June when Lloyd George was pressing for Sarrail's replacement was perhaps more to the point; *La tâche du Commandement en Chef était singulièrement difficile du fait qu'il avait sous ces ordres troupes de six nationalités différentes* (The Commander in Chief's job was particularly difficult in that he had troops from six different nationalities under his orders.)[16] This had not been foreseen on his original appointment as Commander of the *Armée de l'Orient*; the

---

12 Schiavon, *Front d'Orient*, p.287 quoting letter from Clemenceau to Sarrail 9 December 1917 (Service Historique de la Défense).
13 Repington, *First World War Vol. 2*, p.151.
14 Sarrail/Porte, *Mon Commandement*, foot note to p.249. Porte is quoting from Mermeix, *Le Commandement Unique Vol. 2*.
15 Palmer, *Gardeners*, p.163.
16 Ribot, *Lettres à un Ami*, p.322.

management of an international force was not on his original job-description, it had just developed this way. He had not been selected for any particular skills in this field, and had never really risen to the task, which was, unquestionably, a difficult one.

Sarrail concludes his own report on his time as Commander in Chief of the Allied Army of the East with a five page summary of his final troop dispositions and their readiness to face attack. This is followed by a brief and bitter 'Conclusion' given over mainly to complaints about the lack of resources he was given to do the job, and the absence of cooperation from the Allied forces under his command.[17] He does himself less than justice. He could have called up several examples of positive achievements during his almost two years as Commander in Chief.

Sarrail's advance deep into Serbian Macedonia and subsequent staged withdrawal with the only three divisions at his disposal in autumn 1915 was a masterpiece of mobile warfare and adaptive planning. Had he been able to set out on this mission while the Serbian Army was still in play, and with the active support of the British Army, the war in the Balkans might have taken on a different shape from the outset. It could be argued that whatever his political obsessions and administrative weaknesses, both of his greatest successes as a military leader, here and at the First Battle of the Marne, were at the level of Corps Commander.

The fast establishment of the Entrenched Camp around Salonica – which the enemy never challenged, and probably never considered challenging, even after the success of their two-pronged offensive of August 1917 – was executed under his leadership. And having secured Salonica his was the decision to proceed immediately to secure advanced positions on the borders of Greek Macedonia before the enemy could infiltrate the Krusha Balkan range.

It was Sarrail who recognized the absolute necessity of removing the enemy consulates from Salonica, of destroying bridges on the Constantinople railway to deny the enemy any access, and, critically, of capturing the Kara Burun forts at the mouth of the Bay of Salonica; then subsequently taking control of the railways and telecommunications in order to enable his forces to operate on a proper military footing within the Salonica area – whatever the Greek Government might think, and despite the timid reservations of Allied governments.

Neither the reconstitution of the Serbian Army in Corfu nor its trans-shipment to Salonica were directly handled by Sarrail, but he must take credit for its incorporation into the Allied Army, and for providing training and much equipment. From late 1916 onwards the first three Greek 'nationalist' divisions were also brought to a state of battle readiness on his watch.

That Sarrail was wrong-footed by the enemy's pre-emptive strike in August 1916 must be put on the negative side of the balance, particularly with regard to the apparent failure of his intelligence services. However, but for the delay in the Romanian declaration of war – totally out of his hands and totally mismanaged by the Allied governments – he would have moved earlier in accordance with his planned timetable, and the Bulgarians would not have been given this opportunity. On the positive side, his response to this setback was fast and effective; and that he was able to block it, counter it, and return to the offensive by September was a significant achievement.

During this offensive, and under his overall command, the Serbs took Kaymakcalan, effectively providing a base and springboard for the final breakthrough two years later.

The capture of Monastir in face of long-prepared enemy defences and the critical support of German crack regiments and artillery must count as the military highlight of Sarrail's command, albeit at the cost of a considerable weakening of his forces.

It could be said that Sarrail's principal contribution to the final success of the Macedonian Campaign was the removal of King Constantine. It might also be said that this, like the taking of Monastir, could have been achieved earlier or in a different way.

---

17   Sarrail/Porte, *Mon Commandement*, pp.339–350.

Casson wrote that nowhere in the armed world in those years was there anywhere to be found 'a more disastrous collocation of extreme opposites than Sarrail and Constantine.'[18] Constantine's distaste for Sarrail was clear but rarely broke the surface, and anyway was connected with the maltreatment he felt he was receiving from the Allies in general. Sarrail's antipathy for Constantine on the other hand was personal, and towards the end verging on the obsessive. He only saw a resolution of the deadlock in military terms, and this mindset may well have delayed or impeded the construction of a more pragmatic or diplomatic solution. Nevertheless, of all the legacies of his Command in Macedonia, this was by far the most valuable to hand on to his successor.

Sarrail was succeeded by General Marc-Louis Adolphe Guillaumat, formerly Commander of the French Second Army on the Western Front. They probably spent only a few hours together before Sarrail left for France on 22 December. Guillaumat wrote of their meeting:

> *Il m'a reçu comme un frère; Il n'avait jamais été si cordial et si confiant avec moi ... Je m'attendais néanmoins à quelques coups de boutoir. Il n'y en a eu un seul, et nous avons causé amicalement de beaucoup de choses* (He received me like a brother ... He had never been so cordial or so open with me. I had expected at least some cutting remarks. There wasn't one. We discussed a whole load of things in a friendly manner.)[19]

Whatever the ups and downs, political, military and personal of his long months of command, General Sarrail ended them on a high note.

* * *

At the end of the year the '*War Cabinet Report for the Year 1917, Presented to Parliament by order of HM. Price one shilling*' devoted half of one of its 248 pages to the Salonica Front. This document was designed for general consumption by those members of the public willing to part with a shilling, and a certain amount of gloss is to be expected:

> On the Salonica Front no important operations have taken place since the capture of Monastir. In accordance with General Sarrail's orders an offensive took place in May-June, and in this the role allotted to the British Army was an attack west of Lake Doiran designed to precede the main offensive by the French, Serbs and Italians east of Monastir and to draw the enemy to our Front. The British attack achieved its objectives in capturing a large number of Bulgarian prisoners and inflicting severe losses to the enemy. But the main attack did not achieve any results of importance. During the past year the British army has captured 1095 prisoners. During the summer our troops withdrew from the Struma valley to higher and healthier ground. We have recently re-established our line on the left bank of the river.
>
> Only minor engagements have taken place since, but the Allied Army continues to hold the greater part of the Bulgarian army on the Macedonian Front ...'[20]

Or, as Signaller Bailey prosaically observed, 'Another Christmas in Macedonia. Wet day.'[21]

---

18 Casson, *Steady Drummer*, p.152.
19 Sarrail/Porte, *Mon Commandement*, foot note to p.350. Porte is quoting from *Correspondance de Guerre du Général Guillaumat* (Paris: l'Harmattan, 2006), 23 décembre 1917.
20 *War Cabinet Report for the Year 1917* (London: HMSO, 1918), p.45.
21 E Bailey, 25 December 1917

28

1918
On the Defensive

Schlieffen had not foreseen a Bolshevik revolution. Although the first part of his plan – a lightning conquest of France – had proved illusory, the second part was taking care of itself. At Brest-Litovsk on 15 December 1917 the Russians agreed a cease-fire with the Central Powers. Between this date and the final peace treaty the talks broke down, and the Germans piled 52 divisions across the armistice line and, 'using the Russian roads and railways as if they were on a civilian excursion,' advanced over 200 km, taking prisoners, seizing Russian war materials, and effectively establishing a new front line.[1]

When the final peace treaty between the Bolshevik government and the Central Powers was signed on 3 March 1918, the Russians were forced to cede territory containing a third of their population, a third of their arable land and nine-tenths of their coalfields.[2] This included Poland, White Russia, Finland, the Ukraine, the Caucasus and the Baltic states, all of which of were of great value in reducing the effects of the Allied food blockade. Further, over 600,000 Austrian prisoners of war were released, extra manpower at the disposition of the Central Powers.

The Treaty of Brest-Litovsk coincided with the Peace of Buftea, leading within a couple of days to the Treaty of Bucharest, which finally removed Romania from the war as a belligerent. Ludendorff's memoirs at this point are, unsurprisingly, upbeat:

> The situation on the Eastern Front was eased to an extraordinary degree by the peace of Brest-Litovsk on 3 March and on the preliminary peace of Buftea on 5 March.

But he goes on:

> A real peace with Russia had however not been arrived at. There was still the danger that a new Eastern Front might be formed…..what we had in the East was admittedly a strong force, yet all we had achieved there was an armed peace, and many elements of danger remained.[3]

The new borders had to be stabilised, the populations controlled and policed. The two 'peaces' still called for a strong German presence on the Eastern Front. Even in Romania a force of six divisions was considered necessary. Nonetheless, Ludendorff reports that 'more than forty divisions were transferred' (to the Western Front).[4] With these extra forces the Central Powers would, at last, outnumber those of the Allies on the Western Front. In March 1918 the 178 Allied divisions faced 192 Central Powers divisions. And it would be some time before the Americans, arriving in early

---

1　Gilbert, *First World War*, p.398.
2　Gilbert, *First World War*, p.401.
3　Erich von Ludendorff, *My War Memories* (Berlin: Mittler und Sohn,1919), p.527.
4　Ludendorff, *My War Memories*, p.572.

1918 at the rate of 120,000 a month, would provide a counter-weight.⁵ And Salonica? If ten of these forty German divisions, battle hardened on the Eastern Front, had been assigned in March 1918 to the Macedonian Front where the Central Powers already enjoyed numerical superiority, they could have created havoc. A determined three-prong thrust through Monastir, and down the Vardar and Struma valleys could have enforced the withdrawal of the Allied Army of the East and overrun the Allies' latest recruit while its forces were still at an early stage of preparation.

Conquest of Greece would have led to the availability of its ports to German shipping and the setting up of submarine bases, control of the Eastern Mediterranean, the re-opening of the Dardanelles, the exposure of southern Italy to invasion while its army was fighting for its life on the Piave, the stiffening of Bulgarian resolve, and the removal of the Italian Corps from Albania. These risks are developed further in a post-war lecture, probably written by George Milne 'Communication with Egypt and further with Mesopotamia and India through the Suez Canal would have been entirely disrupted. The Cape route with all its disadvantages would have had to be used and the morale of our Allies would have been correspondingly depressing.'⁶

Ludendorff's memoirs give no indication that this course of action was ever considered. With the probability of half a million American soldiers being in France by mid-year, with British and American factories and shipyards raising the production of war materials and ships to ever higher levels, and with the Allied blockade causing increasing physical and moral distress, particularly to the Austrians, Hindenburg and Ludendorff decided to go for a conclusive attack on the Western Front.

As the Allies prepared themselves for the storm, General Marc-Louis Adolphe Guillaumat arrived in Salonica on 22 December 1917 to take over the command of the Allied Army of the East. As it happened, while the tenure of Sarrail had been nearly two years, Guillaumat was to remain at the post for less than six months before being withdrawn by Clemenceau for what he considered a more important assignment.

Born in 1863, Guillaumat was seven years younger than Sarrail. He had passed out top of his class at St Cyr in 1884. Then, unlike Sarrail, most of whose pre-war career had been in staff positions, he spent nearly twenty years in line operations before returning to St Cyr in 1903. He served in Tunisia, Algeria (for two years as part of the Foreign Legion), Indochina and China where he was wounded during the Boxer uprising. Much of his operational career had been with colonial units, which was helpful in that three of France's eight divisions in Macedonia were colonial ones. By the time War broke out he had risen to divisional command. In 1915 he became a Corps commander, and in 1916 had replaced Nivelle as head of the Second Army on the Western Front. He was recognised for his intellect and his ambition. A major characteristic was his love of order and organisation, something soon to become evident.⁷

As it happened General Franchet d'Espèrey was Clemenceau's preferred candidate as Sarrail's replacement. Despite his deep interest in the Balkans however, Franchet d'Espèrey, now Commander of the Northern Group of Armies in France, turned the offer down, and was supported in this by both Foch and Pétain.⁸ Franchet d'Espèrey backed up his refusal to take the post by pointing out that his politics were known to be essentially right wing. As Schiavon reports it:

> *Le parlement, qui s'intéresse souvent plus aux opinions des généraux qu'à leur compétence militaire prendrait très mal que Sarrail soit limogé pour être remplacé par un calotin royaliste* (Parliament, which was often more interested in the political opinions of generals than in their military

---

5   Gilbert, *First World War*, p.411.
6   Nicol, *Uncle George*, p.149.
7   Schiavon, *Front d'Orient*, p.289.
8   Palmer, *Gardeners*, p.166.

capabilities would take it very badly if Sarrail had been shelved in favour of a priest-loving royalist).

Guillaumat on the other hand although leaning towards the left had no particularly strong political affiliations.[9]

On the face of it Guillaumat's new appointment was a difficult one, the leadership of a force composed of soldiers from five different nations with very different military cultures, responsibility for a vast territory, and much uncertainty as to the part he was expected to play in contributing to overall Allied war objectives. He had, however, the advantage of bringing a fresh mind to the situation, unencumbered with the historical baggage which had hung so heavily around the neck of Sarrail.

Structures and procedures which Sarrail had set up and built upon since the early beginnings in 1915 often no longer had sense or relevance and could be re-addressed. Unquestionably the greatest treasure bequeathed by Sarrail to Guillaumat was a Greece now firmly in the Allied camp. But here also Guillaumat had the advantage of being able to pick up the situation as it was rather than concerning himself with how it got there. Whether for example Sarrail would have had the vision to launch the best prepared of the Greek divisions against the enemy in May 1918 for a showpiece offensive – rather than the French or the Serbs – is debatable.

In the early uncertain days of his tenure Sarrail had often found it expedient to be secretive about his purposes, unsure where his trust could be placed. By 1918 greater clarity had been achieved, and anyway Guillaumat's instincts were more consultative, and he soon established professional relationships with Milne and the heads of the other national contingents.

The change of command in Macedonia coincided with changes in the Allied procedures of consultation and joint decision making. Lloyd George in a letter to the French government of 30 November 1917 had suggested that the Allies lacked a central management structure for determining military priorities, and that trying to run the war in a series of separate compartments had been inefficient and had not made the best use of the resources available.[10]

As a result of this letter, or, at least, shortly afterwards, a Supreme War Council (*Conseil Supérieur de Guerre*) was decided upon during an Allied conference at Rapallo on 6 November 1917. It was to consist of Allied Heads of Government and Chiefs of Staff, with a permanent military staff. The SWC therefore replaced the ad hoc conferences with floating lists of attendees which had been the practice until then. Larcher compared it admiringly with the British War Cabinet. The SWC provided a structure for identifying issues but not necessarily for decision taking. One clear decision which at least put the Allies on a par with the Central Powers' command structure was to appoint Foch as Commander in Chief of all Allied forces on the Western Front from 26 March 1918. By this time he no longer had direct responsibility for the Macedonian Front, something the SWC reserved for itself.[11]

At the time of Guillaumat's appointment however, Foch still had such a responsibility, and he sent the new Commander of the Allied Army of the East out to Salonica with a short but very clear statement of objectives. These were dated 16 December 1917, were counter-signed by Clemenceau, and came with a back-up set of notes covering some of the issues and challenges which would have to be addressed and faced.[12]

Guillaumat was given four main objectives:

---

9   Schiavon, *Front d'Orient*, p.288.
10 Larcher, *Grande Guerre*, pp.214–215 quoting Mermeix, *Le Commandement Unique*.
11 Larcher, *Grande Guerre*, pp.214, 223.
12 Larcher, *Grande Guerre*, Annexe 15 p.280–281,Instructions from Clemenceau to Guillaumat of 16 December 1918. Translation in Falls, *Macedonia Vol II*, Appendix 5 p.318–21.

- To base his operations on the whole of Greece, not just on Greek Macedonia
- To prevent the enemy from conquering Greece, by maintaining '*en premier lieu l'intégralité du terrain conquis*'; to ensure the solidity of defences along the current Allied line, from the Aegean to the Albanian lakes while maintaining contact with the Italian forces at Valona
- To consider offensive action (only) after the defensive lines had been completed, or were in the final stages of completion
- To determine the role of the Greek army and its location in the battle line, respecting as far as possible its independent status.

Guillaumat was also asked to provide, working with General Ferrero (Italian XVI Corps) and the Greek government, for the protection and security of the island of Corfu.[13]

The emphasis on checking and perfecting defences along the currently held lines was very clearly a reaction to the liberation of vast enemy forces following the Treaties of Brest-Litovsk and Bucharest, and before it was known with any certainty where they were to be directed. The objectives concerning possible offensive action and the integration and employment of the Greek divisions are also interlinked.

An Italian input, probably following the first SWC meeting in Rapallo on 6 November is also clear, with the two references to working with the Italian XVI Corps based on Valona.

Despite the brevity of these instructions, Foch and Clemenceau managed to slip in a contentious corollary:

> *Dans le cas où les forces alliées seraient dans l'obligation de céder du terrain, elles devront continuer à interdire à l'ennemi l'accès de la Grèce…en maintenant aussi longtemps que possible la possession du camp retranché de Salonique* (Should the Allied forces be obliged to give ground, it will be their duty to deny the enemy any access to Greece … maintaining as long as possible possession of the Entrenched Camp at Salonica).[14]

To Milne, and very shortly after he had found his way around, to Guillaumat, the idea of being able to hold Greece after relinquishing Salonica was an absurdity, and both stepped quietly around this issue until the SWC sent a commission to Salonica in May to quiz them about it and Guillaumat put them right on the matter. And just as Foch and Clemenceau misunderstood the indispensable nature of the Salonica port and stronghold, no mention is made of the role played by the mainly British base at Mudros, back-stop to Salonica and as critical in its way to Allied interests as the island of Corfu.

The back-up notes which were attached to Guillaumat's instructions were headed 'Points to which the attention of the General Commander in Chief of the Allied Army of the East are directed.'

Firstly Guillaumat's attention is directed to the need for an audit of all defences, defensive materials, telecoms, communications, roads, railways, the distribution and condition of the troops, artillery numbers and positions. (Curiously no reference is made to air forces or air fields). Since this would be an obvious first step for any incoming commander, the fact that Foch felt it necessary to spell it out suggests a lack of confidence in Sarrail's staff to keep such records.

Guillaumat is then tasked with improving rail and road links between Greek Macedonia and Old Greece. The instruction on how and when to use the Greek troops is expanded with a suggestion that they might be used on the Struma Front 'in contact with the British forces' for the eventual

---

13 Essential for the control of the route across the Adriatic, but also as the seat of the Serbian government.
14 Larcher, *Grande Guerre*, Annexe 15 p.280.

re-conquest of East Macedonia. The Italian influence is again evident in the request that the Italian 35th Division should be moved to the extreme left of the Allied Front in accordance with the demand of the Italian High Command. (Guillaumat managed to side-step this one just as Sarrail had before him). The notes then give Guillaumat *carte blanche* on when the Russian troops should be withdrawn from the front.

The next point calls for the establishment of the *Armée Française de l'Orient* (AFO) as an independent formation by providing it with an Army organization and the necessary services, combined with a review of the command structure and all staff. This is revealing in showing that both Foch and Clemenceau were aware that Sarrail had been commanding the French forces under his control as a personal fief, without any formal apparatus of central staffs. The need for this would have seemed as obvious to Guillaumat as it never was to Sarrail.

But the central theme of these notes is defence; strengthening the current positions, the provision and siting of supporting positions, the need for telephone contact all along the line, and the positioning of reserves to support the front and successive lines.

On 30 December Guillaumat went through his instructions with Milne.[15] There is no record of him having shown them to any other of the Allied commanders, but then Milne was by far the longest serving among the Allied commanders and represented the other nation bank-rolling the whole campaign. Milne may also have been shown the accompanying notes, and if so he would have approved of the use of the Greek army for the eventual re-conquest of East Macedonia. This would have permitted a wry smile at Foch's demands relating to the reorganization of the French forces. Overall Milne had no problem with the Terms of Reference Guillaumat had brought with him, except of course to the concept of holding on to Greece after having lost Salonica.

Guillaumat spent his first two weeks reviewing all the sectors under his command. On 3 January he visited BSF's XII Corps and then on 9 January the XVI Corps. *Equipement, tenue, discipline impeccables. Moral excellent* he reported back to the French war ministry.[16] This was a tribute to Milne and his Corps Commanders given the depredations of malaria, and above all the heavy casualties sustained only six months earlier from what turned out to be a wholly pointless attack on the Doiran defences.

From his side, Milne, when asked by Robertson on 15 January for his views on Guillaumat, was also full of praise:

> General Guillaumat has created a favourable impression ... he appears to be essentially a soldier and to regard the situation from a military point of view ... he appears to be a firm believer in thorough organization and is willing to listen to the views of others, although at the same time he has clear views of his own ... I do at least feel that there is a strong hand at the helm, and that all orders given will be part of a general plan, and not merely the whim of a moment.[17]

In other words, quite different from Sarrail and much closer in outlook to Milne himself.

A major re-evaluation of defences across the whole Allied Army sector was put in motion. After a sullen period of inactivity the whole front was dynamised. Front line defences were strengthened and stabilized. Gun and machine gun positions were fixed. There was a major expenditure of concrete. The concept along the whole of the Allied line was to create lines of secondary defence, not necessarily contiguous, behind the front line.

---

15 Falls, *Macedonia Vol. 2*, p.49.
16 Falls, *Macedonia Vol. 2*, p.52.
17 Nicol, *Uncle George*, p.149.

On the Monastir Front three defensive lines were to be built behind the front line, the first between three and twelve kilometers back, the second between two and fifteen kilometres behind these to 'stop the enemy on the Crna and to set a barrier across the base of the Monastir valley' and the third much further back, 15 to 25 kilometres basing itself on the mountain ridges. Budgets and manpower (including local labour) were allocated to improving access roads, and, in line with the instructions, north-south communications with Old Greece. Each division was to be provided with an access road, and these roads were to be crossed by a system of east-to-west *rocades*.[18] Beyond their immediate – and long term – value, these networks were far better than those built by the Bulgarians on the other side, a factor to prove crucial when the Allies finally broke through and the enemy's ability to move men and armour to pressure points was hampered by inadequate transport links.

A new *service industriel* was set up to exploit local resources, mines, forests and crops.[19] It had been Clemenceau who called the Allied Army of the Orient 'The Gardeners of Salonica'. Guillaumat took him up on the idea, except that the whole of Greece, not just Salonica, was now available for gardening.

On the east side of the Vardar Milne had already set in motion a very extensive set of fallback defensive lines right across the middle of his territory. These ran from Berovo, through Lahana to reach Lake Arjan via Kirkut and Yanesh and incorporated the Beshnik Dagh heights. This ambitious programme, begun in September 1917, was 'practically finished by September 1918' and 'formed a strong and shorter line of defence at a distance varying from five to fifteen miles behind the front line, and covered all lines of advance from the north or north-east.'

Here on the BSF sector attention was also given here to communications. Above all, the key Seres Road, from Salonica to the Struma, virtually the only supply route for XVI Corps, was strengthened to the point where it never disintegrated over the winter of 1917-18, as it so frequently had the previous year. Metalled roads were also built from Salonica to Doiran and to Karasuli on the Vardar. Light railway lines were built to Snevce, as well as to Stavros on the Gulf of Rendina.[20] On the Struma front concrete gun emplacements were set up and the dikes on the right bank of the river were heightened to prevent flooding.[21]

Following the arrival of Guillaumat, and in view also of the importance given to Salonica in his joining instructions, the Entrenched Camp around Salonica was given particular attention. The 'Birdcage' defences had been installed two years ago; a mass of knowledge of successful defensive structures had been gathered since then, including the skills deployed by the enemy. Also, since they had never been used or threatened, they had fallen into neglect. Guillaumat set up a commission under General Génin, and the Birdcage defences were upgraded to state of the art with concrete machine gun emplacements, artillery observation posts, and improved access and lateral roads. Much use was made of local paid labour. In January 1918 the BSF had over 25,000 local labourers on its ration strength. As was the case in 1916, such labour was used in non-sensitive areas, front line defence work being conducted by 'entrenching battalions'.

On 25 February Guillaumat sent a progress report with plans of the final defensive structures he envisaged to the French War Ministry. He also reported that his work was being hampered by *le très petit nombre d'officiers aptes à faire des études de cette nature* (the very small number of officers available capable of performing this sort of work). He had already written to Foch three times on the lack of qualified staff officers. It was a subject dear to his heart and in due course he began to receive some.[22]

---

18   Schiavon, *Front d'Orient*, p.302.
19   Larcher, *Grande Guerre*, p.217.
20   Milne, *Despatch of 1918*, pp.1–2.
21   Falls, *Macedonia Vol. 2*, pp.53 and 55.
22   Lieutenant-Colonel Lepetit, *La Genèse de l'Offensive en Macédoine* (Paris: Institut de Stratégie Comparée 1922), p.4, quoting the Report of General Guillaumat of 25 February 1918. Lepetit's

Despite this, and with the staff resources at his disposal, Guillaumat now set about defining how the comprehensive defence network in course of realisation was to be used, and the role of reserves in the case of an enemy offensive. By 3 March he had prepared, effectively, an 'order of defence' as thorough in its detail as any 'order of battle.' For the purposes of defence the Allied Front was divided into three army groups; from the Struma to the Gandach plateau the BSF and the French First Group (including the Greek National Corps) under General Milne, the centre from the Gandach plateau to the Crna the Serbian Army under Voivode Bojović, and from the Crna to Lake Prespa the *Armée Française de l'Orient* and Italian 35th Division under General Henrys. Mobile reserves behind each of the three sectors were to be controlled by Guillaumat.[23] It was a long front, and just as the Allies in September would break through by applying immense pressure on one part of the line, the same option was open to the enemy, and Guillaumat's forces had to be prepared with procedures for the deployment of *masses de manoeuvre* and the fast cross-transfer of support to the sector in danger. This was a step-change in planning from the days of Sarrail.

By end January Guillaumat had knocked another item off his check-list. From the beginning of the month the Russian brigades on the Crna were withdrawn in small units, disarmed, and given the choice of either joining the French Foreign Legion, or remaining on the front as labourers, or internment.[24] The majority were interned in Tunisia and repatriated in 1919–1920.[25] The withdrawal of the Russians also created for Guillaumat a plausible reason for not fulfilling another of his instructions, that of moving the Italian 35th Division to the extreme west of the Allied Army's front. The Allied line within the Crna bend would have been seriously compromised if both the Russians and the Italians moved out, so the Italians would have to stay.

In tandem with his work on perfecting the defences along his long front, Guillamaut started work immediately on organizational issues. He was fortunate – indeed, he may have had a hand in his selection – in the choice of General Henrys as the new commander of the *Armée Française de l'Orient*. He also brought with him a new Chief of Staff, General Charpy, who had served with him in the Second Army on the Western Front. Together they set about providing the central staffs for the French Army called for in Guillaumat's instructions.[26] They were underwhelmed when they went through their predecessors' files on arrival. Guillaumat reported in the same letter of 25 January to the War Ministry that when he had asked to see the orders given to the Allied Army relative to organizational and defensive plans, his staffs couldn't find anything more recent that December 1916. No doubt he used this as further evidence of his need for more and better staff officers.[27]

Among Guillaumat's other decisions was the logical one of creating a common reserve of artillery which could quickly be directed to the part of the front where it would be of most use.[28] Conscious of the lack of collaboration at operational level between the individual national armies which he had inherited (particularly between the British and the French), Guillaumat set up inter-allied commissions, an example of which was the one set up to review and reconstruct the Entrenched Camp defences. The Allied Railway commission was an early example of the success of these joint bodies where the British and French Directors of Railways shared the same office.[29]

---

    calculation of the length of the Allied line from the mouth of the Struma to the western shore of Lake Prespa was 295 kilometres p.2.
23 Falls, *Macedonia Vol. 2*, p.73, Schiavon, *Front d'Orient*, p.304.
24 Schiavon, *Front d'Orient*, p.298.
25 Hall, *Balkan Breakthrough*, p.98.
26 Falls, *Macedonia Vol. 2*, p.50.
27 Schiavon, *Front d'Orient*, p.302.
28 Palmer, *Gardeners*, p.168.
29 Falls, *Macedonia Vol. 2*, p.53.

Implicit in the notes accompanying Guillaumat's joining instructions was the need for training. The science and practice of warfare had changed out of all recognition since the beginning of the war on the Western Front. During this period the Allied Army of the East had been living in a sort of time-warp down in Macedonia. Aware of this Guillaumat and his recently arrived staff officers set up divisional training centres along the lines of those put in place by Pétain in France, to cover both technical and tactical training. They hoped that the example being set by the French Army would be taken up by other elements of the Allied Army of the East.[30]

Milne, who had withdrawn all units in succession for training during the summer-line period of 1917, needed no persuasion. In January 1918 he issued new instructions to formalise training throughout the BSF. These included specialist schools for artillery, signals, engineers, as well as gas training and infantry training for all officers and NCOs.[31] In addition to these usually month-long courses, in-the-field training was seen as a productive use of down-time for units in reserve.[32]

In addition to the need for central staffs for the *Armée Française de l'Orient* Guillaumat realized immediately the need for central staffs to serve and direct the Allied Army of the East as a whole. *La première constatation que j'ai pu faire en arrivant ici, c'est qu'il n'existait pas un Etat Major des Armées Alliées en Orient* (The first thing I discovered when I arrived here was that there wasn't a General Staff for the Allied Army of the East). He went on to say that even if it were not a case of five armies from different countries, but five all-French armies, a central staff would be equally necessary. To him this was an obvious first principle. And so it would have been to Sarrail had he been serving on the Western Front, but his command in the East had developed on such an ad hoc and unplanned basis, and he had never seen it this way. Guillaumat split this inter-allied central staff into two sections, the one covering services and logistics, the other covering military operations. He called for officers from all of the Allied contingents to take up positions in these.[33]

By the close of 1917 all of the Allies on the Macedonian Front had been calling for Sarrail's recall, the British, the Serbs, the Italians, even, and stridently, the Greeks. There seems no doubt at all that they were all satisfied with his replacement – even the Italians who were not on speaking terms with Sarrail when he left. The new Commander of the Allied Army of the East had made a good start, and within a couple of months had gone a long way to fulfilling the initial objectives he had been given. But he himself was under no illusions that the road was long, and much remained to be done before his forces would be in a position to move onto the offensive. His position is succinctly summarised in his report to his leaders on 14 February:

> I am sure that those in high places never questioned the difficulty of leading and bringing to a common objective forces of five different nationalities; the problems resulting from such a diversity are found in all coalitions, and, naturally, they are here in Macedonia. For the moment you can't call for too much from the Allied Army of the East. Several months will be necessary for training these armies, allowing time for the Serbs to absorb their new recruits, organising the Greek army in a manner to enable it to play its part, and above all to gain everyone's confidence and create a proper offensive spirit. One can't foresee setting up a major offensive before the Autumn.[34]

---

30 Schiavon, *Front d'Orient*, p.300.
31 Falls, *Macedonia Vol. 2*, p.57.
32 In January 1918 Signaller Bailey reports that he was giving semaphore, buzzer and morse training to classes of forty, while in February he attended gas training and engaged in regular rifle practice. Then in May he was sent to Salonica for ten days for a formal train-the-trainer course at the BSF's central Signals School.
33 Schiavon, *Front d'Orient*, pp.291–292.
34 Schiavon, *Front d'Orient*, p.299, Report from Guillaumat to War Office, 14 February 1918.

29

1918
Greek and Other Reinforcements

On his appointment at the end of 1917, Guillaumat took command of an Allied Army nominally of 23 divisions: eight French, four British, six Serb, three Greek, one Italian and one Russian.[1] The reality was much less than this. The Russian division had already disintegrated and been disassembled in the first days of the year. Of the remaining contingents only the Greeks and Italians were numerically at strength, although the Greeks were short of equipment and artillery.

The *Armée Française de l'Orient* in November 1917 was over 40,000 men short due to absences (leave and those whose leave had been transformed into service on the Western Front).[2] In addition, the two latest of the French divisions to arrive (30th and 76th) were under establishment at 9 battalions instead of 12.[3] The French forces also suffered from *paludisme* as Sarrail's angry exchanges with his Health Services in 1917 attest.[4]

But the *paludisme* was far worse among the British forces. Hospital admissions of BSF troops due to malaria had risen by the end of 1917 to over 16,000 a month.[5]

As for the Serbs, sickness and above all casualties had exacted a severe toll. After the 1917 restructuring each of the six divisions was reduced from twelve to nine battalions.

The force actually passed on from Sarrail to Guillaumat was for all these reasons in manpower terms much closer to the equivalent of 17 divisions than 23: six French, three British, four Serb, three Greek and one Italian.

As Guillaumat completed the audit of his forces and resources as required by Foch and Clemenceau all this would have become clear to him, and no doubt he reported it back. If the purpose of the audit had been to ensure that he had the strength to meet his primary objective of holding his long front and keeping the enemy out of Greece, the results were not encouraging. One of the pay-backs of Guillaumat's report was a steady flow of newly trained recruits to fill out the depleted French divisions during January and February.[6] For both political and personal reasons Clemenceau would not have wanted his own newly appointed Chief Gardener to be deprived of the means of doing his job. According to *Armée Française de l'Orient* staffs, total French manpower in Macedonia increased by 50,000 between July 1917 and June 1918.[7] In due course as the threat on the Macedonian Front declined, and that on the Western Front increased, 10,000 of these were called back.

---

1   Larcher, *Grande Guerre*, p.207.
2   Larcher, *Grande Guerre*, p.209, quoting Allied Army Staff statistics.
3   Falls, *Macedonia Vol. 1*, p.255.
4   Sarrail/Porte, *Mon Commandement*, p.321.
5   Falls, *Macedonia Vol. 2*, pp.58 and 351. Falls points out that a much-reduced level of malaria in 1918 was perhaps mainly due to the repatriation programme, which removed a major source of infection.
6   Palmer, *Gardeners*, p.165.
7   Larcher, *Grande Guerre*, p.208.

Reinforcements to the British Salonica Force came in the form of materials rather than men. Milne had long been calling for more powerful guns, particularly to attack the Doiran defences. In January 1918 he finally received an 8-inch battery. This was followed by twelve 6-inch trench mortars, an ideal weapon for dislodging the enemy in their fortified positions between the hills and ravines of the Doiran to Vardar sector. These came from Palestine where they had become surplus to requirements following Allenby's entry into Jerusalem in December.[8]

During the first months of 1918 Milne's air forces were also increased on a regular basis. He reported that in March 'almost every day the Air Force raided the enemy's country, bombed his camps, dumps and railway stations and attacked his troops with machine gun fire from low altitudes. In the fighting that these raids entailed our airmen more than held their own.'[9] When the RAF was formed on 1 April from the merging of the RFC and the RNAS a third squadron was added to the force in Macedonia, equipped with a new generation of high performance fighter planes. From this time the British dominated the skies in their sector.[10] From April to September the new squadron, No.150, destroyed 34 enemy aircraft and captured two for the loss of only one plane.[11]

In February Guillaumat informed Milne that due to the departure of the Russians he would have to move the three French battalions from 122nd Division, currently on the British side of the Vardar, back to the other side. In exchange Milne would get the first Greek Royalist division, 1st Larissa, now ready for deployment. This division however had limited artillery and was anyway to be assigned to the Struma front. Since 122nd Division would take its artillery with it, Milne asked the War Office for the return of the heavy artillery he had been obliged to send to Egypt in mid-1917. Perhaps to his surprise the three 6-inch howitzer batteries were returned to him, together with another one from Mesopotamia.

On 18 February Sir William Robertson was replaced as Chief of the Imperial Staff by Sir Henry Wilson. Robertson had been Chief of Staff, then CIGS, from December 1915. As has been seen he had been a long-term fellow officer, and at times senior officer, of Milne, and may well have had a hand in his appointment as Commander of the British Salonica Force. It is arguable that the very closeness of their relationship and the frequency of their correspondence worked against rather than in favour of Milne's interests, Robertson finding it easier to gloss over Milne's requirements, whereas a more formal reporting structure may have seen Milne's problems being assessed more objectively. However, the situation did not improve much under Wilson, who was to remain CIGS for the rest of the war. It has to be said that Wilson entered into the job as the war on the Western Front was building up to an almighty climax and had little time for the 'side-show'. When in September 1918 the breakthrough was made he was among the first to realise the importance of it and was full of praise and support for the achievements of Milne's army. And it was Wilson who finally saw to Milne's promotion to full General in July 1918.

On the day of his departure from the job Robertson concluded his long correspondence with Milne on 18 February with a short and rather sad note:

> I am today handing over my duties to General Wilson. I desire to thank you most warmly for the cordial and efficient manner you have co-operated with me in carrying out your difficult and irksome task. Good luck to you.[12]

---

8   Palmer, *Gardeners*, p.170.
9   Milne, *Despatch of 1918*.
10 Wakefield, *Under the Devil's Eye*, p.196.
11 Falls, *Macedonia Vol. 2*, p.59.
12 Nicol, *Uncle George*, p.158.

In addition to official correspondence during the 18 months of their collaboration, Milne and Robertson had also exchanged no less than 137 'Secret and Personal' telegrams. Wilson set up a similar conduit with Milne but rarely used it.[13]

The most welcome and unlooked-for reinforcements were those received by the Serbs. The plan to create after the war a new state uniting Serbia, Croatia and Slovenia had been formalized on 20 July 1917 in the 'Corfu Declaration'.[14] Interestingly, although the Declaration runs to 13 points, no mention is made of Bosnia. The Declaration does however assure freedom of profession for the 'Orthodox, Catholic and Musselmann religions.' Montenegro announced its intention to join the new state on 1 December 1918.

But, long before this, a unity of purpose and objective had been growing among the South Slav nationalities, including those which in 1914 formed part of the Austrian Empire. The composite Austro-Hungarian army contained any number of them. In 1916 Serbian representatives had gone to Russia to negotiate the release of any South Slav prisoners of war (some of which were ethnic Serbs) who were prepared to switch sides and fight for the Allies. From these a force of two divisions was formed, initially to be sent to Romania to fight alongside the Russo-Romanian armies. When the Romanian campaign came to an end it was agreed that they should be sent to join the Serbs on the Macedonian Front. Since the Central Powers stood astride any southern route, a first detachment of 10,000 men was sent via Archangel and arrived in Salonica in January 1918. A further 6,000 men were caught up in the Bolshevik revolution and had to travel across Siberia to get out. They finally arrived in Salonica on 1 April having travelled more than 20,000 kilometres in three months.[15]

As a result of these new arrivals, the six Serb divisions were more or less brought up to strength, and the Cavalry Division was recreated. Many of the new recruits were put into the Vardar Division which was appropriately renamed the Yugoslav Division.[16]

Retrieving South Slav prisoners of war from the Italians proved less easy. There were 30,000 of these, including many who had taken part in the great Serbian retreat of November 1915 as prisoners of the Serbs and had been subsequently interned in Italy.[17] The Serbian military attaché in Rome reported that he had received 4,000 written applications from South Slav prisoners of war in Italy who wanted to serve in Macedonia, but the Italians refused to release them.[18]

The Italians were of course unenthusiastic about the creation of a South Slav nation since they expected much of Slovenia and parts of Croatia to accrue to them after the war. Villari makes a brave effort to explain that these were a different sort of South Slav, untrustworthy and still attached to the Dual Monarchy, but he is not very convincing.[19]

Nevertheless the 16,000 recruits ex-Russia made an excellent impression, enabled the Serbian army to regain much of its strength, and above all had a good effect on morale.

But it was from Greece that the most significant reinforcements to the Allied Army of the East were expected. The three 'Venizelist' divisions – Seres, Crete and Archipelago, forming the Corps of National Defence – had already been operational for almost a year. Some battalions of Seres had seen minor action with the BSF on the Struma Front in 1917, but all three divisions now formed part of the French First Group based to the west of the Vardar and guarding the Vardar valley.

---

13 Nicol, *Uncle George*, p.190.
14 The Corfu Declaration, the text in English is given in <firstworldwar.com> under Primary Documents, the Corfu Declaration 20 July 1917.
15 Gray and Argyle, *Chronicle Vol. 2*, p.152.
16 Falls, *Macedonia Vol. 2* p.69.
17 Villari, *Macedonian Campaign*, p.194.
18 Falls, *Macedonia Vol. 2*, p.70.
19 Villari, *Macedonian Campaign*, p.195.

The first Greek Royalist Corps was then formed very quickly. Guillaumat had decided that when complete the whole Corps should take over the whole Struma front, while remaining under the command of General Milne.[20] Its Larissa Division was already trained, equipped and on the Struma by 12 March. When it was joined in May by 13th Division (Calchis) and June by 2nd Division (Athens) Milne was obliged to redefine the line positions of all the forces under his command.

This exercise, complex in itself, was complicated by three other factors. First, this reorganisation coincided with the period for withdrawal of troops from the Struma to the summer camps in the hills. This year however Milne decided to leave a stronger presence in the valley, partly in view of a strengthened enemy presence, and partly because the Greeks were more resistant to malaria than the British.

Second, although the new Greek divisions made an excellent impression on British officers in terms of their physique, turn-out and motivation, they were lacking in much essential equipment and very short of ammunition and pack animals, and the supply of such shortages and its transport fell to the BSF.[21]

Third, while all this was going on Milne received reports from deserters that the Bulgarians were planning a major offensive on the Struma. In the end this came to nothing apparently as a result of mutinies in the Bulgarian ranks. Further, in June, the Bulgarians opened up with a major artillery bombardment on the Doiran sector. As it happened this was found to be not the prelude to an offensive but a sort of public relations operation to encourage their infantry.[22] Despite Bulgarian claims, British casualties as a result of this bombardment were minimal. But all this caused extra delays in the roll-out of Milne's overall movement plan.

Following this move, the Greek forces under Milne's command were almost as numerous as the British ones, and in XVI Corps they outnumbered the British by three divisions to one, 27th Division having been transferred to XII Corps.

The final configuration involved the three Greek Divisions taking over the entire Struma Front, from the Gulf of Rendina to south of Lake Butkovo; Chalchis nearest the sea, Larissa in the centre replacing 27th Division, and Athens taking the northern part of the sector up to Lozhitsa, replacing 83rd and 84th Brigades of 28th Division. These two Brigades were now placed in reserve based on Yanesh, while 28th Division's other two Brigades, 85th and 228th retained their previous positions on the Butkovo sector between Lake Butkovo and Lake Doiran.

West of Lake Doiran, 22nd and 26th Divisions (XII Corps) retained their long-held positions between Doiran and Vardar. The largest move had to be made by 27th Division, now part of XII Corps, which found itself on the far side of the Vardar with 26th Division on its right, and the Greek Cretan Division on its left. Remarkably, this was the first time during the whole Macedonian campaign that a British Division had 'crossed the river'. Unsurprisingly, the move of 27th Division was the last brick to fall into place and was not completed until 9 July.

As an early part of this overall movement 228th Brigade was ordered out of the Struma valley to take up a line between Lake Butkova and Dova Tepe, where it remained for the rest of the war. Signaller Bailey's Battalion, 22/Rifle Brigade executed this transfer by making four silent night marches, often outside British lines and latterly also with pack and wheeled transport, from Turbes to Radile, and thereby achieving an honourable mention in the pages of the Official History.[23]

---

20 Milne, *Despatch of 1918*, p.2.
21 Falls, *Macedonia Vol. 2*, pp.95 and 98.
22 Falls, *Macedonia Vol. 2*, p.99. quoting Nedev.
23 Falls, *Macedonia Vol. 2*, p.63. E Bailey 21 March 1918 'Another march by night, no smoking, no talking in danger zone mostly on the plain to Radile and Todovaro. Marched well but tired each night. Glad when finished.'

The Peloponnese had been the heartland of pro-Constantine sentiment but Venizelos was prepared to raise a second Royalist Corps there if required by the Allies. Clemenceau gave his go-ahead and work started in April, with three divisions becoming operational by August. In common with the Serbian and some French divisions, the new Greek Corps divisions were established at nine battalions instead of twelve. A further division was mobilized for service in Epirus, to prevent any Austrian incursions down the west coast of Greece, or perhaps more to the point, to enable the Greeks to keep an eye on the doings of their Italian ally across the Albanian border. This division did not come under the orders of the Allied Army commander. By the end of the war Greece had mobilized an army of over 250,000 men, of whom 160,000 were to serve on the Macedonian Front before the ending of hostilities.

All this did not come without a cost. In December 1917, Britain France and America each voted a budget of £10,000,000 to equip and supply the Greek Army, and a commission was set up to decide how the money should be spent. In general non-military materials (food, forage, clothing, transport) were to come from Britain while armaments and aviation were to be provided by the French. The French military mission of 150 officers from all branches made an indispensable contribution to the organization, training and operational readiness of these new Greek formations.[24]

Inevitably there were problems. Desertion was a problem with soldiers serving so close to home. Then in February 1918 two detachments mutinied at Lamia on their way to Salonica, requiring the personal intervention of King Alexander. Two of the ringleaders were executed, and no one was left in any doubt that the new King was supporting his Prime Minister.[25]

* * *

Due partly to Guillaumat's actions and interventions, partly to events which were already underway before his arrival, and partly to good fortune, the Allied Army of the East grew significantly in size and fire-power during the first half of 1918, without being troubled in any serious way by the enemy.

On the Western Front it was otherwise. The expected enemy offensive was launched on 21 March, and the Allies were pushed back to the Marne. Within a few days the Germans had taken 45,000 British and French prisoners, were threatening Arras, Amiens and Compiègne and were within 75 kilometres of Paris.[26] On 23 March the War Cabinet were yet again thinking of withdrawing the remaining four British divisions in Macedonia.[27] They decided not to because these divisions were 'riddled with malaria.'[28] The line was stabilized but subjected to further all out offensives on 27 May and 7 June.

On 2 May at a meeting at Abbeville the Supreme War Council concluded that due to the new Greek Corps coming on line, it should now be possible to withdraw several British and French battalions for use on the Western Front, where they were needed, *sans pour cela mettre en péril la situation en Salonique* (but without endangering the situation in Salonica). They agreed to send a delegation headed by two Generals, one French and one British to Salonica to discuss the matter with Guillaumat, and *si possible d'arranger avec lui l'enlèvement immmédiat des bataillons alliés* (to arrange if possible for the immediate withdrawal of some Allied battalions).[29]

---

24 Falls, *Macedonia Vol. 2*, p.64.
25 Palmer, *Gardeners*, p.171.
26 Gilbert, *First World War*, p.409.
27 Gray and Argyle, *Chronicle Vol. 2*, p.146. Gray and Argyle also report that on 24 January 1918 Haig had suggested at Compiègne that all French and British forces in Macedonia should be removed to the Western Front.
28 Falls, *Macedonia Vol. 2*, p.76.
29 Larcher, *Grande Guerre*, Annexe 17 p.282. Minutes of SWC Meeting of 2 May 1918.

One can imagine the forceful arguments brought to bear by the delegation, and in the end Milne was obliged to accept the reduction of all his brigades (except 228th Brigade) to three battalions, adding another major element of complexity to his task of moving his entire force northwards and westwards to accommodate the Greek First Corps in the Struma valley. Twelve battalions were subsequently sent to France.[30] These left Greece on 1 June and indeed when they arrived many were found to be suffering from malaria. Very unwillingly Guillaumat agreed to reduce French forces by 10,000 men, about the equivalent amount.[31]

Independently of the troop withdrawal negotiations, the delegation had been tasked by the SWC to quiz Guillaumat on the plans he had developed for relinquishing Salonica should it prove necessary. At a conference on 29 May at which Milne was also present Guillaumat rose to the occasion. Firstly, he pointed out that for the Greeks (and Serbs) any talk of abandoning Salonica, even as a theoretical staff exercise, would be tantamount to treason. Secondly he told them that with the original Entrenched Camp fortifications, and the additional work performed over the winter months, protected as it was also from the sea, Salonica could hold out until hell froze over. Thirdly the whole Allied Army of the East depended almost totally on Salonica for supply, and the idea of supplying the army through Volos, Itea and Piraeus was pie in the sky; these ports were not only physically detached, they were incapable of handling the traffic.

Finally Milne's staffs produced figures showing that 140 days would be required to evacuate all base and military personnel and their supplies, even assuming that shipping were available.[32] That the investigative commission had received and understood the message is clear from their report to the War Cabinet, upon which Robertson himself commented 'in the event of an attempted evacuation it is quite possible that there might be a bad disaster for our troops in that theatre of war.'[33]

The Official Historian, who so many times must have come across crass staff stupidity in the course of his research, but felt that his job was to record rather than comment, could not help remarking on this occasion that an obsession with plans for relinquishing Salonica as the Army's base indicated the potential danger 'of a council or junta with no link with armies in the field being made responsible for military policy.'

---

30 One of the Battalions sent from 26 Division was 7 Battalion, the Wiltshire Regiment. Falls p 94. This was the Battalion of Owen Rutter, author of Tiadatha, and explains why no account of the Second Battle of Doiran is included in the poem.
31 Larcher, *Grande Guerre*, p.224. He notes that BSF establishment levels at May 1917 were 240,000. At 17 November 1917 they were, 152,000 and at June 1918 137,000. From a high of 270,000 in April 1918, French levels had fallen to 247,000 by mid-year
32 Falls, *Macedonia Vol. 2*, p.75.
33 Birch, *No Sideshow*, p.94, quoting the Report by the Military Mission to Salonica 18 September 1918.

The remains of the Bulgarian defensive fortifications on the Doiran hills are still very visible today. (Author)

French troops from 156th Division consolidating trenches taken from the Bulgarians on the Tservena Stena, 17 March 1917. (MCM, Opérateur K)

French troops from 57th Division about to launch an attack on Hill 1248, 19 March 1917. (MCM, Opérateur K)

Generals Sarrail and Milne. Not a happy relationship. (SCS)

General Sarrail and Commissioner Jonnart in Athens on 4 July 1917 following the abdication of King Constantine. (MCM)

The Great Fire of Salonica, August 1917, destroyed between a third and a half of the town. (SCS)

Refugees from the Great Fire. 80,000 inhabitants of the town were made homeless.
(*Nottingham Evening Post*)

Field gun in action on the Struma front, 1917. (SCS)

The Struma plain from the Turbes hills. During the summers of 1917 and 1918 General Milne withdrew most members of XVI Corps to the hills to avoid the worst of the malarial season. (Author)

British Hospital encampment Number 36 with Number 37 in the background, Vertekop 1918. (MCM/Opérateur K)

British troops digging drainage channels to eradicate mosquito breeding grounds. (SCS)

In early 1918 the new King of Greece, Alexander, paid visits to all parts of the Allied Army in turn; here with General Milne on 8 February following a review of parts of the BSF. (MCM, Opérateur T)

Church parade for a brigade of Yugoslav Division on 28 June 1918, the anniversary of the Battle of Kosovo Polje, a triangle formed by the three battalions. (MCM, Opérateur K)

Italian troops facing Hill 1050 in the Crna bend. (NAM)

A French 155 cannon. Seven 155 batteries were hauled up the Moglena mountains to support the Serbo–French attack on Dobropolje, September 1918. (MCM, Opérateur T)

General Marc-Louis Guillaumat, Commander of the Allied Army of the East from December 1917 to June 1918, with General Ernesto Mombelli, Commander of the Italian 35th Division and General Henrys. (MCM, Opérateur T)

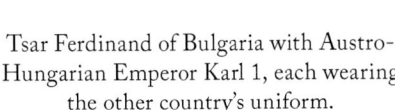

Tsar Ferdinand of Bulgaria with Austro-Hungarian Emperor Karl 1, each wearing the other country's uniform.

General Louis Franchet d'Espèrey, Commander of the Allied Army of the East From June 1918 to the end of the Campaign. (MCM/Opérateur Z)

Prince Regent Alexander, Commander in Chief of the Serbian Army. (MCM)

Voivode Zivojin Mišić, Chief of Staff of the Serbian Army from June 1918.

Voivode Stepa Stepanović, Commander of the Serbian 2nd Army.

Voivode Petar Bojović, Chief of Staff of the Serbian Army from January 1916 to June 1918, Commander of the Serbian 1st Army for the Final Offensive.

General Franchet d'Espèrey and General Henrys consulting the map between Monastir and Prilep, September 1918. (MCM)

Members of a Spahi Regiment. (MCM/Opérateur K/F)

The French Military Cemetery at Monastir (now Bitola) contains the graves of over 6,000 French soldiers, with a further 7,000 – 10,000 interred in two ossuaries. (Author)

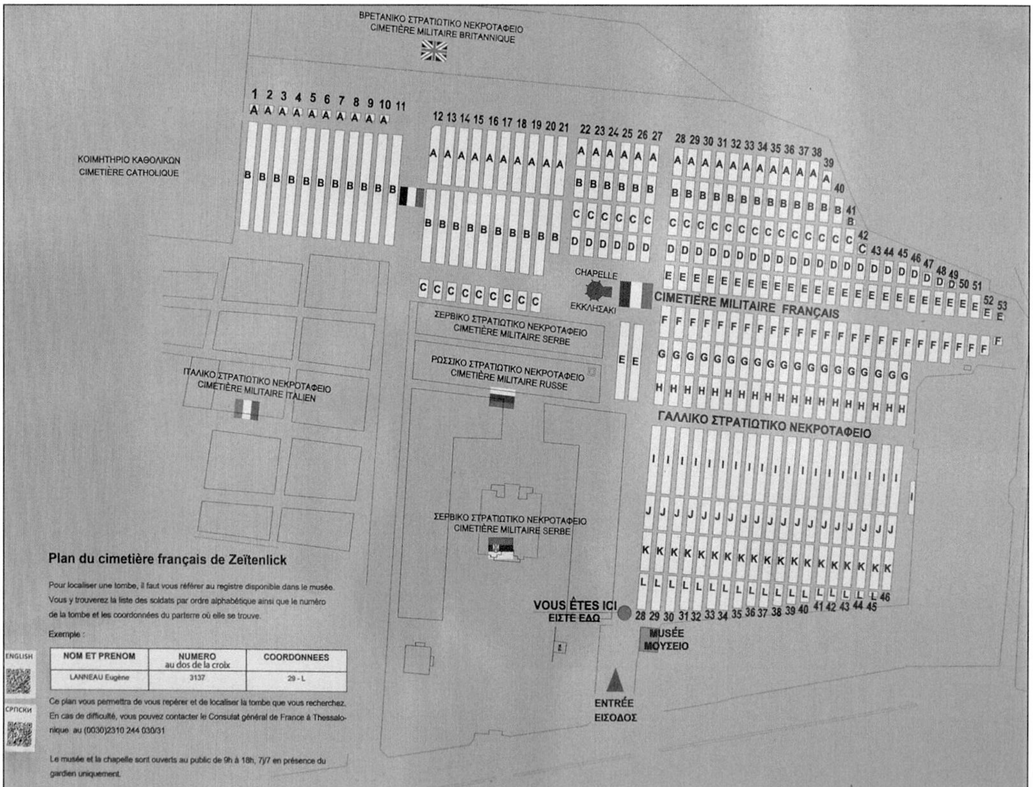

Plan put up by the French at the entrance to the Zeitenlik international military cemetery in Thessaloniki, the largest in Greece with over 20,000 graves; 8,098 French, 7,441 Serbian, 3,500 Italian, 1,634 British and 393 Russian. (Author)

Part of the French cemetery at Zeitenlik. (Author)

The British section of the Zeitenlik Cemetery, beautifully kept. There are 15 other British First World War cemeteries in Greece. (Author)

Memorial to 22nd Division to the rear of the Doiran battlefield. (Author)

Signallers from 22nd Battalion, the Rifle Brigade in Egypt prior to their transfer to Salonica. Edward Bailey standing on the left. (Author)

Key to credits/abbreviations:
NAM: Image Courtesy of the National Army Museum.
SCS: Image reproduced with the permission of the Salonica Campaign Society from the SCS Trench Map DVD.
MCM: Copyright accorded by *Photo (C) Ministère de la Culture – Médiathèque de l'Architecture et du Patrimoine. Dist. RMN – Grand Palais.*
IWM: Imperial War Museum

30

1918
Guillaumat Completes his Mission

(Maps 8, 9 & 10)

By the end of February Guillaumat had been in the job for a little over two months but had already ticked off most of the items on the check-list given to him by Foch and Clemenceau at the start of his mandate. A total overhaul of defences was well advanced. With a heavily armoured front line and two sets of fallback positions along the whole of the front, he could soon be confident about 'maintaining the integrity of the conquered territory'. In addition to the physicals he had developed a defensive plan for their use, and for the deployment of reserve forces.

He could now turn his attention to the remaining major item on his list of objectives *Etudier les possibilités d'une offensive à entreprendre, pour agir au mieux des intérêts de la Coalition contre les armées de l'ennemi, suivant les circonstances du moment* (Consider the possibilities of an offensive against the enemy's armies, according to the conditions of the moment, which best serve the interests of the Coalition).[1]

On 1 March he sent Clemenceau a detailed report and proposal for future offensive action on the Macedonian Front. He immediately discounted the possibility of launching in 1918 an all-out attack of the sort which would aim at the re-conquest of Serbia, or knocking Bulgaria out of the war, 'unless final victories on the Western or Italian Fronts totally change the situation'.[2]

However, operations of more limited scope could be considered, aimed either at extending the Allied Army's front line to more favourable positions, or at disconcerting the enemy, preventing him from moving forces away, or even obliging him to call for reinforcements. Guillaumat identified three 'lesser' areas where such objectives could be met; the Monastir and Crna valleys aiming at Prilep, the Vardar–Doiran Front aiming at the Strumitsa valley, or the Struma valley aiming either at Demi Hasar–Seres or Kavalla.

He excludes the mountain range between the Crna and the Vardar as not being very suitable for an offensive. (An assessment totally at odds with that of Franchet d'Espèrey later in the year). Each of these three 'lesser' actions was in fact more ambitious than any yet achieved by the Allied Army of the East, with the exceptions of Kaymakcalan and Monastir in 1916.

As he extends his analysis, Guillaumat excludes his first option - the advance on Prilep from Monastir – in that it would stretch a very long front even further and would seriously test supply lines back to Salonica.[3] A push up the Vardar valley and to the west of Lake Doiran he finds

---

1   Larcher, *Grande Guerre*, Annexe 15 p.250. Instructions from Clemenceau to Guillaumat of 16 December 1918.
2   Louis Cordier, *Victoire Éclair en Orient* (Aurillac: Editions U.S.H.A., 1968), Annexe 2 p.261. Report of General Guillaumat to the French War Office of 1 May 1918.
3   Lepetit,, *Genèse de l'Offensive*, p.5.

more promising. If Allied forces could reach the line Miletkovo – Rabrovo the enemy's flexibility of movement would be restricted to the defile of the Vardar – at its narrowest here – or along the Strumitsa valley. The idea of establishing a position with the Doiran hills and Lake Doiran behind, and with the massif of the Marianska Planina to the west was obviously appealing. Also, Guillaumat goes on, an attack in this area would be closing in on Bulgaria itself, and therefore likely to oblige the enemy to retain heavy defensive forces and bring forces in from other parts of his line. Further, he points out, distance would be added between the enemy front line and Salonica.[4] One wonders whether Milne had fully debriefed Guillaumat on the action of Machukovo in 1916 and the battles of Doiran in 1917 and the strength of Bulgarian defences in this sector.

Turning to his third option, action across the Struma, he identifies three directions of advance, Demi Hasar *en liaison avec celle du Vardar* (therefore presumably involving moving up the Struma to its junction with the Strumitsa), Demi Hasar and Seres, or thirdly along the coast from Orfano up the river valley to Kavalla. This one, he says, would be quick to set up, and would attract a lot of enemy attention.[5]

He concludes with a preference for a combined Vardar–Struma offensive. For these he would use three French, two British and two Greek divisions, noting that since such an offensive could not be mounted before the Autumn, he would by then have three more Greek divisions available.[6]

A feature of Guillaumat's presentation, and an unstated reason for the choice of the Vardar corridor for his main offensive rather than the Moglena–Crna sector is his obvious lack of rapport with the Serbian army. In his lengthy proposal of 1 March he refers only in passing and in very negative terms to the Serbs: *L'armée Serbe si celle-ci décide de faire quelque chose* (The Serbian Army if it decides to do something). *L'incertitude qui plane toujours sur les véritables dispositions de l'Armée Serbe* (The uncertainty which always surrounds the mood of the Serbian Army) and then to his lack of knowledge as to *les intentions de l'Armée Serbe quant à une action éventuelle* (The intentions of the Serbian Army relating to an eventual action).[7]

Clemenceau, no doubt with his mind on the forthcoming German offensive on the Western Front replied to Guillaumat on 17 March. He noted Guillaumat's proposals and while generally agreeing with them stressed the *nécessité de réaliser d'urgence, rapidement et complètement l'organisation défensive dont dépend la sécurité des Armées Alliées de l'Orient et de la Grèce'* (the urgent need to ensure a complete and speedy defensive organization on which the safety of the Allied Army of the East and that of Greece depend).[8] From a hundred years on this sounds very much like a staffer's reply put in front of his boss to sign while vastly more important priorities were crowding in on him.

During February and March massive activity was detected on the Bulgarian Front. Aerial photographs showed railways in constant action, the build-up of major dumps close to the front, and guns, troops and equipment being gathered for a major offensive. Plans were obviously afoot to support the major German offensive on the Western Front with one in Macedonia. But as it turned out the expected launch date came and went and nothing happened. Intelligence sources later discovered that the Bulgarians had waited for a crashing victory by their allies in France, and when it didn't happen, decided to carrying on sitting tight and waiting on events.[9]

---

4   Lepetit, *Genèse de l'Offensive*, p.6.
5   No further attention seems to have been given to this last idea. It is not clear whether Guillaumat was intending to use Greek Royalist divisions together with the BSF for this. An attack on Kavala could have been well supported from the sea.
6   Armées Françaises, *Tome VIII Vol. 3*, p.9.
7   Cordier, *Victoire Éclair*, Annexe 2 p.261.
8   Lepetit, *Genèse de l'Offensive*, p.8, quoting telegram from War Ministry to Guillaumat of 17 March 1918.
9   Casson, *Steady Drummer*, p.195.

By 1 April the German make-or-break offensive of 21 March on the Western Front had been held, and Foch could try to assess what the enemy's next moves would be. But one thing was now clear; contrary to reinforcing their Bulgarian allies with a view to mounting a parallel offensive on the Macedonian Front, the Germans were more likely to bring their troops in Macedonia back to France, and even appeal to the Bulgarians to support them. By the end of January there were only three German battalions, 49 batteries and 17 machine gun detachments as well as central staffs remaining in Macedonia.[10] The collapse of the Eastern Front, far from endangering the Allied forces on the Macedonian Front, was relieving the pressure on them, and, with the increasing loss of morale among the Bulgarian forces, was putting them very definitely on the front foot.

The need to prevent the enemy from transferring forces from the Macedonian to the Western Front suddenly became of critical importance, and on 4 April Guillaumat received another message from Clemenceau (in agreement with Foch) which completely countermanded that of two weeks earlier:

Contrairement aux prescriptions de ma lettre du 17 mars, l'obligation s'impose donc pour vos armées de se tenir prêtes, si les circonstances l'exigent, à passer à l'offensive. (Contrary to my letter of 17 March, you now need to prepare your army, should it prove necessary, to move onto the offensive).

He goes on to say that offensive plans (one assumes he refers to those detailed by Guillaumat in his report of 1 March) should be brought forward, the integration of the (Greek) forces coming into line speeded up, and that whilst this is going on:

Il importe que, sur l'ensemble de votre front, vos troupes redoublent l'activité pour inquiéter l'ennemi, entraver sa liberté d'action, vérifier son ordre de bataille, déceler ses mouvements. (It is necessary, on the whole of your front, that your troops re-double their work of troubling the enemy, blocking his freedom of action, checking his dispositions, and uncovering his movements).

This should be achieved, he continues, by carefully prepared local attacks with well-defined objectives, limiting the use of infantry as far as possible, but with massive use of artillery.[11]

This letter represents a turning point in the history of the Macedonian Campaign. As Lieutenant Colonel Lepetit puts it 'the date of 4 April marks a complete change in direction in the mission of the Allied Army of the Orient, this, up to now strictly defensive, becomes progressively offensive.'

Guillaumat now asked Milne for his views on the three options for offensive action which he had identified to Clemenceau. Milne in his reply of 9 April was in favour of an attack fanning out northwards and eastwards from the mouth of the Struma. The light railway he was building from Sarakali to Stavros was almost completed, in the Gulf of Rendina he could call on significant naval support, and it was known that Bulgarian defences were not strong in this area.[12] Guillaumat however retained his preference for the Vardar–Doiran option.

Milne doubted, in view of the troop movements involved, the arrival and insertion of the next Greek Division, and the build-up of the necessary artillery support, that this could be achieved within the next two months. In response however to Clemenceau's call for local actions to 'trouble, block, check and forestall', while plans for the major offensive were in train, Milne was able to offer immediate action on both the Doiran and Struma fronts.

---

10   Larcher, *Grande Guerre*, p.218.
11   Lepetit, *Genèse de l'Offensive*, p.9. quoting telegram from War Minister to Guillaumat, 4 April 1918.
12   Falls, *Macedonia Vol. 2*, p.78.

On the Struma with the 1st (Larissa) Greek Division on the right, 28th Division in the centre and 27th Division on the left the objective was to re-establish a line from Beglik in the south through Prosenik and Homondos to Ormanli in the north. Considerable resources were deployed. The attack was launched on 14 April.

The record of the BSF in anything from skirmishes to full scale attacks against enemy positions across the Struma had over the two previous campaigning seasons been almost uniformly successful. The Bulgarians however had obviously been analysing the reasons for this, and this time they were ready with appropriate countermeasures.

Only the Greek division met its objectives, meeting limited resistance except at Salmah where it absorbed an enemy attack and then pushed the Bulgarians back over the Meander river. Villari reported that 'although the action was of small importance, the Greek press … extolled the episode to the skies as if it were a first class victory. Even in the restaurants of Athens bouquets were given and an abundance of champagne to celebrate the great triumph.' Much better was to come a month later.[13]

In the centre however four battalions from 27th Division were driven back with serious losses from Prosenik by alert and determined Bulgarian units, while on the left two battalions from 28th Division ran up against strong enemy forces at Kyupri and were subjected to heavy fire and forced to retire over open ground without adequate artillery cover.[14] This calamitous action, shortly to be the subject of a Court of Enquiry, was called off on 18 April. Total casualties were significant for an action of this sort and included 225 dead or missing.

Concurrent with this attack XII Corps was once again to take on the formidable Bulgarian defences west of Lake Doiran, and on this occasion with much more success than XVI Corps on the Struma. A full scale attack similar to that of April–May 1917 was not planned; this was above all a heavy artillery demonstration with limited territorial aims. Nonetheless successful raids were made on Petit Couronné and two of the heavily defended neighbouring hills, and enemy trenches were invested before withdrawal. Casualties were 136 of which 26 dead or missing, considerably lighter than those which XVI Corps had taken a few days before, and a fraction of those suffered by XII Corps in their attempted assaults of the Doiran defences a year before.[15]

The aims of this attack were more modest, but the four day artillery bombardment incorporating all of BSF's recently acquired hardware, combined with new more effective machine gun tactics had been successful, and had paved the way for much less costly advances by the Corps' infantry towards the enemy positions.

On the other side of the Vardar French and Serbian forces and Italy's 35th Division were engaged from February onwards in *nombreuses reconnaissances et petits coups de main* – exploratory skirmishes and raids – in order to keep the enemy engaged, and to establish the composition of opposing forces. Between 15 and 25 March four larger attacks were mounted by the Italians around Hill 1050 and by 156th and 30th Divisions around Monastir, where the presence of a Turkish Brigade and a strengthening of the Austrian presence was discovered.[16] On 4 May the Serbs were engaged on the Dobropolje sector and captured some enemy trenches.[17]

Then in mid-May Guillaumat mounted a joint exercise with the Italian XVI Corps in Valona. Such an exercise would have been unthinkable during Sarrail's command; indeed in October 1917 when Sarrail's expeditionary force was advancing almost unopposed up the western shore of Lake Ohrid he had been told to stop. As he subsequently observed, 'Italy had spoken.'[18]

---

13 Villari, *Macedonian Campaign*, p.196.
14 Palmer, *Gardeners*, p.175.
15 Falls, *Macedonia Vol. 2*, p.86.
16 Armées Françaises, *Tome VIII Vol.3*, p.10.
17 Gray and Argyle, *Chronicle Vol. 2*, p.164.
18 Sarrail/Porte, *Mon Commandement*, p.338.

Things had changed. After the disastrous Battle of Caporetto General Cadorna had been replaced by General Diaz. Diaz's colleagues on the Supreme War Council would have pointed out to him that with the Allies fighting for their lives on all fronts, mid 1918 was scarcely the time to debate eventual post-war arrangements in Albania. General Ferrero and the staffs of XVI Corps would anyway have found it easier to work with Guillaumat and his staffs than with those of Sarrail, and Guillaumat would have had no difficulty in convincing Ferrero that France had no long-term military or political ambitions in Albania.

The objective of the joint action was to push the Allied line between Lake Ohrid and the Adriatic further north, to cut off an Austrian salient which had resulted from the French seizure of Pogradec in September 1917, and to push the enemy much further north of the Koritsa – Santi Quaranta road. The French force, carefully selected for the purpose, consisted of two infantry battalions, the equivalent of a battalion of Albanian gendarmerie, three mountain batteries, and a squadron of Moroccan cavalry. The Italian XVI Corps advanced across the Osun to join up with the French at Backe near Cerevoda.[19] The attack opened on 15 May and was all over in three days.

By removing the salient, the Allied line was shortened by 40 kilometres, the average depth of the terrain gained was 10 kilometres, and casualties were minimal. The advance encompassed the mountain range of Ostravitsa, around 20 kilometres west of Koritsa, control of which was considered by Guillaumat as essential for the protection of lines of communication with the Italian XVI Corps.[20]

The whole exercise was a model of Franco–Italian cooperation perhaps unmatched until the completion of the Mont Blanc tunnel in 1962. On June 10, in fact the day after Guillaumat's departure, the French launched another attack on the Austrians in Albania, this time between the Devoli and the upper Skumbi. The main objective was Mount Kamia, 2,150 metres, captured after five days of intensive fighting. Over 400 prisoners were taken and ten guns. French casualties were less than fifty.[21] In July French and Italian forces were to combine in another joint operation, pushing the Austrians yet further back. Besides perhaps helping to advance Italy's post-war Albanian ambitions, these well-conceived and well planned actions, with limited forces and few losses, also served to reduce any serious possibility of Austrian intervention when the Allied Army of the East made its final breakthrough into Serbia in September.

Meantime, Guillaumat had been working on his longer term objective of an offensive in the Vardar–Doiran sector. He came to the conclusion that an essential preliminary to this was the elimination of a Bulgarian position ten kilometres to the west of the Vardar known as Skra di Legen.[22] This was a two kilometre long rocky escarpment, 1,000 metres high with a virtually sheer southern face. It represented a minor salient into Allied territory and was in fact on the Greek side of the border. From this position enfilade fire could be brought to bear covering the Epernon, a ridge to the west fronting two kilometres of open ground, and, critically, for several kilometres to the east, threatening any Allied advance over the hills on the right bank of the Vardar.

For the Bulgarians it was key to the control and defence of a twelve kilometre length of their front line. It was heavily fortified with shelters, dug outs and gun emplacements rising up from the face of the cliffs, and resembled on a smaller scale the rocky approaches to the Grand Couronné on the other side of the Vardar. From the Allied side of the line, wheeled transport could only reach Skra di Legen by a winding track from the Gumendje station on the Vardar railway climbing over

---

19 Villari, *Macedonian Campaign*, p.202.
20 Armées Françaises, *Tome VIII Vol. 3*, pp.50–64, Lepetit, p.10.
21 Villari, *Macedonian Campaign*, p.203.
22 Hall, *Balkan Breakthrough*, whose history of the Macedonian campaign is mainly from the Bulgarian viewpoint, calls this feature Yerbichna, presumably the Bulgarian name. p.114.

two mountain passes to the village of Ljumnitsa.²³ In this particular sector the Bulgarians were provided with better access roads from their side. In addition to the tactical advantage of removing this dangerous enemy salient, Guillaumat could well have reasoned that this was an excellent target by virtue of its inaccessibility; the Bulgarians could scarcely have expected an Allied attack here.

For his attack on the Bulgarian positions of Skra di Legen, and the associated spurs and ridges to both side of it, Guillaumat selected an all-Greek force, consisting of two brigades of the Archipelago Division, and one brigade each from the Seres and Crete Divisions. A French brigade was to be held in reserve for consolidation purpose. Although the three divisions of the National Defence Army had been part of the Allied force for over a year they had never been involved in any action remotely approaching the scale of this one. All four brigades were withdrawn from the line in early April to undergo intensive training. Although risky, Guillaumat's decision was enlightened. Failure would not result in a collapse of the Allied front, whereas success would have an effect well beyond the immediate military advantage.

The track to Ljumnitsa was surreptitiously upgraded by French engineers. Significant numbers of French and British guns were dragged up mostly by night, to Ljumnitsa, including the British 8-inch howitzer battery. British heavy batteries at Smol on the other side of the Vardar were also to contribute.²⁴

Increased air reconnaissance and artillery action in the second half of May convinced the Bulgarians that an attack, somewhere along the line, was in the offing, but the Allies kept them guessing till the last moment. The British pounded the Doiran defences and further confused the enemy with raids and incursions until 28 May. (Had the Bulgarians been listening carefully they could have guessed from the absence of the 8-inch howitzer battery that the real attack was not to take place at Doiran). Simultaneously the Serbs and the French 122nd Division opened up on their fronts to either side of Skra di Legen.²⁵

The assault was launched at 0500 on the morning of 30 May. The Greeks advanced under the protection of a creeping artillery barrage and within an hour they had scaled and taken the Skra as well as the further objective of the Piton Dénudé 800 metres behind it. Within the same timescale elements of Archipelago Division had crossed the two kilometres of open ground to the Greek left to take the Epernon position. So complete was the surprise that many of the gun emplacements were found to be untenanted. On the Greek right flank the Cretan brigade secured the ridge between the two branches of the Ljumnitsa river by early afternoon. All objectives had been achieved. The Greeks and their leader General Iannou had fought a hard, swift and well planned action with courage and tenacity. The expected Bulgarian counter-attacks in the afternoon and during the night were repulsed.²⁶

The Bulgarians had not suffered such a set-back since the fall of Monastir. Bulgarian and German prisoners taken, including wounded, were around 2,500. Fifty machine guns and fifty trench mortars were taken, and 800 dead were left on the battlefield.²⁷ The whole of one Bulgarian regiment, the 49th, was eliminated.²⁸ Allied losses, almost entirely Greek, were of the order of 600 killed and 2,000 wounded.²⁹

---

23   Palmer, *Gardeners*, p.176.
24   Villari, *Macedonian Campaign*, p.196.
25   Armées Françaises, *Tome VIII Vol. 3*, p.43.
26   Armées Françaises, *Tome VIII Vol. 3*, p.43.
27   Falls, *Macedonia Vol. 2*, p.90, quoting Emile Bujac, *Les Campagnes de l'Armée Hellenique* (Paris : Ch. Lavauzelle, 1930), p.57.
28   Palmer, *Gardeners*, p.177.
29   The sources give varied information. '5-600 dead and wounded' Villari. '500 dead' Palmer. '600 dead, 1,700 wounded' Col Feyler, *La Campagne de Macédonie'* quoted by Hall. Armées Françaises give Greek losses at 2,500, French losses at 150. Falls gives total casualties of 2,795, Grey and Argyle 2,659,

Their job done, Guillaumat withdrew the Greeks and replaced them with more experienced French troops to hold and secure the line. But there was no doubt to whom the victory belonged. 'The success of Skra was a veritable revelation' records Larcher, not normally given to hyperbole. 'It opened the eyes of the Allies to two facts of which they should not have been unaware; the diminution of Bulgaria's powers of resistance, and the value of the Greek troops. Against the demoralised and hungry Bulgarians the new Greek formations gave proof of their training, discipline and dynamism.'[30]

Skra di Legen proved a number of things: the Bulgarians could be outwitted, their defences were not impermeable, meticulous planning could be rewarded with success (the mind is drawn back to the shambles of Sarrail's 1917 campaign). The coordination between artillery support and infantry movement had been of copy-book standard.

But by far the most important feature of Skra di Legen was that the victors had been Greek. Guillaumat and Venizelos played this for all it was worth, which was a great deal. Suddenly all of Greece was behind the war; a traditional enemy backed and supported by the greatest military power in Europe had been vanquished by Greek forces. Minds harked back to the victories against Bulgaria in the Second Balkan War. A new impetus was given to the formation of the new Greek divisions.

But this was not only a turning point for Greece, it breathed life into the whole Macedonian campaign. Bulgarian morale had been very severely dented. The Germans may have regretting withdrawing almost all of their troops but could now do very little about it. Above all the victory at Skra di Legen suddenly put the inactive Serbs on their mettle. It was in many ways the launch pad for the final allied breakthrough later in the year.

On 1 March in his overall proposal to Clemenceau for offensive action on the Macedonian Front, Guillaumat had proposed a number of options and come down in favour of a two-pronged attack, up the valleys of respectively the Vardar and the Struma. On 14 April in a further report to the French War Ministry he updated his original concept by dropping the attack up the Struma and concentrating on the Vardar–Doiran front. Insufficient artillery was quoted as a reason for this. The Vardar–Doiran attack would be undertaken by two Greek Divisions and three French brigades on the west side of the Vardar, and five British brigades on the east side with, as primary objective, the salient of Machukovo.

But in the short period between mid-April and June much had changed. The force under Guillaumat now outnumbered the enemy facing him by about 3:2.[31] Superiority in the air had been achieved. Most of the German forces who had served to stiffen the Bulgarian army had been withdrawn to France. Bulgarian morale was reported to be at a low ebb. The Greek First Royal Corps had now been brought into line and was twitching its fingers facing the Bulgarian and Turkish enemy who were occupying Greek Eastern Macedonia. The Greek Second Royal Corps was well on its way and would become operational in August–September The Joint Italian–French action in Albania had pushed the Austrians with relative ease beyond any possibility of threatening the Allied right flank.

But above all the victory at Skra di Legen had re-invigorated the whole Allied army and convinced its Commander that the moment was ripe for a much broader offensive that that proposed on 14 April. He revised his plans. To supplement the attack on the Vardar–Doiran front he reinstated a push across the Struma by the Greek First Corps directed at Seres and Kavalla, and further,

---

    figures of great precision, which seem high for such a short action with only 4 brigades engaged. The slaughter on the second night of the first battle of Doiran resulted in casualties of around a thousand less than this.
30 Larcher, *Grande Guerre*, p.225.
31 Larcher, *Grande Guerre*, p.225.

envisaged bringing the Serbs into action over their mountain front. These three offensives, Vardar–Doiran Struma and Moglena were to be *échelonnées*, or undertaken in staged progression to allow best use of transport, air cover and artillery

This ambitious programme developed by Guillaumat was not actually presented to the French War Ministry until 13 June, five days after his departure from the Macedonian theatre, but it then formed the basis for the instructions given to his successor on 23 June.[32]

On 6 June Guillaumat received a telegram from Clemenceau calling him back with extreme urgency to Paris. He was to leave as quickly and discreetly as possible, handing over in the interim to General Henrys.[33]

Guillaumat was being recalled, officially, to become Military Governor of Paris. On 27 May the Germans had broken through on the Aisne and advanced twenty kilometres.[34] They were now threatening the road to Paris. Guillaumat was no doubt seen as a rising star as well as a safe pair of hands in these dark days. Clemenceau's purposes in repatriating Guillaumat probably went deeper than this. He may well have been providing himself with immediate and competent cover should anything happen to Foch or Pétain.[35] Or, should Pétain have faltered in his current task, he may have been keeping an accomplished and acceptable alternative up his sleeve to present to Parliament if they called for Pétain's removal. It is unlikely that this possibility for his recall had not crossed Guillaumat's mind.[36] Indeed Milne reported to his diary on 8 June 'Guillaumat tells me he is off to France. Seems to have all the luck … Don't know if he is pleased or not. Thinks he might replace Pétain or Foch.'[37] But Pétain kept his job, allowing Guillaumat, as it turned out, the opportunity and time to give massive support from Headquarters for the Macedonian project over the next few critical months.[38]

He left Salonica on 9 June, and arrived in Paris on 12 June, passing his successor like ships in the night. On this occasion there was no time or opportunity for a man-to-man exchange, cordial or otherwise, as had been the case between Sarrail and Guillaumat.[39]

Guillaumat had been Commander in chief of the Allied Army of the East for less than six months. He had amply fulfilled the objectives set for him by Foch and Clemenceau at the start of his mandate. In early 1918 he had strengthened, renewed and created defensive structures and communications to protect his forces against eventual enemy offensives in early 1918, and articulated a Plan of Defence for operation along the whole length of his extended line.

He had brought the Nationalist Greek divisions to the field as a fighting force far faster than anyone had thought possible and given them pride of place in his cornerstone offensive action. The First Royalist Corps of the Greek Army, with the aid of the French Military Mission was coming on stream in record time. He had collaborated productively with the Italian XVI corps at Valona, both strategically and militarily. He had lost no time in disbanding the tainted and now ineffective Russian division, and by so doing had removed the risk of it spreading discordance within the Serbian army.

He had developed excellent relationships with the BSF and made good contacts with the Italian division under his control, while preventing it from moving further west, and thereby partly out of his control. His holistic approach to the structuring of the Allied Army, however, had gone down

---

32 Lepetit, *Genèse de l'Offensive*, p.12. quoting Instruction from War Minister to Franchet d'Espèrey of 23 June 1918.
33 Schiavon, *Front d'Orient*, p.309.
34 Gilbert, *First World War*, p.425.
35 Falls, *Macedonia Vol. 2*, p.101.
36 Schiavon, *Front d'Orient*, p.309.
37 Nicol, *Uncle George*, p.166.
38 Palmer, *Gardeners,* p.178.
39 Larcher, *Grande Guerre*, p.225.

less well with the Serbs, and he found it difficult to understand their obsession with retaining an integrated force. A demand on Bojović on 11 April for example to move one of his divisions to the general reserve had met with a blank refusal on 16 April.[40]

He had re-organised the staffs of the *Armée Française de l'Orient* and of the Allied Army of the East. As instructed he had completed his audit of the resources, human and material, at his disposal, and had reorganized the staffs of the AFO and of the whole Allied Army. The French divisions under his command had been brought back to establishment. Welcome reinforcements to the Serbian Army had been received, enabling him to establish more cordial relationships with the Serbian High Command. He had set up training centres and procedures for the French forces and encouraged the commanders of the other national armies to do the same. Above all he had created an air of purposeful optimism.

The forces under his command learnt of his departure with disappointment if not dismay. Milne's valediction is unreservedly complimentary. 'During his short period of command', he wrote in his annual report, 'General Guillaumat had gained, by his tact, courtesy and soldierly qualities, the respect and admiration of all those with whom he came into contact, and I am deeply grateful to him for his cordial and sympathetic assistance.'[41] He was to be replaced by General Franchet d'Espèrey.

---

40 Cordier, *Victoire Eclair*, p.15.
41 Milne, *Despatch of 1918*, p.3.

31

1918
Franchet d'Espèrey Picks up the Reins

General Louis Franchet d'Espèrey was seven years older than Guillaumat. Their careers however had followed similar patterns, both were from army families, both had graduated from St Cyr, both had served many years in North Africa and Indochina; both had fought in the Boxer uprising. Both therefore had spent more of their formative years in operational rather than staff roles before returning to St Cyr as instructors.

Unlike Guillaumat and indeed most of his contemporaries, Franchet d'Espèrey was also widely travelled in Europe and his military horizons were not limited to Germany. Prior to the First World War he travelled extensively in Austro-Hungary, even meeting the Austrian Head of Staff Conrad von Hoetzendorf. He visited select Napoleonic battlefields.[1] Above all he had made lengthy visits to the Balkans, much of it still under Ottoman control, and mentions this in the short but excellent Preface he wrote to Commandant Larcher's *La Grande Guerre dans les Balkans*.[2] Between 1908 and 1910 he visited Bosnia, Croatia, Serbia, Montenegro and Greece.[3] He may have become aware of the tensions between the Turks and the emergent Balkan nations, but politics was not his major suit; he would have been more interested in assessing the military possibilities of the terrain.

Following the success of his Fifth Army at the First Battle of the Marne in September 1914 his fertile mind returned to the Balkans. Together with Colonel de Lardemelle, his Chief of Staff, he had developed a detailed plan for attacking the Central Powers from the south, through Serbia, which was then still intact. He presented this plan first to President Poincaré and then to Joffre in November. However, the moment had passed, the Allies were then on the defensive in France, and, effectively, Franchet d'Espèrey's proposal was overtaken by the Gallipoli campaign.

His star continued to rise on the Western Front. It can be assumed that he kept himself up to date with the progress of the Allied Army of the East, but when offered Sarrail's job at the end of 1917 he turned it down. By this time the situation in Macedonia was so far at odds with the premises on which his original plan had been based that he probably thought of it as a demotion – and was at that time in a sufficiently strong position to say so.

By June 1918 this was no longer the case. His Army Group North had not acquitted itself well during the major attack launched by the Germans on 27 May. A scapegoat had to be found, and Clemenceau decided at this critical moment that neither Foch nor Pétain could fulfil this role.

On 6 June Franchet d'Espèrey was told to relinquish his command and go to Salonica to replace Guillaumat. The following morning he had a curious interview with Clemenceau who explained his reasons and told him he was being '*Limogé*', code for being retired, although in his particular case Limoges was Salonica.[4] He left Paris on 11 June.

---

1   Palmer, *Gardeners*, pp.21–22.
2   Larcher, *Grande Guerre*, pp.8–9.
3   Schiavon, *Front d'Orient*, p.312.
4   Paul Azan, *Franchet d'Espèrey* (Paris: Flammarion, 1949), p.176.

As he travelled to Salonica he may have been consoled by two thoughts. Firstly that the considerable distance from the War's epicentre would make his command a more independent one. And secondly that he might in this new environment find opportunities to indulge his natural preference for fast-moving rolling offensives, virtually impossible on the battlefields of France.

His predecessor Guillaumat on his appointment to Macedonia in December 1917 had been given a list of well thought-out instructions and relevant guidelines. Franchet d'Espèrey arrived with nothing like this. His biographer General Azan maintains that 'the Commander of the Allied Army of the East left knowing nothing of the treaties and agreements concluded with the Balkan powers, and without any more extensive military directives than a colonel taking command of a regiment.'[5]

As has been seen, Guillaumat's ambitious programme for a 'staged' (*échelonné*) series of offensives concentrating on the Vardar corridor but also involving a thrust into Eastern Macedonia and action by the Serbs on their mountain front had been presented to the French War Office in the form of 'notes' on his return to Paris on 13 June. His notes were transformed by French army staffs into a formal set of instructions to Franchet d'Espèrey dated 23 June. These incorporated other elements clearly at Guillaumat's dictation, stressing that the strength of the Allied Army of the East had now reached a high-water mark in men and materials, while the morale of the Bulgarian Army, now deprived almost entirely of German support was at its lowest ebb since the onset of the conflict.[6]

On 12 June the Bulgarian Chief of Staff Zhekov had written to Tsar Ferdinand; 'Today it is impossible to have any illusions that the spirit of the soldiers is the same as at the beginning of the war, or even of last year.' Both the Bulgarian troops and the civilian population were very short of food, a situation exacerbated by poor harvests in 1917 and 1918. At the end of 1917 rationing was introduced. Army officers reported that their soldiers lacked boots. Basic supplies from clothing to medicine were lacking, There was widespread resentment over German domination of the economy and their attribution of half of the conquered Dobrujah to the Turks.[7]

From this point no decisions were made by French staffs or government relating to the Macedonian Front without Guillaumat being consulted, and his forceful advocacy over the next three months was decisive in securing the agreement of the Supreme War Council for the final major offensive in Macedonia.[8]

Compared with the taut and numbered instructions given by Clemenceau to Guillaumat six months earlier, the *Instructions du Gouvernement Français au 23 juin 1918 pour les Armées de l'Orient* (agreed between Clemenceau and Foch the day before) read more like a manifesto. The points about the Allied strengths and the enemy weaknesses are stressed again:

> *L'état matériel et moral des Armées Alliées n'a jamais été meilleur. L'armée bulgare abandonné par les allemands souffre d'une crise morale manifeste qui diminue sa capacité de résistance* (The material condition of the Allied Army and its morale has never been better. The Bulgarian army abandoned by the Germans is suffering from a clear moral crisis which reduces their capacity to resist).

In this light the aim of the Allied Army of the East should be to:

> *rompre le système de défense Bulgare afin d'obliger l'ennemi à un recul important susceptible d'ouvrir aux armes Serbes et Grecques l'accès du territoire perdu* (break through the Bulgarian defences in

---

5   Azan, *Franchet d'Espèrey*, p.177.
6   Lepetit, *Genèse de l'Offensive*, p.13.
7   Hall, *Balkan Breakthrough*, pp.100–108.
8   Falls, *Macedonia Vol. 2*, p 102, Lepetit, *Genèse de l'Offensive*, p.27, Palmer, *Gardners*, p.189

order to force them to make a significant withdrawal, giving the Serbs and Greeks access to their lost territories).⁹

Also carried over from Guillaumat's notes was the caveat that although 'all the forces forming part of the Allied Army of the East should be involved' insufficient artillery and air cover was available for a general attack on all fronts, and that the offensive actions should follow each other in succession. Account should also be taken of the climate: *La saison chaude s'oppose au développement d'opérations importantes dans les régions impaludées des bases plaines et des vallées*. (Major operations should not be taken in the summer season in the malarial plains and valleys).

In summary Franchet d'Espèrey is told that in the short term he should build on the base provided by the recent successes in Albania and at Skra di Legen, and to disrupt the enemy with actions of increasing intensity, which should make possible the launch of a general offensive before the autumn from which major results would be expected.¹⁰

This document was sent by hand of Commandant Enaux, liaison officer, on 24 June, but on 22 June Clemenceau had already informed Franchet d'Espèrey of its imminent arrival and enjoined him to proceed with the implementation of the plans established by General Guillaumat before his departure.¹¹

So it was that while Guillaumat's joining instructions six months earlier had been almost exclusively of a defensive nature, Franchet d'Espèrey was ordered immediately to go on the offensive. He needed little persuasion, and by the time Enaux arrived on 2 July with the written instructions he had already reviewed the situation on the ground and decided on the form and location of the offensive he wanted to launch. Sadly this account of the irrepressible momentum built up by Guillaumat for further exploitation by his successor must be broken off at this point.

* * *

The agreements taken at Doullens and Abbeville on 25–26 March 1918 had made Foch supreme commander on the Western and Adriatic Fronts. The Allied Army of the East however did not come under his orders but reported to the Supreme War Council. Lloyd George had not been consulted on the withdrawal of Guillaumat and the nomination of Franchet d'Espèrey in his place, and naturally enough was very displeased when he heard.¹² The next meeting of the SWC was set for 2 July in Versailles, as it happened the same day that commandant Enaux arrived in Salonica with Franchet d'Espèrey's written instructions. To rub further salt into the wound, Clemenceau had not circulated copies of his instructions to Franchet d'Espèrey until two days before this meeting of the SWC.¹³ And on this occasion, the British Chiefs of Staff were not forewarned by Milne because he had not been informed either. Franchet d'Espèrey's management style was different from that of Guillaumat.

In presenting this *fait accompli* Clemenceau (certainly under the tutelage of Guillaumat), correctly predicting that the British would try to apply the brakes, was above all concerned with losing no time in preparing an autumn offensive. It was already end June. But, despite the fact that the British Salonica Force now only amounted to four divisions – recently reduced to nine battalions each - out

---

9 Larcher, *Grande Guerre*, Annexe 18 p.283. Instruction from War Minister to Franchet d'Espèrey of 23 June 1918.
10 Lepetit, *Genèse de l'Offensive*, pp.14–15, Larcher, *Grande Guerre*, Annexe 18, p.283.
11 Lepetit, *Genèse de l'Offensive*, p.16 quoting a telegram from War Ministry to Franchet d'Espèrey of 22 June.
12 Schiavon, *Front d'Orient*, p.313.
13 Falls, *Macedonia Vol. 2*, p.104.

of a total of twenty five allied divisions on the Macedonian Front, and that the Greeks and Serbs who together accounted for twelve divisions were not represented at all, the British position on the SWC was so strong that effectively Lloyd George wielded a veto. He pointed out at the July 2 meeting that at the SWC in December a defensive posture in Macedonia had been agreed, and that was still his position.

Clemenceau, making great play of all his previous Salonica-sceptic credentials – he had indeed at one stage proposed the recall of all troops in this theatre – convinced Lloyd George that no action was intended which would weaken in any way the overall Allied position.[14] He further pointed out that the minutes of the December SWC, reporting Guillaumat's instructions, contained as an objective 'to study ... the possibilities of an offensive to be undertaken to best further the interests of the Allies against the armies of the enemy, as the occasion arose.[15] The occasion, Clemenceau contended, had now arisen.

Inevitably the matter was referred to a sub-committee of the military and political representatives on the SWC. One can wholly sympathise with Larcher's view that:

Le théâtre de l'Orient ne bénéficiant pas du commandement unique, une offensive allait être étudiée, plaidée, combattue et jugée au cours d'une longue procédure, comme un procès entre parties averses, dans une confusion inextricable de la direction politique et de la direction militaire (Since all the benefits of a central command had not been extended to Macedonia, the proposal for an autumn offensive on this front was now to be studied, discussed, fought over and judged over a long period, as if by two opposing parties, with conflicting political and military interests creating total confusion).[16]

The military and political representatives of the SWC duly met a week later, on 11 July. Eight delegates, one military and one political from each of the four members of the SWC (France, Britain, Italy, United States) were convened under the chairmanship of the French Foreign Minister, Stephen Pichon. General Guillaumat, whose new responsibilities as Military Governor of Paris were not at that moment involving him on a full-time basis, was also present in a consultative capacity.

On the 'political' side the British Foreign Office position, advanced by Lord David Cecil, Minister for the Blockade, was that rather than mounting an offensive against Bulgaria, efforts should be made to detach them from the Central Powers by explaining to Tsar Ferdinand that this would be in his best interests, and by offering territorial recompense.[17] Sadly, it seemed, Foreign Office understanding of the Balkan situation had remained in a time capsule since 1915 and the days of Grey. Bulgaria was now facing a united alliance, two members of which, Greece and Serbia, far from being disposed to cede territory to the Bulgarians were on an active war footing as members of the Allied Army of the East to regain what they had lost to them. Perhaps Lord David Cecil's intention was to reward the repentant Bulgarians with the Dobrujah, to be taken after the war from allied Romania, or with Constantinople after Turkey had been conquered.

Pichon pointed out that the Bulgarians would only use such an approach as a means of extorting concessions from the Germans, greater military support in the immediate, and greater post-war territorial promises – just as they had during the 1915 negotiations.[18]

---

14 Palmer, *Gardeners*, p.189.
15 Lepetit, *Genèse de l'Offensive*, p.20.
16 Larcher, *Grande Guerre*, pp.226–227.
17 Larcher, *Grande Guerre*, p.227.
18 Lepetit, *Genèse de l'Offensive*, p.22.

Fortunately sounder counsels prevailed, and, after the intervention of Guillaumat, the recorded 'political' conclusions of the meeting were that:

- there was a case for studying an offensive in the Balkans in view of the effects it could have on the Bulgarian situation and
- that such an offensive would only be justified if it led to a victory of more than local importance.

This second conclusion, put in apparently on British insistence, turned out to be in tune with the thoughts of Franchet d'Espèrey, already crystallising around achieving one major breakthrough rather than the general programme of staged offensives favoured by Guillaumat.[19]

When the Council sub-committee turned to the 'military' part of the agenda, Guillaumat's input was decisive. He stressed again the strength and readiness of the Allied Army compared with the weakened and demoralized Bulgarian forces, pointed out that the Germans were for the next three months anyway in no position to provide reinforcements, and explained that the Serbs and Greeks in particular were straining at the leash, and that public opinion in Greece demanded the action promised by Venizelos after Greece had finally swung behind the Entente. If no offensive were mounted in 1918, these key forces could well fade away.

Despite this, the football was kicked further down the road. The 'military' conclusions of the meeting were that the military representatives should 'examine the conditions of a general offensive with a view to its probable results', and that the French Government would provide the military representatives with 'complete information on the projected general offensive as well as the method of execution.'[20]

Four days later on 15 July and following on from these resolutions, General Sackville-West, the British military representative on the SWC submitted a list of eleven questions to the French. These covered the proposed plan of attack, objectives, forces to be employed, estimated casualties, reasons for believing that the Bulgarians could be beaten, transport, communication and equipment requirements, timing etc. The list of questions was passed, inevitably, to Guillaumat to answer.[21] His reply four days later repeated much of the information provided at the previous meeting and in general could act as a template for the exposition and demolition by a field operator of the fatuities of central staffs. It was interesting however in revealing that Guillaumat considered Franchet d'Espèrey still to be following the lines of his own 'staged' offensive plan of 11 June, which was not at all the case.

Guillaumat also replied at the same time to questions put to him by General Bliss, the American military representative on the SWC. The Americans of course had no operational involvement in the Macedonian campaign and were not even at war with Bulgaria. General Bliss' intervention may be seen as a classical example of someone who having been given a job, feels a necessity to do something to fill the space.

Bliss also thought it would be useful to consult Milne. As it happened it was, in the sense that from his reply to Bliss on 22 July – more than a month after Franchet d'Espèrey had arrived in Salonica – it was clear that Milne was also still under the impression that his new Commander in Chief was following the guidelines put down by his previous one. Milne even took the opportunity to disagree with Guillaumat's 'staged' plan. He said he was as convinced as ever that if the Bulgarian line were turned or broken their forces would begin to disintegrate. 'In my opinion an offensive here at the psychological moment may have more than local effect and should be planned

---

19 Palmer, *Gardeners*, p.190.
20 Lepetit, *Genèse de l'Offensive*, p.37.
21 Falls, *Macedonia Vol. 2*, pp.106–107.

for.'²² Milne copied his reply to the War Office.²³ He re-states his preference for an action at the mouth of the Struma by his forces rather than the Doiran front where he considered that the enemy's forces outnumbered his.

None of this was perturbing Franchet d'Espèrey who, having decided where and how his offensive was to be launched was working with demoniac speed and application to put everything in place for mid-September.

As early as 29 June Franchet d'Espèrey had decided on a strategy which dispensed with the 'staged' approach and went straight for the major breakthrough, not up the Vardar corridor at all, but over the Dobropolje in the central Moglena mountains. His plan was at the most a complete re-write of the one inherited from Guillaumat, or, at the very least, a fundamental change of emphasis.

Although preceded by Clemenceau's telegram of 22 June, the letter containing Franchet d'Espèrey's joining instructions had not reached him until 2 July. But by then he had already moved on from his strategic concept, had the main structure of his revised offensive clearly in mind, and was moving on to its definition and documentation. As early as 7 July he was sending Mišić, the Serbian Chief of Staff, not only a complete statement of the objectives of the offensive, but also a detailed plan for their execution.²⁴

It was only on 13 July that he sent the French War Office a formal reply to the instructions he had received on 2 July. In it he explained in general terms how he intended to meet the objective he had been given of exploiting the Bulgarian weaknesses to achieve a breakthrough of their defences. His letter did not reach Paris until 22 July.²⁵ This formality dealt with, Franchet d'Espèrey continued with the detailed planning for his offensive, which included ensuring that the national armies under his command were ready and equipped to play the parts he envisaged for them within the planned timescale.

Working on an obviously need-to-know basis he issued instructions to his subordinate commanders on a staggered basis. General Henrys, Commander of AFO on 26 July, General Anselme, Commander of the First Group of Divisions on 6 August, Voivode Mišić (these in the form of confirmation) also on 6 August, and General Danglis, Commander in Chief of the Greek Army only on 27 August. Milne had received his on 24 July, only two days after he had replied to Bliss.²⁶

Only at this point was Milne informed of the part the BSF was to play in the campaign being developed by Franchet D'Espèrey.²⁷ But that was as far as it went. His instructions contain no description of the overall strategy. There is however a reference to 'the general action, the broad lines of which I have explained to you verbally.'

On 25 July Milne sent a telegram to the War Office saying that he had received instructions from Franchet d'Espèrey 'to make preparations for a serious offensive with my force in the second half of September.' He expresses himself to be in favour of this offensive 'Taking all things into consideration it seems sound and right that we in this theatre should be prepared to take advantage of the situation which might present itself this autumn.' But he also makes it clear that 'This action on the part of my force will be likely to be successful only if you are prepared to bring us up to fighting

---

22 Palmer, *Gardeners*, p.191.
23 Birch, *No Sideshow*, p.186.
24 Cordier, *Victoire Éclair*, Annexe 2 p.261. Franchet d'Espèrey's Plan for the Final Offensive of 7 July 1918.
25 Lepetit, *Genèse de l'Offensive*, p.30, quoting letter from Franchet d'Espèrey to the War Minister 13 juillet 1918 (arrived 22 July).
26 Lepetit, *Genèse de l'Offensive*, p.40.
27 Falls, *Macedonia Vol. 2*, Appendix 7 p.323. Instruction from Franchet d'Espèrey to Milne of 24 July

pitch by sending the necessary reinforcements and ammunition by the date mentioned.'[28] The cat had once more been unleashed amongst the pigeons.

Sir Henry Wilson following his elevation to the role of CIGS in February was no longer a member of the SWC. He had not thus been party to their discussions during the month of July and in particular to the persuasive interventions of Guillaumat, and was still working on another plane. On the very day he received Milne's telegram he had prepared a paper for the War Cabinet declaring that 'I am adverse to undertaking an offensive in the Balkans, and recommend that we economise British troops to the utmost by the gradual substitution of Indian troops …'[29]

In his almost totally negative response to Milne on 27 July he maintains that an autumn offensive would be dangerous because the Germans would be able to reinforce the Bulgars (a view which seems to cut across all current thinking on the matter), and that it would be better to wait until spring before the onset of the malarial season.[30]

Querulous messages were then exchanged between the British and French war offices, leading to another meeting – supposedly the last on this subject – of the military representatives on the SWC in Versailles on 4 August. The two conclusions of the meeting were as follows:

- *Qu'il y a lieu de pousser activement les préparatifs d'une offensive en Macédoine sur les bases prévues, afin de mettre les armées alliées d'Orient en état de passer à l'exécution, au moins à partir du 1er octobre 1918* (That there is a need to press on actively with preparations for an offensive in Macedonia along the lines foreseen, in order to enable the Allied Army of the East to proceed to the execution of the offensive no later than 1 October 1918).
- *Qu'il convient en principe de laisser le général commandant en chef des armées alliées d'Orient libre de réaliser cette offensive au moment qu'il jugera le plus favorable, à moins que des circonstances nouvelles et imprévues n'imposent au conseil supérieur de guerre d'en fixer lui-même l'époque ou d'y renoncer complètement* (That it is appropriate, in general, to leave the Commander of the Allied Army of the East free to launch this offensive at the moment which seems to him most suitable, as long as new and unforeseen circumstances do not oblige the SWC itself to decide on the timing, or to call it off completely).[31]

The American representative, General Bliss, although arguably he should have had no voice on Macedonian matters, insisted on adding a condition that these preparations should in no way divert men, materials or shipping required for the execution of plans for the Western Front. Otherwise, except in the case of unexpected developments, Franchet d'Espèrey had the SWC's authority to proceed with his offensive.

Having been persuaded by his colleagues to sign up to this, the British military representative on the SWC, General Sackville-West justified his deviation from the British party line firstly by reporting that Foch was in favour, there was no conflict with his actions on other fronts, indeed it supported his plans. Secondly that he had been given to understand that the offensive was essential to preserving the support, even the continued existence, of the Greek Army, and thirdly that since Milne would get no reinforcements (as a result also of the Bliss condition), the 'deficiencies would limit the scope of his operations.'[32] It is to be hoped that he did not appreciate the consequences of

---

28 Falls, *Macedonia Vol. 2*, Appendix 8 p.325. Telegram from Milne to the War Office 25 July.
29 Falls, *Macedonia Vol. 2*, p.109.
30 Nicol, *Uncle George*, p.168.
31 Lepetit, *Genèse de l'Offensive*, p.24, quoting from report of the military representatives of the SWC, Versailles 3 August.
32 Falls, *Macedonia Vol. 2*, p.111.

this absurd logic, or his conscience would have been mightily troubled by the casualty list following the Second Battle of Doiran.

Franchet d'Espèrey continued unremittingly with his plans for a make-or-break offensive starting on 14 September. By 1 September along the whole of the Macedonian Front all components of the Allied Army of the East had received their full instructions, were in place, and were ready to play their part in by far the biggest action yet undertaken in this theatre.

But even at this late stage Guillaumat was obliged to rush to London on 4 September to secure agreement for the launch of the offensive from France's reluctant ally. Once again he gave a convincing presentation, and Lloyd George duly gave his consent to an Allied offensive in which his own troops were severely handicapped through deficiencies of men and equipment, although probably this was not explained to him.

To ensure that all angles were covered Guillaumat then went to Rome on 7 September where the Italian government also gave him their agreement to proceed.[33] Thus it was that on 10 September, only four days before the day planned for the launch of the offensive, Clemenceau was finally able to give Franchet d'Espèrey the go-ahead:

> *D'accord avec gouvernement Britannique, je reçois ce matin l'agrément du gouvernement Italien. Vous êtes en conséquence autorisé à commencer les opérations quand vous le jugez convenable* (The British Government agrees. This morning I have received the agreement of the Italian Government. You are therefore authorized to begin operations when you consider best). [34]

Franchet d'Espèrey noted in his diary for 10 September 'I have Clemenceau's agreement to commence operations when I consider it suitable. Artillery fire to start on 14 September. *Jour J* 15 September.'[35]

It was less than three months since he had arrived in Salonica. In that time he had covered the ground, fixed his objective, and worked relentlessly to have all his forces in battle-readiness for 15 September. He had played little part in the political games being played around him, leaving this to the French Foreign and War offices, and particularly to Guillaumat. Fortunately they won their battle just in time for him to open his.

---

33 Villari, *Macedonian Campaign*, p.212.
34 Lepetit, *Genèse de l'Offensive*, p.28, quoting telegram from War Minister to Franchet d'Espèrey, 10 September.
35 Palmer, *Gardeners*, p.196.

32

1918
Final Offensive: Decisions and Preparations

(Map 11)

General Franchet d'Espèrey had arrived in Salonica on 18 June 1918. Nearly three years had elapsed since the arrival of the Allies in Macedonia. During this time advances against the enemy had been minimal, despite a progressive increase in resources and personnel allocated to this theatre and the arrival of new national components within the Allied Army of the East. Some territory had been gained west of the Vardar; Monastir, the Crna bend, at the western end of the Moglena mountain range and at Skra di Legen. In conjuction with the Italian XVI Corps in Valona the allied line west of Lake Ohrid had been pushed somewhat further north. Greece's Eastern Macedonia province had been overrun by the Bulgarians. Some of it had been clawed back by the BSF during the campaigning season and then largely relinquished during the malarial summer. The necessary removal of the pro-German King of Greece had taken almost two years of poorly coordinated diplomatic, military and naval effort. Plans, offensive and defensive had been made, modified, or overtaken by events. Despite the limited military achievements, casualties had mounted, and malaria had taken a dreadful toll, particularly but not only in the British sector. From beginning to end the British and French Governments and Central Staffs had fundamentally disagreed over the purpose and direction of the whole enterprise.

Within two weeks of his arrival however, Franchet d'Espèrey had taken the whole project by the scruff of the neck, identified the centre of the Moglena mountain range as the most vulnerable part of the enemy's defences, and had developed around this a full-blown offensive strategy which bore almost no relation to the directions he had been given. One of the most intriguing questions relating to the whole Macedonian Campaign is, how did he get onto this so quickly?

He had visited the Balkans ten years earlier during his holidays, but at that time they were largely at peace, there were no opposing lines to be broken, and it is unlikely that he gained any first-hand knowledge of the Moglena.[1] These trips may well have provided the stimulus for the paper he had prepared in November 1914 with de Lardemelle proposing an assault on the Central Powers through Serbia, but at that time there would have been no need to enter it across the mountains.

As has been seen, his journey to Salonica crossed with that of Guillaumat; there was no opportunity for a debriefing from his predecessor. It would have been totally in character if between his meeting with Clemenceau on 7 June and his departure from Paris on 11 June he had explored the Campaign archives, but there is no record of this.

Cordier maintains that before he left Paris Franchet d'Espèrey was given by General Alby, Chief of the Army General Staff, a copy of Guillaumat's proposal of 1st March; the one in which he had

---

1   Franchet d'Espèrey's Introduction to Larcher's *La Grande Guerre dans les Balkans, p.8.*

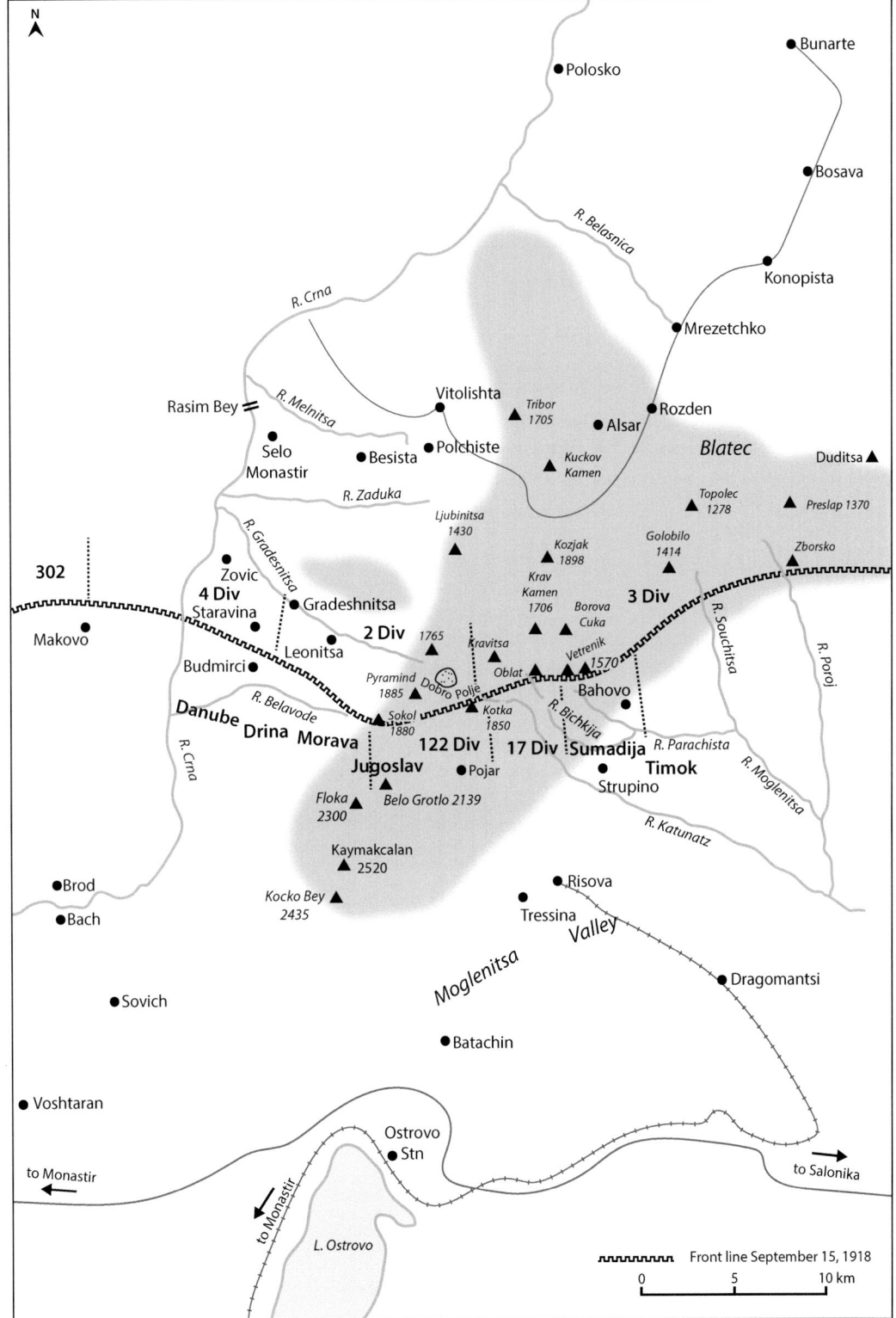

Map 11. Battle of Dobropolje September 1918.

identified three possible areas for offensive action and come down in favour of the Vardar–Doiran sector.² During his week-long journey to Salonica he would have had plenty of time to study this in detail, and perhaps come to some initial conclusions.

But this document was not even Guillaumat's latest proposal – that of 13 June which formed the basis for Franchet d'Espèrey's joining instructions when they finally arrived on 2 July also included a role for the Serbs, but in the most general terms, almost as a throw-away line.³ Neither the proposal of 1 March nor the instructions of 2 July make any mention of the Dobropolje, and neither of them aimed at advancing any further than Prilep, the Strumitsa valley or the Rupel pass.

Guillaumat had left behind him General Henrys, Commander of the French Army of the East, an officer of great competence, as well as General Charpy, head of a completely re-vamped staff. Charpy had been promoted to Lieutenant Colonel by Franchet d'Espèrey during the Battle of the Marne and enjoyed his full confidence.⁴ But neither Henrys nor Charpy was able to offer their new Commander in Chief any plan other than that which had been developed under Guillaumat. *Ce plan* wrote Franchet d'Espèrey in his diary on 22 June, *le seul qui figure dans les archives et le seul qui me fut présenté par mon Chef d'Etat Majeur ne correspondait pas du tout à mes intentions* (This plan, the only one which features in the archives, and the only one which was presented to me by my Chief of Staff, doesn't in any way satisfy my intentions).⁵ The question remains, how could he have developed such clear intentions after only four days on the job? Appropriately enough, this entry was made on the very day he received the advance telegram from Clemenceau enjoining him to proceed according to '*ce plan*'.

Time spent on *rencontres protocolaires* was cut to an absolute minimum. Milne travelled to Salonica on the evening of 18 June to meet the new Commander in Chief shortly after his arrival. 'Seems a smart-looking little man' he noted in his diary. As it happened Milne and the smart-looking little man had already served together at the First Battle of the Marne in 1914, but at rather different management levels; Franchet d'Espèrey as head of the French Fifth Army, Milne as GOC Artillery in the British 4th Division.⁶ During his first few weeks in Macedonia Franchet d'Espèrey paid little attention to the BSF after this '*rencontre protocolaire.*'

On enquiring from Wilson whether Franchet d'Espèrey's arrival 'portends any change of policy in this theatre', Milne was told that it didn't.⁷ Neither of them had any inkling that, in fact, it did until Milne received on 24 July his instructions from Franchet d'Espèrey on the role planned for the BSF in the forthcoming offensive.⁸

While Guillaumat had immediately shared his instructions and objectives with Milne, Franchet d'Espèrey's contacts with the BSF were limited and formal. Even as far back as his proposal to Poincaré and Joffre in 1914, his conviction had been that the thrust into Serbia should be made west of the Vardar and should be made solely by French forces; for him the Struma and Butkovo Fronts were of peripheral importance, and their main function was to hold the Bulgarian Second Army, and parts of its First Army in place.

It was on the same 22 June, the fourth day after his arrival, that he first met Voivode Mišić, now Chief of Staff of the Serbian Army, who was to play the key role in the final offensive and the liberation of Serbia. '*Un homme sérieux et sévère*' he noted approvingly in his diary:

---

2   Cordier, *Victoire Eclair*, p.14.
3   Larcher, *Grande Guerre*, p.284.
4   Cordier, *Victoire Eclair*, p.89.
5   Cordier, *Victoire Eclair*, p.19.
6   Nicol, *Uncle George*, p.66.
7   Nicol, *Uncle George*, p.166.
8   Falls, *Macedonia Vol. 2*, Appendix 7 p.323

Le Voivode Mišić me dit combien les Serbes sont désireux de marcher. Ils sont prêts à faire autant que les Grecs au Skra di Legen, s'ils sont soutenus comme eux par une masse d'artillerie française (Voivode Mišić told me how much the Serbs were keen to advance. They are ready to do as much as the Greeks at Skra di Legen if provided like them with a mass of French artillery).[9]

At this meeting Mišić must also have persuaded him that the Dobropolje was the direct and logical place to effect a complete break-through of the Bulgarian line and strike a killer blow on the Bulgarian HQ and centre of operations at Gradsko on the Vardar. The Serbs had already had a go at this fortified steep sided ridge, falling like a limestone wall into the Moglenitsa plain in May 1917, and had failed for reasons mostly outside their control. But Mišić remained totally convinced that this was the best way back into Serbia.

Two days later Franchet d'Espèrey accepted the invitation of the Prince Regent Alexander to come to Yelak, the Serbian advanced HQ on the slopes of Mt Kaymakcalan, 'for at least two days to study the configuration of the terrain.'[10] The Prince, by no means simply the nominal head of the Serbian Army, had also impressed Franchet d'Espèrey during his *visite protocolaire*.

The new Commander in Chief wasted no time. Three days later, he was taking the forest track to the top of Mt Floka on horseback accompanied by Mišić and the Prince. Floka, 2,300 metres, captured by the Serbs in 1916 at the same time as its twin peak Mt Kaymakcalan, offered a superb view over the enemy positions of the central Moglena from Mt Sokol, only five kilometres to the north, and across to Mt Vetrenik, by way of the Dobropolje ridge. Franchet d'Espèrey noted in his diary:

28 juin. 1800 heures. Départ à cheval par un sentier forestier pour atteindre le sommet dénudé de Floka (2,300 mètres). Le soleil oblique fait ressortir les lignes Bulgares qui s'étalent au-dessus de nous. On voit jusqu'à leur deuxième position sur le Kozjak ainsi que les chemins qui relient les deux positions (28 June, 1800 hours. Leave on horseback along a forest track to reach the bare summit of Mt Floka (2,300 metres). The declining sun lit up the Bulgarian positions beneath us. One could see as far as their second line on Mt Kozjak, as well as the tracks which connected these two positions).

They were met at the top by Voivode Stepanović, Commander of the Second Army whose sector this was, and Voivode Bojović, Commander of the First Army.[11] The Serbian High Command was complete.

Franchet's visit to Yelak and his ascent of Mt Floka on the 28 June 1918 – which as it happened was the Serbian National day and the 529th anniversary of the defeat of Prince Lazar at Kosovo Polje – was the key moment in the Macedonian Campaign. The plan for the final victorious offensive against the Bulgarian army was born here.

Two days later, on 30 June, Franchet d'Espèrey records that he had a 'long and serious conversation' with the Prince and Mišić, and as a result of this:

J'arrête les bases de notre opération… au lieu d'une opération locale, ce sera une attaque décisive à laquelle participera toute l'armée Serbe renforcée de deux divisions Françaises (I decided on the nature of our action. Instead of a purely local operation, it would be a decisive attack involving the whole of the Serbian army reinforced by two French divisions).

---

9   Cordier, *Victoire Éclair*, p.20, quoting Franchet d'Espèrey's diary of 22 June.
10 Cordier, *Victoire Éclair*, p.19.
11 Cordier, *Victoire Éclair*, p.20. Diary of 28 June.

He told them that by relieving the Serbian units currently serving on other parts of the Allied front, he would re-unify the whole Serbian army, that he would then reinforce it with two French divisions, and that he would support it with as much French heavy artillery as possible:

> *Ils sont emballés. Mišić me demande si les deux divisions françaises seront sous ses ordres. Sur ma réponse affirmative, le Prince se lève, et, sans mot dire, vient me serrer la main. L'accord est complet* (They were overjoyed. Mišić then asked me whether the two French divisions would be under his orders. I replied affirmatively. The Prince got up, and without saying anything, came across to shake my hand. The deal was done).[12]

Over the following week Franchet d'Espèrey worked with his staffs to prepare a detailed definition of the plan he had agreed with the Serbian High Command, and on 7 July went through it with them.[13]

The report begins by confirming that while the planned initiative would involve almost all elements of the Allied Army 'The main action is entrusted to an Army Group under the command of Voivode Mišić, Chief of the Serbian Staff.' The purpose of the action, could scarcely have been expressed more clearly or concisely:

> *L'action principale qui développe dans la région Dobropolje–Vetrenik et au nord a pour but de couper en deux l'Armée Bulgare séparant les forces qui opèrent dans la région Vardar–Struma de celles qui tiennent la région de Monastir* (The main action to be directed at Dobropolje–Vetrenik and to the north of them will have the objective of cutting the Bulgarian army in two, separating their forces operating in the Vardar–Struma sector from those centred around Monastir).[14]

The action was to be in two phases, the first phase of which was to be conducted by the Serbian Second Army (Voivode Stepanović) incorporating the two French divisions.

The objective of Phase 1 (the 'Rupture') was to break through the whole enemy front between the river Souchitsa and Mt Sokol, about 14 kilometres. Each topographical feature between these two points is identified in the report. Three divisions were charged with the initial assault, Sumadija Division on the right, French 17th Colonial Division in the centre, and French 122nd Division on the left. The territorial objectives of each division are defined.

These three divisions were to be supported by Timok Division on the right and Yugoslav Division on the left, who after the three assault divisions had broken the first line of enemy defences would pass through them and take the Bulgarian rear defences in front of and on the Kozjak ridge. Timok and Yugoslav would then combine with Sumadija to implement their Phase 2 (Exploitation) objectives by forcing their way to the Vardar via Rozden, Mrezetchko and Bosava. Maps were provided; 1: 50,000 for Phase 1, 1:200,000 for Phase 2.

To the left of the Second Army, the First Army (Voivode Bojović) consisting of three divisions, from left to right Danube Drina and Morava, would cover the front from Budmirci to Sokol, and on the successful completion of Phase 1 by the Second Army, would push across the rivers Gradeshnitsa, Zaduka and Melnitsa to Vitolishta.

The other elements of the Allied Army, French, British, Italian and Greek are only mentioned as needing to be ready to support the Serbian Armies; their roles in the 'Exploitation' phase were to be fleshed out later.

---

12 Cordier, *Victoire Éclair*, p.21. Diary of 30 June 1918.
13 Cordier, *Victoire Éclair*, Annexe 2 p.261. Franchet d'Espèrey's Plan for the Final Offensive of 7 July 1918.
14

This was to be, from the outset and very clearly, a Serbian show, whose success would depend on one heavily concentrated and supported thrust through the centre of the long Bulgarian line; a total sea-change from Guillaumat's *'echelonné'* one-after-the-other plan or Sarrail's blanket everyone-together approach.

Issues of communication, transport logistics, the movement of artillery, air support and services were left to be completed later by the appropriate staffs. But the main infantry tactics to be employed are already covered in this report; rolling artillery barrages to support the initial assault, the necessity of reserves to advance right on the heels of the shock troops (Franchet d'Espèrey was always insistent on this), the use of light columns advancing in parallel during the Exploitation Phase, the need to disguise preparatory movements of men and equipment and to indulge in no abnormal pre-battle air reconnaissance.[15]

Leaning on his long experience on the Western Front, Franchet d'Espèrey stressed that surprise and the tight maintenance of secrecy were paramount in the launching of a major initiative. But overall the strategy which Franchet d'Espèrey agreed with the Serbian High Command on 7 July of rupture and pursuit across a high mountain range had nothing at all to do with the largely static warfare on the plains of Northern France which he had known for the past four years.

A sudden visionary flash of enlightenment, or an open-minded analysis of a totally new military environment, or something of both?

The logistical difficulties of storming well-defended mountain positions, and positioning assault troops and guns without attracting too much enemy attention were obvious. However, the plan had many things going for it. Firstly, the enemy would not be expecting the Allies to attempt the major breach here; a supportive artillery demonstration could be expected to disguise Allied intentions, but the major attack would surely occur elsewhere. Even after the Allied armies had achieved the break-through the commanders of the German Eleventh Army still thought it was a feint. Secondly, the Serbs already held a strong position at Kaymakcalan–Floka. They were proven mountain fighters, and would be fighting to liberate their own country. Thirdly, although the Bulgarian defences on Dobropolje and surrounding ridges were strong, their artillery concentration here was weaker than on any other of their fronts.[16] Also, their positions lacked depth; apart from the Kozjak there were no significant successive lines of defence. Fourthly, roads and tracks from the rail head at Risova in the Moglenitsa valley extended a long way towards the mountains across the plain and up the river valleys, easing movement of men and materiel to their take-off positions. Fifth, once over the mountains, the rivers and streams, tracks and finally roads ran essentially south–north straight down to the Vardar. There were no troublesome river valleys to be continually crossed or bridged (as would have been the case had the main attack been planned to the east of the Crna river).

Above all, this was actually the shortest route available to the Allies to the nerve centre of Bulgarian operations, the stretch of the Vardar between Krivolak and Gradsko. Control of this area would give the Allies command over the roads running west and south to Prilep and Monastir and east to Stip and Sofia, essential to the Bulgarians as a link between their two army groups.[17] In addition, the Allies would have side-stepped the narrow defile of the Vardar south of Demi Kapu, and isolated enemy troops south of the defile. They would control the river and the railway at this point, for further exploitation north along the wider river valley. Moreover, since the Crna exits into the Vardar at Gradsko, its possession would allow control of the Crna valley.

In view of its strategic position as a centre of road, river and rail communications, Gradsko was also the main supply centre for the Bulgarian armies. This was obviously the place to get to. This had no doubt been clear to everyone – even Hindenburg who rarely turned his attention in

---

15 Cordier, *Victoire Eclair*, Annexe 2 p.261.
16 Cordier, *Victoire Eclair*, pp.57–60.
17 Lepetit, *Genèse de l'Offensive*, p.17.

this direction had noted that Gradsko was the most important centre of communication in the Macedonian theatre. Franchet's touch of genius, with the prompting of the Serbs, was to realise that the best way to get there was not up the heavily defended Vardar or Monastir valleys, but over the top.

As Falls said 'As a strategic concept it will without doubt always hold a very high place in the estimation of military students.'[18]

The concept now needed to be put into practice. Franchet d'Espèrey was determined to launch his offensive in mid-September, two weeks earlier than the day envisaged by the Supreme War Council at their meeting of 3 July.[19] But the SWC had no real idea of the offensive's as yet unstated final objectives, and to Franchet d'Espèrey an extra two weeks before the arrival of the Balkan winter were critical. Within this tight time scale an immense amount of planning, preparation, briefing and training needed to be done.

Leaving his staffs to flesh out his instructions for his review and handle the mass of administrative detail attendant upon such a major undertaking, Franchet d'Espèrey personally visited all the key personnel and formations on whom the success of the action would depend. On 4 August he was with Stepanović (whose ideas he found rather '*arriérées*', particularly on the speed with which reserves should follow on the heels of assault troops) and planned with him the dispositions to be taken up by Sumadija Division. On 6 August it was the turn of Timok Division.[20] In between he made a second reconnaissance of the enemy positions on Vetrenik and Dobropolje from another viewpoint, Belo Grotlo, a peak slightly to the north-east of Floka and almost as high.

As he completed his tour of the other Serbian divisions he concluded that '*Les Serbes sont braves et disciplinés, mais les problems d'Etat Major les laissent froids.*' (The Serbs are brave and disciplined but are totally uninterested in Staff matters).[21] In view of this he put his own deputy Chief of Staff, Colonel Trousson at the disposition of the Serbian Army, put General Bonoust in charge of artillery planning and execution for the offensive, and placed senior French artillery officers in each Serbian army. The vital functions of supply and ambulance services to support the offensive he put in the hands of French officers. That such impositions were achieved without offending any sensibilities he puts down to the whole-hearted collaboration of the Prince Regent.[22]

He saved what was for him the pleasant task of visiting the two French divisions selected for the initial attack, 122nd and 17th Colonial, until 22 and 23 August. Both had served with him before, and he was sure of their qualities. He told them:

> *Nous aurons une préparation d'artillerie comme on n'en a jamais vu ni entendu sur ce front … une fois sauté la croute, nous irons très loin, peut-être jusqu'au Danube* (We will start with an artillery barrage of an intensity never seen or heard on this front … once we have made the breakthrough we will advance a very long way, perhaps even to the Danube).[23]

Between 24 July and 27 August he sent his instructions to those parts of the Allied Army not involved in the main Franco–Serbian attack.

Each of these sets of instructions related solely to the part to be played by the forces of the recipient; there is at this point no statement of the overall objective of the offensive, nor of the strategy for its realisation. When a degree of collaboration with a neighbouring Army Group was required,

---

18   Falls, *Macedonia Vol. 2*, p.124.
19   Lepetit, *Genèse de l'Offensive*, p.24.
20   Cordier, *Victoire Eclair*, p.23.
21   Cordier, *Victoire Éclair*, p.23. Diary for 6 August.
22   Cordier, *Victoire Éclair*, p.23. Diary for 8 August.
23   Cordier, *Victoire Éclair*, p.24. Diary for 23 August.

the instructions for that group would be forwarded for information. On 4 August Milne received a copy of the instructions which had been sent to the Commander of the First Group of Divisions, Milne's neighbour on the west side of the Vardar.[24]

It was not until 31 August, fifteen days before the planned launch date that Franchet d'Espèrey sent out to the Allied Commanders an *'Instruction Générale'* on the role all parts of the Allied Army should play in the 'Exploitation' phase.[25] Since this was the first document covering the whole campaign and the whole Allied Army, security was essential:

> *Tous les exécutants, jusqu'au commandants de division inclus devront être orientés sur le plan en ce qui les concerne. Mais les exemplaires entiers de la présente instruction ne devront pas dépasser l'échelon armée.* (Its executants, down to Divisional level, should be made aware of the contents of the plan where it concerns them. But complete copies must not go below Army level).

The purpose of the offensive, and the plan for 'Rupture', whose success is already taken for-granted, are summarized in four lines. The rest of the six page document deals with the follow-up ('Exploitation'), which is now designated 'First Phase.'

For its execution Franchet d'Espèrey divides the Allied Army of the East into five Army Groups, and an introductory summary lays down the positions which each of these Army Groups should have reached by the end of this First Phase of the 'Exploitation.'[26]

From Allied left to Allied right:

French Army of the Orient (AFO); Uskub (Skopje)
Serbian Armies; Veles/Stip
First French Group of Divisions; Udovo
British-Greek Army; Strumitsa Valley
Greek Army; Demi Hasar, Rupel, Petrica

For the veterans of the Macedonian Campaign, these must have seemed breathtakingly ambitious objectives.[27]

The *Instruction Générale pour l'Exploitation* then goes into detail on how the goals of the First Phase of the 'Exploitation' are to be reached, for each Army Group, by division, with specific routes to be followed.

The instructions relating to the Serbian Armies are basically unchanged from those of the seminal report of 7 July. The importance of holding bridges, both on the Vardar and on the Crna is stressed, together with the need to combine efforts with the AFO, advancing on their left.

The British Army Group, (strengthened with the addition of two Greek divisions, Seres and Crete), after breaking through the Doiran defences was exhorted to strengthen both flanks, right towards the Blaga Planina and left towards the Vardar, where it should recuperate 27th Division, until now working with the First French Group of Divisions on the west bank of the river.

---

24 Falls, *Macedonia Vol. 2*, Appendix 10 p.326. Instruction of Franchet d'Espèrey for the French 1st Group of divisions of 4 August 11918.
25 Cordier, *Victoire Éclair*, Annexe 5 p.271. General Instruction for the Final Offensive from Franchet d'Espèrey to all Allied Commanders of 31 July 1918. Translation in Falls, *Macedonia Vol 2*, Appendix 11 p.327.
26 Falls, *Macedonia Vol. 2*, p.328. This part of the Instructions, and the paragraphs which follow it relating to Phase 2 are excluded from Cordier's Annexe 5.
27 See Map 9

The instructions for the First French Group are spelt out in some detail; theirs was a complicated mission, on the left with one division collaborating with the Serbian right, and on the right with two divisions moving up the western side of the Vardar valley. Essentially this involved circling the Marianska plateau from different sides with the two contingents coming together at Udovo.

The AFO was the largest of the component armies, with 5 French divisions, two Greek divisions, six mixed battalions (including one Albanian), and the Italian 35th Division whose long watch over Hill 1050 was finally to come to a successful conclusion. It also incorporated the French cavalry, later to play a dashing role in the advance. This AFO Group faced the very well prepared defences of the so-called German Eleventh Army north of Monastir and in the Crna valley, against which many unsuccessful actions had already been mounted in the past. Franchet d'Espèrey had set it the objective of breaking through to Prilep and then advancing on Skopje in conjunction with the Serbian Second Army, while protecting the Allied left flank and isolating enemy forces from around the lakes, and west of the Tetovo–Kicevo line.

The Greek Army's orders are for the moment left open. *Les opérations de l'Armée Hellénique feront l'objet d'une instruction spéciale.* (The operations of the Greek Army will be covered in a special instruction). At the outset of the offensive, six Greek divisions were in fact attached to other Armies. Franchet d'Espèrey took the opportunity once more to stress the need for the early deployment of reserves. He was to be proved right about this, particularly in mountain territory.

The objectives of the 'Second Phase' are not defined, although it is clear that Franchet d'Espèrey had his sights set on the Danube. His feeling was that in the Second Phase territorial goals would be easier to reach; 'In the Second Phase we are unlikely to find ourselves faced by considerable organized forces on large fronts; the resistance of an enemy whose morale will have been gravely weakened will probably be met with only in patches, and with weak artillery. It is therefore likely, even if the Germans intervene, that we shall be able to impose our will, on the condition that our operations are coordinated and our system of communication with the rear functions normally.' General Franchet d'Esperey, the third Commander in Chief of the Allied Army of the East, was so sure of the outcome of his campaign that he was writing its history even before it had taken place.

33

1918
Final Offensive: The Battle of Dobropolje[1]

(Maps 11 & 12)

As clearly explained in Franchet d'Espèrey's general instruction of 31 August, the 'Rupture' was the sole responsibility of the Serbian Army Group, but the 'Exploitation' would involve all the other Army Groups immediately afterwards.

Facing the five Allied Army groups there were four Bulgarian Army Groups. The so-called German Eleventh Army Group of seven divisions (essentially Bulgarian with German staffs) on the Allied left covered the long front from Lake Ohrid to Skra di Legen, incorporating Dobropolje and the whole area ear-marked for the Serbian assault. The Bulgarian First Army Group, 3 divisions, covered the Vardar corridor up to Lake Doiran. The Bulgarian Second Army Group, three divisions, then took over from north east of Lake Doiran, across the Belasitsa range and down the Struma valley to Lake Tahinos.

On the extreme Allied right the Bulgarian Fourth Army Group, one division and assorted other troops, was principally involved with policing the occupied territory of East Macedonia and guarding the coast from the mouth of the Struma to the Maritsa.

In terms of 'morale' however, all the sources stress that the Allies had very much gained the upper hand since their failed offensive of 1917. Hall devotes a complete chapter to the decline in Bulgarian morale during 1918, with reports and examples from the battlefront.[2]

Poor morale in the field was matched by increasing unease at Bulgarian government level. On 2 September General Ganchev, Bulgaria's representative at German military HQ at Pless reported to his government that the Germans were preparing to open peace negotiations with the Americans without consulting their allies. On 13 September Tsar Ferdinand received a telegram from the Austrian Emperor Karl saying that it seemed to him that they could no longer rely on German resistance. On top of this, traditional Bulgarian–Ottoman hatreds were resurfacing. A report prepared for Prince Boris just before the Allied breakthrough suggested that if the Germans failed on the Western Front, Bulgaria should turn to Britain for help against the Turks.[3]

In mid-September there were only three German battalions left on the Macedonian Front. There were however six more arriving on the Struma Front, with the aim of 'turning' the Greek First Corps in the mistaken belief that its loyalties remained with the Kaiser's brother-in law. They

---

1   Falls, *Macedonia Vol. 2*, p.147 notes that this is the name attributed to the battle by French and British sources. The Serbs called it, perhaps more justly, the Battle of the Moglena. Dobropolje translates as 'nice field', probably a good upland pasture for shepherds in the summer. To access it they would have had to come from the north-west.
2   Hall, *Balkan Breakthrough*, pp.101–25. Chapter 31 above.
3   Hall, *Balkan Breakthrough*, pp.127–128.

Map 12. Armies, 15 September 1918.

soon found out that this was untrue, and in due course were drawn into the main battle. A curious misuse of precious manpower by the Germans.[4]

At the start of his offensive Franchet d'Espèrey's force consisted of 289 infantry battalions. This faced up against 297 on the enemy side, although of these 33 were with the Bulgarian Fourth Army Group which was only marginally involved in the offensive. As to cavalry, the Allies held the advantage with 47 squadrons compared against 26. Allied totals of around 2,000 heavy guns and 2,600 machine guns compared with 1,850 and 2,500 on the enemy side.[5] In the air the Allies had a superiority of 200 planes against 80. Apart from this, the forces were fairly evenly balanced.

In the Serbian Army Group sector, however, Franchet d'Esperey had seen to it that this was not all the case. In May 1917 as part of Sarrail's spring offensive the Serbian Second Army had already attacked the Dobropolje and had got no further than gaining a few footholds on the lower slopes. On that occasion Serbian morale was at a low ebb following the Apis affair, late snow up to 3 metres thick had impeded the placement of troops and guns, and above all artillery support was woefully inadequate.

Franchet d'Espèrey's 1918 Autumn campaign was not hampered by snow, although he was keenly aware that not a day was to be lost if he were to achieve his objectives before winter fell. By giving the Serbs the dominant role in the offensive – and command over two French divisions – he gave their morale a tremendous boost and addressed the lingering resentment that the Skra di Legen action had been monopolized by the Greeks.

But above all he understood from the outset that frontal assaults on 14 kilometres of well-prepared defences on high and precipitous mountain territory would require an overwhelming superiority in men and armaments. If this necessitated, at least at the outset, a considerable thinning out of cover on the other parts of the line, so be it; once into 'exploitation' mode, guns, men and materials could be redistributed.

Consequently, although in September 1918 Allied and enemy forces along the whole Macedonian Front were virtually at parity, in the sector covered by the Serbian Army Group the Allied strength exceeded that of the enemy by a factor of 3:1. In terms of manpower the Allies had amassed 75 battalions to confront 26 (excluding Bulgarian reserves) The Allies had 500 guns and trench mortars compared with 146 on the Bulgarian side, and their 36,000 rifles and 756 machine guns faced up against 12,000 and 245.[6] In men and fire-power this represented around a third of the strength of the whole Allied Army of the East. Not to mention superiority in the air with 81 Allied planes against 24 Germano–Bulgarian.[7] Mišić had told Franchet d'Espèrey on 22 June that given the same artillery support which the Greeks had enjoyed at the battle of Skra di Legen, the Serbs would do wonders. Franchet d'Espèrey had more than responded to the challenge.

But this was to be an incomparably bigger operation than that of Skra di Legen, whose objectives had been limited to removing a powerful and dangerous enemy salient with no intention of advancing any further. At Skra di Legen artillery support had been of copybook standard but was largely static. Guns had had to be pulled into the mountains, but the distances were shorter, a usable track already existed as far as Ljumnitsa, and the gradients involved were about a third of those facing the engineers below the peaks of the Moglena.

---

4   Larcher, *Grande Guerre*, p.232.
5   Cordier, *Victoire Éclair*, p.260. Estimates vary slightly. Cordier's figures are from Serbian sources (Kalafotovic, Belgrade 1923) which are those used by Gordon-Smith, *From Serbia*, p.331. Falls, *Macedonia Vol. 2*, p.145 quotes figures slightly at variance from Bulgarian post-war sources which may not include reserves.
6   Ducasse, *Balkans,* p.197. These are the French figures. Falls, *Macedonia Vol 2*, p.128 quotes the Serbian ones, the same except that the Serbians counted 580 guns instead of 500.
7   Hall, *Balkan Breakthrough*, p.134.

In the Moglenitsa valley the 60 cm decauville line ran as far as Dragomantsi, 200 metres above sea level, and then on to Second Army HQ at Tressina–Risova.[8] Tracks then ran to the foothills of the mountains, but from here guns had to be hoisted at least another 1,000 metres up the slopes north of Pojar, where they had to be high enough to cover not only the initial assault on the enemy front lines between Vetrenik and Dobropolje, but also far enough up the mountain to provide support for the attacks on the second enemy line around Kozjak. No fewer than seven 155 mm batteries were dragged into positions along the mountain face to achieve this dual purpose.

Further west guns offloaded at Ostrova Station, 360 metres above sea level, had to be moved along the Kaymakcalan ridge for positioning on Floka and Belo Grotlo, both over 2,000 metres with a sharp col between them. This necessitated the construction of a 40 kilometre surfaced track with gradients in part of 20 percent to enable the heavy guns to be pulled up with tractors, one tractor for 105mm guns, two for 155mm guns.[9] Other routes were created, including one on the north side of the Kaymakcalan massif. Thousands of labourers, including members of the disbanded Russian brigade as well as Bulgarian and Turkish prisoners of war were employed in the initial stages of this Herculean task. French pioneer regiments and engineers took over for the final more sensitive stretches.[10]

The movement and final deployment of the guns themselves remained the responsibility of the divisional artillery units, and it was the final parts of the ascent which were the hardest: *Le début de ces déplacements s'effectuait au moyen de tracteurs, d'attelages de chevaux, mais il se terminait par des manoeuvres de force au moyen d'agrès et de cordage* (Moving these guns was effected by tractors and teams of horses in the first instance, but finished with physical effort in pulling on ropes and pulling apparatus).[11]

Two batteries were pulled up to the top of Floka and a further two were placed on Belo Grotlo. These dominated the enemy positions below them from Sokol to Vetrenik. They were so positioned that they could initially support the main assault of the Serbian Second Army, and when this had succeeded, could switch round to support the advance of the Serbian First Army. It took seven days for the bigger guns to be hoisted into place, but the tracks and paths built for their ascent had to be good enough for the guns to be quickly withdrawn after the initial break-through and returned within three days to the AFO units from which they had been borrowed. Ammunition was carried up by teams of buffaloes, and also by horses of the French cavalry regiment, eight shells per horse.[12]

Inevitably most of this work had to be carried out at night, as silently as possible, and traces of the night's work camouflaged by day; equally inevitably, given their grandstand views over the Moglenitsa plain, the Bulgarians had a good idea that something was going on, but as was to be proven on 15 September, no clear idea of the scale of it.

There was no doubt on the Bulgarian side that a major Allied attack was forthcoming. In addition to the much increased movement of troops and materials which they could observe on the ground and from aerial reconnaissance, information inevitably filtered down to their spies in Salonica. In early September the Bulgarians captured a Serbian NCO and three private soldiers who told them of a huge Serbian offensive being planned against Dobropolje including two French divisions.[13] Further, a major breach in confidentiality somewhere in staff headquarters in France had been

---

8   Villari, *Macedonian Campaign*, p.221, Gordon-Smith, *From Serbia*, p.332.
9   Cordier, *Victoire Éclair*, pp.103–108. Cordier devotes an entire chapter to the movement of guns to support the attack.
10 Palmer, *Gardeners*, p.192.
11 Schiavon, *Front d'Orient*, p.327 quoting Colonel Abadie *Etude sur les Opérations de Guerre en Montagne* (Paris : Ch. Lavauzelle, 1924), p.80.
12 Cordier, *Victoire Éclair*, p.105.
13 Hall, *Balkan Breakthrough*, p.132.

reported back to the Bulgarians through Geneva with accurate information on the place and exact date planned for the Allied offensive.[14]

However, the Allies tried to keep them guessing. On the AFO Front actions were mounted in the Ohrid and Monastir areas, the last of which was made as late as 13 September.[15] But the major diversionary attack was made by the BSF on the west bank of the Vardar. Two battalions of 27th Division were set the task of eliminating a well-defended salient extending southwards from the Bulgarian line known as the Roche Noire, about ten kilometres east of Skra di Legen, and directly across the river from Machukovo. This was a well-planned operation, artillery support was precise and effective, infantry follow-up and tactics were of the highest order, the objectives were met, and the new line now extended down to the Vardar. Casualties however of 300, including 50 dead and missing, were high for an operation of this nature.[16]

The Geneva telegram had been forwarded, obviously, to General von Scholz, commander of the so-called 'Army Group von Scholz' which incorporated both the German Eleventh Army Group and the Bulgarian First Army Group. On 1 September Bulgarian central staffs wrote again to General von Scholz bringing his attention to the massing of Allied forces beneath the Dobropolje. 'An attack on the Dobropolje becomes more certain every day – preparations are running at fever pitch – in the Serbian sector we have counted the arrival of 17 new batteries, and every day we discover more – massive campments have appeared beneath the Moglena – all of which shows that an attack in the direction of Dobropolje will be on us in a matter of days.'[17]

Despite the seeming inevitability of a major Allied offensive in mid-September, in all probability centred on the Moglena, the Commander of the Bulgarian Army General Zhekov chose this moment to travel to Vienna for treatment on his ear. Even more amazingly, his replacement General Todorov spent the day of 14 September in Sofia as part of a delegation to welcome King Frederick Augustus of Saxony.[18]

As a result of the information he had received von Scholz made minor adjustments to the deployment of the German Eleventh Army and sent an infantry brigade with associated artillery to strengthen the rearward defences on the Moglena.[19] He remained convinced however, that the Allies would not make their main attack over the mountains. All his experience in the trench-by-trench warfare of the Western Front, where he had commanded the Eighth Army until being sent to Macedonia in mid-1917, told him that the main Allied advance would be made up from Monastir and the Crna towards Prilep, specifically between Hill 1248 north of Monastir and Hill 1050 (the 'Italian Hill') in the centre of the Crna bend north of Makavo.[20]

---

14 Cordier, *Victoire Éclair*, p.74. Cordier prints a handwritten letter he had received from Franchet d'Espèrey in 1937 recounting how when the Allied forces arrived in Sofia after the Armistice they were given the run of the Bulgarian secret service archives. Here they discovered a telegram received from Geneva in early August with the information that the Allies were planning to launch an attack in the area of the Moglena on 15 September. Even after nearly 20 years Franchet d'Espèrey's comments on the matter have lost nothing of his contempt for central staffs and arm-chair soldiers 'I was obliged to send the Supreme War Council my plan of operations to be reviewed by four worthy generals of limited competence, Belin, Bliss, Sackville-West and Robilant. Each of these had a staff, no doubt all honest persons, but a secret known to twenty people is no longer a secret, which explains the telegram from Geneva. This learned assembly (he uses the word *aréopage*, immensely more cutting in French) then had the nerve to send me advice on how I should conduct my operations...
15 Schiavon, *Front d'Orient*, p.382.
16 Falls, *Macedonia Vol 2*, p.144.
17 Schiavon, *Front d'Orient*, p.329.
18 Hall, *Balkan Breakthrough*, p.137.
19 Cordier, *Victoire Eclair*, p.79.
20 Ducasse, *Balkans*, p.200.

In addition von Scholz had fallen for a very creative piece of counter-espionage mounted by Commandant Cartier, Head of the Second Bureau in Salonica, whereby pictures fed to his staffs through an intermediary in Romania purported to show a major build-up of tanks around Florina. On the back of this von Scholz had assigned three reserve divisions to this front rather than to the Moglena, despite the reiterated demands of the Bulgarians. Cordier devotes a whole chapter to this deception and its consequences.[21]

On 13 September, the day before the artillery offensive was to start, and to throw the hostile spy network off the scent, Franchet d'Espèrey drove across to the Struma where he inspected the Greek First Corps. Everything was ready, there was nothing more that he could do in Salonica.

It is to be recalled that due almost entirely to the efforts of Guillaumat, it was only on 10 September that Clemenceau had finally given Franchet d'Espèrey the go-ahead to 'begin operations when you consider best.' It is pretty certain that on that date no one in Paris or London, even Guillaumat, had a clear idea of what their man in Macedonia was setting out to achieve. All were conditioned to a form of warfare where success was judged by moving the front line forward, and then digging in to new positions.

A flurry of doubt in Clemenceau's mind that this was not at all what Franchet d'Espèrey had in mind may have prompted a telegram from him dated 14 September with the staggering message; *Il est bien entendu que l'action qui doit se déclencher demain quinze septembre sera engagé sur votre seule responsibilité* (It must be understood that the action which is to be launched tomorrow 15 September is undertaken entirely on your responsibility).[22] According to Cordier, Franchet d'Espèrey took the message from Captain Pichéry, Transmissions Officer, who had brought it to him, lit a candle, and burnt it. Of course this may be apocryphal, but Cordier's account is minutely researched, and it is a good story, in spirit not too far from Clemenceau's known feelings about his 'Gardeners of Salonica.'

Franchet d'Espèrey had been basing his plan for over a month on a launch date of 15 September preceded by an all-out artillery attack on 14 September. He and Mišić had discussed tactics for the latter – a four day pounding, or a lightning blitz of 4-5 hours? They compromised on one day, long enough to readjust bearings and re-select targets, but not long enough for the enemy to realise where the main infantry follow-up was to take place – or if they did, not long enough to move troops and guns to cover the main area of attack.[23]

Franchet d'Espèrey left the final timing for the start of the artillery barrage to Mišić, who would be the best suited to assess the suitability of the weather from his mountain stronghold on Mt Floka.

The morning of 14 September dawned fine. Mišić had no hesitation in sending the code message to all battery commanders '*mettez en route quatorze officiers et huit soldats,*' and at 0800 on 14 September 500 guns spoke out along the whole Allied front of 80 kilometres from the Vardar to Monastir.[24]

Franchet d'Espèrey had promised the officers of 122nd and 17th Colonial divisions 'an artillery barrage the likes of which had never been seen or heard in Macedonia,' and he was true to his word. General von Scholz could hear it in Skopje, 60 miles to the north, but it was only in the evening that he realised that by far the heaviest shelling was being directed at the Bulgarian defences between Sokol and Vetrenik and had finally to accept that the Bulgarian intelligence services had been right.[25]

---

21 Cordier, *Victoire Eclair*, pp.221–225.
22 Cordier, *Victoire Eclair*, p.118.
23 Ducasse, *Balkans*, p.197.
24 Palmer, Gardeners, p.197.
25 Palmer, *Gardeners*, p.199.

The guns rolled on all day, with short breaks from 0900 to 0930 and 1500 to 1600 to allow French and Serbian planes to review and report. The bombardment ceased at 2030, to re-open the following morning solely in the area chosen for the Franco–Serbian assault.[26]

The offensive which was to bring the whole Macedonian Campaign to a victorious conclusion; which was to liberate Serbia, knock Bulgaria out of the war and accelerate the departure of Turkey, put the final nail in the coffin of the Austro-Hungarian Empire and hasten the final capitulation of Germany was unleashed beneath the Moglena mountains in northern Greece at 0530 on the morning of 15 September 1918. A scenario uncannily similar to the one presented by Franchet d'Espèrey to Joffre in December 1914 was about to be played out four years later.

The plan of attack and the units involved had not changed since those discussed and agreed between Franchet d'Espèrey, Prince Alexander and Voivode Mišić on 7 July. On the left Sokol and Dobropolje were to be taken by 122nd Division. In the centre 17th Colonial Division was to occupy the Kravitsa plateau, and take the Kravitsa, Kravitski Kamen and Goliak heights, and on the right Sumadija Division was to attack and overcome Bulgarian defences on both peaks of Vetrenik and the hills behind.

These three divisions were to move forward simultaneously. Their objectives achieved, Timok and Yugoslav Divisions, moving up no more than 1,000 metres behind them, were to take over the assault on the Bulgarian second and then third lines across the wide mountain spur behind the Dobropolje–Vetrenik ridge.[27]

The key responsibility lay with 122nd Division. The Bulgarians had started to fortify the Dobropolje ridge and plateau in 1916 after the Serbs had taken Kaymakcalan. They had further improved their defences here following the failed Allied spring offensive of 1917, and Crown Prince Boris had reported to his father in autumn 1917 that the Dobropolje front 'had been strengthened and could resist attack.'[28] These defences now consisted of a front line of trenches along the ridge with traverses every 50 to 200 metres, a secondary line two kilometres behind, and both protected by artillery batteries to the rear. The positions were strengthened with barbed wire and obstacles.[29]

Unless the Dobropolje defences were taken, there was little chance of holding on to the Kravitsa plateau or advancing beyond it, and the capture of Vetrenik in isolation would represent little more than advancing the Allied line by a few kilometres and gaining a useful mountain artillery position for some new offensive in the future. Taking out the Bulgarian gun position on Sokol was also of critical importance since this not only covered their Dobropolje defences but overlooked the Serbian First Army's planned direction of advance.

Since the Vetrenik massif bulges southwards out of the main Moglena ridge it formed a salient into the Allied line. Sumadija attacked the Bulgarian positions from both flanks. The western peak, 1,570, was taken by 0730 with 300 prisoners and six guns.[30] Behind on the higher eastern peak, heavy Bulgarian resistance was finally overcome in the early afternoon, and the Serbs were able to advance in support of 17th Colonial on their left.

To the west of Vetrenik, the Bichkija stream runs down a high mountain valley. The 17th Colonial advanced to the left of this aiming directly at Kravitsa, leaving the Bulgarian lines along the valley to be mopped up in a subsequent operation. By 0800 17th Colonial was already in possession of Kravitsa, and by 1000 the nearby summit of Goliak. Due to its decision to side-step the Bichkija valley, however, it was now in advance of the other two Divisions, and was subjected to repeated counter attacks, at one point losing the Kravitsa plateau. These were finally driven back

---

26 Cordier, *Victoire Eclair*, p.125.
27 Cordier, *Victoire Eclair*, p.111.
28 Hall, *Balkan Breakthrough*, p.130.
29 Hall, *Balkan Breakthrough*, pp.129–130, quoting Krivorov.
30 Cordier, *Victoire Eclair*, p.187.

and the Division's exposure relieved by the arrival of Sumadija to their right. In the view of General Plunkett, the British staff representative with the Serbian armies, this intervention was critical to the success of the whole offensive.[31] By 1600 17th Colonial with the aid of Sumadija had also taken Kravitski Kamen. The initial objectives of both divisions had now been met.

To their left 122nd Division were faced with the main Dobropolje defences They made good initial progress but were subjected to bitter fighting as the day wore on. The Sokol and Kotka peaks were separated by a deep ravine, totally unsuitable terrain for advancing into enemy territory. The Commander of 122nd Division decided to send two battalions to the left of this ravine and the rest of his force to the right. One of the battalions on the left was to assault and take Sokol. The other was to circle the 'cuvette', a marshy area in the centre of the Dobropolje and capture a heavily defended rise with an elevation of 1,765 metres with a commanding view of the whole battlefield.

The main body of 122nd Division had stormed their way over the Kotka and the Dobropolje defences by 0730. The advancing forces were protected by an immaculately timed artillery barrage moving at 100 metres every four minutes, but also by the fact that once within 500 metres of the Bulgarian trenches the trajectory of the enemy guns could not be adjusted to fire below that distance.[32] By 0800 they had taken the Pyramid, at 1,885 metres the high point of the Dobropolje massif with a commanding view of the entire battlefield.

The two detached battalions however had fared less well. The intensive artillery bombardment of 14 September had not succeeded in neutralizing the Bulgarian gun emplacements on Sokol. By 0615 the right wing of Drina Division had taken the right peak of the mountain, but it took until nightfall for them in conjunction with the detached battalion of 122nd Division to take the left peak and complete Allied occupation of this key position.

The other detached battalion had missed their artillery barrage and were pinned down in front of their objective until fresh artillery support became available from Yugoslav Division. This, following Franchet d'Espèrey's instructions on the close support of second line forces, joined the battle and enabled point 1,765 and its adjoining ridge to be taken at 1400 hours.

* * *

The Serbian Second Army had met its 'rupture' objectives of overcoming the Bulgarian first line defences and taken possession of the central Moglena ridge on a front of 14 kilometres with a depth of around 2,000 metres, all on the first day. Given the enormity of the achievement casualties were not excessive, around 2,000 across the three divisions (less than half the number the BSF and Greek divisions were to suffer three days later at Doiran). Three thousand prisoners had been taken and 50 guns.[33]

By the middle of the afternoon when the success of the initial 'rupture' phase was apparent, the two pursuit divisions, Timok on the right and Yugoslav on the left were already on the move. By 1800 they had joined up with Sumadija and were able to take over the advance.

There were emotional scenes as the Serbs assumed the relay from the French 122nd and 17th Colonial Divisions, as it happened right on the Greek–Serbian border. French officers from 17th Colonial tell how troops from Yugoslav Division broke into a run and as they saw the white border markings shouted 'Granitsa! Napred' (The Frontier ! Onwards !), and how young men and grizzled old soldiers:

---

31 Falls, *Macedonia Vol. 2*, p.150.
32 Hall, *Balkan Breakthrough*, p.136.
33 Hall, *Balkan Breakthrough*, p.137.

Le regard extasié s'agenouillent à la limite du sol sacré de leur pays et en baisant pieusement la terre sans se soucier des balles de mitrailleuses qui rasent encore la crête (With wonder in their eyes kneeled down at this sacred spot and reverently kissed the ground, indifferent to the machine gun bullets which were still flying around).

Crying 'Merci, Franzousi' they shook hands and embraced their French allies as they passed through their lines singing patriotic songs.[34] Similar scenes were reported by soldiers of 122nd Division as the Serbs passed through their lines.

To the right Timok Division was already well over the frontier, had found Golo Bilo undefended, and was advancing towards Topolec, north east of Kozjak. Having passed through the French lines Yugoslav Division pressed on through the night to be ready to attack the defences of Kozjak on the morning of 16 September.

During 15 September due to the delay in neutralising the enemy guns on Sokol, the Serbian First Army made little progress. At 1500 and again at 1700 attempts to advance were driven back. Once Sokol had fallen fast progress was made on 16 September, by 0530 the whole of the Bulgarian front line on this sector was in the hands of the First Army, they were advancing on Leonitsa and by 1000 they were across the Graneshnitsa. The Danube Division on the left met fierce resistance as the enemy fought rearguard actions on their way to the Rasim Bey bridge, but during the day the whole Army, also using its cavalry, advanced upward of ten kilometres. By the evening of 16 September it joined hands with the Serbian Second Army on its right, and all six Serbian Divisions were able to move forward in concert.[35] On their left the right wing of the AFO Group had taken Staravina and Zovic.

The Bulgarian second line of mountain defences ran from Preslap in the east through Kozjak to the heights above Gradeshnitsa in the west, but by far the strongest fortifications on this line were on the Kozjak massif itself which rose up in the middle of a wide north–south mountainous spur descending gradually from Dobropolje–Vetrenik through Rozden to the Vardar. This was the last major nut to crack and the Bulgarians held out all day on the 16th. General von Scholz ordered General von Reuter, commander of the joint reserve, to rush troops, particularly a crack German Jaeger battalion, to the defence of the Kozjak. Despite heavy resistance by the Germans and with the support of the Serbian First Army's Morava Division on its left, Yugoslav finally prevailed just before nightfall. Even then the German unit held out on a position north of the Kozjak while von Reuter, pistol in hand, tried to stem the retreat of the Bulgarian 2nd Division.[36]

But it was in vain. By this time the whole of the Bulgarian second line had been taken by the Serbs, and von Scholz authorized von Reuter to combine his reserves with the residue of the 2nd and 3rd Divisions and retreat to the even more rudimentary 3rd line of defence. This ran from Mt Duditsa to the east, through the Blatec Plateau, then south of Polchiste and Belsitsa to the Crna at Chebren.[37]

But any chance of an orderly retreat was forestalled by the unilateral decision already taken by the commander of the Bulgarian 2nd Division, General Rusev, to retreat once again, this time to the Crna. Unsurprisingly he was relieved of his command the following day, but the damage had been done, and given the slowness of the division's transport, much of it by oxen, many guns were left behind.[38] This withdrawal enabled Danube and Drina Divisions to occupy a line from Selo

---

34 Cordier, *Victoire Éclair*, p.210 reporting on-the-spot memories of Lieutenant Roguet and Captain Hugues.
35 Gordon-Smith, *From Serbia*, pp.340-344.
36 Palmer, *Gardeners*, p.204.
37 Ducasse, *Balkans*, p.205.
38 Hall, *Balkan Breakthrough*, p.138.

Monastir to Vitolishta before the evening of the 17th. On their right however Morava and Yugoslav Divisions faced stiff opposition from the Bulgarian 3rd Division. This resistance was not overcome until 1700, when the enemy retreated to Mrezetchko. Simultaneously Timok Division on their right overran the Bulgarian third line at Blatec, while to their right, the French First Group of divisions broke through to Preslap.

To the west of the Crna the AFO Army Group were heavily engaged, making slow progress, but preventing Bulgarian 4th Division from releasing forces to help their stricken colleagues on the other side of the river in stemming the inexorable advance of the Serbian Armies. By the evening of 17 September the Bulgarian army had been forced to abandon their third line of defence and had fallen back, in considerable disorder, to behind the Belasnica river.

Within a period of only three days a breach in the enemy line fifty kilometres across and thirty kilometres deep had been created.[39] Some 4,000 prisoners and 90 guns had been taken.[40] Much heavy fighting remained before the Serbs would reach the Vardar, but the 'Rupture' had been achieved, and Franchet d'Espèrey could now move to 'Exploitation' mode.

---

39 Falls, *Macedonia Vol. 2*, p.193.
40 Schiavon, *Front d'Orient*, p.335.

34

1918
Final Offensive: Second Battle of Doiran

(Map 10)

There has been some debate over the degree of operational flexibility and timing enjoyed by General Milne before and during the Second Battle of Doiran. A good summary is provided by Charles Packer, who was there, and had a special interest in the subject.[1]

On 24 July Franchet d'Espèrey had given Milne his instructions on the action to be taken by the British Army Group following the launch of the main Franco–Serbian offensive. There was to be a two-pronged attack, to the left and to the right of Lake Doiran. These attacks were to be made 'when the attacks on the other parts of the Eastern Front have made a certain progress.' It did not say who should decide 'when a certain progress' had been achieved, but the final list of instructions issued by Franchet d'Espèrey on 31 August it is very clearly stated that the action would be launched *sur l'ordre du Général Commandant en Chef lorsque l'avance de l'attaque central aura ébranlé la 1ère Armée Bulgare* (on the orders of the Commander in Chief when the central attack has shaken up the first Bulgarian Army).[2]

During the almost two years when their service had overlapped, Milne and Sarrail had developed a sort of modus operandi, neither harmonious nor particularly fruitful, but involving a degree of dialogue and exchange. Following Sarrail's departure Milne worked well with Guillaumat during his brief period in charge, appreciating his more consensual approach and willingness to share views. The arrival then of a Duke of Wellington type of Commander in Chief whose management style was to give orders and expect them to be obeyed clearly took Milne by surprise.

He had not been consulted beforehand about the part the BSF was to play in Franchet d'Espèrey's offensive and must have found the 'certain progress' element particularly open-ended. His initial preference, as in 1917, would have been to concentrate his main attack over the Struma, restricting activity at Doiran to a holding operation; artillery attacks and demonstrations.[3]

With the experience of Kosturino, Machukovo, Roche Noire and of course Doiran set against the almost perfect record of his forces on the Butkovo and Struma fronts, Milne knew perfectly well, and had said so, that the BSF's strengths were more suited to the flat than to any form of mountain warfare – particularly if he did not enjoy overwhelming artillery superiority. 'Gallant as our men are, they are not a match for the Bulgar over difficult ground, though they are superior over the flat' he had written to Robertson on 15 May 1917 after the First Battle of Doiran.

---

1 Packer, *Return to Salonica*, pp.110–114.
2 Cordier, *Victoire Eclair*, Annexe 5 p.273.
3 See Chapter 17, Palmer, *Gardeners*, p.115, Falls *Macedonia Vol. 1*, p.294, Larcher, *Grande Guerre*, p.195.

However, as in 1917, he recognised that an attack on the very far right of his and the Allied front would have no strategic sense as part of an offensive whose major push was to be made west of the Vardar, said so to Wilson in his letter of 25 July.[4]

The key outstanding issue was when his attack was to be launched. In the event, for want of any definite instructions to the contrary from his staff controllers in London, Milne followed the clear instructions of his superior officer, despite any reservations he may have had about the degree to which 'certain progress' had been achieved.

* * *

There were other, more material, elements leading up to the Second Battle of Doiran which are worth rehearsing and which certainly reinforce any claim that the attack was launched prematurely and against any probability of success.

During the sixteen months which had elapsed since the First Battle of Doiran the Bulgarians had strengthened their formidable defences even further. Under the resourceful and capable General Nerezov, Commander of the Bulgarian 1st Army, reinforced concrete around trenches and gun emplacements had been installed against which the artillery which the BSF had at its disposal would have little impact. The Doiran defences were still manned by Bulgaria's elite Plevna Division. Plans captured after the Battle showed that they had very accurate information on the disposition of the British forces, and above all knew exactly where their batteries were located.[5]. The strengthening of Bulgarian defences had extended also to the Belasitsa foothills and the Blaga Planina plateau.[6]

On 25 July when Milne had warned Wilson of Franchet d'Espèrey's upcoming offensive and the part the BSF was asked to play, and told him that such an action could only be undertaken 'if you are prepared to bring us up to fighting pitch by sending the necessary reinforcements and ammunition' he had been told by Wilson in his reply of 27 July that he could not expect any 'reinforcements or ammunition in excess of the normal allotment.'[7] Wilson went on to say that he was averse to an offensive at that time in the Balkans, and thought spring 1919 would be a better idea.

In June the BSF had been obliged to send 12 battalions to France. In July Milne had 22,000 men in hospital, mainly with malaria. He told Wilson on 27 July that he was short of 8,000 fit men.[8] But far from sending extra forces to Macedonia, Wilson told him he was planning to 'economise' British troops for Indian ones, who could not anyway arrive for several months.[9]

With regard to artillery and ammunition, Milne had been on the case since June, when he told the War office that for some of his guns available ammunition was less than half of establishment level. He asked for another battery of 8-inch howitzers, and for the return of 6-inch guns sent to Egypt. He sent his Deputy Quartermaster-General to England to plead his case, all to no avail.[10]

On 27 July Milne returned to the charge pointing out again 'ammunition is far below establishment levels. I do not have enough heavy artillery to compete with the Bulgar. Gas shell is urgently required.'[11] In the end it required the intervention of Clemenceau, prompted by Franchet

---

4   Falls, *Macedonia Vol. 2*, Appendix 8 p.325. Telegram from Milne to the War Office of 25 July 1918.
5   Mann, *Salonica Front*, p.56.
6   Packer, *Return to Salonica*, p.115.
7   Falls, *Macedonia Vol. 2*, p.325.
8   Nicol, *Uncle George*, p.170.
9   Falls, *Macedonia Vol. 2*, p.109.
10 Palmer, *Gardeners*, p.194.
11 Nicol, *Uncle George*, p.170.

d'Espèrey, to get London to promise him 15,000 6-inch gas shells. Of these only 3,000 arrived, the day before the attack was launched.[12]

CIGS Wilson was of course Milne's interlocutor, but both were bound also by the vagaries of the Supreme War Council, whose negative input on the planned offensive is covered above.

The result of all Milne's demands, pleas and representations was that while on the eve of battle on the Franco–Serbian Dobropolje Front the Allies were to have 3:1 superiority in all areas over those of the enemy, the Allied forces charged with assaulting the main Doiran Front were effectively operating at less than parity.

Including Seres Division, the BSF XII Corps had 27 battalions.[13] The forces of 9th Plevna Division facing them including reserves were 26 battalions.[14] On paper therefore the infantry strengths were more or less equal, but many of the Battalions of 22nd and 26th Division were indeed on paper only, due to the ravages of malaria. Prior to the Second Battle of Doiran British some battalions had been reduced to around 400 useful men.[15] There had also been an outbreak of Spanish influenza so serious that on the eve of battle one brigade – the 65th – was completely removed from the front line. Milne reported in his despatch of 1918; 'The effective strength of the British troops had fallen to below one-half of normal establishment.'[16]

By denuding 27th Division and drastically reducing the cover on 26th Division, Milne had amassed 231 artillery pieces, totally inadequate for the job in hand of attacking the strongest defensive structures anywhere on the Macedonian Front.[17]

'What happened,' concluded the Official Historian, allowing himself one of his rare critical comments, the more devastating for their simplicity, 'was that the British authorities had given their approval to an attack, but did not supply the means.'[18]

* * *

In his instructions to Milne of 24 July, Franchet d'Espèrey had defined the objectives of the British Army Group, after the attacks on the other Fronts had 'made a certain progress' to:

> Attack with determination the enemy's positions east of the Vardar so as to drive back the Bulgarian forces and cut their communication with Strumica.

In order to obtain this result, he goes on:

> The first objective should be the P Ridge, and the neighbouring heights west of Lake Doiran … It appears that the best means of capturing the P Ridge will be a heavy frontal attack *with artillery preparation* west of the lake with two divisions, one British and one Greek, combined with a surprise flank attack, *without artillery preparation* by one Greek division on that part of the enemy's front extending from the Belasitsa Planina to Lake Doiran (north of the lake). The means at the disposal of the British Army, in addition to its own resources, will be: two Greek divisions, one group of three Greek 6-inch batteries, and the armoured train of 19 cm (two guns).[19]

---

12 Falls, *Macedonia Vol. 2*, pp.115–16.
13 Villari, *Macedonian Campaign*, p.230.
14 Palmer, *Gardeners*, p.206.
15 Nicol, *Uncle George*, p.177.
16 Milne, *Despatch of 1918*, p.3.
17 Wakefield, *Under the Devil's Eye*, p.201.
18 Falls, *Macedonia Vol. 2*, p.113.
19 Falls, *Macedonia Vol. 2*, Appendix 7 p.324. Instruction from Franchet d'Espèrey to Milne of 24 July 1918.

Now attached to XII Corps, 27th Division would remain on the west bank of the Vardar. Its role in the offensive, defined in Franchet d'Espèrey's global instructions of 31 August, was to 'grapple with the enemy in the direction of Gevegli and Pardovica, and to rejoin the rest of XII Corps on the east bank of the river once the French First Group of divisions had reached the Vardar.[20]

Aware no doubt of Milne's manpower shortages, the offer of the pick of the Greek Divisions, Seres and Crete was a generous gesture. These two 'nationalist' divisions had been in the field for a year, had gained operational experience, and had distinguished themselves at Skra di Legen. The drawback was that they had had no experience of working with the BSF, and Franchet d'Espèrey's timetable left little time for training and assimilation. Milne would have preferred divisions drawn from the Greek Royalist I Corps, who had been working alongside XVI Corps for several months, and in particular Larissa Division who had already put in useful work on the Struma Front, but Franchet d'Espèrey didn't see it this way.[21] Subsequently Milne was also given a Zouave regiment, which, as it turned out, he would have been better off without.

The new element of Franchet d'Espèrey's plan for 'rupture' on the Doiran Front was the separate attack from the other side of the lake. As recently as 1913 the Greek Army had outflanked the Bulgarians here and forced them to evacuate Doiran in the Second Balkan War.[22] The fact that this had never featured in any of Milne's proposals was perhaps due to the known the difficulties of approach.

From receipt of Franchet d'Espèrey's instructions of 24 July any lingering preferences Milne may have had for a Struma-based campaign were abandoned, as he and his staffs set about gathering forces and guns for the frontal assault on the main Doiran defences.

On 3 September he wrote gloomily to Wilson 'I consider the odds against us will be great. The season of the year after the summer is trying on the army. Effectives are at their lowest. It has been impossible to gain the reinforcements, guns and ammunition I have asked for, six inch howitzers have not arrived, and owing to the strength of enemy artillery a great deal depends on silencing his guns.'

He goes on, presciently, 'provided the attack is delayed until the Bulgarians are moving their guns and reserves we stand a fair chance.' In this he was absolutely right; had his assault on the Doiran heights been delayed by two days until 20 September, he would have been pushing at an open door. But, had the British–Greek army not heavily engaged the enemy on the Doiran Front on 18 and 19 September, the transfer across the Vardar of considerable elements of the Bulgarian First Army may have influenced if not halted the advances being made by the Serbs.

* * *

Apart from 27th Division, Franchet d'Espèrey had left the decision on the roles to be played by the other British and Greek divisions under his command entirely to Milne. He had only specified that the frontal attack on the Doiran defences should be made by one Greek and one British division, and that the other Greek division should be used for the 'surprise flank attack' over the top of the lake. In the attack on Skra di Legen Seres had made the frontal attack, Crete a flanking attack on the right, and Milne gave them similar roles for the Doiran offensive. Crete therefore came under the orders of XVI Corps (General Briggs), while Seres became part of XII Corps (General Wilson).

Two Brigades of 28th Division (84th and 85th) were to be engaged with Crete in the 'flank' attack, with one (83rd) in reserve and with the ever-present 228th Brigade covering the Butkovo

---

20 Falls, *Macedonia Vol. 2*, Appendix 5 p.330 quoting from Franchet d'Espèrey's General Instruction to all Allied Commanders of 31 August.
21 Wakefield, *Under the Devil's Eye*, p.200.
22 Palmer, *Gardeners*, p.206.

Front to Lozhista against any incursions by the Bulgarian 2nd Army. The long stretch from Lake Butkovo to the mouth of the Struma was now covered by the Greek I Corps (Athens, Larissa and Calchis divisions).[23]

With 27th Division across the river, this left 22nd and 26th Divisions together with Seres Division facing the major Bulgarian defences between Lake Doiran and the Vardar.

Last year the major attack on the Doiran defences had been undertaken by 26th Division on the right with 22nd Division performing a reduced role on their left. This year the roles were reversed with 22nd Division, together with Seres Division, making the frontal attack between Pip Ridge and the lake, while 26th Division was to make smaller diversionary attacks to their left, and with 27th Division across the Vardar to prevent a Bulgarian flanking attack down the Vardar valley. Had this happened they would have found themselves in some difficulty, Milne having denuded them of most of their guns to maximise his fire-power on the enemy's main Doiran defences.[24]

It is interesting that for the two Battles of Doiran, by far the most important military actions undertaken by the British Army during the whole Macedonian Campaign, Milne in both cases used his two Volunteer 'K3' Divisions (22nd and 26th) leaving his two regular army divisions (27th and 28th) in supporting roles. It may simply be that this was the way the divisions were distributed at the time between the two Corps.

The landscape facing XII Corps was depressingly familiar; on the right, the hills to the west of the lake rising to the enemy's third line of defences, in the centre the dreaded ravines in front of a range of fortified hills leading up to the major fortification of the Grand Couronné with its ever visible 'Devil's Eye' observation point, and on the left 'Pip Ridge' running on a virtually south-north axis and gaining height as it rose. From the lake to the base of Pip Ridge was about five kilometres, from the British front line to the Grand Couronné about three kilometres with an upward gradient to climb, not counting the ups and downs of the ravines and ridges of around 400 metres.

General Henrys, Commanding Officer of the AFO, when he visited the Doiran Front said it was 'the most terrible position to assault that I have ever seen'. Possibly his boss had not given it the same scrutiny, but XII Corps needed no convincing.[25]

The plan of attack was for two brigades of Seres (1st and 2nd) to take the right hand sector between the lake and Petit Couronné, while 22nd Division took the left hand sector between Petit Couronné and Horseshoe Hill, 67th Brigade to the right, 66th Brigade to the left. For reasons unexplained in the sources the 3rd Brigade of Seres was detached from the rest of the Division and placed between 67th and 66th Brigade of 22nd Division, and under the orders of its Commander, General Duncan.

The objective of Seres Division (1st and 2nd Brigades) was to seize the Bulgarian first line of defence (Petit Couronné and the 'O' Ridge as far as O5) and advance up to the line between Doiran Hill and Hill 340. Having secured this they were to assault and take the Orb on the second line of the Bulgarian defence, then, with this position having been occupied and supported by 22nd Division on their left they were to go for the Grand Couronné.

The objectives of 22nd Division were for the 67th Brigade to take O6 and then advance up to the Bulgarian second line of defence between the Hilt and the Sugar Loaf, before advancing on the Grand Couronné. In this it would be supported by Seres 3rd Brigade, advancing on both sides of the Vladaja Ravine who would then push on to Koh-i-Nor. To 66th Brigade was allotted the well-nigh impossible task of picking off the successive enemy defences, one after another, on the Pip Ridge.

---

23 Falls, *Macedonia Vol. 2*, p.175.
24 Wakefield, *Under the Devil's Eye*, p.201.
25 Packer, *Return to Salonica*, p.114.

The other Brigade of 22nd Division, 65th, was considered unfit due to the influenza epidemic to take part in the battle was withdrawn and replaced in reserve by 26th Division's 77th Brigade. To the left of 22nd Division, covering the sector from Pip Ridge to the Vardar, the remainder of 26th Division was to make small incursions and demonstrations.[26]

* * *

The Franco–Serbian attack of 15 September on the Dobropolje had been a resounding success, such that Franchet d'Espèrey now felt confident that 'sufficient progress' had be made for the British assault on the Doiran defences to be launched within two days. On the evening of 15 September Milne noted in his diary that he had been informed that '18th is our day. Bombardment begins tomorrow.'[27]

The bombardment which began on the 16th and was continued on the 17th was essentially wire-cutting, with Milne in the main withholding his limited gun power and gas shells to support the attack on the morning on 18th September. A heavier artillery attack on the night of 17-18 September was to be followed with a creeping barrage by field guns when the advance by the two divisions was underway.[28] The effectiveness of a creeping barrage however was to prove limited by the nature of the terrain to be crossed, deep ravines and dry stream beds running in all directions preventing any regularity in the pace of advance, restricting visual control, and hindering communication.[29]

The Second Battle of Doiran opened at precisely 0508 on the morning of 18 September 1918, a daylight action having been preferred this time to the night-time chaos of last year. The Bulgarians can scarcely have been surprised.

The Seres Division on the right made a good start. By 0700 they had overrun the complete first Bulgarian line of defence including Petit Couronné, had taken the Doiran and Teton Hills and the heavily defended Hill 340, and nearly 700 prisoners. Securing this line in accordance with their instructions, they then pressed on and took the Orb, a key point on the enemy's main defence line and within a kilometre of the Grand Couronné. However in the face of furious counter-attacks, and unsupported by 22nd Division, they were forced to give up this position and return to the Doiran Hill–Hill 340 line. This they held despite every attempt to dislodge them.[30]

To the left of Seres Division, 22nd Division's 67th Brigade also started well, with two battalions taking the O6 position and reaching the Knot and the Tassel before being driven back, also by the lingering effects of the British gas bombardment. A third battalion, finding that the Sugar Loaf and Tongue positions had largely been cleared, as planned, by Seres 3rd Brigade, were able to assault the Grand Couronné defences at the Rockies. Here they were met with lethal machine gun fire from three sides. Only 55 men and one officer survived the assault by the battalion, leaving wounded on the field their Commanding Officer, Lieutenant Colonel Burges.[31]

The Seres 3rd Brigade, having taken the Sugar Loaf and the Tongue were brought up short at the Feather, the northern extremity of the Jumeaux Ravine, and were driven back with heavy losses. The Sugar Loaf was held until the early afternoon, when they were finally forced to withdraw.[32]

26　Falls, *Macedonia Vol. 2*, pp.164–168.
27　Nicol, *Uncle George*, p.174.
28　Wakefield, *Under the Devil's Eye*, p.201.
29　Mann, *Salonica Front*, p.56.
30　Falls, *Macedonia Vol. 2*, p.167.
31　Wakefield, *Under the Devil's Eye*, pp.205-206. Lt Col Burges was subsequently awarded the VC. 'Although wounded, but quite regardless of his own safety, he kept moving to and fro through his command, encouraging his men and assisting them to maintain formation and direction. He led them forward through a decimating fire until he was again hit twice and fell unconscious.' He was taken by a Bulgarian stretcher party to a dugout behind the lines where he was found, alive, two days later.
32　Falls, *Macedonia Vol. 2*, p.170.

Pip Ridge could only have been taken by frontal attack, the ridge being too narrow to allow any form of flanking approach. From the point of departure on Horseshoe Hill, the Ridge rises steadily to its highest point at P1, and each of the small natural steps in the Ridge – the 'Pips' – was heavily defended.[33]

Only an overwhelmingly strong and accurate pre-assault Artillery bombardment followed by an equally heavy and precise rolling barrage in front of the advancing troops would have given 66th Brigade any sort of chance. In the event the preceding artillery bombardment was completely inadequate and then, as a result of a delay in taking P4½ the barrage was lost and three successive battalions hurled themselves forward, at one point taking P4, but being faced with intense frontal and enfilade fire as they struggled towards P3 were forced to retire taking crippling casualties.[34] 'In their heroic attempt,' reported Milne in his Despatch 'they had lost about 65 percent of their strength.'[35] None of the 'Pips' was taken.

By 1700 Milne called off the attack. The Allied forces had sustained crippling casualties in taking no more than the Bulgarian first defensive line from the lake to O6, which anyway the Bulgars had always regarded as expendable should the men within it risk capture or encirclement.[36] Terrain south of a line from Doiran Hill to Hill 340 had also been taken, together with around 800 prisoners. As to 67th and 66th Brigades, they had virtually ceased to exist, and Seres 3rd Brigade had been savagely mauled.

However, conscious that the continuing success of the Serbo–French break-out to the west of the Vardar also depended on the enemy being unable to divert forces from the Doiran front and having received a message to that effect from Franchet d'Espèrey, Milne announced that another attack on this front would take place the next day.[37]

Meanwhile the planned 'outflanking' action by XVI Corps north of Lake Doiran had been an abject failure. Since from the base of the Krusha heights to the enemy positions on the Blaga Planina about seven kilometres of completely flat country would have to be crossed, success would depend on watertight planning, close cooperation, faultless communications, impeccable timing by the artillery, and as much as possible of the advance being made under cover of darkness. All of these essential features were absent on the day.

The main attack was to have been made by the Cretan Division with two Brigades of 28th Division in support. These units were in place in the valley before daybreak on 18 September, the Cretans having arrived during the night of 16 September and remaining under cover throughout the day.[38] Crucially however there was only one route for wheeled vehicles coming down from the Krusha heights, along which all of 28th Division's artillery had to pass. When, at 0530, in accordance with plans, the Cretans sent up flares to announce the start of their advance, the artillery support was by no means in place. According to Packer, who was there as part of 99 Brigade, the Allied bombardment did not commence until 0645, and some field guns were not operational until 0800 am.[39] Unsurprisingly the enemy's artillery, now fully alerted, was immediately in operation, and quickly homed in on the Allied gun positions on the plains as well as the advancing Cretans.

The Greeks made two attacks on the enemy positions on the Blaga Planina but were driven back twice by enfilade machine gun fire and, above all, by uncut wire. One of the Greek brigades was also caught up in a bush fire caused by enemy shelling. The enemy defences were breached in two

---

33 SCS Trench Maps DVD Doiran 20-8-19.
34 Wakefield, *Under the Devil's Eye*, pp.206–207.
35 Milne, *Despatch 1918*, p.4.
36 Packer, *Return to Salonica*, p.125.
37 Falls, *Macedonia Vol. 2*, pp.171–172.
38 Falls, *Macedonia Vol. 2*, p.174.
39 Packer, *Return to Salonica*, p.127.

places, but any consolidation proved impossible. To the right of the Greeks 84th Brigade advanced to Dervishli, but made no further advance on the enemy trenches, while 85th Brigade, holding a position west of Popovo along the Constantinople railway line was not called into action.

The Greeks retired at 1600. At this point some artillery units were still moving forward and the two Brigades of 28th Division were not aware of the Greek withdrawal until the evening.[40] No follow-up was attempted on 19 September. The Cretan Division was sent back behind the lines to recuperate while 28th Division and 228th Brigade returned to their old positions facing the enemy defences on the Belasitsa Range. Compared with those of XII Corps on the other side of the lake, however, XVI Corps casualties on 18 September were light, the Cretans having lost 150 dead or missing, while the total British casualties were less than 100, half of which were gunners.[41] Far from meeting its stated objective of linking up with Seres and 22nd Division around the north of the lake, this sorry action had, apart from clearing a few Bulgarian advanced posts in the valley and the subsequent construction of a line of trenches from the railway to the lake, achieved nothing of strategic or even tactical value.[42]

In the anodyne words of his Official Despatch Milne wrote 'at dawn they (the Cretan Division supported by troops of 28th Division) carried the enemy's outpost line and pressed forward to his main line. This they penetrated in two places on a narrow front but a permanent foothold could not be maintained. Nothing was now to be gained by pressing this attack and I therefore authorised a return to the line of the railway.'[43]

In later years he wrote 'Tanks would have altered the whole complexion of the Campaign.'[44] Interestingly on 24 August 1918 a Captain Mackay of the Tank Corps arrived in Salonica to assess the use of tanks on the Macedonian Front. A bit late in the day. Anyway, the visiting expert ruled them out.[45] His arrival did not go undetected by enemy intelligence and gave rise to rumours that the BSF was equipped with tanks. A captured order to a German Air Squadron read; 'The arrival of tanks from the western front is reported. Behind the Vardar–Doiran Front is a lorry park. Characteristic tracks lead one to suppose the presence of a tank station. The Squadron is ordered to proceed to take photos of this.' The report of tanks on the Doiran Front did not have such an unsettling effect as those conjured up by the Deuxième Bureau (Chapter 33 above) before the Battle of Dobropolje, but certainly did no harm.[46]

* * *

The survivors of the frontal attack on the Doiran defences of 18 September were spared that of 19 September. In their place 65th Brigade had been recalled, by no means recovered from the influenza epidemic, 77th Brigade was brought across from 26th Division, and 2nd Regiment Zouaves was brought up from reserves. Seres 1st and 2nd Brigades were retained on the right, where they fought with the same determination as the previous day. Again both the Hilt and the Orb were taken and then lost. By 1000, five hours after the opening of the day's hostilities they were forced back to the Doiran Hill–Hill 340 line which they held.

The centre was divided between the Zouaves on the left and 77th Brigade on the right. The Zouave objective was to reach the third Bulgarian line at the Warren, then swing left to take Pip 3.

---

40 Wakefield, *Under the Devil's Eye*, p.211.
41 Falls, *Macedonia Vol. 2*, p.177.
42 Wakefield, *Under the Devil's Eye*, p.212.
43 Milne, *Despatch of 1918*, p.4.
44 Nicol, *Uncle George*, p.175.
45 Gray and Argyle, *Chronicle Vol. 2*, p.206.
46 Casson, *Steady Drummer*, p.198.

On their right 77th Brigade were to attempt similar objectives to those of 67th Brigade the previous day, Sugar Loaf, Tongue, Tassel before advancing on the Rockies. Ambitions for Pip ridge had been reduced to taking Pip 4, and this was assigned to one battalion of 65th Brigade with two in reserve. The whole enterprise miscarried this time because the Zouaves failed to advance more than a few hundred metres from their starting blocks.

Messages were sent to the advancing 77th Brigade that if the Zouaves did not finally advance they were to go no further than the Tongue. The message didn't get through, and the Brigade continued towards their stated objectives, the Fang, the Knot and the Tassel. Unsupported on their left the mission was hopeless, and all three battalions were forced back to the Tongue, from which they withdrew with crushing casualties at 1030.

General Duncan's message about the delay in the timing of the barrage on the P Ridge didn't get through either. The assault battalion, leading off at the planned time, captured P4½ despite the lack of artillery cover, but by the time they reached P4, came under the fire of their own guns – the Howitzer 8-inch moreover – as well as enemy fire. By 0615 they had been driven back to their starting point.[47]

Milne called a halt to the Battle at 1100 am. Nothing new had been added to the small gains of yesterday, although this might not have been the case if the Zouaves had participated. His laconic diary entry for the day reads 'watched the battle till 1000. Another failure. We had neither the men nor the guns for the task. The Zouaves seem to have let us down badly.'[48]

It is worth noting however that in the Second Battle of Doiran the Allied troops advanced much further than in the First Battle of 1917, reaching the enemy's third line of defence in several cases, as well as taking and holding the first line of defence. The task in both cases was next to impossible, but in addition to the folly of attacking by night, a lot had obviously been learnt, particularly about negotiating ravines and the positioning of enemy guns and artillery. This was apparently not lost on Franchet d'Espèrey who awarded the French Croix de Guerre to three battalions of 66th, 67th and 77th brigades for the parts they played during this Second Battle of Doiran.[49]

The Second Battle of Doiran, 18 and 19 September 1918 cost the British–Greek Army Group 7,103 casualties, 3,575 British and 3,528 Greek. Of these 88 percent were sustained by XII Corps. Bulgarian losses, according to Nedev, were 2,726, less than 40 percent of those suffered by the Allies.[50] In the face of these statistics comfort however could be gained in that of the two objectives set by Franchet d'Espèrey for the British Army Group:

- To drive back the Bulgarian forces and cut their communications with Strumica, and
- To deprive the Bulgarian First Army of any freedom of movement by attacking it and pinning it down,

the second and certainly the most important had been met. Of all their forces between Lake Doiran and the Vardar, the Bulgarians had only been able to release one reserve regiment, the 66th, for subsequent action against the Serbs.[51] This has been uniformly recognised as the positive side-effect of a disastrous military engagement, a useful contribution to the success of the Franco–Serbian break-through west of the Vardar. But it was much more than this. The real importance of the role of the Second Battle of Doiran to the Allied victory is admirably summarised by Schiavon:

---

47 Falls, *Macedonia Vol. 2*, pp.178–184.
48 Nicol, *Uncle George*, p.175.
49 Falls, *Macedonia Vol. 2*, p.182.
50 Wakefield, *Under the Devil's Eye*, p.218.
51 Falls, *Macedonia Vol. 2*, p.190, Wakefield, *Under the Devil's Eye*, p.218.

It was essential to stop the enemy from re-forming in the centre of the war theatre. In this respect the action of General Milne was crucial. He prevented two Bulgarian divisions from establishing themselves on the Belasitsa massif on the left bank of the Vardar, taking control of the Vardar valley and its communications and eventually mounting a counter-attack on the Allied right as they were advancing on Gradsko.[52]

Schiavon could have added 'and control of the Strumitsa valley'; this access to Bulgaria, the shortest route to Sofia, could have been blocked at need by the Bulgarian forces without significantly reducing the strength of the two divisions in question.

More 'what ifs' surround the Second Battle of Doiran than any other action by the British on the Salonica Front. What if Milne had received the men, guns and shells he had so desperately asked for? What if Seres Division had fought as a unit without one of its brigades being put with 22nd Division? What if Larissa instead of Crete had been used for the 'flanking' attack as Milne and Briggs would have preferred? What if there had been no flanking attack and both Seres and Crete had been thrown against the Grand Couronné, with 22nd Division supported by heavy artillery concentrating on the P Ridge? What if the Zouaves had gone into action and fulfilled the mission assigned to them? What if Franchet d'Espèrey had ordered the battle for the 20th rather than the 18th of September? Writing to Wilson on 24 September, Milne was in no doubt that it was ordered prematurely.[53] But this is already with hindsight, for at this point of the story, following the long grind since 1915 and the intense pressure and bloodshed of the last two days, events began to move at a bewildering pace.

---

52   Schiavon, *Front d'Orient*, p.334.
53   Nicol, *Uncle George*, p.174.

35

1918
Final Offensive: Pursuit and Rout

(Map 9)

In his *Instruction Général pour l'Exploitation* issued on 31 August 1918, Franchet d'Espèrey with breath-taking self-assurance takes the success of the '*Rupture*' over the Moglena for granted two weeks before this decisive offensive was even launched. In fact the '*Rupture*' is no longer defined in the '*Instruction*' as the first phase of the operation. *La Première Phase* is now the *Exploitation* of the Rupture with territorial objectives set for each of the Allied Army Groups.[1]

The student of the Macedonian Campaign cannot be other than impressed – if not amazed – at the precision with which these objectives were met. The Serbian armies did indeed reach the Vardar, take Gradsko and advance to the Veles/Stip area. The AFO made it as required to Prilep and Skopje. The British Army Group reached the Strumitsa valley, with the French First Group cleared the Vardar valley to Udovo, and advanced into Bulgaria. As to the residual Greek Army on the Struma, plans for it to advance into Eastern Macedonia were overtaken by the Bulgarian capitulation.

Significantly Franchet d'Espèrey sets no timing objectives for the programme laid down in his *Instruction Général pour l'Exploitation* of 31 August. Nor does he include, as an over-arching objective, forcing the Bulgarian government to capitulate. This suggests that he remained wary to the end of the pressure the Germans could apply to their increasingly unwilling ally, and of the military support they might provide to prop them up.

Other than for ongoing operational orders, Franchet d'Espèrey only found it necessary to issue three further *Instructions* to all the Army Groups after the launch of the offensive right up to the Bulgarian armistice. The first was on 21 September enjoining the Groups to 'widen the breach made in the enemy's array to complete our success'. The second on 23 September was an update necessitated by the speed with which plans were falling into place. The third was on 25 September and was largely a touch on the tiller except for an order correcting the distribution of forces under General Henrys putting greater emphasis on Skopje than on the Kicevo–Resan axis.[2]

In his '*Instruction*' of 31 August Franchet d'Espèrey had referred to a '*deuxième phase*' with 'distant and audacious objectives.'[3] But after the Bulgarian collapse he issued no new comprehensive '*Instruction*' covering this promised second phase. He no longer had the same freedom of action; as a result of the enormous and unexpected success of Phase One, the matter had been taken out of his hands. Everyone now wanted a slice of the action, and Franchet d'Espèrey's plans

---

1   Cordier, *Victoire Éclair*, Annexe 5 p.271.
2   Falls, *Macedonia Vol. 2*, Appendix 20, p.349. Instruction from Franchet d'Espèrey to all Allied Commanders of 25 September 1918.
3   Falls, *Macedonia Vol. 2*, p.329.

for the *deuxième phase* were largely overtaken by the conflicting views and aspirations of the various members of the Supreme War Council, and the governments in Paris, London and Rome.

As Larcher points out, during the whole period of the Rupture and the Exploitation the central allied staffs and war offices left him alone, *ne lui donna aucune instruction pendant toute la deuxième partie de septembre*.[4] This was partly because they were pre-occupied with the Western Front and the Allied advance leading up to the Fifth Battle of Ypres. But mostly because they didn't realise what was going on in Macedonia, or if they had vague preconceptions, wanted no part of it.

On 21 September, for example, when the Bulgarian army was in disarray and disorganised retreat, the French War Office issued a note saying that more troops should be moved from the Macedonian to the Western Front, and that the Commander in Chief of the Allied Army of the East should consider limiting his offensive and stabilising a new front line.[5]

As late as 25 September when Gradsko and Prilep had fallen the British Representative on the Supreme War Council was forecasting that the Allied Army would soon have to fall back on its old lines or create new ones.[6]

* * *

Over the three-day period 15-17 September the Franco–Serbian forces had crossed the Moglena massif at Vetrenik–Dobropolje and over-run the Bulgarian 1st, 2nd and 3rd lines of defence. Having driven the enemy across the Belasnica they now stood in front of Mrezetchko. A breach of 50 kilometres had been created in the enemy lines with a depth of 30 kilometres.

The next three days, 18–20 September saw a consolidation of the main advance, and a widening of the breach on the flanks. Timok and Yugoslav Divisions continued to represent the arrow-head of the Allied advance. By the evening of 20 September Yugoslav had taken Kavadarci and crossed one of the enemy's main access roads from Prilep to Gradsko. Timok, meanwhile, was closing on Demi Kapu, as planned. Sumadija and French 17th Colonial Divisions were following up behind, but their rate of advance was constrained by the lengthening supply chain, and also by the relentless speed of advance of the lead divisions. Ducasse, who was there with 17th Colonial gives a graphic account of the search for food and water, and the sabotage wrought by the retreating Bulgarians.[7]

Pressurised by the Serbian advance, the Bulgarian 2nd Division had retreated to the west bank of the Crna on 18 September, joining up with its 4th Division. These put up a strong resistance, also with the holding of two bridgeheads at Rasim Bey and Selo Monastir. The Crna was crossed and the bridgeheads were finally overtaken on 20 September by the Serbian First Army and the AFO, paving the way for an advance on Prilep.

To the right the French First Group (General Anselme) on 18 September had captured Nonte. Then in a well-prepared and brilliantly executed action over 19 and 20 September they encircled and took the Bulgarian positions on the Dzena mountain, at that point the pivot of the enemy's mountain defences.[8] Within a total period of five days the Allied forces had virtually expelled the Bulgarians from the entire Moglena mountain range.

During this three day period 18-20 September – the opening, as Franchet d'Espèrey would have it, of the Exploitation Phase – by far the fiercest fighting was on the other side of the Vardar with the assault by British and Greek forces against the Bulgarian defences west and east of Lake Doiran. The tale has already been told in Chapter 34.

---

4   Larcher, *Grande Guerre*, p.233.
5   Larcher, *Grande Guerre*, p.232.
6   Falls, *Macedonia Vol. 2*, p.203.
7   Ducasse, *Balkans*, pp.205–208.
8   Falls, *Macedonia Vol. 2*, p.197.

There was however an unexpected outcome of the Second Battle of Doiran. After the British Army Group had been repulsed on 18 September, the Commander of the Bulgarian First Army, General Nerezov, was so confident of the superiority of his forces that he proposed to General Todorov, acting Bulgarian Commander in Chief, that this was the moment for his Army to break through and march on Salonica. This should be combined, he told Todorov, with a simultaneous break-out by the Bulgarian Second Army across the Struma, also directed on Salonica. And eventually, evoking the 'pincer' campaign of 1917, involving the as yet intact divisions of the Eleventh Army between the lakes of Prespa and Ohrid.

Nerezov may or may not have been aware of a number of other factors which would have made such a counter-attack on Salonica an interesting possibility. Salonica itself was only lightly defended. Most of the Greek army was engaged on the other side of the Vardar or with the BSF, only three divisions remained on the Struma, with relatively limited artillery. The British 27th Division, guarding the other side of the Vardar was also very short of guns. The French First Group was not there, being engaged on the Dzena. The physical strength and health of the BSF, low before the second Battle of Doiran, was now worse. Above all, Franchet d'Espèrey would have found it difficult to extricate French or Serbian forces to face up to a determined attack on Salonica, only two days' march from Doiran, and then effectively wage war on two fronts.

No doubt Nerezov put these points to Todorov. Only on the previous day as the severity of the 'Rupture' across the Moglena was brought home to him Todorov had written to Hindenburg asking for at least six more German divisions.[9] Now he would have some good news, or at least convincing evidence of the aggressive intent of his Bulgarian forces and rushed off to Prilep to sell the plan to the Germans. It was obvious that if such a daring and unexpected operation were to be mounted, it should be done immediately, before the BSF recovered, and before the Serbs reached the Vardar. General von Steuben, commander of the Eleventh Army, and his staff quickly did the numbers and came to the conclusion that they didn't have enough troops, and above all that available transport was quite inadequate to do the job.[10]

Von Steuben and von Scholtz's staff did however recognise that the situation west of the Vardar called for a withdrawal of some of their forces in order to contain the Allied advance and make counter attacks. They decided to fall back north of Monastir, but to continue to hold the line westwards to Lake Ohrid. This was partly to maintain alignment with the Austrians in Albania. But perhaps mainly as a result of the intervention of the Bulgarian Tsar Ferdinand, who, pushed by his General Kantardjiev on the spot, refused to give up Ohrid, sacred centre of Bulgarian culture in the 12th Century.[11] This turned out to be a grave mistake since when the Allies approached Skopje a significant part of the Eleventh Army would find itself bottled up south of Kicevo having participated little in the struggle against the Allied Armies.

Falls quotes Bujac who suggests that at this stage a major withdrawal by the whole Eleventh Army to a line Tetovo–Skopje–Stip and the Bulgarian mountains east of Stip would have been the safest policy.[12] But this would have involved abandoning most of North Macedonia, and as a probable consequence, Bulgarian-occupied Thrace, the reasons for which Bulgaria had gone to war in the first place. The AFO and the First Serbian Army would have harried mercilessly such a retreat extending over 100 kilometres. Allied dominance in the air might have created scenes of chaos among the retreating troops similar to those shortly to be seen in the approaches to the Strumitsa valley. Even during the Prilep meeting of 20 September Allied bombers had obliged the

---

9   Hall, Balkan Breakthrough, p.150. Hindenburg's oily and entirely negative reply arrived on 19 September and is presented by Casson, *Steady Drummer*, p.206.
10 Palmer, *Gardeners*, pp.211–212.
11 Cordier, *Victoire Eclair*, p.229.
12 Falls, *Macedonia Vol. 2*, p.198 quoting Bujac *Les Campagnes de l'Armée Hellenique,*, p.123.

participants to descend to the cellars.[13] In addition, much of the Bulgarian transport was pulled by teams of oxen, moving at only half normal marching pace.[14]

Besides, the German Command with its experience of the Western Front was inevitably drawn to the concept of 'snuffing out the pocket' by attacking the ever-lengthening Allied salient on both sides. Besides, they expected, not without justification, that the Franco–Serbian force would soon outrun its supply back-up, and get bogged down by the absence of roads and other logistical difficulties. It became apparent however over the next couple of days that the pocket was not for snuffing. From the left of the Allied salient the Bulgarian 4th and 2nd Divisions were being pushed even further westwards, while on the other flank the Bulgarian 3rd Division which had borne the brunt of the battles of the 'Rupture' was on the point of breakdown, despite the efforts of Crown Prince Boris who drove from unit to unit at the wheel of a light lorry in an attempt to rally the troops. He reported to his father that he had gone to the front to 'save everything that could be saved' but that the 'condition of the army is worse than I could have imagined' and that he feared that retreat would lead to disintegration.[15] The Bulgarian 66th Brigade and two Landwehr battalions were being rushed in to reinforce the Bulgarian 3rd Division. The 66th Brigade had been the only one released by Nerezov during the Second Battle of Doiran. The Landwehr battalions were two of the seven mistakenly sent by the Germans to the Struma to 'fraternise' with the Greek First Corps. They would all arrive too late and would have to be withdrawn themselves in view of the gains made by the Serbian Second Army and the French First Group.[16]

Meanwhile trouble was brewing in Bulgaria. On 20 September Tsar Ferdinand presented himself at von Scholz's headquarters at Skopje asking for support in facing the Allied offensive but also for support in putting down uprisings against his government in Sofia. On the same day he telegraphed the Austrian Emperor Karl asking for his help in squeezing more troops and arms from the Germans, and also wrote to Kaiser Wilhelm cunningly warning him of the dangers and consequences to Germany of losing Niš should the Allied advance continue unchecked. Kaiser Wilhelm told him that Germany was doing everything possible, and that perhaps the Bulgarians had retreated too early. Emperor Karl was much more helpful offering through his military attaché in Sofia two Austrian divisions, one from the Ukraine, one from Italy, to arrive 27–28 September.[17]

The German High Command took the issue of civil and military unrest in Bulgaria more seriously than that of the Allied advance. At a point, they reasoned, the latter would be held, ground would be lost (as Hindenburg had confessed to Todorov in his oily reply of 19 September), but this would not affect the outcome of the war. On the other hand losing control over the Bulgarian Government did worry them. Initially they thought of making von Scholz military dictator in Bulgaria, protecting a puppet regime by force. In the end they sent General Reuter who got the uprising under control with the aid of the German 217th Division, hurriedly sent from the Crimea.[18]

By 20 September the Germans had already abandoned all hopes of 'snuffing out the pocket', and von Scholz decided on a more substantial withdrawal, reconstructing a line from Topalcani (about half way between Monastir and Prilep) to Kavardarci. But events were moving faster than plans, and before the end of the day he was obliged to move the withdrawal line much further north,

---

13   Cordier, *Victoire Éclair*, p.229.
14   Schiavon, *Front d'Orient*, p.235.
15   Hall, *Balkan Breakthrough*, p.150 quoting from Hindenburg's memoirs p.450. Hindenburg, notes Hall, was a fan of the Crown Prince.
16   Falls, *Macedonia Vol. 2*, p.198.
17   Hall, *Balkan Breakthrough*, pp.150–153. Confirmed by Larcher, *Grande Guerre*, p.239, who refers to these two divisions as '*médiocres.*'
18   Larcher, *Grande Guerre*, p.235.

running from Prilep to the mouth of the Crna, and abandoning the railway south of Gradsko.[19] The breach in the enemy line of 50 kilometres on 18 September was now effectively over 100.

For the BSF the momentous consequence of this decision by the enemy to move their line of defence significantly further north was that the First Bulgarian Army was instructed to relinquish their beloved – and unconquered – Doiran stronghold and retreat to the Strumitsa valley. The military logic of this was clear – to prolong the newly defined Bulgarian line eastwards from the Crna's confluence with the Vardar to the natural lines of defence provided by the Plachkovitsa and Ograzden ranges. [20] But the dismay of Nerezov, who only two days before had been set on advancing on Salonica with his victorious army can only be imagined.

So it was that on 21 September Milne's exhausted and depleted British and Greek forces found the Doiran defences, the assault of which over 18-19 September had cost them over 7,000 casualties, empty, untenanted and abandoned.

* * *

It was only six days since Franchet d'Espèrey had launched his offensive against the heights of Dobropolje and Vetrenik, but the enemy had already been obliged to withdraw to positions up to 50 kilometres north of a front line which they had held, virtually unchanged, for over two years. And the length of the breach in this line, from Lake Doiran to Hill 1248 north of Monastir was now around 150 kilometres.

On 21 September Franchet d'Espèrey issued another general 'Instruction' to all Army Groups, the first since that of 31 August which had defined and launched the campaign. His key demand was to 'widen the breach made in the enemy's array, and to complete our success.' The Serbian Second Army should establish itself between Demi Kapu and Gradsko, creating a bridgehead at Krivolak. On its right it should help the French First Group to reach the Vardar and force a bridgehead at Udovo, at the southern end of the 20 kilometre gorge. The Serbian First Army should advance on Prilep 'outflanking the enemy's successive positions of retirement' and support AFO on its left. The AFO was to have the double objective of working with the Serbian First Army in clearing the Crna bend and preventing the three still intact divisions of the Eleventh Army holed up between the lakes from escaping north through Kicevo to Skopje. [21]

Essentially therefore the Allied Army now had three main directives, on the right to gain control of the Vardar valley up to and including Gradsko. In the centre to take Prilep and advance to the Vardar at Veles. And on the left to prevent the Eleventh Army from reaching and re-consolidating at Skopje before the Allies got there.

By this time, Franchet d'Espèrey knew that he was winning. He had forced the enemy to retreat perhaps even further and faster than his expectations, and he realised that they had left it too late, particularly on their right flank. His intelligence came from his forces on the ground, but also from the air. The rôle of air surveillance, according to the *Histoire des Opérations de l'Armée de l'Orient*, was of major importance *Par elle le commandement a été constamment tenu au courant non seulement de la progression de nos troupes, mais aussi de la situation de l'ennemi* (Air surveillance enabled the Command not only to follow the progress of our own troops, but also of the enemy's situation).[22]

Such was his confidence that he felt able, on 22 September, exactly one week after he had launched his offensive, to issue a short one paragraph order, probably the most satisfying of his career:

---

19 Falls, *Macedonia Vol. 2*, p.199.
20 See Map 3
21 Falls, *Macedonia Vol. 2*, p.201 quoting J. Revol *La Victoire de Macedoine* (Paris: Ch. Lavauzelle,1931), p.79.
22 Quoted by Schiavon, *Front d'Orient*, p.336.

The enemy is in retreat on the whole front between Monastir and Lake Doiran. We now have to rout him, take prisoners from his ranks, and capture his material by an unceasing pursuit… the cavalry, whose hour has come, should precede the infantry columns and prepare the way for them.[23]

Or, as Signaller Bailey succinctly remarked, 'Johnny Bulgar on the run.'[24]

The next day, 23 September, Franchet d'Espèrey issued a new 'Instruction' to all Army Groups. This updated that of 21 September, many of whose objectives had now been overtaken by the speed of the Allied advances. The Serbian First Army, having already by-passed Prilep was to move towards Veles. The Serbian Second Army, having already achieved its bridgeheads over the Vardar was to go for Stip. The French First Group, also having achieved its bridgeheads was to advance up the Gradeska Planina. The AFO was to send a division north east to support the Serbian First, and, significantly, orient the Cavalry Brigade towards Skopje. The British Army Group were to continue in the direction of the Strumitsa valley, and the Greek Corps on the Struma should be ready for an advance up the Rupel Pass.[25]

* * *

On the right of the Allied line the British Army Group were suddenly faced with a new reality. Against all expectations the enemy had retreated and must be pursued. But to do this Milne reckoned that of the 12 Brigades of his four divisions, only 7 were fit for the job, and two of these were with 27th Division across the river. Before news of the Bulgarian retreat reached him he had planned to completely withdraw 22nd Division, as well as Seres and Crete, and had written to CIGS Wilson asking for reinforcements. Wilson had replied that he would try to bring forward the arrival of 12 Indian battalions originally planned for November to October, but that he had no knowledge of any further offensive operations for the BSF having been approved. This was before either of them had heard about the retreat of the Bulgarian First Army.

In light of the new situation Milne reorganised his depleted forces into three parts. The first (Seres) was to occupy the deserted Doiran battlefield. The second (XII corps) was to move from the east of Lake Doiran onto the Blaga Planina and the Belasitsa range. The mission of the third group (XVI Corps) was to advance in pursuit of the main body of the retreating Bulgarian First Army which was retreating to the Strumitsa valley via the Kosturino pass.[26] This decision to swap the positions of the two Corps was forced on Milne by the depleted strength of XII Corps following the battle, and this change-over took its toll particularly on support services.[27] Milne did not need the urgings of Franchet d'Espèrey to get this underway as quickly as possible. The iron was hot, it needed to be struck immediately. But, however understandably, time was wasted, and Milne's dissatisfaction comes through in his diary entry of 23 September; 'the difficulties of getting the Army on the move are very great' he wrote two full days after the Bulgarian retirement 'administrative staffs are not getting a move on, and there seems extraordinary delay.'[28]

No such lethargy affected the RAF. On 21 September they had found all the roads and defiles leading north from the Doiran battlefield packed with endless columns of the retreating enemy. From that afternoon and for the following thirty-six hours 45 RAF planes bombed and machine

---

23 Palmer, *Gardeners*, p.315. Telegram from Franchet d'Espèrey to all Allied Commanders.
24 Signaller Bailey, 21 September.
25 Falls, *Macedonia Vol. 2*, p.219.
26 Falls, *Macedonia Vol. 2*, pp.121, 203 and 207.
27 Seligman, *Salonica Sideshow*, p.134.
28 Nicol, *Uncle George*, p.176.

gunned in relays the helpless enemy lines of troops, vehicles and transport creating havoc, blockages and congestion which made their attacks even more lethal. The 'gradual, orderly withdrawal' foreseen by Todorov turned into a massacre for which, obviously, they were totally unprepared, and against which the German air force scarcely put in an appearance.[29] Initial attacks were on the Doiran to Strumitsa road where the Kosturino defile was a particular target. Inevitably the British and Greek troops along this road two days later found signs of devastation. Later attacks covered also the Rupel pass, and the Kresna pass in Bulgaria.[30]

It so happened that Crete Division, which was attached to XII Corps, was once again part of the force advancing from the east of Lake Doiran towards the Blaga Planina. This time they met very limited opposition, mainly sniper posts and the crest of the Planina was reached by the evening of 23 September. Signaller Bailey noted with approval 'Greek Division coming through our lines. Going to storm Belasitsa. Thousands of Greeks, fine looking men, just the stamp for hill warfare.'[31] As it happened, 228th Brigade was ordered to accompany them. Milne notes 'Cretan Division, in conjunction with the 228 Infantry Brigade, swept along the slopes of the Belasitsa down to the Butkovo valley against Rupel and Demi Hasar.'[32]

XVI Corps initially made slow progress, to the evident frustration of General Milne, with 26th Division getting no further than the Bayemia river on 24 September, while its heavy artillery was still at Stojakovo, 15 kilometres to the rear. After which they advanced at an increasing pace to pass through the Kosturino defile on 25 September, reaching Strumitsa on the 26th, from which they fanned out to cover the exit roads from the town. Material and ammunition discarded by the Bulgarians was found all along the way. Between Kosturino and Strumitsa early on 25 September the Derbyshire Yeomanry entered Bulgaria, the first Allied troops to do so since 1915.[33]

The retreat by the Bulgarian First Army up the east bank of the Vardar to a line beneath Stip and the Plachkovitsa highlands was in accordance with the retirement plan of Todorov 'to a natural mountain defence line through southern Serbia and the ranges south of Sofia.' The Belasitsa was however a different proposition. This mountain range dominated the lower Strumitsa valley and access to the Strumitsa river's confluence with the Struma, which then ran north into central Bulgaria. The Bulgarian army was not going to give this up easily.

Milne had called for the Vishoka Chuka (known to the BSF as Signal Allemand), at 1,845 metres the dominant peak of the range, to be taken on 24 September. This was something of a tall order; the mountain was some 7 kilometres from the north of Lake Doiran and represented a climb of around 1,000 metres from the Blaga Planina. The Belasitsa ridge including the Signal Allemand was finally taken in the early hours of 27 September by 28th Division, the Cretans, and the Zouaves, redeeming themselves in some way for their failure to advance during the Battle of Doiran.[34] Further east, British and Greek forces were driving the Bulgarian army back across the Struma into Bulgaria, a final offensive before the armistice came into effect which resulted in 1,300 prisoners being taken and 790 guns.[35]

On the evening of 19 September Franchet d'Espèrey had written to Milne that after the success of the French First Group in breaking the enemy line at the Dzena he was now ordering them

---

29 Palmer, *Gardeners*, p.212.
30 Wakefield, *Under the Devil's Eye*, p.222.
31 Signaller Bailey, 27 September.
32 Milne, *Despatch of 1918*, p.3. 'Swept' might have been a good word to describe Cretan progress, but it is difficult to imagine the veterans of the ex-garrison 228th Brigade who had never expected to serve on the front line, let alone be involved in an armed pursuit, 'sweeping'.
33 Milne, *Despatch of 1918*, p.4. The Strumitsa enclave was then part of Bulgaria. After the war it was ceded to Yugoslavia. It is now in North Macedonia.
34 Falls, *Macedonia Vol. 2*, pp.208 and 227.
35 Hall, *Balkan Breakthrough*, p.161.

down to the Vardar to drive the enemy across the river and bottle him in from the north. He asked that 27th Division be assigned temporarily to Anselme for this, to which Milne agreed, and the switch was made at noon on 21 September. On the same day the RAF reported that the enemy was streaming north to cross the Vardar from west to east at Pardovitsa and Miletkovo. On 22 September 27th Division found Gevgeli abandoned, and, joining up with First Group's Archipelago Division to its left, advanced on Pardovitsa. That the retreating Bulgarians would blow up the bridge here had been foreseen, and a bridging train was already on the way. It arrived at 4 am on 24 September, and the new pontoon bridge of 150 metres was in place at midday. The Division with most of its artillery crossed to the left bank, and returned to the orders of XVI Corps.[36]

In the meantime the three divisions of the French First Army (two of which were Greek) made contact with the southernmost wing of the Serbian Second Army on the Marianska Planina and proceeded to roll the enemy up the west bank of the Vardar from Pardovitsa to Davidovo. On 24 September they crossed the river at Strumitsa Station, just south of the steep defile carrying both the road and railway, between Udovo and Demi Kapu. The day before, Timok had crossed the river at Demi Kapu and made its way up the Gradeska Planina on the other side. Further north Yugoslav had crossed the river at Krivolak and pressed onwards to the Kara Hojali heights controlling the road to Stip, overcoming strong opposition from the Bulgarian First Army. By 25 September the Serbs, moving at their now habitual speed had taken Stip and were advancing on Kočani. Even Franchet d'Espèrey was impressed.[37]

With control of the Vardar on both sides up to Krivolak, the Serbian Second Army could now turn to its key objective, Gradsko. A hurriedly reconstituted Bulgarian defence – in fact in this case with a German General and the seven re-assembled Landwehr battalions from the Struma Front – put up a strong fight, particularly in the hills south of the Vardar and west of the Crna confluence. This had been a major scene of contention, around the Arcangel Monastery, during Sarrail's campaign of 1915. Yugoslav had to call on the French 17th Colonial Division, which had been following close behind them, to deal with this.[38] The Vardar was crossed and Gradsko taken on 24 September. In spite of last minute destruction by the retreating army, the booty exceeded all expectation:

> *Des dizaines de milliers de tonnes de matériels, de munitions et de vivres sont récupérés par les Alliés. Des canons, des avions, des trains remplis de matériel sont capturés* (Tens of thousands of tons of material, ammunition, arms and food were recuperated by the Allies. Guns, planes, trainloads of equipment were taken).[39]

Hindenburg had described Gradsko as 'the most important centre of communications in the Macedonian theatre of war.'[40] Well, now it was lost to them, as was all their previously held territory to the east of the Vardar up to and including Stip.

* * *

---

36   Falls, *Macedonia Vol. 2*, p.215.
37   Falls *Macedonia Vol. 2*, Appendix 20 p.349. Instruction from Franchet d'Espèrey to Allied Commanders of 25 September 1918.
38   Ducasse, *Balkans*, p.207.
39   Schiavon, *Front d'Orient*, p.336.
40   Palmer, *Gardeners*, p.217.

With the capture of Gradsko the battle of Dobropolje had been brought to a brilliant conclusion. Franchet d'Espèrey's objective now was to apply the killer blow to the enemy and win the war on the Macedonian Front.

It will be recalled that on 28 June, only ten days after his arrival in Salonica, Franchet d'Espèrey had accompanied Voivode Mišić and Prince Alexander to the summit of Mt Floka and decided on his plan of campaign. By 7 July he and his staff had codified this plan. The objective, right from the start, was to *couper en deux l'Armée Bulgare, séparant les forces qui opèrent dans la région Vardar/Struma de celles qui tiennent la région de Monastir* (cut the Bulgarian Army in two, separating their forces operating in the Vardar/Struma sectors from those centred around Monastir).[41]

Franchet d'Espèrey had never wavered from this core objective and in his definitive *Instruction pour l'Exploitation* of 31 August he stresses the importance of *le développement de nos succès vers le nord est l'ouest jusqu'à la région d'Uskub* (the development of our success to the North and West up to Skopje).[42]

Following the heroics of the Serbian Second Army, the successes of the French First Group and the defensive victory of the British Army Group, attention now turned to the First Serbian Army and the AFO.

Facing them was the 'German' Eleventh Army (almost entirely Bulgarian) under General von Steuben. The left flank of the Eleventh Army, 2nd and 3rd Divisions, had borne the brunt of the attacks of the Serbian Second Army and the French First Group, and were to play only a limited role for the remaining days of the campaign. In the centre of the Eleventh Army line was its LXI Corps, 302nd and 4th Divisions whose initial instructions under the withdrawal order were to retire to a line running east from Prilep to Gradsko, and south west to Monastir.

To the right of the Eleventh Army line was LXII Corps, three divisions holding a line from north of Monastir running over the Lakes Prespa and Ohrid to Albania. This had been its line at the opening of the Allied offensive, and as has been seen, at the behest of Tsar Ferdinand and his cultural general, was not to be included in the withdrawal. Remarkably this order was only formally rescinded by Todorov and Prince Boris on 24 September,[43] although von Steuben partially anticipated this two days earlier by ordering a retirement further north to a line Debar–Kicevo–Brod.[44]

The Allies had already been progressing west of the Crna before the Bulgarian withdrawal order. The Serbian First Army, over the Crna on 20 September, had been instructed by Franchet d'Espèrey in his order of 21 September to advance on Prilep supporting the AFO on its left. By 22 September they were at Shivets, well up the Crna, only 20 kilometres short of its confluence, and were advancing through the Drenska Planina south of Prilep. Just south of Shivets they had captured a bridge intact at Vosartsi, an appropriately positioned contact point between them and the Serbian Second Army. This strategically placed bridge had been gained by the French Expeditionary Force almost exactly 3 years previously, the high water mark of its attempt to link up with the retreating Serbian Army.

Then, leaving Prilep to the AFO, the Serbian First Army continued through the Babuna Pass to Veles, which was to fall on 26 September. To their left the right flank of AFO, Greek 3rd Division, French 11th Colonial Division and Italian 35th Division were advancing up the bend in the Crna. On 22 September the Italians finally took 'their' Hill 1050 as the enemy retreated. They were as amazed at the sophistication of the fortifications as the BSF had been at Doiran. 'Immense caverns cut out of the solid rock illuminated by electricity, and special appliances whereby detachments were warned of different kinds of bombardment…nothing had been neglected to make this

---

41   Cordier, *Victoire Eclair*, Annexe 2 p.262.
42   Cordier, *Victoire Eclair*, Annexe 5 p.272.
43   Ducasse, *Balkans*, p.208.
44   Falls, *Macedonia Vol. 2*, p.218.

mountain an impregnable fortress.'⁴⁵ These AFO divisions found little trace of any rearward lines of defence, and moved on to the Krivogastani plain reaching Krushevo on 25 September. On 27 September battle was joined with elements of LXI Corps south of Kicevo.

To the left of the AFO line, the remaining four divisions finally took Hill 1248 from which the Bulgarians had been able to bomb Monastir and its railway ever since Sarrail's battle of Monastir in 1916. By 23 September they were at Topolcani. On the afternoon of 23 September the Cavalry, who had left Florina on 22 September on General Henrys' orders, entered Prilep with 11th Colonial Division on their heels. The delighted local inhabitants showed the arriving troops where the Eleventh Army HQ had been, now deserted. Only five days previously Todorov had proudly presented Nerezov's plan to von Steuben here.[46]

Other elements of AFO moved westwards challenging the northward retreat of LXII Corps, taking Resen on 26 September, Ohrid on 29 September, and blocking any possibility of a retreat through Albania.[47] It would have been one of the greatest ironies of the Macedonian Campaign if this had been forced upon them. Unlike the Serbs in 1915, however, the passage would have been much easier in September than December, and there were no mountain ranges to cross. It is interesting to speculate what the Austrians would have made of three large divisions of Bulgarians appearing in their midst.

The Bulgarian LXI Corps finding its original objective unattainable was now divided into two parts, one trying to reach to Vardar via the Babuna Pass to help stem Allied advances up the river towards Skopje, the other supporting the retreat of the LXII Corps up the Kicevo/Tetovo corridor.

A major divergence of opinion between General Henrys and his boss emerges here. Franchet d'Espèrey was not happy with so much of AFO being used to the west and north. In his *'Instruction'* of 25 September (which was, in fact, almost entirely directed at Henrys) he notes that 'Five divisions are now taking part in the pursuit of Resen and Kicevo; their directions are convergent ... on the contrary our weight should be shifted more and more in the direction of Skopje. This is at the same time the direction in which we shall achieve the greatest success, and that in which German intervention may threaten us most seriously.' He asks that the equivalent of two divisions be directed immediately at Skopje.[48] Two days later came another stronger message, just to Henrys 'the bulk of French divisions should be pushed as quickly as possible on Skopje…only small detachments should be left facing Kicevo.' He even added a hand-written note at the bottom *la direction est au nord et à l'est.*

As early as 23 September Franchet d'Espèrey must have realised that the extent and timing of the Bulgarian withdrawal was rendering the 'outflanking movement on Skopje via Tetovo' foreseen in the *Instruction* of 31 August obsolete, or at least secondary. The priority now was to prevent the enemy from using the same outflanking route and getting to Skopje first. There was a branch railway line from Tetovo to Skopje which would have speeded up the last leg of the journey to Skopje by LXII Corps, making the taking of Skopje and its railway station by the Allies even more urgent.[49] The main Allied push should be up the Vardar from Veles. With one exception.

In his exultant note of 22 September, Franchet d'Espèrey had declared that 'the cavalry, whose hour has come, should precede the infantry columns and prepare the way for them.' The *Groupement de Cavalerie* of the *Armée Française de l'Orient* consisted of 1st and 4th Chasseurs d'Afrique and a regiment of the Spahis Marocains. This combined force fielded 3,000 horsemen, supported by a

---

45 Villari, *Macedonian Campaign*, p.235.
46 Palmer, *Gardeners*, p.216.
47 Villari, *Macedonian Campaign*, p.241.
48 Falls, *Macedonia Vol. 2*, Appendix 20 p.349.
49 Villari, *Macedonian Campaign*, p.223.

section of armoured cars.⁵⁰ It was known as the 'Brigade Jouinot-Gambetta' after its charismatic commander.⁵¹

After they had taken Prilep, General Henrys had told them to wheel westwards towards Kicevo, but at this point Franchet d'Espèrey arrived in his car and redirected them towards Skopje. As Alan Palmer has it 'probably the last great cavalry march on the continent of Europe had begun.'⁵² Jouinot-Gambetta's plan was to make for Dolgace and follow the Tresta river valley to Skopje, but found the area around Brod well defended, and turned back to the Prilep–Veles road.⁵³ He passed through the Babuna gorge without much difficulty, but at Izvor ran up against the Serbian First Army heavily engaged against LXI's 4th Division who were defending Veles. Jouinot-Gambetta realising that the road route to Skopje was now barred to him decided to leave it at Starigrad, and set off across the mountains, leaving the Spahis who had got drawn into the battle to follow on when they could. Between Starigrad and Skopje lay the Golesnica massif, mostly untracked mountainous terrain rising to 2,000 metres in places. The distance as the crow flew was around 60 kilometres, but nearer 100 on the ground. This is not cavalry territory, as a glance at a contemporary map shows.⁵⁴ For much of the journey the horsemen had to dismount and lead their horses.⁵⁵ The armoured cars were left behind with the Serbs. The Cavalry Brigade had no arms beyond 37 mm guns carried by packhorses.⁵⁶

The cross-country march of the Cavalry Brigade which was to bring an extraordinary fortnight's offensive to a fitting conclusion, and put the seal on the Allied victory, began in the evening of 25 September. By the next day they had arrived at Drenovo. Along the narrow goat tracks the column stretched for 6 kilometres. After Drenovo a climb up to 1,800 metres, and then a sharp descent of 300. On 27 September after a night march they arrived at Aldince on the Kaidina river, where they waited for the Spahis to catch up, and found a grassy plateau with barns and hay where finally they were able to feed their horses and rest a little.⁵⁷ On 28 September they descended from the mountains to Dracevo, near the railway line, just short of Skopje.⁵⁸ In three days they had completely side-stepped the Veles–Skopje road, only 40 kilometres for the famous crow, but around 70 with twists and turns, where the German led Bulgarian forces were doggedly resisting the Allied infantry advance.

Early on 29 September the Jouinot–Gambetta Brigade charged into Skopje. Surprise was total, panic followed. The Spahis were sent to take the Karshjak ridge to the south of the town, which commanded the Skopje–Tetovo road. This was achieved with little resistance by 0930.⁵⁹ The Chasseurs d'Afrique went for the centre of the town and the railway station. They were greatly outnumbered; Skopje, formerly the HQ of the Army Group von Scholz,⁶⁰ was garrisoned with seven battalions, four artillery brigades and an Armoured train. It was the latter, German

---

50 Larcher, *Grande Guerre*, p.233.
51 Schiavon, *Front d'Orient*, p.338. His uncle Leon Gambetta played a key role during the Franco-Prussian War and then in the establishment of the Third Republic. He is remembered for escaping from Paris in 1870 in a hot air balloon ahead of the Prussians and effectively running the French Government for five months from Tours. His nephew's exploit was more spectacular than this, but is less well known.
52 Palmer, *Gardeners*, p.216.
53 Schiavon, *Front d'Orient*, p.338.
54 GSGS 2097 Uskub OSO1915.
55 Schiavon, *Front d'Orient*, p.339.
56 Palmer, *Gardeners*, p.219.
57 Ducasse, *Balkans*, p.212.
58 See Map 3
59 Schiavon, *Front d'Orient*, p.340.
60 Von Scholz seeing the writing on the wall had transferred his HQ to Lescovac, 50 km south of Nis on the day the Allies took Gradsko, 24 September.

controlled, which posed the greatest problem, but when the Spahis having left a squadron to guard the Karshjak heights, suddenly roared in from the north of the town, the train pulled out in the direction of Niš, and victory for the Cavalry, against all the odds was assured.[61]

Over 300 prisoners had been taken, five guns and ammunition, and plenty of food for the famished men and their mounts. At 1000 am the Brigade wrote a message on the ground to communicate to a French reconnaissance plane that Skopje had been taken, confirming to the Allied Commander in Chief that, once again, he had been right.[62]

Efforts were now redoubled to get the Allied infantry up to consolidate the achievement of the Cavalry. It was a very close run thing. On the morning of 30 September, twenty four hours after Skopje had fallen to the French Cavalry, leading units of the LXII Corps were within 5 kilometres of the town and were de-training from the Tetovo railway. They had brought their guns with them, of a calibre far superior to those with which the Jouinot-Gambetta Brigade were equipped, had crossed the Vardar and were preparing to attack the town from the west.

The heroics of the Cavalry may well have counted for nothing but for three factors. Firstly, on hearing of the fall of Skopje General Suren, Commander of the LXI Corps decided, instead of attacking Skopje from the east, to march north to protect the Kumanovo road. Secondly, in the nick of time, around noon on 30 September, news of the Armistice was brought to General Fleck, Commander of the LXII Corps. Thirdly any lingering thoughts he might have had – the Armistice did not of course cover Germany – of ignoring it and pressing on with his Bulgarian troops to clear Skopje and escaping with them towards Bulgaria on the Kumanovo road, were dispelled by the arrival of the French and Serbian infantry on the morning of 1 October.[63] From this moment the Bulgarian Army was really 'coupée en deux' and Franchet d'Espérey's key objective had been achieved.

Around 60,000 men were now blocked west of Skopje. There was no way to escape back to Bulgaria, or even press on to Serbia. Apart from the narrow and treacherous Kačanik Pass, which even if taken would only lead further into the depths of Serbia, the only other road to Bulgaria through Kumanovo required first passing through Skopje.

The whole campaign from the assault by the Serbian Army on the Dobropolje to the capture of Skopje by the AFO Cavalry had taken exactly two weeks, from the morning of 15 September to the morning of 29 September. It had been a brutally unremitting offensive conducted by troops from five separate national armies working to a masterpiece of a plan. The objectives set by Franchet d'Espèrey on 31 August for the five Army Groups had been met with almost metronomic precision – AFO, Skopje; Serbian Armies, Veles and Stip area; French First Group; Udovo, Demi Kapu and Gradeska; Greek Army, Demi Hasar and Rupel; British Army Group, Strumitsa valley. And most of these Army Groups had gone even further.

The enemy had made mistakes in the face of this furious assault – notably the under-utilisation of LXII Corps, the vain attempt to 'snuff out the pocket', and the precipitous withdrawal of their First Army from the valley of the Vardar – and Franchet d'Espèrey had seized on them. He was not, although he may have provoked them, directly responsible for the conflicting agendas and disagreements between the Bulgarian and German political and military leaders, but he was able to benefit from them. Just as he exploited the advantages he had to hand – dominance in the air for attack and reconnaissance, the hill-fighting qualities of the Serbian, Greek and French Colonial forces, the quality of the staffs and also of the communication networks left to him by Guillaumat. And, as Larcher said, total lack of interference during the critical period from the French or British war offices.

---

61 Schiavon, *Front d'Orient*, p.341.
62 Palmer, *Gardeners*, p.220.
63 Falls, *Macedonia Vol. 2*, pp.248–249.

It was a collective success for the five Allied nations collaborating on the Macedonian Front, working in mixed Army Groups according to need and competence rather than nationality. But it was Franchet d'Espèrey who was indisputably the architect of the victory over the Bulgarians. The Germans and the Austrians still needed to be driven from the Balkans. But the hard bit had been done.

36

1918
Armistice

The Treaty of Berlin in June 1878 had effectively recognised four new countries in the Balkans. In all cases any nominal Ottoman suzerainty had been thrown off by the end of the 1890s, and Princes adopted the title of 'King', or in the case of Bulgaria, 'Tsar.' Of these countries only Serbia and Montenegro had home-grown kings. Bulgaria and Romania – just as Greece fifty years before – adopted kings of German extraction, with a preponderance of Saxe-Coburg Gotha, the candidates placed before the National Assemblies having been vetted by the Great Powers. All of these Balkan kingdoms were short-lived, none surviving beyond the Second World War.

Tsar Ferdinand was well integrated in European royal circles and appears in the iconic photo of nine kings at the funeral of Edward VII. It is to be presumed however that the blind and disastrous pro-Bulgarian attitude of the British Government in 1915 was not necessarily the result of royal connections. Queen Victoria is reported as having said on his appointment in 1887 'He is totally unfit. It should be stopped at once.'[1]

Whatever his foreign origins and his probable total ignorance of Bulgarian affairs when he took up his rôle, it would not have taken his subjects long to acquaint him with the long history of their country, of the martial doings of earlier Tsars, and of Bulgaria's territorial aspirations, above all of the promise held up of 'Greater Bulgaria' at the Treaty of San Stefano in March 1878. He had received not only a crown, but a mission, and one in no way conflicting with the interests of his former country.

Having been outwitted and defeated in the Second Balkan War, he had declared for the Central Powers in 1915. Until the end of 1917 the dream of 'Greater Bulgaria' still seemed to be within his grasp. His troops just had to stay put on the Greek and Albanian frontiers, and in Eastern Macedonia, and his German and Austrian allies just had to win the war up there.

But by mid 1918 all this seemed less certain, and the nature of his worsening vassal-status was coming home to him. Of its small population of 4.5 million, more men had been conscripted per head of the population than in France or Germany. The economy was in chaos, as was agriculture with few men to tend the land, and the requirement to feed the Bulgarian and German armies. The demands of the Germans who were seen more and more as an occupying force increased. The menace of starvation loomed.[2]

In June 1918 Tsar Ferdinand replaced his pro-German (and German educated) Prime Minister Vasil Radoslavov with Aleksander Malinov, who had already served two terms, and who had been against the alliance with Germany in the first place.[3]

Malinov, however, despite all that was going on around him, proved to be as obsessed with territorial aggrandisement as all his predecessors. His particular objective was to gain all of the

---

1 Theo Aronson *Crowns in Conflict* (London: John Murray,1986), p.83.
2 Palmer, *Gardeners*, p.222.
3 Ducasse, *Balkans*, p.214.

Dobrujah for his country, not just the southern half conceded to them by the Germans at the Treaty of Bucharest on 7 May 1918.[4] Following the tumultuous Allied break-through on the Moglena he noted on 17 September that 'events have taken an unfortunate turn', but then turned back to the Dobrujah. On 24 September he had his wish – desperate to keep Bulgaria in the war, the Germans agreed that Bulgaria could have all of the Dobrujah if they conceded some territory to the Turks on the Maritsa.[5]

But by this time the Dobrujah issue had become totally irrelevant. Bulgarian soldiers on the Macedonian Front were deserting en masse, particularly those of the Bulgarian First Army who were being pushed across the Vardar and up the Strumitsa valley by the British Army Group and the French First Group.[6] On 21 September Malinov had sent a parliamentary commission, including Finance Minister Ljapcev, to investigate the situation on the front. They reported back that 'A great part of our Army has demobilised, and in the rest a determination to retreat in difficult circumstances has set in.'[7] By the same day, Hall notes, the Serbs had only taken 5,000 prisoners despite their unrelenting advances from the Dobropolje to the Vardar. This could only mean that significant numbers of Bulgarian soldiers, particularly from 3rd Division, were now voting with their feet.

On 24 September rebellious soldiers seized control of Kyustendil, the Bulgarian Army HQ.[8] They drove out the Bulgarian General Staffs, pillaged the town and continued their march on Sofia.[9] Over the next two days 30,000 insurgents moved into Gornja Dzumaja and Radomir, thirty kilometres south west of Sofia and started to move on the capital.

On 25 September, having been told that an army of 20,000 'Bolsheviks' was advancing on Sofia to liberate the imprisoned leader of the pacifist Agrarian party, Aleksander Stamboliski, Tsar Ferdinand had authorised his release.[10] Stamboliski, together with the majority of deputies to the Bulgarian Parliament, had been totally against Bulgaria's entry into the war in 1915. 'It is our deep conviction that this adventurism will lead Bulgaria to the grave.'[11] He had been incarcerated for the whole of the war, but his release did not help much as he inevitably became a rallying point for the anti-war movement.

In Radomir on 27 September Raiko Daskalov, a leader of the Agrarian party declared a republic with himself as commander of the armed forces and Stamboliski as President. He announced that 'Today the Bulgarian people broke the fetters of slavery, toppled the despotic regime of Ferdinand and his aides … and declared itself a free people with a republican government.' The next day five train loads of rebellious soldiers set out for Sofia. On 29 September, their ranks swelled with other army deserters, they moved on Sofia in three columns by night.[12] They were held off by cadets of the military academy, the Tsar's guard force, and above all by the German 217th Division commanded by General Reuter which had been rushed across from the Crimea, the first units of which arrived in Sofia on 25 September.[13] The Tsar, who had been with von Scholz in Skopje, and then watching events before Gradsko, now felt sufficiently secure to return to his capital.[14]

---

4   Falls, *Macedonia Vol. 2*, p.257.
5   Hall, *Balkan Breakthrough*, p.153.
6   Villari, *Macedonian Campaign*, p.245.
7   Hall, *Balkan Breakthrough*, p.150.
8   See Map 11
9   Larcher, *Grande Guerre*, p.235.
10 Hall, *Balkan Breakthrough*, p.156.
11 Glenny, *Balkans*, p.337. After the war Stamboliski fulfilled many government functions including Minister of Defence, Foreign Minister and Prime minister before being assassinated in 1923.
12 Hall, *Balkan Breakthrough*, p.162. quoting Ljubomir Ognyanov '*The 1918 Soldiers Insurrection in Bulgaria*'. Ognyanov reports that in the conflict 2,500 rebels were killed and 2,000 taken prisoner.
13 Falls, *Macedonia Vol. 2*, p.251..
14 Larcher, *Grande Guerre*, p.235.

General Lukov, Commander of the Bulgarian Second Army on the Belasitsa and Struma Fronts, had already recognised that the game was up as soon as the Allies had reached the Vardar and von Scholz had ordered the major retreat, and had begged the Tsar to seek an armistice and was told 'Go and get killed in your present lines.'[15] On 25 September he returned to the charge this time supported by General Nerezov, whose Bulgarian First Army had now been forced back in disarray and dissolution following the Battle of Doiran. Together they called on Malinov's Government to seek terms with the Allies.[16] It was less than a week since the triumphant Nerezov had proposed to Torodov a lightening pincer movement on Salonica with his victorious troops and those of the Second Army on the Struma.

On the same 25 September General Todorov himself, acting Commander in Chief of all Bulgarian forces, told the Crown Council that the military situation was 'hopeless.' His view was not shared by his boss, General Zhekov, still recovering from his operation in Vienna, and still convinced that fighting should continue in the expectation of help from the Central Powers.[17] But Zhekov was out of touch and not there, and after the Crown Council meeting Malinov had no alternative but to report to the Tsar that 'The Crown Council has concluded to its deep regret, that the war is lost, and that there is no alternative but to ask for peace. Only this way can we protect our country from ruin and all those evils which Bulgaria could expect if the enemy crosses its borders.' He wanted, for very obvious reasons and at all costs to keep the vengeful Greeks and Serbs out of Bulgaria.[18]

Tsar Ferdinand finally realised that he had come to the end of the road. He sent a telegram to Emperor Karl:

> The destruction of my unfortunate army proceeds at a rapid pace. The First Army of Nerezov is fading away. The Second Army is threatened by the superior power of the Greeks and the English. Revolutionary troops, burning and murdering everywhere are already threatening Sofia. The Malinov Government demands an armistice and an immediate peace from me. I have submitted my abdication to the Ministerial Council.[19]

In a similar message to the Kaiser of 25 September the Tsar predicted that defeat on the Macedonian Front would prove to be a disaster for the whole (Central Powers) alliance *(Der Schlag an der mazedonischen Front ist das Verhaengnis fuer alle).*[20]

Either Kaiser Wilhelm didn't get this message, or it was withheld from him, or (more likely) he didn't want to understand the gravity of the situation, for on 27 September he wrote to the Tsar, 'German and Austrian troops arriving from all sides will bring necessary help to your army and push back the enemy further.' Further? In due course the Central Powers did pull together six divisions, who were to delay but in no way prevent the Allied Army of the East from clearing all enemy forces out of Serbia by the end of October.

Having reached his decision Malinov wasted no time. At 0800 on the morning of 26 September a delegation consisting of two Bulgarian officers 'headed by a Major Trianov approached the British lines in a motor car.'[21] They had brought a letter from General Todorov stating that the

---

15 Ludendorff, *My War Memories*, p.712, Villari, *Macedonian Campaign*, p.246 and Palmer *Gardeners*, p.222.
16 Hall, *Balkan Breakthrough*, p.155.
17 Hall, *Balkan Breakthrough*, p.160.
18 Hall, *Balkan Breakthrough*, p.156 quoting Bulgarian Government sources.
19 Hall, Balkan Breakthrough, p.157 quoting from Austrian and German sources.
20 Larcher, *Grande Guerre*, p.239 quoting Arz. Interesting to note that his correspondence with the Austrian Emperor and with the Kaiser was in German, his native language.
21 Nicol, *Uncle George*, p.177 quoting BSF War Diary.

Bulgarian government, with the consent of the Tsar, requested the mediation of Milne with the Allied Commander in obtaining a 48 hour ceasefire, during which armistice conditions could be discussed. The delegation was passed to Stanley Casson, officer for unusual events, who called his Commander in Chief. Milne instructed him to send them on to Salonica. 'Tell them' he stated, 'there is a war still on and we don't intend to stop it for them.' Milne knew perfectly well that they would get very short shrift from Franchet d'Espèrey, which is what they got.[22]

It is worth recalling that on 26 September the Allies had only just reached Veles. The Serbian Second Army had reached Stip but was still 50 kilometres short of the Bulgarian border. Jouinot-Gambetta was only one day into his epic crossing of the Golesnica (of which the Bulgarians anyway knew nothing). French First Group had only crossed the Vardar the day before. The British had not quite reached Strumitsa. Other than a few Yeomanry units, no one had so far even set foot or hoof in Bulgaria. Control of the Belasitsa range was not yet assured, and Signal Allemand had not been taken. Above all, on the Allied western flank AFO was still heavily engaged with the LXI Corps; a pitched battle was taking place in front of Kicevo, and there was still every possibility that LXI Corps would get to Skopje via Tetovo before the Allies via Veles.

The 'hopelessness' felt by Todorov and shared by Malinov, Lukov and Nerezov was not therefore entirely a matter of the military situation, on which a final conclusion had not yet been reached, but in the realisation that the Germans with their backs to the wall in France were not going to pour in with reinforcements, that the lands for which Bulgaria had gone to war had already been lost, or soon would be, and that they had no particular interest in helping the Germans and Austrians to retain the rest of Serbia. Also, they were faced with mass desertions by the divisions closest to home, and that they didn't want to prolong their country's misery by suffering under Serbian or Greek occupation.

Franchet d'Espèrey's response to the Bulgarian delegation was as Milne had predicted. On 27 September, the next day, he sent it back with the message that he would receive 'with fitting courtesy duly qualified delegates of the Bulgarian Government, who should present themselves to British lines' (the British lines obviously because this is the way they would come). But in the meantime 'I can accord no suspension of arms leading to the interruptions of the operations in progress.'[23]

On the evening of 27 September Milne notes in his diary 'An American Diplomat arrives by night ... a Mr Walker from the American legation in Sofia.' Mr Walker was the representative of Mr Murphy, the US Chargé d'Affaires in Sofia. The purpose of Walker's visit was to 'mediate' between the Allies and the Bulgarians.[24] As previously noted America was not at war with Bulgaria and had held an Embassy there throughout. Here was another example of the sort of interference characterised by General Bliss, who as a member of the Supreme War Council, was able to pontificate on the Macedonian Campaign whilst playing no military part in it.

Franchet d'Espèrey spent the day of 27 September agreeing with Clemenceau the terms he would offer to the 'duly qualified delegates' when they arrived.[25] He probably did not need Clemenceau's confirmation that he should have nothing to do with Mr Walker.

On the morning of 28 September three cars containing the 'duly qualified delegates' were stopped by 3 Troop, B Squadron of the Derbyshire Yeomanry at Bosilov, a few miles east of Strumitsa on the road leading through the Strumitsa valley to Bulgaria.[26] The party consisted of General

---

22 Casson, *Steady Drummer*, p.211. Casson accompanied them to Salonica himself.
23 Falls, *Macedonia Vol. 2*, p.250.
24 Nicol, *Uncle George*, p.177.
25 Schiavon, *Front d'Orient*, p.343.
26 Wakefield, *Under the Devil's Eye*, p.226.

Lukov,[27] Finance Minister Ljapcev, a diplomat Minister Radev, and two officers. They arrived at Milne's HQ at 1300. He interviewed them and gave them lunch, and sent them on their way to Salonica, where they arrived at 1600. Milne immediately sent a report to CIGS Wilson of his meeting, including a one-to-one session with the Finance Minister in which Ljapcev 'appeared to be honestly anxious to cut adrift from the thraldom of Germany, but does not accept to have been thoroughly beaten in the field.'[28]

On their arrival in Salonica, the delegation received a note from Franchet d'Espèrey crisply laying down the lines for the negotiations:

> We could justly behave cruelly towards Bulgaria. She no longer has an army and is at our mercy. However we do not want to ruin her, nor do we want to impose humiliating conditions on her. We will not enter Sofia, nor will we compromise your sovereignty. But we require from you certain guarantees for the security of our operation.[29]

For Franchet d'Espèrey a subdued and acquiescent Bulgaria would now be a side issue to that of driving his forces to the Danube and beyond and confronting the core enemies. Clemenceau accepted this pragmatic approach. When, however, the Bulgarian delegates floated the idea of 'neutrality', eventually employing her forces to help the Allies, Franchet d'Espèrey brought them back immediately to the reality of the situation: 'You are defeated, and you must submit to our terms. Bulgaria is not a neutral country but a military zone, and it is unthinkable that we should not pass through it.'[30]

With his usual precision Franchet d'Espèrey had prepared all his conditions, and had cleared them with Clemenceau the previous day. His hand was strengthened immeasurably by the news of the fall of Skopje which came to him shortly after 1000 on 29 September while negotiations were still taking place. Terms were signed just before midnight on 29 September, to come into operation at noon the following day 30 September:

- Immediate evacuation of occupied territories in Greece and Serbia
- Immediate demobilisation of the Bulgarian Army except for three divisions of 16 battalions each to protect the railways and defend the Eastern Frontier (Dobrujah)
- All arms and military equipment of all sorts, including horses, to be placed in designated depots
- Return to Greece of all military material seized by Bulgaria in Eastern Macedonia
- All Bulgarian troops currently west of Skopje to lay down their arms and be treated until further notice as prisoners of war
- Return of all Allied prisoners of war. Right of the Allies to employ Bulgarian prisoners of war.
- Germany and Austria to withdraw all troops and *organes militaires* within four weeks. Their diplomats and other nationals in Bulgaria to leave similarly

---

27 After the war, the Germans considered that Lukov was the prime mover behind the call for an armistice. Falls, *Macedonia Vol 2*, p.249 quoting *Weltkriegsende an der Mazedonischen Front* p.139. Lukov had been a former Bulgarian Military Attaché in Paris. Schiavon, *Front d'Orient*, p.343. Ducasse maintains that he had been a former pupil of Franchet d'Espèrey at the Ecole Militaire. Ducasse, *Balkans*, p.215. According to Schiavon Ljapcev had also studied in Paris.
28 Nicol, *Uncle George*, pp.177–178.
29 Hall, *Balkan Breakthrough*, p.160.
30 Villari, Macedonian Campaign, p.247.

To which were added four 'secret' clauses:

- Use by the Allies of railways, roads, river transport and ports, telephone and telegram equipment. The details for this to be worked out within 8 days
- *Un certain nombre de points stratégiques seront occupés à l'intérieur du territoire Bulgare par les grandes puissances alliées.* (A certain number of strategic points in the interior of the country will be occupied by the 'major' allied powers). Such occupation to be temporary. Except in particular circumstances Sofia will not be occupied.
- The Allied Commander to enforce a total blockage of any contact between Bulgaria and her former allies
- The opening of all Bulgarian ports to Allied and neutral shipping.

The terms were signed by Franchet d'Espèrey on behalf of the Allies, and General Lukov and Minister Ljapcev on behalf of the Bulgarian Government.[31] Not stated, but implicit, was that Bulgarian Sovereignty was to be maintained – the Allies were not planning to take over the country – that the 1915 borders would be maintained until a final peace treaty, and that there would be no reparations or military indemnities.

With regard to the second of the 'secret clauses' Franchet d'Espèrey's original position was that all of the members of the Allied Army of the East should be allowed as part of the temporary occupying force. Both Prince Alexander and Venizelos to their credit told Franchet d'Espèrey that they preferred to waive this right in the interest of future relations with Bulgaria.[32] This unquestionably would have come as a great relief to the Bulgarian delegates.

As a result of the last-minute news from Skopje the Allied Commander had been able to formalise the rupture of the Bulgarian Army into two halves, and to add over 60,000 prisoners of war to the Allied tally. General Henrys in a message to the AFO a few days later quantified the achievement:

> *La XIème Armée vient de capituler devant l'AFO. Depuis le début de l'offensive 66,629 Bulgares dont 1,287 officiers et 5 généraux, 1,476 Allemands dont 14 officiers, 1,354 Autrichiens dont 3 officiers. 255 canons, 31,159 chevaux ou bœufs sont tombés entre nos mains. La Victoire est complète*
> (The XI Army has just capitulated to the AFO. Since the beginning of the offensive 66,629 Bulgarians including 1,287 officers and 5 generals, 1,476 Germans including 14 officers, 1,354 Austrians with 3 officers, 255 guns, 31,159 horses or oxen have fallen into our hands. The victory is complete).[33]

These numbers did not include 15,000 prisoners captured elsewhere, or indeed the enormous number who must have deserted.

On 2 October the Bulgarian Parliament formally approved the Armistice terms. On 3 October Tsar Ferdinand abdicated.[34] In terms proportionate to the population of his country he had brought as much grief to his people as Kaiser Wilhelm had to Germany. He was succeeded by Crown Prince Boris, the succession possibly being helped by the presence of the German 217th Division in Sofia keeping revolution at bay during these critical days. The Germans left on 5 October. As Falls points

---

31 Larcher, *Grande Guerre*, Annexe 20 p.286 for the full text. Falls, Vol 2 p.252 provides an exact translation.
32 Villari, *Macedonian Campaign*, p.247.
33 Schiavon, *Front d'Orient*, p.345.
34 Larcher, Grande Guerre, p.237.

out, of all the First World War defeated nations, only Bulgaria retained its monarchy.[35] Tsar Boris died in 1943, five years before his father who had retired to Germany.

One of the first to congratulate Franchet d'Espèrey was Guillaumat. He at least would have understood the magnitude of the achievement. Had he remained as Commander of the Allied Army of the East it is doubtful that Bulgaria would have been knocked out of the war at the end of September. But without the relentless political pressure he had applied in Paris, London and Rome during August and September, approval for the Allied offensive would almost certainly never have been given. It was also very much his victory. But had he been still there, he would at least have had the sense and courtesy to keep Milne in the loop, and probably as a co-signatory.

On 29 September when Franchet d'Espèrey was agreeing/dictating the terms of the armistice to the Bulgarians, Milne simply heard 'rumours of peace'. He was woken at 0100 on 30 September by his Chief of Staff to be told that 'hostilities cease at noon' and that Franchet d'Espèrey wanted to see him at 1600. It was not until 1215 when the armistice was already in place that 'a letter arrived at British Headquarters enclosing a copy of the Military Convention between the Entente Powers and Bulgaria. It contained seven clauses and marked the end of hostilities.'[36]

The Macedonian Campaign had been launched as a joint Anglo–French initiative in 1915, but had suffered for the whole three years from disagreements and misunderstandings stemming in the main from totally different views as to its purpose. It had been the subject of mostly uninformed and usually conflicting input from Governments and military staffs in France and Britain.

If, at this critical moment, Clemenceau feared that by submitting the armistice terms to the Supreme War Council and the British Government for analysis and approval, delay would result, and a unique opportunity be lost, he was probably right. Similarly, and this is probably the main point, Franchet d'Espèrey would have known that Milne, if involved in the discussions, would have had to confer with London.

Nevertheless, Milne had been there facing off to the Bulgarians from the start. He had thrown his troops into two murderous battles at Doiran in support of Franco–Serbian offensives, one of which never took place, undertaken countless other actions against the enemy in the highly malarial area which had been allocated to him, and had defended and policed a front which represented more than half of the total Allied front since 1916. He ought at least to have been kept informed of the signing of the Armistice, rather than receiving formal notification by means of a letter after the cease fire had started. This omission is skated around by the Official Historian who provides no information either as to whether the British War Office had been involved in any way with the definition of the armistice conditions, or whether to them it was also presented as a *fait accompli*. Schiavon regrets this '*maladresse*' which he points out led inevitably to the exclusion of the French from the negotiations and signature of the armistice by the British with Turkey on 30 October.[37]

Franchet d'Espèrey had run a momentous campaign, possibly the greatest in the War. The victory was his. A word to his and his country's principal ally as he brought it to a triumphant conclusion would not have been misplaced.

---

35 Falls, *Macedonia Vol. 2*, p.252.
36 Nicol, *Uncle George*, p.178 quoting the War Diary. No mention is made of the 'secret clauses.'
37 Schiavon, *Front d'Orient*, p.345.

37

1918
Aftermath

(Map 12)

With the capitulation of Bulgaria the story of the Campaign on the Macedonian Front comes to an end. The Allies have regained possession of occupied Greek and Serbian Macedonia, restored Greece to her pre-war frontiers, and knocked one of the four enemy nations out of the war. The objectives set by Franchet d'Espèrey in his *Instruction* of 31 August have been achieved, indeed exceeded.

The Allied Army of the East could now address itself to the realisation of the 'distant and audacious' Phase 2 objectives alluded to but not developed in this *Instruction*. Franchet d'Espèrey was at the top of his game. He was Commander of a successful and motivated army of over half a million men. Now he expected to lead them in pursuit of his concept, essentially unchanged since he had presented it to Joffre in November 1914, of advancing to the Danube and the frontiers of Austro-Hungary and attacking the Central Powers from the south.

In this light, and scarcely pausing to take breath, he gave orders on 30 September as an immediate first step for the Serbian First Army to advance on Niš, and for the Serbian Second Army to secure control of the Kumanovo–Kustendil road. The French Cavalry went with the Serbian First Army. Both General Mombelli Commander of the Italian 35th Division and Prince Alexander would have liked the Italians to go with them as well, but Franchet d'Espèrey wanted them in Bulgaria on garrison duty.[1] Given the post-war friction between the Italians and the Yugoslavs, possibly this was an opportunity missed for some beneficial fraternisation.

By 4 October Franchet d'Espèrey had developed his plans for the rest of the Allied Army and briefed his army commanders.[2] On 5 October he sent Clemenceau a summary of these plans. The main thrust would be to the north '*avec l'objectif de libérer la Serbie et menacer l'Autriche-Hongrie.* (with the objective of liberating Serbia and threatening Austro-Hungary)' A total of 17 divisions would be employed here, three British on the right, eight AFO in the centre, and the six Serbian divisions on the left. A French division would be sent through Bulgaria to '*tendre la main à la Romanie et couper les communications entre Centraux et Turquie*' (to hold out a hand to Romania and cut communications between the Central Powers and Turkey). A group of five divisions, one French, one British and three Greek under a French General (Anselme) would be sent towards Turkey '*pour débloquer les Dardanelles.*' (to unblock the Dardanelles). Tactical reserves of two French divisions in Bulgaria and three Greek divisions on the Struma were to be held.

---

1 Villari, *Macedonian Campaign*, p.263.
2 Falls, *Macedonia*, Vol. 2, p.257.

In this brief communication the only unit to be identified by name, curiously enough, was the humble British 228th Brigade, who were to garrison the Bulgarian Black Sea ports of Varna and Burgos.

In conclusion he observed, *nos forces sont intactes et en belle forme, mais prisonnières de leurs communications* (our forces are intact and in good form, but are prisoners of their communications), and he calls for the immediate despatch of *personnel technique, et le matériel de réparation de voies ferrées, ainsi que du matériel de transport automobile* (technical personnel, material for repairing railways, and material for automotive transport). Completely confident in the justness of his mission he concludes with the words *j'agirai sans attendre* (I shall go ahead without waiting.)[3]

George Milne had considerable doubts about Franchet d'Espèrey's plan. To him the priority now was to knock Turkey out of the war. Turkey was teetering or defeated on all her other fronts, and now that Bulgaria had capitulated, her European front was very vulnerable. Furthermore, liberating the Black Sea for Allied shipping would help to reduce the Allied Army of the East's supply train by a significant factor; Salonica was now far behind them, and the main lines of communication through Serbia to Niš and beyond had been sabotaged in dozens of places by the retreating enemy. The Bulgarian rail network however was intact, and in the hands of the Allies. If Allied shipping had access to the Black Sea the use of the Bulgarian Black Sea ports would provide an invaluable supplement to Salonica.

Although Milne immediately set about moving three divisions into Bulgaria in accordance with his orders, he wrote to the War Office and to Wilson with his views on the matter:

> He (Franchet d'Espèrey) intends to form a mixed force to operate against Turkey, but whether French or Greek Generals are to be placed in charge I cannot say. I recommend that the British Government insists on their troops being employed in this direction and not northwards. The French are naturally anxious that advances in every direction remain in their hands … what is required here is to give every Army its separate task and line of communication and leave it to carry it out. In my opinion ours ought to be to open up the Dardanelles … the French do not appear to realise to what extent our sea power can now be turned to our advantage.[4]

This time he was pushing at an open door. At the Supreme War Council meeting of 7 October Lloyd George, always a closet Easterner, insisted that Turkey was a British affair, and that Milne should lead the force against Turkey with three British divisions, one French, and eventually three Greek. He also opened the issue of terms to be imposed on Turkey when, as now seemed likely, the Turks asked for an Armistice. It was also agreed that such negotiations would be opened with whichever Allied Power the Turks first approached. It must have been obvious to everyone that this would be the British, and as a result the French and Italians asked for the inclusion of a number of harsh conditions.[5]

Wilson confirmed to Milne after the meeting that 'the Prime Minister took a very strong line in Paris with the result that you have been given a very considerable force to operate against Turkey in Europe.'[6]

---

3   Larcher, *Grande Guerre*, Annexe 21 p.286 quoting telegram from Franchet d'Espèrey to Minister of War of 5 October.
4   Nicol, *Uncle George*, p.179.
5   McMeekin, *Ottoman Endgame*, p.406.
6   Nicol, *Uncle George*, p.180.

Without rejecting Franchet d'Espèrey's plan in its entirety, the Supreme War Council made significant modifications. These were summarised in two telegrams sent by Clemenceau to Franchet d'Espèrey on 7 October.[7]

The four future objectives of the Allied Army of the East were now defined as; to liberate Serbia, to occupy Bulgaria, to make contact with Romania with the aim of eventual joint offensive actions, and to force Turkey to seek an armistice, thereby opening the Black Sea to the Allies. *Porter la guerre à les frontières meme de l'Autriche* (Carry the war even to the frontiers of Austria), is now only listed as *une possibilité*.

General Berthelot, formerly head of the French Military Mission to Romania is now re-introduced into the picture as head of an Army of the Danube with four divisions, a thinly disguised attempt on the part of the SWC probably even piloted by Clemenceau, to clip the wings of a too-successful general.[8]

Play is made of handing much of the responsibility for the Balkan theatre to the Balkan armies, another recurrent SWC theme. Mention is also made, surprisingly, to 'the participation of part of the Bulgarian army in our operations.' Even after all these years the spirit of Grey still hovered somewhere above British Foreign Office deliberations. The appointment of Milne as head of the army to 'march on Constantinople' is also covered.

As a final example of SWC thinking the Allied Army of the East is now enjoined to prepare a '*front défensif de l'Albanie au Danube et à la Mer Noire.*' (A defensive front from Albania to the Danube and the Black Sea.)

One can imagine, even after all these years, the delusion and disappointment of Franchet d'Espèrey in reading all this. A sadness captured well by Schiavon:

> Officially Franchet d'Espèrey retained his command over all the forces of the Allied Army of the East. In reality, now that the menace of the enemy was diminished, everyone wanted to further their own interests and pursue post-war geo-political objectives. It became clear that the Allied Army would break up in the near future. *La magnifique campagne dont rêvait le Général français, toutes forces réunies, n'aura pas lieu* (The magnificent campaign which the General dreamed of wouldn't take place.)[9]

While the Supreme War Council was digging paper trenches and drawing a defensive line from Albania to the Black Sea, the German Supreme Command were recognising the full impact of the defeat of Bulgaria on their war effort.

They had been taken completely by surprise. Ludendorff records that at the beginning of September 'we still had reason to hope that we would maintain our position in Italy and Macedonia; our flanks and rear were covered'. Even by the time he was writing his memoirs, he had not come to terms with the collapse of Bulgaria, and his report of the Battle of Dobropolje makes for compulsive reading:

> On September 15 the armies of the Entente attacked in Macedonia, east of the Vardar, in the mountains between the Vardar and the Crna, and with weaker forces near Monastir. In the centre where the attack was faced with the greatest obstacles the Bulgarian 2nd and 3rd Divisions offered no resistance. No other explanation accounts for the rapid advance of the Entente troops over that wild and broken country, eminently suited for defense. The 2nd and

---

7   Larcher, *Grande Guerre*, Annexe 22 p.287, Telegrams from War Ministry to Franchet d'Espèrey of 7 October 1918.
8   Falls, *Macedonia Vol. 2*, p.261.
9   Schiavon, *Front d'Orient*, p.347.

3rd Divisions retreated as in on a definite plan without any show of resistance; they simply surrendered their position, behind the Crna in one direction, behind the Vardar in the other. The Bulgarian Army went home. Entente propaganda and money had done their work. Possibly, too, Bolshevik influences from Russia had crept in.[10]

On 28 September Hindenburg and Ludendorff held a crisis meeting at Spa. They were forced to conclude that the defeat of Bulgaria would lead to the crumbling of the whole south-eastern front, and that this combined with major setbacks in France left no alternative to asking for peace. On 29 September in Spa they met with Foreign Minister von Hinze who convinced them of the necessity for 'a complete change of system, and the foundation of a Parliamentary Ministry in Berlin'. They took their conclusions to the Kaiser, who had joined them in Spa, and convinced him of the necessity of calling for the intercession of the American President to bring the war to an end. They pointed out to him however that President Wilson would not deal directly with him, nor with his senior military staff.[11] His Majesty', reported Ludendorff 'was unusually calm'. The same evening an Imperial Proclamation was sent to Chancellor von Herting for the introduction of a parliamentary system in Germany. The next day, 30 September (the day, as it happened of the Bulgarian Armistice) the Kaiser and Hindenburg returned to Berlin, a new ministry was set up, and von Herting was replaced as Chancellor by Prince Max of Baden.[12]

It was all too late. On the same 30 September having heard of the Bulgarian capitulation, Ludendorff informed his staff, 'The Bulgarian Army has collapsed and signed an armistice today – Turkey, the frontiers of Austria and the South-East are menaced. There are no troops available. The Field Marshal and I are convinced that in the interests of the Army an end must be put to hostilities.[13]

On 3 October Hindenburg presented his (subsequently much-quoted) statement to the new Chancellor:

> The Supreme Army Commander repeats his request, already made on 29 September, for an immediate peace offer to be made to our enemies. As a result of the collapse on the Macedonian Front and of the weakening of our reserves in the West which this has necessitated, and in view of the impossibility of making good the losses of the last few days, there seems now no possibility, as far as human judgement goes, of winning peace from our enemies by force of arms ... In these circumstances it will be best to stop the struggle and save the German people and its allies from useless losses. Every day will cost the lives of thousands of brave soldiers.[14]

The next day, 4 October, a 'peace note' was sent to President Wilson asking him to agree to an armistice. Both the Germans and the Austrians stressed that this was not a surrender, but an attempt to end the war without any preconditions.[15]

The day after the new regime had been established in Berlin, the spokesman for the Supreme Command, Major von den Bussche, briefed the newly empowered parliamentary leaders:

---

10   Ludendorff, *My War Memories* Vol.2, p.712
11   Gilbert, First World War, p.467.
12   Ludendorff , *My War Memories Vol.2* pp.721–731.
13   Larcher, *Grande Guerre*, p.240 quoting Ludendorff, *Documents di GHQ* (Paris: Payot, 1922) Vol.2 p.345.
14   Ludendorff, *My War Memories,* Vol 2 p.729.
15   Gilbert, First World War, p.474.

The military situation has completely changed over the last few days. The collapse of the Bulgarian Front has profoundly affected our operations. Contact with Constantinople is menaced, as well as control of the Danube, essential for our supplies. We have been forced to send to the Balkans German and Austro-Hungarian divisions destined for the Western Front.[16]

On 8 October Wilson rejected the 'peace note' on the basis that an essential precondition was the evacuation of all Central Power forces from occupied territory.

The war went on. The Germans were fully aware that the stronger their position on the ground during armistice negotiations, the better terms they would get. With this intention, hurriedly and belatedly, the Germans and Austrians put together six divisions to try to stem the Allied tide in the Balkans. Two further German divisions were to be sent from Russia via the Crimea, in addition to von Reuter's 217th Division, already present. An Alpine division had been sent from France and parts of it were already in Niš on 30 September. The two Austrian divisions promised in extremis by Emperor Karl to Tsar Ferdinand on 20 September were already in or near Bulgaria. Hindenburg however had no illusions about the fighting qualities of these divisions 'How weak those troops were' he wrote in his memoirs 'our Alpine Division had scarcely any effective units, while one of the Austrian divisions was full of Czechs who presumably would not fight.'[17]

Meanwhile the Serbian First Army was pressing on relentlessly towards Niš and Belgrade along the Morava river. Efforts by the Austrian 9th Division and the remnants of LVI Corps to hold a line from Pristina to Vranje while the other five divisions completed their detrainment and deployment to the north were swept aside. On 5 October Danube Division entered Vranje and on 6 October Grdelica.[18] On 7 October the Serbs took Lescovac, and the next day were at Brestovac twenty kilometres south of Niš and continued moving.[19]

As a transport hub and military depot, Niš was of critical importance to the Central Powers. Whoever controlled Niš controlled the rail to Sofia and Constantinople; in 1915 when the Germans took Niš, then the military headquarters of the Serbian Army, the Kaiser came in person to witness the event. For the Allies the importance of taking Niš was up there with Gradsko and Skopje; with Niš in their hands the rest of Serbia was open to them. The speed of the Serbian advance once more confounded the enemy. Two of the German divisions were still de-training, the Austrian 30th Division had not yet arrived. The Serbs arrived in Niš on 10 October and had invested the town by midday. By the next morning the enemy were in retreat.

While the Serbian First Army was powering its way up the Morava valley, other Serbian units and the Italian XVI Army were driving Austrian forces out of Albania, the Serbs taking Tirana on 10 October, and the Italians Durazzo on 15 October. By 30 October units of Yugoslav Division had taken Skadar, and with elements of the Montenegrin Army liberated Podgorica on 3 November and seized the port of Kotor on 6 November.[20]

On 10 October, the day of the fall of Niš, the Serbian Armies had been on the march for 25 days, almost continually in contact with the enemy. They had covered 300 kilometres. Major efforts by Allied engineers to re-open the Vardar railway had got as far as Veles by 15 October, but by this time the Serbs were well out of reach, living on their own provisions, supplies captured from the enemy, and the willing support of the local populations as well as extra recruits into their ranks.[21]

---

16   Cordier, *Victoire Eclair*, p.249.
17   Larcher, Grande Guerre, p.247 quoting Hindenburg p.372.
18   See Map 11
19   Babac, *Serbian Army*, p.123.
20   Babac, *Serbian Army*, p.123.
21   Falls, *Macedonia, Vol. 2*, p.272.

North of Niš the Serbs waited for four days to let the French catch up with them. By 20 October the enemy had regrouped sufficiently to offer serious resistance at Paraćin, but by 23 October had been soundly beaten by the Franco–Serbian force and began an obvious if orderly retreat to the Danube. Paraćin turned out to be the last battle in the magnificent campaign conducted by the Serbian Armies across the whole length of their country.[22]

By the end of October Serbia had been cleared of all enemy forces, and on 1 November the Serbian First Army entered Belgrade. General Jouinot-Gambetta whose Cavalry Brigade had accompanied them and fought alongside them through the whole month of October wrote a moving tribute to the Serbian army on their inexorable advance from Skopje to Belgrade:

> *Jamais hommes ne montrèrent plus de silencieuse persévérance, plus de stoïque volonté têtue, un plus tenace désir de vaincre … les yeux fixés vers le Danube, vers Belgrade que rien désormais ne semblait capable de les empêcher d'atteindre* (Never again will men show such quiet persistence, such stoical and obstinate determination, such a fixed desire to win through … their eyes set so firmly on the objective of the Danube and Belgrade that nothing seemed capable of preventing them from attaining.)[23]

On the same day, the Serbian Second Army having moved up to the west along the Morava reached the Drina on the Bosnian border.[24] Almost three years had passed since, overwhelmed by the joint armies of the Central Powers, the Serbian armies had retreated across the mountains of Albania to the Adriatic. The same armies under the same leaders had now played the major role in expelling the enemy from their homeland. It was by any standards a phenomenal achievement.

Only two days later, on 3 November, Austria signed armistice terms with the Allied Powers following their crushing defeat on 24 October at the hands of the Italian Armies, with the support of British and French divisions, at the battle of Vittorio Veneto.[25]

By this time the Austro-Hungarian Empire had virtually ceased to exist. The Czechs had declared independence on 28 October, joined two days later by the Slovaks. On 29 October the interim 'State of Slovenia, Croatia and Serbia' was formed, (to be replaced on 1 December by the 'Kingdom of Serbia, Croatia and Slovenia', by this time also incorporating Bosnia, Montenegro and the Vojvodina).[26]

Hungary had broken away from Austria on 31 October and set up a revolutionary government headed by Count Karoli. Hoping for special treatment from the Allies, Karoli began separate armistice negotiations with Franchet d'Espèrey, to whom the Supreme War Council had given the authority. These were concluded in Belgrade, very much along the lines of the Bulgarian armistice, and with no special treatment having been conceded, on 13 November – two days, as it happened, after the date of the General Armistice with Germany.[27]

The Allied Army of the East's final military action was by the 'Army of the Danube', elements of which crossed the river at Ruschuk (now Ruse) to confront the few remaining German troops in Romania. They met with little resistance, but their action may have helped Romania to hurriedly re-declare war on Germany on 9 November, a perfect example of just-in-time

---

22 Villari, *Macedonian Campaign*, p.258.
23 Schiavon, *Front d'Orient*, p.351 quoting F-J Deygas, *L'Armée d'Orient dans la Guerre Mondiale* (Paris: Payot, 1932), p.270.
24 Babac, *Serbian Army*, p.123.
25 Gray and Argyle, *Chronicle Vol. 2*, p.240.
26 Alan Palmer, *Victory 1918* (London: Weidenfeld and Nicolson, 1998), p.297, Gray and Argyle, *Chronicle Vol 2*, p.237.
27 Larcher, *Grande Guerre*, p.252, Gray and Argyle, *Chronicle Vol 2*, p.246.

diplomacy and rewarded in due course by the virtual doubling of their territory at the expense mainly of Hungary.[28]

On 27 October Franchet d'Espèrey received a bizarre request from Clemenceau to develop with General Berthelot a plan for the 'economic encirclement' of Bolshevik Russia, ' intervention in southern Russia would form a natural extension of the mission of the Allied Army of the East.' Franchet d'Espèrey poured cold water over the whole project (which could well have originated from Berthelot) citing military, political, cultural and climactic reasons.[29]

His refusal to play ball here may have been a contributing factor in Clemenceau's refusal to consider a new plan which he submitted to Clemenceau on 3 November. It was, in fact, the old plan, the one he had nurtured in his mind since 1914 and which, remarkably, he had come very close to be able to put into effect; crossing Austro-Hungary into Bohemia and then on to Berlin. The attack would be led by the AFO and the Serbian Armies, with eventual Italian participation on the east flank.

On 5 November he was told by Clemenceau that an Allied strike on Germany had already been approved at a SWC meeting of 2 November. It would be led by Foch, would be launched from France and Italy and would aim at Bavaria. On top of this, Franchet d'Espèrey was told that from now on he reported to Foch.[30] His extraordinary exploit of getting his army from Greece to Belgrade and the Hungarian frontier in 45 days had already been archived in the minds of the Allied Supreme Command, who had never really understood it or appreciated its consequences, or its contribution to bringing the war to an end in 1918. He and his army were now just elements to move around on the map during the armistice process. He was not even pre-informed of the forthcoming armistice with Germany, simply receiving a telegram from Paris giving him the news:

Je n'ai pas été consulté ni même avisé des pourparlers, et pourtant mes troupes étaient en Hongroie, et, fait unique dans cette guerre, j'occupais deux capitales ennemies, Sofia at Constantinople (I was not consulted or even informed about the negotiations, despite the fact that my troops were in Hungary and, uniquely in this war, I was in occupation of two enemy capitals, Sofia and Constantinople).[31]

* * *

On 30 October, the day before the Serbs arrived in Belgrade, an armistice had been signed with Turkey. Cut off from the Central Powers, with Bulgaria no longer providing a buffer on her European frontier, the fall of Turkey following that of Bulgaria was only going to be a matter of time. When told by the Bulgarians on 29 September that they were seeking an armistice, the Turkish Grand Vizier Talat Pasha didn't take long to work out the consequences. 'We're done' was his immediate reaction.[32]

Milne had been allocated by the SWC four divisions, three British and one French, for his attack on Constantinople. These were to be the BSF 22nd, 26th and 28th Divisions and the French 122nd Division. BSF's 27th Division, was sent into Bulgaria to form part of the Army of the Danube. Milne was also given the Greek First Corps in support.

---

28 Falls, *Macedonia Vol. 2*, p.280.
29 Ducasse, *Balkans*, p.237 quoting Telegram from Franchet d'Espèrey replying to Clemenceau's of 27 October.
30 Schiavon, *Front d'Orient*, p.351.
31 Schiavon, *Front d'Orient*, p 355.
32 McMeekin, *Ottoman Endgame*, p.397.

By 23 October 26th Division had arrived by train at Jsir Mustapha Pasha north of Adrianople (now Edirne) and 22nd Division was arriving at Dedeagach. Once French 122nd Division was in place at Demotica 30 kilometres south on the Maritsa river, the plan was for 26th Division to take Adrianople, which was lightly defended, while the French made a bridgehead over the Maritsa. Due to the delay in arrival of 122nd Division, however, this plan was held over by four days until 28 October.[33]

But by this time peace discussions were well under way. On 11 October Admiral Gough-Calthorpe, British Commander in Chief in the Mediterranean arrived at Mudros on the island of Lemnos to await developments and provide naval support to Milne as necessary. On 20 October the new Turkish Vizier, Izzet Pasha sent General Townshend who the Turks had held prisoner for two and a half years following the fall of Kut, to tell the Admiral that the Turks were prepared to talk peace. On 26 October Turkish emissaries arrived on the island to agree armistice terms. Agreement was reached on 30 October to come into effect on 31 October.

The Straits were to be opened to Allied shipping. Otherwise the other conditions were very similar to those of the Bulgarian armistice; demobilisation of Turkish forces except for small units to preserve order, all German and Austrian personnel to be expelled, war ships to be surrendered, Allied rights to occupy ports and strategic points. As with Bulgaria, no attempt was made for regime change, and the Allies did not propose to occupy the capital.[34] The sting however was in the tail: Clause 11, the surrender and withdrawal of garrisons from the Transcaucasia to Persia, Clause 15, the evacuation of Bakum and Batu, which the Allies would take over, and Clause 16 'the surrender of all Ottoman garrisons in the Hejaz, Asir, Yemen, Syria, Mesopotamia and Cicilia to the nearest Allied Commander or representative'. Although not yet formalised in a post-war peace treaty, this effectively represented the start of the dismemberment of the Ottoman Empire outside Anatolia.[35]

Although they had agreed a draft set of negotiating terms with their Allies, the British had side-stepped the French by not inviting their representatives to the armistice negotiations – an early move in the chess game to be played out between the two Powers in the Middle East up to, into, and beyond the Second World War. The British pointed out with some warmth that they had not been present at the signing of the Bulgarian Armistice. Lloyd George in a secret meeting with the French on the same 30 October went further 'we have half a million men on Ottoman territory. We have destroyed three or four Turkish armies. We have fought alone against Turkey for three years.'

As Commander of the Allied Army in Salonica Franchet d'Espèrey had had the right to sign the Bulgarian armistice, retorted Clemenceau, Calthorpe did not have that authority. *On nous fait violence,* he concluded, *mais nous renonçons à notre droit pour maintenir l'accord nécessaire entre la Grande Bretagne et nous* (We are being subjected to force. But we are renouncing our rights in order to maintain the necessary accord between ourselves and the British). A week later he sent a telegram to Franchet d'Espèrey telling him to cede the command in Constantinople to General Milne.[36]

At the moment of signature, Milne had assembled three divisions ready on the Turkish border, 22nd Division at Dedeagach (now Alexandroupolis), 26th Division just north of Adrianople and 122nd French Division at Demotica. The Greek First Hellenic Corps was not far behind, spread out between Kavalla and Drama.[37] Two battalions of 228th Brigade, before fading out of the story, were sent to garrison the Black Sea ports of Varna, Burgos and Constanza.

---

33   Falls, *Macedonia Vol. 2*, p.263.
34   Palmer, *Victory 1918*, p.266.
35   McMeekin, *Ottoman Endgame*, p.409.
36   Ducasse, *Balkans*, p.239 quoting J Delaunay *Secrets Diplomatiques 1914 – 18* (Bruxelles : Brépol, 1963)
37   Milne, *Despatch of 1918*, p.5.

Milne had planned to occupy the Straits with one division. Since the port of Dedeagach was inadequate for embarking quantities of troops to the Dardanelles, 22nd Division was once again returned to Salonica overland. The honour of occupying the Dardanelles therefore fell to 28th Division, shipped direct from Salonica, who occupied both sides of the Straits and took over the Turkish forts on 10 and 11 November. The Allied fleets passed through the Dardanelles on 12 November, three and a half years after they had failed so disastrously at the first attempt. British forces reached Constantinople and the Bosphorus on 14 November.[38]

On the same day the BSF HQ was formally transferred from Salonica to Constantinople. Formal command of European Turkey and the Balkans still rested with the Commandant of the Allied Armies of the East, but the process of implementing the terms of the Armistice was left largely to the British. Further east, and beyond the remit of Franchet d'Espèrey, British forces were to be engaged for an extended period policing Turkish disarmament and in peace-keeping missions as far afield as the Caucasus and the Caspian Sea.

The 'New Army' divisions, 22nd and 26th, were disbanded in mid-1919. The 'Regular Army' Divisions, 27th and 28th, remained in the field, in some areas to 1923, as the re-designated 'Army of the Black Sea'.

The remainder of the Allied Army of the East was now widely scattered. Formally, Franchet d'Espèrey maintained his HQ in Salonica until 6 February 1919. On that date he moved it to Constantinople, where he retained his command until March 1920, coordinating policing and reconstruction work throughout the Balkans, mainly with residual French, British and Italian forces. The Greeks, for their part, had gone home after a successful late intervention in the campaign, to sort out their post-war destinies and re-possess Eastern Macedonia. The Serbs having achieved the re-conquest of their country in spectacular fashion, were now engaged in rebuilding the shattered lives of the Serbian people, and at the same time setting up the new Kingdom of Serbs, Croats and Slovenes with the incorporation of lands previously part of the Austro-Hungarian Empire.

Most of the Italian 35th Division remained in Bulgaria until July 1919, overseeing the process of reconstruction, and ensuring the application of the terms of the Bulgarian armistice. The 'Army of the Danube' under General Berthelot had the task of removing the last vestiges of von Mackensen's army from the north bank and shepherding them back through Hungary, and in so doing giving Romania the opportunity to re-join the war during its last few days. Other AFO units were engaged in policing and peace-keeping activities in Bulgaria and Hungary, while some were sent to oversee potentially difficult transfers of power and territory in Montenegro and Dalmatia.

These were all valid post-war activities, but as a fighting unit the Allied Army of the East had completed its mission. It had achieved one of the greatest victories of the war and would now pass into history, which would promptly ignore it.

---

38 Gray and Argyle, *Chronicle Vol. 2*, p.246.

38

Conclusions

As Bismarck had foreseen, the First World War had its origins in the Balkans. No one, however, could have predicted that one of the results of the 'damned foolish thing' would be close on a million men facing off to each other for three years in Macedonia.

This could very well not have happened. If the Anglo-French fleet had forced the Dardanelles in November 1914 before the Germans had mined them, gained the Sea of Marmara, joined forces with the Russians in the Black Sea, and subsequently brought in troops, including those offered by Greece, to secure the Straits, the Macedonian Campaign in the form it took may not have been necessary. With the Allied Fleet before Constantinople and in the Black Sea, Romania might have declared earlier for the Allies and marched into Hungary. Above all, there is a strong chance that Bulgaria would have remained neutral.

Instead of which in March 1915 the Allied fleet was driven back by mines and the 480,000 men sent in from April onwards were also driven out, with horrendous casualties.[1] As this major Allied setback unfolded, Bulgaria increasingly saw that her chances of achieving the fabled frontiers of San Stefano lay with joining the Central Powers, who in turn needed an alliance with Bulgaria to enable a means of overland communication with Turkey.[2]

Before any of this took place, the idea of an Allied attack on the Central Powers through Salonica and Serbia had been floated, by Franchet d'Espèrey among others, in late 1914. The case for exercising this option became stronger as the war progressed into 1915, but by this time Gallipoli was totally overshadowing any other 'Eastern' approach.

Unquestionably the potential rewards of the Dardanelles Campaign as originally designed were immediate, dramatic and game-changing. But by mid-1915 it was already clear that it was not turning out this way. If at that time losses had been cut, and a large part of the forces committed to Gallipoli had been diverted to Salonica while Serbia and her roads and rail to Belgrade remained intact and available, by the end of 1915 an Allied Army of the East including the full Serbian Army could have been facing Austro-Hungary across the Danube; a much more productive role than facing the Bulgarian Army across the Greek frontier. In this second scenario also, Bulgaria would probably have remained neutral and Romania would have declared earlier. And the Central Powers would have been denied overland communications with Turkey.

At the close of this volume, setting out to describe what happened on the Macedonian Front between 1915-18, perhaps a short descent into the hypothetical may be permitted. Moving on however from the hypothetical to the historical, two main questions remain open at the end of a study of the Macedonian Campaign; why has the Campaign been so denigrated and neglected, and what did it achieve?

---

1 Laffin, *Gallipoli*, p.222.
2 Falkenhayn, *German Headquarters*, p.161.

Throughout its life the three-year campaign on the Macedonian Front had been subject to public indifference and political ambivalence. Media coverage in both France and Britain was minimal, generally misinformed and often pejorative. In Britain the BSF was the butt of music hall jokes. Clemenceau (before he came to power, but even then his feelings changed little) referred to Sarrail's forces as 'the gardeners of Salonica'. Even the Germans referred to them as 'the inmates of a great concentration camp'.

Such was the overwhelming attention given to the Western Front in British and French press that Bulgaria and Turkey came to be considered second-class enemies in the public mind. Politically, the Macedonian venture had been set up unwillingly and under false premises and was to suffer from uncertainty as to its purpose through its whole duration. Conflicts of interest and differences over strategy between the French and the British repeatedly beset the whole enterprise.

These attitudes sadly outlived the triumphs on the Macedonian Front in September–October 1918. No campaign medals were struck in either Britain or France. As has been seen, Franchet d'Espèrey was virtually side-lined after having led his troops to perhaps the most spectacular victory of the whole war. In Britain titles and monetary rewards were given to senior army commanders, but Milne was overlooked.[3] Falls, on the last page of his superb *'Official History'* relates with bemusement if not disbelief that:

> When victory in the Great War had its apotheosis in Paris on 14 July 1919, and in their triumphal march the troops passed the august winged figures, each symbolic of a victorious battle, in the Champs Elysées, the only Macedonian names upon the scrolls which met their eyes were 'Pogradec' and 'Skra di Legen.' No Monastir, no Dobropolje upon those tablets of glory![4]

Charles à Court Repington's controversial *The First World War 1914–1918* can be cited as a prime example of British lack of interest in the Macedonian Campaign. In his diary for 1918 he mentions Milne once in passing, Guillaumat not at all, and Franchet d'Espèrey twice, once relative to his earlier service on the Western Front, and once as a sort of afterthought following an issue which was obviously of equal importance to him; 'I saw Cecil Higgins at David's HQ. He is much wasted in his present work there and is a good man. The victories of Franchet d'Espèrey at Salonika and Allenby in Palestine add to the prevailing happiness.'[5]

Repington and his peers obviously rushed to get their books out as quickly as possible after the war. Dozens of full-scale histories of the First World War have been published over the last 100 years, however, whose authors have had much greater opportunities for research and analysis than Repington. Sadly, in most of these works coverage of the Macedonian Campaign remains close to negligible. An analysis of ten such works made by Nigel Birch revealed that some don't mention the subject at all, and those who give it a few paragraphs, use them mainly to downplay the achievements of the Allied Army of the East.[6] The otherwise wide-ranging and comprehensive *Great War* by Ian Beckett gives Macedonia a total of five pages, and mentions Franchet d'Espèrey once. Disconcertingly the only Milne to be found in the index is not the Commander in Chief of the BSF but the author of *Winnie the Pooh*. Two exceptions are Martin Gilbert's *The First World War* and Alan Palmer's *Victory 1918*, which both give more space and credit to the Macedonian Army.

Following the early output of personal memoirs by soldiers or medical staff who served in Macedonia, there have been few histories of the Campaign as a whole since the end of the First World War. The classics are Cyril Falls' *Official History of the Great War – Macedonia* and on the

---

3 Nicol, *Uncle George*, p.189.
4 Falls, *Macedonia Vol.2*, p.283.
5 Repington, *First World War Vol.2*, p.412.
6 Birch, *No Sideshow*, pp.22–24.

French side *Armées Françaises dans la Grande Guerre, Tome VIII*, both published in the 1930s. The most recent is Max Schiavon's *Le Front d'Orient*, published in 2014. He is obliged to concede, in the centenary year of the First World War, that *'le rôle considérable des operations dans les Balkans reste méconnu'* (the importance of the part played by operations in the Balkans remains unrecognised).[7]

And a century on he makes a determined effort to identify the reasons for this. The main factor, he concludes, is that no one was expecting this long-term static front to suddenly break out and within a couple of weeks bring Bulgaria crashing down, threaten the borders of Austro-Hungary, and cause the Germans to realise that the end was nigh.[8] 'It wasn't supposed to happen this way', one might continue. 'It had featured in no one's plans. The victory was to be secured on the Western Front, this year or probably next year, everyone was planning for this, not for a motley five nations army to appear out of nowhere and completely upset the odds. The best thing to do is to ignore it or send it off to Russia.' In fact, to pick up Schiavon's point in reverse, any commentator or historian who found the two week defeat of Bulgaria in September 1918 freakish or accidental,[9] had not been following the story.

The development and execution of an outstanding plan conceived by General Franchet d'Espèrey led to the defeat and rout of the Bulgarian Army in fifteen days, faster perhaps than he himself had expected, and certainly faster than the Germans thought possible.

But he did not start from a zero base. From 1915, right after the setback of Sarrail's expedition to Serbia, the platform for a final successful offensive against the Bulgarians was gradually being created.

There was certainly no master plan, but over 1916 and 1917 defences were perfected, reinforcements were received, notably from Serbia but also from Russia and Italy, and incorporated into the Allied Army. Control of railways and essential facilities was wrested from the Greeks, a programme of roads and decauvilles to support troop movements was constantly ongoing, training was undertaken, relationships between the various national forces bedded down at both personal and operational levels, and all components of the international army from the Struma to Koritsa were battle-hardened with regular raids and actions against the enemy. Familiarity was gained with the battle terrain, and its particular demands on both infantry and artillery. Provision had been made for the special medical needs of troops operating in Macedonia.

In 1916 Monastir was taken, together with the mid-Crna bend and above all Kaymakcalan and the southern peaks of the Moglena, all of which were valuable starting points for further advances. Successful actions were fought on the Struma. At whatever cost the Greek problem was solved, and Greek divisions were being formed to join the Allied Army.

During these two years, despite the lack of any consistent political direction from central governments and staffs, a military competence was being forged which survived the pre-emptive enemy attacks of 1916, and the failed offensive of 1917.

When Guillaumat arrived at the end of 1917, the process accelerated, but he very definitely had material to work with, as he transformed what he had inherited into a well-structured and professional army.

Meanwhile, Bulgarian morale was slipping. They also had been there for three years, but were now suffering from lack of food, clothing, direction and motivation. The German 'stiffening', key in 1917 to successful holding operations from Lake Prespa, Hill 1248 and the Crna bend to Doiran and the Vardar corridor, had by now almost all been removed. Guillaumat's copy-book success at

---

7 Schiavon, *Front d'Orient*, p.14.
8 Schiavon, *Front d'Orient*, p.367.
9 Or, according to Ludendorff, equally dumbfounded, the result of cynical match-fixing. *My War Memories Vol 2* P.712.

Skra di Legen and his joint action in Albania with Ferrero's XVI Corps had also served notice to the enemy of what was likely to come.

In June 1918 he passed on to Franchet d'Espèrey a well-formed, well-integrated army of 24 Divisions, with further Greek divisions in preparation, an army close in numbers to that of the enemy, but far superior in morale, equipment, air power and rearward communications.

Had Guillaumat remained in place, it is unlikely that the final victory over Bulgaria would have happened in 1918; even after he had left he was still envisaging a 'stepped' offensive. Franchet d'Espèrey's stroke of brilliance was to break through the 'crust' of the enemy defences at Dobropolje with an overwhelming force, three times that of the enemy, and then give the Serbs their head, but his military genius was evident in the precision of his planning, and the use of all his forces for the follow up. Only he could have done it.

He benefitted unquestionably from being left alone without HQ interference, for the critical period of the 'rupture' and 'exploitation', but the groundwork put in place particularly by Guillaumat since the beginning of the year, had made the success of the final offensive, if not inevitable, then highly probable. Far from being taken completely unawares, the Allied Governments and the Supreme War Council should have been planning for it, and above all for its exploitation.

* * *

Finally, what did the Macedonian campaign achieve, and what was its contribution to the overall Allied victory in the First World War? First, and as it turned out significantly, Sarrail's belated expedition into Serbia in late 1915 may have diverted Bulgarian attention sufficiently to allow a major part of the remaining Serbian Army to escape to the Adriatic.

Second, the Allied Army for three years held down almost the entire Bulgarian Army. In itself, this was a rather mixed achievement. The Bulgarian Army was never likely to have been used on any other front, except in small numbers on the Romanian one. Nor was it likely to invade Greece, although had the Allied Army not been there it might have tried to take Salonica, missed by a hair's breadth in the First Balkan War. Further, although German support to their Bulgarian allies probably never amounted to more than three full infantry divisions, they also provided significant engineering, technical, material, artillery and staff support, which could have been diverted to other fronts had it not been required in Macedonia. The long Allied line from Italian XVI Corps to the Adriatic also discouraged any Austrian penetration into southern Albania, Epirus and the Gulf of Corinth. It could also be noted that at the other end of the Allied line, BSF troops were close to European Turkey, and when the balloon finally went up in 1918, this proved to be of considerable value. The Allied Army of the East was also at hand, after the conclusion of hostilities, to police the implementation of peace agreements, protect civilian populations and prevent ethnic strife, while much of the Balkans and the Near East settled down within new borders and under new governments.

Third, if the Allied Army had not been there, King Constantine may well have declared for the Central Powers, or have been pressurised by his brother-in-law to do so, with the consequent risk of German submarine bases in Salonica and the Greek ports. All sorts of collaborative linkups with Turkey would have been facilitated. Disruption and danger to Allied sea traffic in the Mediterranean and to British interests in India would have been immense. Even had he not, the likelihood of nine Greek divisions being added to the Allied headcount by the end of the war was extremely remote. Similarly, without the Allied presence in Salonica in 1916 the Serbian Army following its withdrawal over the Albanian mountains would have had nowhere to go, and probably would have remained 'as fugitives, scattered and useless to the end of the war'.[10]

---

10 Lake, *In Salonica*, p.217.

Value was also added of a non-military nature in the form of a network of roads, railways, bridges, wells and canals where none had existed before in this 'mother naked land, little short of a wilderness'.[11] Milne in his preface to Mann notes that 'like the Romans of old, the roads of the British Army in Macedonia will long remain as the best memorial to its presence',[12] and this applied also to the land to the west of the Vardar, particularly during Guillaumat's tenure.

These are all solid points. But keeping a force of around half a million troops on the Macedonian Front could only really be justified if its over-riding aim was to destroy the Bulgarian Army, and to liberate the occupied territories in Serbia and eastern Macedonia. Three major campaigns were mounted with this objective, one in each year.

The aim of the 1916 campaign, to collaborate with Romania on her entry into the war, was compromised by her late declaration. Bulgaria's pre-emptive strikes into Greece then forced the Allies onto the back foot. Counter-attacks resulted in hard-won victories at Monastir and in the southern Moglena.

The 1917 campaign was conspicuously unsuccessful, considerable casualties were incurred and gains were miniscule. Much of Sarrail's attention was taken up by his almost paranoiac pre-occupation with the Greek situation. His leadership came under increasing criticism from the other national components of the Allied Army and finally led to his removal by the end of the year, a few months after his great adversary in Athens had been forced to abdicate.

A more successful campaign in 1918 seemed assured. Both Sarrail and Constantine were out of the way, Greek and other reinforcements had arrived, and Guillaumat in the space of a few months had re-organised and re-motivated the Allied Army. Guillaumat was replaced in June by Franchet d'Espèrey whose final offensive in September drove Bulgaria out of the war.

Most commentators on the Macedonian Campaign have concluded that the triumphant outcome of the 1918 campaign more than offset all the expenses and sacrifices involved in keeping the Allied Army in Macedonia for those three long years.

There are also those who maintain that the defeat of Bulgaria by the forces of Franchet d'Espèrey was the major factor in bringing the First World War to an end, citing above all the German reaction.

Hindenburg's statement of 3 October 1918 is frequently quoted; 'As a result of the collapse on the Macedonian Front and the weakening of our reserves in the West which this has necessitated … there seems now to be no possibility of winning peace from our enemies by force of arms.'[13] So also is Ludendorff's retrospective conclusion; 'the events of 15 September which took place on the Bulgarian Front sealed the fate of the Central Powers'.[14]

Franchet d'Espèrey himself was in no doubt about this. Even in his 80s when he was addressing a Reunion of the Salonica Army hosted by Lord Milne he was telling his (no doubt appreciative) audience, 'Though the Armies of the East were often treated by the strategists in London and Paris as of little account, it was they who decided the war.'[15] The normally reticent Milne expressed the same sentiment in a *Times* article in 1928.

The position that 'it was they who decided the war', has been endorsed by other writers and historians who have studied the campaign over the years, including even Winston Churchill.[16] Perhaps the most complete vindication of the Macedonian Campaign is contained in the War Memoirs of

---

11 It is to be recalled that Greece had only taken control of Greek Macedonia in 1913, and that the area had been devastated during the Balkan Wars.
12 Mann, *The Salonica Front*, Preface.
13 Larcher, *Grande Guerre*, p.247, Cordier, Victoire Eclair, p.250, Falls, Macedonia Vol.2, p.284.
14 Ludendorff, *My War Memories* Vol.2, p.679.
15 The Mosquito, June Edition 1937
16 Churchill, Letter to *The Times*, 25 November 1931.

Lloyd George, published in 1936. Eighteen years had elapsed for him to be able to put his thoughts in order, and he covers the ground with forensic thoroughness.

In an unstated *mea culpa* (he was, after all, prime minister at the time) he admitted that in the summer of 1918 with everyone's attention taken up with the 'colossal struggle' on the Western Front, other theatres were completely ignored except as potential sources of reinforcement. He concedes that for the French this was understandable; the war was on their doorstep, but for the British it was inexcusable and 'quite contrary to the military and naval traditions which built up the Empire.' Nevertheless, 'The events in those forgotten and despised theatres in the East brought the war to an end; but for them it might have continued its bloody course until spring or summer 1919', which, he confirmed, all Allied generals (and he himself) were predicting at the time.

Lloyd George's analysis of the mistakes made by the Allies in the Balkans in 1914 and 1915 is brief but incisive. He picks up on the potential advantages of an earlier attack on the Dardanelles, with Greek support. He runs through the catalogue of errors leading up to the Allied arrival in Salonica:

> We failed to save Serbia when we could have saved that country from disaster and turned it into a corridor for Allied attacks on Austria. Then, too late, we planted an expeditionary force in Salonica, too small to carry out serious offensives against the enemy, yet unduly large for mere garrison and defence purposes. We failed to keep Bulgaria from joining the enemy, and for a time we so muddled our relations with Greece that instead of being an ally, she was a peril in our rear.

However, despite all his initial reservations about the purpose and value of the Macedonian Army, he was in no doubt whatsoever that it was its sudden and comprehensive elimination of Bulgaria from the war which forced the Germans to realise that the game was up:

> Of all the 'side shows' the most important turned out to be the despised Salonica Front. Here it was that the deadly thrust was delivered against the Central Powers which crumpled their resistance and finally compelled them to abandon hope of continuing the war. The Balkans are the Back Door of Europe, and when it had been forced, the end was in sight.

He backs up his case with the irreproachable testimony of the Reichstag Commission of Enquiry set up after the war to investigate the cause of the collapse of Germany in 1918. This, after exhaustive researches, came to the conclusion that:

> The war was lost in a military sense when, during the retirement of the German Western Front in September 1918, the collapse of Bulgaria which was followed by that of Austro-Hungary completely changed the situation of the German Army in the field. From then on every attempt to obtain peace by purely military means was obviously vain.[17]

In this debate however, less attention has been given, even by Lloyd George, to the underlying reasons for German despair on the loss of Bulgaria. Certainly they realised at once that the situation on the Western Front was already too precarious to allow the release of significant forces to plug the holes left by Bulgaria.

But the major concern which weighed on the minds of the Central Powers as Franchet d'Espèrey pressed on remorselessly towards the Danube was that they were not expecting him to stop there.

---

17 Lloyd George, *War Memories*, pp.1910–1920.

The threat to the virtually undefended southern frontiers of Austria and Hungary from the apparently unstoppable Allied Army of the East must have seemed inevitable. Ludendorff wrote 'It was obvious that the Entente would attempt to liberate Serbia and to make an attack from there on Hungary, thus giving the *coup de grace* to the Dual Monarchy'.[18] He goes on to observe that following the Bulgarian collapse the Entente could at any time march over the Maritsa where the Turkish forces were minimal, since Bulgaria had been protecting them back on the Struma Front.

In desperation General Arz von Straussenburg, Austrian Chief of Staff was already contemplating calling for peace with Serbia and Romania, withdrawing from Albania, and resolving the 'Yugoslav issue' within the Empire.[19] (Since it was Austria's determination at all costs to declare war on Serbia in the first place which had unleashed these four years of horror and bloodshed this was a staggering proposal.)

Indeed, even after allowing for operations in Turkey, Romania and Albania, and for the occupation of Bulgaria, Franchet d'Espèrey on 4 October had earmarked 17 divisions to advance on Austro-Hungary.[20] For the central Powers to assemble a force capable of resisting such an invasion would have crippled their armies on the Western and Italian Fronts, already under immense pressure. Franchet d'Espèrey knew all about this of course, it was what he had been working for. In his excellent Preface to Larcher he above all stressed the effect on the Central Powers of the threat posed by his relentless advance on the Danube in October 1918; *C'est grâce à cette poursuite sans merci que la chute des Empires Centraux fut précipité irrémédiablement* (The collapse of the Central Powers was precipitated irremediably thanks to our merciless pursuit.)[21]

Meanwhile, as the Allied Army of the East was knocking away the props under one of Germany's three allies and were about to deal the same fate to a second, the Allies were gaining the upper hand on all other fronts, in France, Italy, and the Middle East. Foch's major autumn offensive on the Western Front was launched on 26 September and the success in Macedonia took place at almost exactly the same time as the breaking of the Hindenburg Line. Even before the defeat of Bulgaria the initiative was passing to the Allies. It was beyond doubt that the final decisive battles of the war would be fought on the Western Front. But when?

Before the armistice with Bulgaria, the Allied Powers were very definitely expecting the war to carry on at least until 1919.

- On 16 August Lloyd George in a briefing prepared for Dominion leaders was contemplating a conclusive offensive in 1920.[22]
- Later in the month he and his Secretary of State for War were writing to Haig telling him to reserve manpower for the battles of 1919.
- On 14 August the Interallied Munitions Council met to determine arms requirements for 1919, including a new tank factory in France.[23]
- On 20 August Foch was promising Clemenceau victory in 1919.
- On 27 August CIGS Wilson was telling Milne that the conditions for an offensive on the Macedonian Front would not be favourable until spring 1919.[24]

---

18   Ludendorff, *My War Memories*, p.716.
19   Larcher, *Grande Guerre*, p.246, Quoting Arz, *A History of the Great War* p.300.
20   Larcher, *Grande Guerre*, p.286.
21   Larcher, *Grande Guerre*, Preface, p.9.
22   Gilbert, *First World War*, p.452.
23   Gilbert, *First World War*, p.466.
24   Falls, *Macedonia Vol.2*, p.325.

- On 3 September a British Government memorandum predicted that the 'supreme military effort' would be made in July 1919, a view with which Marshal Pétain agreed a few days later.[25]
- As late as 4 October, Foch and the Americans were planning for a decisive battle in 1919.

To quote but a few examples. Despite the despair it generated in Berlin and Vienna the defeat of Bulgaria did not of itself cause the end of the war. But all the evidence indicates that it was the major factor in bringing it to a close before the end of 1918.

If, by eliminating Bulgaria from the war in September 1918 and making the early capitulation of Turkey inevitable, the Allied Army of the East had reduced the length of the war by even six months, the contribution made in terms of lives saved and relief to the battered European economies would have been inestimable, certainly justifying the whole Macedonian venture.

---

25 McMeekin, *Ottoman Endgame*, p.393.

Appendix I

Composition of the Allied Army of the East 1915–1918

French Divisions	Arrival Date
156th	October 1915
57th	October 1915
122nd	November 1915
17th Colonial	March 1916
11th Colonial	December 1916
16th Colonial	January 1917
76th	February 1917
30th	March 1917

British Divisions	Arrival Date
10th	October 1915 (Left September 1917)
22nd	November 1915
26th	November 1915
28th	December 1915
27th	January 1916
60th	December 1916 (Left July 1917)

Serbian Divisions	Arrival Date
Danube	May 1916
Drina	May 1916
Timok	May 1916
Sumadija	May 1916
Morava	May 1916
Vardar (Re-named 'Yugoslav In February 1918)	May 1916

Russian Brigades	Arrival Date
2nd and 4th	August 1917

Italian Division	Arrival date
35th	August 1917

Greek Divisions	Arrival Date
Seres	February 1917
Crete	March 1917
Archipelago	April 1917
1st Larissa	April 1918
13th Calchis	June 1918
2nd Athens	July 1918
3rd	August 1918
4th	September 1918
14th	October 1918

Appendix II

Post-War Careers

Of all the major actors in the story of the Macedonian Campaign, only three played a major part in their nation's affairs after 1918, Venizelos, von Hindenburg and Milne.

Eleutherios Venizelos. As Prime Minister of Greece he represented his country, brilliantly according to US President Woodrow Wilson, at the Versailles peace negotiations, securing for his country eastern and western Thrace, the Dodecanese and other islands, Smyrna and parts of western Anatolia. He remained Prime Minister until the return of King Constantine in 1920. He was Prime Minister again in 1924, 1928-32 and 1933. Out of power during the Greco–Turkish War of 1921-22, Venizelos returned to negotiate Treaty of Lausanne terms, which provided for a massive exchange of populations. In later years as Greek politics became even more fractious, he led an unsuccessful revolt, after which he retired to France where he died in 1936 at the age of 71.

Field Marshal Paul von Hindenburg. After the 1918 Armistice he oversaw the retreat of the German Army. He stood down from the Central Staff in 1919. He became President of Germany in 1925 and remained in this post until his death in 1934 at the age of 87. In an intervening Presidential election of 1932 he defeated Hitler. Hitler became Chancellor in 1933 but was unable to overthrow constitutional government until von Hindenburg's death.

Field Marshal Lord Milne of Salonica and Rubislaw. Following the Turkish Armistice in 1918 he remained based in Turkey as Commander of the Army of the Black Sea until 1920, with responsibilities as far as Transcaucasia and the Caspian Sea. From 1922-26 he was general Officer Commanding Eastern Command. In 1926 he was appointed CIGS and promoted to Field Marshal in 1928. As CIGS he served two four year terms and retired in 1933, when he was raised to the peerage. In the Second World War he served in the Home Guard, and then as commandant of the Royal Pioneer Corps. Throughout his life he remained in touch with the Salonica Reunion Association. He died in 1948 at the age of 80

* * *

Alexander, Prince Regent and Commander in Chief of the Serbian Army became Prince Regent of the Kingdom of Serbs, Croats and Slovenes in 1918, and King on the death of his father in 1921. He officially changed the name to the Kingdom of Yugoslavia in 1929. In 1934 on a state visit to Marseille he was assassinated by a Bulgarian member of IMRO, the long-standing Macedonian liberation organisation, possibly in alliance with the Croatian Ustase. He was 46.

Voivode Petar Bojović was appointed Chief of Staff of the Yugoslav Army in 1921 and retired from active service in 1922. At the beginning of the Second World War he was appointed Deputy

Chief of Staff to the young King Petar II but played little part in the war. In 1945 he was murdered by communist partisans at the age of 87.

Georges Clemenceau famously represented France at the Treaty of Versailles. In 1918 he was appointed to the Académie Française. He remained Prime Minister until 1920, when he stood for President but was not elected. In retirement he wrote and travelled widely. He died in 1929 at the age of 88.

Constantine I. Following the death of his son in 1920 he became King of Greece for the second time following a plebiscite. He led the Greek force into Turkey in 1921 and suffered a major defeat. He abdicated in 1922 and was succeeded by his son George II. He died in exile in Sicily in 1923 at the age of 56.

General Erich von Falkenhayn retired from the German Army in 1919 and wrote his memoirs and books on military strategy. He died in 1922 at the age of 61.

Maréchal Louis Franchet d'Espèrey. was sent with the AFO to fight the Bolsheviks in southern Russia and the Ukraine in 1918. He was promoted to Field Marshal in February 1921, after Clemenceau had left the scene, and from 1921 was Inspector General of France's North African Forces. He was made a member of the Académie Française in 1934 and received the Grand Croix de Legion d'Honneur. In the Second World War he refused to support Pétain and died in the French 'free zone' in 1942 at the age of 86.

General Adolphe Guillaumat led an active life after the end of the War. In 1919 he was General Inspector of the Army, in 1920 a member of the Supreme War Council, from 1922 - 31 President of the Defense Commission, and from 1924 to 1930 Commander of the French Army of the Rhine. He retired in 1932 and died in 1940 at the age of 77.

General Erich von Ludendorff. After the war he became involved in an outlawed political movement, at one point having to flee the country. On his return he participated in Hitler's Beer Hall putsch of 1923. From 1924 – 28 he was a Nazi member of the Reichstag. He died in 1937 at the age of 72 having broken with both Hindenburg and Hitler.

Voivode Zivojin Mišić was appointed Chief of Staff of the Army of the Kingdom of Serbs, Croats and Slovenes in 1919, but died in 1921 when he was succeeded by Bojović. He was 66.

Field Marshal Sir William Robertson. In June 1918, following his replacement by Wilson as CIGS, Robertson was appointed Commander in Chief of Home Forces. In 1919 he was knighted and created Baronet, and in 1920 promoted to Field Marshal. In 1919 he became Commander of the British Army of the Rhine. In 1920 Churchill put his name forward as Commander in Chief in Ireland, and then India, both times being overruled by Lloyd George. On retirement to augment his low savings he became director or Chairman of four companies including the London Omnibus Company. In his leisure time he wrote and enjoyed hunting and fishing. He died in 1933 at the age of 73.

General Maurice Sarrail. Following his replacement by Guillaumat in 1917 he retired to Montauban to write his memoirs. In 1919 he stood for parliament as a radical socialist but was not elected. In 1924 he was nominated High Commissioner to the French Republic of Syria, and commander in chief of the French Army of the Levant. Accused of brutality in suppressing a revolt of the Druzes he was recalled in 1925. He died in 1929 at the age of 73.

Appendix III

Diary of Signaller Bailey

(Map 4)

Edward Bailey enlisted with the 4th Devon Territorials on 29 October 1914. Until 1916 Territorial units were employed on home defence and were not sent overseas. But at the end of 1915 Edward volunteered for overseas service and joined 22nd Battalion, the Rifle Brigade as a signaller. The Rifle Brigade Battalions 18–24 were formed essentially for garrison service in India and Egypt. For unknown reasons 22nd Battalion was sent to Salonica and became the only one of these seven Rifle Brigade battalions to face the enemy on the front line.

On 3 January 1916 the Battalion embarked on the troop ship Olympic bound for Egypt. Here Edward spent three months on signalling and defence work as well as visiting the Pyramids and the sights of Cairo.

On 23 April 1916 the Battalion was shipped to Cyprus and spent a month laying out large fake camps and airfields in an effort to deceive the Turks into thinking that the British were planning a sea-borne invasion of Iskenderun on the Turkish coast. At the end of May the Battalion was dispatched to the Greek island of Lemnos in the northern Aegean on lines of communication and garrison duties. Lemnos had been the rear operational HQ for the Dardanelles Campaign and was to remain a key naval base and staging point for the Macedonian Campaign.

On 15 September 1916 while the rest of 22nd Battalion remained on Lemnos, Edward and a signalling colleague were sent to form part of a small detachment on Rabbit Island,[1] a small two square kilometre speck of land only ten kilometres from the mouth of the Dardanelles, to observe and report shipping movements through and around the straits. They remained there for three months, probably the closest Allied troops anywhere to the European Turkish frontier and were frequently shelled from the mainland and bombed from the air. Edward also visited Tenedos (now Bozkaada), a larger island to the south, and served for a short period on Imbros (now Gokceada), a much bigger island to the north which had an advanced Allied naval base.

His assignment on Rabbit Island ended on 15 December 1916. He landed in Salonica six days later. His Battalion had already been on the Greek mainland since November. They were now engaged in building trenches and defensive lines about forty kilometres north of Salonica and Edward joined them on 29 January 1917. This work continued until 15 March, when 22nd Battalion and three other ex-garrison battalions were put together to form 228th Brigade for service on the front line attached to 28th Division.

Edward and his Battalion then spent three months on the Butkovo Front between Lakes Butkovo and Doiran, firstly on the 'winter' line based on Dova Tepe, then on the 'summer line' based on Mahmudli. This front was relatively quiet, with both sides exchanging occasional artillery fire and mounting small raids.

---

1   As per *Google Maps* as Tavsan Ada, Tavsan being Turkish for rabbit.

In July 1917 the Battalion was withdrawn to Mirova, thirty kilometres south of the front line, for training. On 20 August they returned again to the Butkovo Front, this time to the eastern end at Kairak-Mah. This was a particularly bad sector for malaria, and on 1 October 1917 Edward succumbed to it for the first time. On this occasion he recovered quite quickly and was able to march with the Battalion on 9 October to their next destination, the much more active Struma Front. The objective here was to regain part of the advanced line across the River Struma which had been given up during the summer.

The Battalion remained on the Struma Front either on the front line or in reserve until March 1918, when the order was received to return once more to the Butkovo Front. This time they took the direct route and made four silent night marches through no-man's land outside the British front line wire from Turbes to Radile. The Battalion remained on this Front, either on the 'winter' or 'summer' line, until September 1918. Enemy shelling and occasional raids continued. In May Edward had a ten day break when he was sent to Salonica for an examination to become a signals instructor, which he passed. He returned to his Battalion on the 'summer' front line on 18 May. Three weeks later he had another bout of malaria but carried on with his work at forward observation posts and on patrols towards the enemy line.

After the Bulgarian retreat on 21 September following the Franco-Serbian break-through west of the Vardar, 228th Brigade advanced with the Greek Cretan Division towards the Belasitsa mountains. Immediately after the Bulgarian capitulation on 30 September however 228th Brigade was disbanded, and 22nd Battalion was set to work repairing sections of the Salonica to Seres railway.

On 18 October Edward came down with malaria again, this time requiring hospitalisation in Salonica and then repatriation. He left Salonica on 21 December and arrived in Liverpool on 4 January 1919 'three years almost to the day since the Battalion left the same landing stage'. After a long period of treatment and convalescence he received his demobilization papers on 23 March.

As it had turned out, his had been an unusually varied war experience, with service in Great Britain, in Egypt, in Cyprus, on Rabbit Island at the mouth of the Dardanelles, and on the Greek islands of Imbros, Tenedos and Lemnos before arriving in Salonica in December 1916.

* * *

Signaller Bailey kept the record of his war service in a small black 10 x 16 cm. notebook, and during the course of the war covered nearly two hundred pages. The last few pages are written in a slightly bluish pencil which is also used for the heading on the front page suggesting that he didn't give his account a title until he'd finished it. As a twenty-word summary of his war service it is as complete as it is succinct:

> Notes kept of my journeys and visits to various places during my soldiering experiences in this the War of Wars 1914-1919.

He makes no claim to having written an account of any historic significance or literary merit; these are just 'notes', not a diary; a framework record of his own actions and movements with occasional observations and comments.

He writes with a good hand and the quality of his handwriting remains even throughout. A peculiarity is the almost total absence of full stops; the story flows along with commas now and then, but the intended periods are clear enough.

He is commendably precise on place names, usually spelling them out in capital letters for greater clarity. This has greatly simplified tracking down his movements on maps of the period, and subsequently on the ground.

Whether he is recording his own doings or relaying news he receives from outside he writes with admirable conciseness:

> Enemy aeroplane came over the harbour, guns spotted her and fired several rounds. Heard afterwards it was brought down. Romania joined Allies. Good news. (7/9/1916)
>
> 'Order to pack up from Imbros to take over signalling station 'Rocky Point' from R.E. (15/9/1916)
>
> Bombarded by Turks, several shells dropped in sea, no casualties. Hunted for pieces, found some. Shells make huge holes in the ground. (22/10/1916)
>
> Good news in the 'Balkan News'. Kut in our hands. 1000 millions subscribed to war loans. (1/3/1917)
>
> Three Bulgar prisoners captured. One speaks English very well. Quiet. Cold. (20/4/1917)
>
> Very heavy bombardment at Doiran three days now. Division on left successfully carried enemy trenches, but Division on right could not establish itself.'(Of the First Battle of Doiran 25/4/1917)
>
> Left DRAGOS for CUKULUK our destination in front line at 1830. Enemy had shelled it day previous. Silent march, absolute silence, had to cross Struma. Ground very marshy, reached village. Nothing doing. Three hours march, carried packs. Had to run telephone wire at once. Difficult. Very dark but got in communication with all posts all right. Up all night. Very cold. (14/10/1917)
>
> 83 and 84 Bde had a go at KUMLI and ORMANLI, served rather bad. (15/4/1918)
>
> Two men drowned, 117 Bty and Kings after heavy rain from Mountain. Water came down river with great rush. Caught men with mules. (2/5/1918)
>
> Johnny shelled our position, no casualties. Otherwise front very quiet. (3/5/1918)
>
> News arrived that convention is signed, cease operations at 1200. Bulgarians notified. (On the day Armistice terms with Bulgaria were signed, 30/9/1918).

That more time is devoted to his outward journey and his time in Cairo than to any similar other period is not surprising; he had the time, and everything was new to him:

> Taken through Alexandria to trams, distance about two miles, very hot, natives, streets, shops, very interesting, very dirty. Native married women wear veils and a sort of cork thing on their foreheads. Boys selling all sorts of things being chased and beaten by policemen, very funny, so different to home. (18/6/1916)

For the rest of 1916 on Cyprus, then on Lemnos and Rabbit Island he prefers to summarise his activities and describe his surroundings in one or two larger entries, reporting incidents of special interest or concern as they occur with short one- or two-line entries.

From the moment he arrived in Salonica at the end of 1916 he spends almost all of the next two years up-country. Sometimes many days pass without any entry, either because he has nothing to say, or because his commitments allow him too little time. As 1918 progresses his entries become even shorter, but more frequent.

Inevitably food was an issue of major importance, and is the subject of numerous diary entries from:

> Messing for the soldiers disgraceful, meat and spuds with skin on. Soup for dinner and dry bread for tea. (2/1/1916) to

> Fine day, great expectation for a good time, were not disappointed. Pint of beer per man (FREE), a very good dinner, Christmas pudding, fish and fruit for tea, plenty free cigarettes and tobacco. Queen Alexandra Christmas gift, nuts, biscuits and coffee. (25/12/1917)

From March 1916 until October 1918 he was living more or less in the open, in tents, bivouacs, dugouts and shelters put together with whatever materials were available. Unsurprisingly the state of the weather is a dominant theme throughout his diary. The Macedonian climate is notoriously one of extremes:

> Weather still lovely. No rain for five weeks and very hot. (20/8/1917) to
> Blizzard, wind very keen, snow seems to cut pieces out of one's face. (2/1/1918)

Edward had come from a sporting family; he and three of his brothers had played league cricket and football for Cambridge town before the war, and anything of a sporting nature during his military service immediately attracts his attention.

He swims, runs, plays cricket and football for his Battalion. Although it was almost certainly new to him, he was very keen to become a good shot. Although he didn't see his signalling duties as a competitive activity, he takes much satisfaction from the high marks he gets from his exam to become a signalling instructor. Nor can he resist reporting that he came second in the whist drive at the hospital on 12 November, the day after the German armistice. He even sees a competitive element to shelling and flying, and is quick to applaud what he considers to be a good performance, even if it is by the enemy:

> Some interesting and clever flying. (15/12/1916).
> Aeroplane duel, fine sight. (14/2/1917).
> Johnny shelled our position. Good shooting but no hits. (9/4/1918).
> Good fight in air. British brought down Bulgar in flames. (20/6/1918)

The sportsman in him placed importance in keeping in good physical condition. He refers several times to not getting seasick while all around are suffering, most notably as Trawler No 11 approaches Rabbit Island for the first time:

> Storm still raging, we had the most awful passage, were battened down while rounding Leakey Point. Seas continually breaking right over the boat and rolling terribly. Major and others sick, but no effect on me. (25/9/1916)

He goes through any number of challenging marches, determined to make it to the end while his companions drop out:

> All held up at TODOVORO until dark. In sight of enemy, off again when dark, kept at it until 0130 next morning, awful time, pack gets very heavy. Men falling out exhausted all along. Managed to stick it to the end. Too tired to put up bivvy, slept out under stars. (24/3/17).
> Marched off again for PICKOVA about 16 kilometres, march much harder, many mountains and ravines to pass, men fagged out, had hard job to get them along. Arrived at camp about midnight. Nothing to eat or drink, starving hungry, slept out in the open again, soon asleep. (23/8/17)

He is dismayed when he gets his first bout of malaria and has to fall out:

> Packing up and feeling too bad for anything. Bivvy packed up, nowhere to lay down. Doctor marked me malaria. March off in afternoon. Had to fall out, first time in soldiering. (6/10/17)

In June 1918, however, when the malaria returns he not only manages to hold out, but also participates in two long overnight patrols towards enemy lines.

For the three years of his foreign service he had no leave. It is even more remarkable that he spent the whole of 1917 and, until hospitalised with malaria, almost all of 1918 in the field. The only trip he made to Salonica during this period was for a training course, and he was not allowed into the town. This apparently was the lot of all Other Ranks. Officers frequently went to Salonica, and many went on leave to the UK. Edward doesn't mention this, and only talks of leave three times in his diary.

But he seems to have enjoyed the work, and fulfilling his duties to his own satisfaction:

> Rabbit Island transmitting station, mainly telephone and helio. Was new to helio … set about getting used to it. Got on very well. (25/9/16)
>
> Enlisted two years ago this date, now entitled to proficiency pay and Good Conduct Badges, Clean sheet so far. (29/10/16)
>
> Inspection with officer of Cuculuk lines … all serene. (12/11/17)
>
> Everything in front line as regards my work OK. (12/3/18)
>
> Doubtful if I will pass but intend having a good try. (Signalling for Instructors exam, 22/4/18).
>
> Awfully hard work. Must stick at it though. (22/10/18)

To today's reader the main characteristic of the diarist is self-detachment. Whatever thoughts he may have had on the purpose and management of the war, or about his colleagues and officers do not feature. His diary entries remained brief, factual, and unemotional.

Throughout his diary he limits expressions of pleasure to 'very acceptable' (food, rum issue, YMCA marquee), 'wanted it' (nice bath in the stream), 'enjoyed very much/immensely' (Swedish drill on the boat, singing, cricket match, tea after the swimming competition), 'worth seeing' (sunset, Mudros harbour), 'very thankful' (parcels). He restricts expressions of pain to 'very sad' (death of a colleague through smallpox, death of his corporal through accidental shooting), 'rough luck' (sinking of a merchant navy ship containing a package of cigarettes for him), 'hard lines' (death through bomb injuries of his friend Peter Snow with whom he had joined up in Devon). Apart from Snow, Bailey only refers to seven or eight other people by name.

Bailey played football with them, he marched alongside them, he enjoyed sing-songs with them, he did training and rifle practice with them. On a great many occasions he must have shared a two-man bivouac with someone, on others rough accommodation in dug-outs. He praises no one and denigrates no one (except perhaps for calling the man who shot his corporal by mistake and then went on the run a 'stupid fellow'). He seems to live beside them rather than with them, just as he stands detached from the group in the photo in front of the Pyramids. Only on the subject of mail does this mask slip. His diary mentions letter writing, receipt of mail, or, more often, disappointment at its absence, more often even than food. Contact with home comes through as the one feature of his life on extended foreign service which matters to him more than any other. He writes frequently to his wife and family – the diary covers about fifty entries on the subject – and his satisfaction on getting letters and parcels is only matched by his sadness when he does not:

> Letter to chicks and Eva. No mail for two weeks. (13/3/16)

> Received snapshots of Eve and chicks. Delighted. (9/9/16)[2]
> No letter from home for several mails. Anxious to hear. (2/12/16)
> Letter received from home, papers and parcel of good things. Very thankful. (21/1/17)
> Mail in, no letter. (1/5/17)
> 'Posted reg. letter with ten shilling post order for Lucy's birthday. (13/5/17)
> Received Christmas cards from Eve and chicks. Very pleased. (21/1/18)
> No sign of parcels from home. (17/2/18)
> Fine parcel of Woodbines from Eve. (20/2/18)

The brevity of his style, with happenings reported immediately after others with which they have no connection sometimes gives rise to unintended humour:

> Visited hospital to see a friend, very nice place, lots of sick and wounded.' (4/3/1916)
> Was vaccinated. Selley dead, very sad. (4/4/1916)[3]
> Stationed along sea coast, very hot day, good bathing, one man shot himself. (5/1916)
> Boat taking small detachment of 22nd Battalion to Thassos Island torpedoed in morning, six drowned. Cricket match ... much enjoyed.' (summer 1916)
> My platoon on fatigue. Managed to get something to eat. One man died of drink.' (16/3/1917).
> Rotten news from France, still falling back. Fine weather, trees blooming, nightingales in song, very nice. (16/4/1918).

This was the diary of a private soldier with no previous military experience, a thirty-seven year old shopkeeper with three children. If he is aware that there is another part of the Allied Army of the East – a much larger part - across the Vardar, he makes no mention of it. His war is against Johnny Bulgar facing him across the Butkovo valley and the Struma River. The wider picture is not his concern. He is doing his bit in that part of the war theatre where chance has thrown him without very much questioning what he is doing there. There must have been millions like him, on both sides. In his case he joined a garrison battalion which fortuitously finished up spending a total of twelve months on the front line, albeit not a very active part of a fairly static front line, but nevertheless with its own share of danger from shelling, bombing, patrols and enemy raids, and, above all, from exposure to malaria.

Bailey's reasons for keeping a diary are as unknown – or perhaps as obvious – as his reasons for enlisting in the first place; it was what one did. Some war diaries are partly or wholly written retrospectively – such was my father's – of the intense ten-day Battle of Arnhem in September 1944. But my grandfather's was, in the main, a more leisurely war, and once his foreign service began in early 1916, his 'notes' were clearly written on the spot and at the time.

---

2   Eva or Eve was his wife. Lucy was his elder daughter. My mother Joyce was one year old when he left for the war and is not mentioned in the diary.
3   Forty-year-old 859 Rifleman G. Selley, 22nd Rifle Brigade is buried in Cairo War Memorial Cemetery.

Bibliography[1]

Published Sources

Abadie, Colonel M., *Etude sur les Opérations de Guerre en Montagne* (Paris: Ch. Lavauzelle, 1924)
Alport, A. Cecil,* *Malaria and its Treatment in the Line and at the Base* (London: Bale Sons and Danielsson, 1919)
Armand-Delille, Felix, et al, *Malaria in Macedonia* (London: London University Press, 1918)
Armées Françaises de la Grand Guerre Tome VIII Volumes 1, 2 and 3 (Paris: Imprimerie National, 1923–1934)
Aronson, Theo, *Crowns in Conflict* (London: John Murray, 1986)
Azan, Paul, *Franchet d'Espèrey* (Paris: Flammarion, 1949)
Babac, Dusan, *The Serbian Army in the Great War* (Solihull: Helion and Company, 2016)
Bailey, Edward,* *Notes of my Soldiering Experiences 1914-1919* (Unpublished, 1919)
Beckett, Ian F.W., *The Great War* (New York; Routledge 2013)
Birch, Nigel, *No Sideshow* (University of Buckingham: Niroad Publications, 2018)
Bjelajac, M., *Generals and Admirals of Jugoslavia* (Belgrade, 2004)
Boardman, J., Griffin, J., and Murray, O., *Oxford History of the Classical World* (Oxford: OUP, 1968)
Bujac, Emile, *Les Campagnes de l'Armée Hellénique* (Paris: Ch. Lavauzelle, 1930)
Burr, Malcolm,* *Slouch Hat* (London: George Allen and Unwin, 1935)
Butcher, Tim, *The Trigger* (London: Vintage, 2015)
Buxton, Noel, *The War and the Balkans* (London: George Allen and Unwin, 1915, Reprint by University of Toronto 2015)
Byron, Lord George, *Don Juan* (London: Thomas Davidson, 1819)
Casson, Stanley,* *Steady Drummer* (London: G. Bell and Sons, 1935)
Chasseaud, Peter, *Mapping the First World War* (Glasgow: Collins, 2013)
Churchill, Winston, *The World Crisis Book 1* (London: Thornton Butterworth, 1923)
Collinson Owen, H.,* *Salonica and After* (London: Hodder and Stoughton, 1919)
Constant, Stephen, *Foxy Ferdinand: Tsar of Bulgaria* (London: Olimpic, 1979)
Cordier, Louis,* *Victoire Éclair en Orient* (Aurillac: Editions U.S.H.A., 1968)
Corrigan, Gordon, *Mud, Blood and Poppycock* (London: Cassell, 2003)
David, R., *Le Drame Ignoré de l'Armée de l'Orient* (Paris: Plon, 1927)
Davis, Richard Harding,* *With the French in France and Salonica* (London: Duckworth and Co., 1916)
Delaunay, J., *Secrets Diplomatiques 1914-8* (Bruxelles: Brépol, 1963)
Deygas, F.J., *L'Armée d'Orient dans la Guerre Mondiale* (Paris: Payot, 1932)
Ducasse, André,* *Balkans 1914/18* (Paris: Robert Lafont, 1964)
Falkenhayn, Erich von, *The German Headquarters and its Critical Decisions 1914–1916* (London: Hutchinson, 1920)
Falls, Cyril, *Official History of the Great War – Macedonia. Volume 1, From the Outbreak of War to the Spring of 1917* (London: HMSO, 1933, Reprint by Naval and Military Press, 2013)
Falls, Cyril, *Official History of the Great War – Macedonia. Volume 2, From the Spring of 1917 to the End of the War* (London: HMSO, 1935, Reprint by Naval and Military Press, 2013)

---

1 *Served on the Macedonian Front in the armed forces or as journalist

Feyler, Colonel, *La Campagne de Macédonie* (Geneva: Editions d'Art Boissonnas, 1920)
Forbes, Arthur, *A History of Army Ordnance Services; Volume 3, The Great War* (London: The Medici Society, 1929)
Frappa, J-J, *Souvenirs d'un Officier* (Paris: Flammarion, 1921)
Fromkin, David, *Europe's Last Summer* (London: Vintage, 2004)
Gauvin, August, *L'Affaire Grecque* (Paris: Bossard, 1918)
Gilbert, Martin, *The First World War* (London: Weidenfeld and Nicolson, 1994, Reprint by London: Phoenix, 2008)
Glenny, Misha, *The Balkans 1804-2012* (London: Granta, 2012)
Gordon-Smith, Gordon,* *From Serbia to Jugoslavia* (New York and London: G.P. Putnam's and Sons, 1920)
Grant, Michael, *History of Rome* (London: Weidenfeld and Nicolson, 1996)
Grant, Michael, *The Classical Greeks* (London: Weidenfeld and Nicolson, 1989)
Gray, Randal with Argyle, Christopher, *Chronicle of the First World War Volume 1, 1914–1916* (Oxford: Facts on File, 1990)
Gray, Randal with Argyle, Christopher, *Chronicle of the First World War Volume 2 1917–1921* (Oxford: Facts on File, 1991)
Green, Peter, *A Concise History of Ancient Greece* (London: Thames and Hudson, 1974)
Guillaumat, Paul, *Correspondance de Guerre du Général Guillaumat* (Paris: l'Harmattan, 2016)
Hall, Richard C., *Balkan Breakthrough* (Indiana: Indiana University Press, 2010)
Hankey, Maurice, *The Supreme Command Vol 1* (London: Allen and Unwin, 1961)
Hindenburg, Paul von, *Aus Meinem Leben* (Leipzig: Hirzel, 1920)
Jones, H.A., *The War in the Air, being the Story of the Part Played in the Great War by the RAF*, *Volume 5* (Oxford: Clarendon Press, 1935)
Laffin, John, *The Agony of Gallipoli* (Oxford: Osprey, 1980, Reprint by Sutton Publishing, 2005)
Lake, Harold,* *In Salonika with our Army* (London: Andrew Melrose, 1917–1918)
Lane Fox, Robin, *The Classical World* (London: Allen Lane, 2005)
Larcher, Commandant M., *La Grande Guerre dans les Balkans* (Payot: Paris, 1929)
Lepetit, Lieutenant-Colonel, *La Genèse de l'Offensive de Macédoine* (Paris: Institut de Stratégie Comparée, 1922)
Livesey, Anthony, *The Viking Atlas of World War 1* (London: Viking 1994)
Lloyd George, David, *War Memoirs* (London: Little Brown, 1934)
Lon, Manuel, *Bulgaria en la Guerra 1915-1918* (Madrid: Talleres del Deposito della Guerra, 1920)
Ludendorff, Erich von, *Meine Kriegserinnerungen* (Berlin: Mittler & Sohn, 1919)
Mackenzie, David, *Apis the Congenial Conspirator* (New York: Boulder, 1989)
Mallainson, Allan, *1914 Fight the Good Fight* (London: Bantam, 2014)
Mann, Arthur James,* *The Salonica Front* (London: A.C. Black, 1920, Reprint by General Books)
Marix-Evans, Martin, *Forgotten Battlefields of the First World War, Salonica* (Stroud: Sutton Publishing, 2003)
Markovic, Lazar, *Serbia and Europe, 1914-20* (London: George Allen and Unwin, 1920)
Mazower, Mark, *Salonica City of Ghosts* (London: Harper Perennial, 2005)
McMeekin, Sean, *The Ottoman Endgame* (London: Allen Lane, 2015)
Mermeix, Gabriel, *Le Commandement Unique Vol 2* (Paris: Société d'Editions Littéraires, 1920)
Milne, George,* *The London Gazette, Despatches* (London: HMSO, 1916, 1917, 1919)
Mitrovic, André, *Serbia's Great War* (London: Hurst, 2007)
Nicholson, Harold, *King George V* (London: Doubleday, 1952)
Nicol, Graham, *Uncle George* (London: Reedminster Publications, 1976)
Norwich, J. J., *Byzantium, The Early Centuries* (London: Penguin Books, 1990)
Norwich, J.J., *Byzantium, The Apogee* (London: Penguin Books, 1993)
Norwich, J.J., *Byzantium, The Decline and Fall* (London: Penguin Books, 1995)
Packer, Charles,* *Return to Salonica* (London: Cassell, 1964)
Palmer, Alan, *The Gardeners of Salonika* (New York: Simon and Schuster, 1965, Reprint by London: Faber and Faber, 2009)
Palmer, Alan, *Victory 1918* (London: Weidenfeld and Nicolson, 1998)

Price, Crawfurd, *The role of Serbia* (London: The Serbian Red Cross Society, 1918)
Reiss, R. A.,* *The Kingdom of Serbia. Infringements of the Rules and Laws of War Committed by the Austro-Bulgaro-Germans* (London: George Allan and Unwin, 1919)
Repington, Charles à Court, *The First World War 1914-1918* (London: Constable, 1920)
Revol, J., *La Victoire en Macédoine* (Paris: Ch. Lavauzelle, 1931)
Ribot, Alexandre, *Lettres à un Ami: Souvenirs de ma Vie Politique* (Paris: Bossard, 1924)
Robertson, William, *Soldiers and Statesmen* (London: Cassell, 1926)
Rogan, Eugene, *The Fall of the Ottomans* (London: Penguin Random House, 2015)
Rutter, Owen,* *The Song of Tiadatha* (London: T. Fisher Unwin, 1920)
Saison, Jean, *De l'Alsace à la Cerna* (Paris: Plon, 1918)
Salandra, Antonio, *I Discorsi della Guerra* (Roma: Tipografia del Senato, 1915)
Sarrail, Maurice* et Porte, Rémy, *Mon Commandement en Orient, Edition Annotée et Commentée* (Paris: Editions Soteca, 2012)
Schiavon, Max, *Le Front d'Orient* (Paris: Tallandier, 2014)
Seligman, V.J.,* *The Salonica Sideshow* (London: George Allen and Unwin, 1919, Reprint by London: F.B. &c Ltd, 2015)
Stebbing, E.P., *At the Serbian Front in Macedonia* (London: John Lane, The Bodley Head, 1917)
Taylor, A.J.P., *The Struggle for Mastery in Europe 1848–1918* (Oxford: OUP, 1954)
Thomas, Nigel, *Armies in the Balkans 1914–18* (Oxford: Osprey 2001)
Thompson, Mark, *The White War* (London: Faber and Faber, 2008)
Thucydides, *History of the Peloponnesian War* translated by Rex Warner (Harmondsworth: Penguin Books Ltd, 1954)
Villari, Luigi,* *The Macedonian Campaign* (London: T. Fisher Unwin, 1922, Reprint by London: F.B. & C Ltd, 2015)
Wakefield, Alan with Moody, Simon, *Under the Devil's Eye* (Barnsley: Pen and Sword Military, 2011)
Ward Price, G.,* *The Story of the Salonica Army* (New York: Edward J. Clode, 1918)
Waring, L.F., *Serbia* (London: Butterworth, 1918)
Watson, Alexander, *Ring of Steel* (London: Penguin Random House, 2014)
West, Rebecca, *Black Lamb and Grey Falcon* (London: Macmillan, 1941)

Miscellaneous

First World War.com <https://www.firstworldwar.com>
Long, Long Trail <https://www.longlongtrail.co.uk/>
OSO Maps 1915 Salonika, Monastir, Uskub
Salonica Campaign Society Trench Map DVD
The Mosquito
The New Mosquito.

Index

GENERAL

Adriatic, ix, 35, 49, 74, 122–23, 150, 153, 160, 180, 190, 205, 272, 279
Agirocastro, 121–22
Albania, 15, 17, 21–22, 34–35, 49–50, 116, 120–23, 165–66, 180–81, 205, 207, 255–56, 269, 271, 282
Alexander the Great, 13–14, 16,
Alexander, King of Greece, 160
Alexander, Prince Regent of Serbia, 45, 74, 152-55, 158, 221, 224, 233, 250, 267, 285
Allied Army of the East, vii–x, 83–85, 89, 114–16, 118, 122–24, 126–27, 163, 165, 167–68, 182–86, 188–95, 199–203, 208–14, 216–18, 224–27, 248–49, 265–69, 275–80, 282
Alport, D., 170–72, 293
Archelaus I, King of Macedonia, 13
Armées Françaises de la Grande Guerre, Tome VIII, 53, 55, 75, 81, 85, 89–90, 95, 118, 128–30, 138, 143–48, 202, 204–6
Asia Minor, 15–16, 33–34, 82, 110, 138, 162
Asquith, Herbert, 58, 74, 109, 113
Athens, 52, 55–56, 72–74, 80, 108, 110–11, 115–17, 156, 158, 160–61, 164–65, 198, 280
Austro-Hungarian Empire, 19, 20, 23, 25, 27–28, 33, 38, 41, 45-46, 82, 84-85, 89, 267, 272, 275, 278, 281-82

Babac, Dušan, 28–29, 35, 38, 45, 75, 271–72, 293
Bailey, Edward, 54, 131-32, 142, 167–68, 173, 175–77, 179, 186, 194, 198, 252-53, 287-93
Bairakli Juma, 104, 114, 141, 178
Balkans, vii, 17–21, 28, 33–34, 36–39, 54, 64–65, 69–70, 87, 92, 164, 210, 218, 231–32, 254–55, 259–61, 273–76, 278–79, 281, 293–95
Balkan News, 56, 289
Belasitsa mountains, 15, 60, 62, 66, 77, 91, 101, 103, 119, 125, 127, 253, 262, 288
Belgium, 33, 53–54
Belgrade, 18, 24–25, 27–28, 38, 40, 47–48, 83, 102, 228–29, 271–73, 276
Berlin, 17, 23, 26, 34, 40–41, 46, 48, 260, 270, 273, 283
Berthelot, Général Henri, 84, 269, 273, 275

Beshik Dagh, 66, 68, 101
'Birdcage' Fortification, 66, 68, 70, 74, 192, 200
Bismarck, Otto von, 26, 54, 276
Black Hand, 23, 25, 153
Black Sea, 17–19, 36, 38, 40, 48, 82, 268–69, 274, 276, 285
Blaga Planina, 77, 225, 238, 243, 252–53
Bliss, General Tasker, 214–15, 231
Bojović, Voivode Petar, 74, 147, 155, 193, 209, 221-22
Bosnia, 23, 25–28, 47–48, 50, 153, 197, 210
Bralo, 166–67
Brest-Litovsk, 182, 187, 190
Briggs, General C.J., 77, 103-4, 132, 141, 178, 240
British Government, 35, 55, 79, 117, 138, 149, 158, 161, 260, 266, 268
Brod, 88, 96–97, 125, 219, 255, 257
Brusilov Offensive, 84, 115
Bulgaria, 18–21, 34, 36–38, 40–41, 43–48, 52–53, 55, 84–86, 89–90, 102, 119–20, 161–62, 213–14, 246–47, 249–50, 253, 258, 260–69, 273–83, 293–94
Bulgarian Armistice, 247, 270, 272, 274–75
Bulgarian Government, 43, 247, 250, 263, 265
Burun, Kara, 65–66, 71–73, 185
Butcher, Tim, 25, 153, 293
Butkovo, 66, 76, 79, 100–101, 105, 141, 143, 237, 240
Butkovo Front, 94, 97, 100, 103, 106, 114, 142, 177, 220, 287–88
Byzantium, 15–16, 20, 294

Caillaux, Joseph, 42, 183–84
Cassander, King of Macedonia, vii, 14
Casson, Stanley, 112, 118, 157, 159, 186, 202, 244, 249, 263, 293
Churchill, Sir Winston, 26, 34, 36, 38, 280, 286, 293
Clemenceau, Georges, 64, 183–84, 188–92, 195, 199, 201–3, 207–8, 210–13, 217–18, 232, 263–64, 266–67, 269, 273
Collinson Owen, 56, 67, 69, 168, 171, 293

Constantine, King of Greece, 33–34, 39, 43, 55, 72, 80, 107–112, 115, 118, 120, 156–62, 166, 279-280, 285
Constantinople, 15, 18, 33–36, 38–39, 41–42, 48, 81, 83, 156, 271, 273–76
Cordonnier, Général Victor, 89, 95–97, 114, 152
Cordier, Louis, 202, 209, 215, 218, 220–25, 229–33, 235, 237, 247, 249–50, 255
Corfu, 18, 24, 50–51, 74, 121–22, 150, 159, 166, 185
Crete, 21, 33, 110, 156
Crna, 60–62, 76, 88, 94–98, 114, 125–27, 131, 143–48, 151–52, 192–93, 218–19, 231, 235–36, 248, 251, 255, 269–70, 278
Cyprus, 19, 178, 287

Danube, River, 14, 17, 19, 24, 27–28, 37–39, 45, 47–48, 82–86, 89, 98, 114, 120, 224, 226, 228, 264, 269, 267, 271–73, 276, 281–82
Dardanelles, 35–43, 46, 52–53, 55–56, 58–59, 62, 64, 267–68, 275–76, 281, 287–88
Debar, 24, 50, 121, 125
Dedeagach, 21, 274–75
Demi Hasar, 71–72, 81, 91, 127–28, 141, 201–2, 225, 253, 258
Demi Kapu, 59, 62, 125–26, 223, 248, 251, 254, 258
Dimitrijević, Dragutin, 23, 25, 52–53, 294
Dobropolje, 125–26, 146–48, 151, 219–24, 227–31, 233–35, 242, 244, 248, 251, 255, 258, 261, 277, 279
Dobrujah, 13, 18, 21, 85, 114, 120, 148, 213, 261, 264
Doiran, 66, 68, 90–91, 100, 102, 119, 132–41, 143–45, 196, 202–3, 206–7, 237–38, 241–42, 253, 289
Doiran Front, 79, 95, 148, 176, 182, 201, 207, 215, 240–41, 243–44
Dova Tepe, 77, 132, 198, 287
Drina, River, 24, 27–28, 47, 272,
Ducasse, André, 92, 95, 97, 229–32, 235, 248, 254–55, 257, 260, 264, 273–74
Durazzo, 18, 24, 35, 50–51, 122–23, 180, 228

Eastern Front, 23, 187–88, 203, 237
Eastern Macedonia, 92–93, 108, 110, 119, 167, 177–78, 180, 260, 264, 275, 280
Edirne, 18, 21, 274
Eliot, Sir Francis, 158
Ersek, 121, 128, 123

Falkenhayn, Field Marshal Erich von, 46, 48–49, 51, 53–54, 64, 72–73, 83–86, 92, 107–8, 112, 114, 120, 286

Falls, Cyril, 47, 53, 86, 102, 118, 182, 200, 224, 239, 277
Ferrero, General Giacinto, 122, 166, 181, 190, 205
Field of the Blackbirds, 19, 49, 221
Floka, Mt.,147, 221, 232–24, 230, 255
Florina, 76–77, 88, 90–91, 93–96, 116, 121, 123, 125, 128, 178, 180
Foch, Maréchal Ferdinand, 188–92, 195, 201, 203, 208, 210–12, 216, 273, 282–83
Fort Rupel, 66, 79–81, 92, 94, 107,156
Fournet, Amiral Dartige du, 108, 111–12
France, 33, 35–37, 41–45, 52–54, 56–57, 69–70, 73–74, 79–80, 97, 111–12, 124, 156–61, 170, 183–84, 186–88, 202–3, 207–8, 210–11, 270–71, 282
Franchet d'Espèrey, Général Louis, ix, 13, 38–39, 42, 105, 118–19, 145, 188, 208–12, 214–18, 220–27, 229, 231–33, 236–40, 242–43, 245–49, 251–59, 263–69, 272–82
Franz Ferdinand, Archduke of Austria, 25-26
French Government, 47, 53, 71, 78, 80, 108–9, 111, 113, 116–17, 158–59, 163, 214, 218

Gallipoli, vii, 20, 34–37, 39, 53, 167, 210, 276, 294
Germany, 23, 33, 35, 37, 40–41, 46, 54–55, 64, 161, 250, 258, 260, 264–66, 272–73, 281–82
Gilbert, Martin, 36, 38, 42, 48, 50–51, 59, 187–88, 199, 208, 270, 282
Glenny, Misha, 23, 28, 36, 41, 43, 84, 153, 261, 294
Gordon-Smith, Gordon, 43, 45, 47–50, 91, 97, 110, 229–30, 235, 294
Gradec, 60, 62
Gradsko, 24, 49, 125–26, 221, 223–24, 228, 246–48, 251, 254–55, 257, 261, 271
Grand Couronné, 128, 133, 135–36, 205, 241–42, 246
Greece, vii, ix, 13–17, 21, 33–38, 40, 43, 52–55, 61–63, 76–77, 79–82, 107–14, 116, 120–23, 156, 158–62, 188–92, 207, 213–14, 280–81
Greek Macedonia, vii, 13, 33, 54, 56–57, 63-64, 68, 81, 91, 135, 185, 190
Greek Government, 52–53, 55, 64–65, 70–71, 74, 79–80, 107–9, 111, 116, 185, 190
Grey, Sir Edward, 26, 34, 44, 47, 109, 113, 213
Grossetti, Général Paul, 128, 166
Guillaumat, Général Adolphe, 89, 155, 184–86, 188–95, 191-12, 198–218, 212-13, 220, 223, 232, 237, 258, 266, 277–80, 286, 294

Hall, Richard C., 147, 193, 205–6, 211, 227, 229–31, 233–35, 249–50, 261–62, 264
Henrys, Général Paul, 193, 208, 215, 220, 228, 241, 247, 256–57, 265

Hill 1050, 131, 145-46, 177.204, 226, 231
Hill 1248, 98, 129-31, 144, 146, 148, 231, 251, 278
Hindenburg, Field Marshal Paul von, 84–85, 188, 223, 249–50, 254, 270–71, 285–86, 294
Homondos, 101, 104, 178–79, 204
Hortiach, 66–67, 72, 168, 171
Hungary, 39, 72, 82, 85–86, 272–73, 275–76, 282

Imbros, 36, 287–89
IMRO (Internal Macedonian Revolutionary Organisation), 19, 285
Iskenderun, 54–55, 287
Italy, 15, 17, 21, 34–36, 50–51, 120, 122, 154, 157, 160, 166, 181–82, 197

Joffre, Maréchal Joseph, 37, 39, 41–43, 53–54, 56, 74, 76–77, 84, 86–87, 89–90, 97–98, 112, 114, 116
Jonnart, Charles, 158–61, 165
Jouinot-Gambetta Brigade, 256- 58, 272
Jumeaux Ravine, 133–34, 136–37, 140, 242

Kačanik pass, 49, 60, 258
Karl, Emperor of Austro-Hungary, 164, 227, 250
Kavalla, 21, 40, 80, 83, 91, 94, 111, 201–2, 207, 274
Kaymakcalan, Mt., 88, 95–96, 114, 125, 150, 185, 201, 219, 221, 223, 228, 230, 233
Kenali, 88, 96, 102, 114, 125
Kicevo, 121, 125, 228, 247, 249, 251, 255–57, 263
King George V, 109–10, 294
Kitchener, Lord, 39, 47, 52, 54–55, 58, 61, 157–59, 189–90, 195, 199–201, 207–8, 212–13, 248, 261–62, 268–72, 282
Koritsa, 121, 123, 125–26, 128, 144, 148, 166, 180, 205, 228, 278
Kosturino, 60, 63-64, 125, 237, 252-23
Kotka, Mt., 146–48, 219, 234
Kozjak, Mt., 146, 219, 221, 223, 230, 235
Kragujevac, 24, 28, 48
Kravitsa, 219, 233
Krivolak, 54, 59–61, 223, 228, 251, 254
Krusha Balkan, 66, 101, 126, 176, 243

Laffin, John, 35–37, 39, 58, 276, 294
Lake Butkovo, 79, 90, 100–101, 106, 132, 198, 241
Lake Doiran, 61, 76–79, 90–91, 100, 102, 128, 130, 132, 135–36, 198, 201–2, 204, 227, 239, 251–53
Lake Ohrid, 122, 166, 180–81, 204–5, 218, 227, 249
Lake Prespa, 90, 129, 143–44, 148, 164, 167, 193, 278
Larcher, Commandant M., 43–44, 53–55, 59–61, 84, 87, 92, 107, 109–10, 112, 114–18, 129–30,
Lardemelle, Général Charles, 38, 42, 61, 210, 218
Lebouc, Général Georges 144, 151-52
Lemnos, 18, 36, 54, 68, 274, 287–89
Lepetit, Colonel, 192, 201–3, 205, 208, 211–17, 223–24, 294
Ljumnitsa, 145, 206, 229
Lloyd George, David, 33, 37, 39, 41, 112–14, 116–17, 119, 156, 163–64, 183–84, 189, 212–13, 217, 281
Ludendorff, General Erich von, 187–88, 262, 269–70, 278, 280, 282, 286, 294
Lyautey, Hubert, 116, 124, 128, 143, 167

Machukovo, 100, 102, 114, 125, 130, 135, 137, 202, 207, 231, 237
Mackensen, Field Marshal August von, 47, 86, 107, 114, 231
Mahon, General Sir Bryan, 43, 52, 58, 61–63, 65, 67, 69–72, 74, 76–78, 87, 89
Malaria, 103, 141–42, 168, 170–75, 177, 191, 195, 198, 200, 238–39, 288, 291–93
Mann, Arthur James,122, 124, 238, 242, 280, 294
Mazower, Mark, 16, 68, 81, 175, 294
Milne, General George, 63, 77–79, 89–91, 97–98, 102, 104, 106, 116–19, 128, 133, 137–42, 141, 144, 151, 164, 170–74, 176–79, 188–93, 196–98, 200, 202–3, 209, 214–16, 220, 225, 237–46, 252–54, 263–64, 266, 268–69, 273–75, 280, 285
Mišić, Voivode, Zivojin, 29, 47, 49, 74, 97, 146–47, 154–55, 215, 220–27, 229, 232-3, 255, 286
Moglena, ix, 39, 88, 95, 125–26, 143–45, 147, 202, 208, 215, 218, 227, 229-32, 247, 248-49
Monastir, 38, 50–51, 60–61, 63, 67, 75–78, 81, 90–99, 102-05, 116, 119, 125–31, 144–48, 150–51, 181, 185–86, 192, 201, 218–19, 222–24, 231–32, 249–51, 255–56, 277–78
Montenegro, 13, 17, 19, 21, 49–50, 180, 197, 210, 260, 272, 275
Morava, River, 24, 27, 83, 228, 271–72
Mudros, 53–54, 68, 190, 274

Nicolson, Harold, 13, 15, 27, 272, 294
Nicol, Graham, 77–79, 117–18, 139–40, 164, 166, 171–73, 188, 196–97, 220, 238–39, 242, 244–46, 262–64, 266, 268
Niš, 27–28, 46, 48, 50, 73, 150, 258, 267–68, 271–72
Nivelle offensive, 124, 127, 143, 149, 166, 182

Ohrid, 24, 88, 121, 125–26, 128–29, 167, 228, 249, 255–56
Ormanli, 60, 62, 101, 104, 176, 204, 289
Ostrovo, 60, 88, 95, 125, 219
Ottoman Empire, vii, 16–20, 33–34, 37-38, 49, 82, 150, 152, 274, 295

Packer, Charles, 103, 133, 135–37, 140, 237–38, 241, 243, 294
Palmer, Alan, 41–43, 58, 91–92, 107, 116, 146, 163–66, 180, 183, 195–96, 210, 213–15, 232, 237–40, 252–54, 256–58
Pardovitsa, 125, 254
Pašić, Nikola, 26, 47, 153–55, 181
Peloponnese, 64, 74–75, 111, 116–17, 150, 156, 199
Peter, King of Serbia, 49, 74, 153
Pétain, Maréchal Philippe, 188, 194, 208, 210
Petit Couronné, 91, 130, 133, 137, 139, 204, 241–42
Philip II, King of Macedonia, 13
Pip Ridge, 133, 135–36, 241–43, 245
Piraeus, 108, 111, 158–60, 200
Pogradec, 121, 165, 180–81, 205, 277
Poincaré, Raymond, 38, 183, 210
Potiorek, General Oskar, 25, 28–29, 46
Prilep, 60–61, 125–27, 131, 201, 220, 223, 226, 228, 231, 247–51, 255, 257
Princip, Gavrilo, 25–26, 28, 153
Putnik, Voivode Radomir, 49–50, 61

Rabbit Island, 287–89, 291
Repington, Charles, 73, 178–79, 184, 277, 295
Ribot, Alexandre, 116, 158, 164, 183–84, 295
Robertson, General Sir William, CIGS, 69–70, 74, 76–79, 84-87, 89–90, 95, 99, 114–19, 127–28, 131, 139–40, 149, 151, 156–57, 161, 163–64, 177–78, 182, 185, 196–97, 200
Romania, 17, 19, 21, 36–38, 40, 46, 48, 82–87, 89, 91, 114–16, 269, 272, 275–76, 282
Rome, 15, 39, 116, 197, 217, 248, 266, 294
Royal Flying Corps (RFC), 79, 131, 133, 178, 196
Rupel Pass, 79–80, 91, 94, 101–2, 119, 141, 177, 220, 228, 252–53
Russia, 17, 19, 23, 33–34, 38, 41, 43, 45–47, 84, 86, 156–57, 159–60, 165, 270–71, 278
Rutter, Owen, 57, 65, 136, 168, 174, 295

San Stefano, Treaty of, 17–19, 34, 40, 260, 276
Santi Quaranta, 116, 121–23, 126, 166, 180, 205
Sarajevo, 18, 24–28, 153–54
Sarrail, Général Maurice, ix, 41–43, 49–50, 58–59, 61–64, 69–74, 76–81, 85, 89–91, 93–100, 10-08, 109, 115–19, 122–24, 126–31, 137–39, 143–48, 151–52, 156–61, 164–67, 173–74, 179–86, 188–90, 193–95, 204, 210, 223, 229, 256, 277-78, 280, 268
Sarrail/Porte, 56, 59, 61–62, 71–73, 91, 127–30, 138–39, 143–45, 157–59, 161, 164–67, 173–74, 177, 180–81, 183–86
Sava, 24, 27–28, 45, 47
Schiavon, Max, 42, 53–54, 73–74, 95–96, 188–89, 192–94, 208, 230–31, 245–46, 250–51, 263–66, 269, 272–73, 278
Schlieffen Plan, 23, 167
Scutari, 24, 50–51, 121
Second Balkan War, 21, 23, 28, 34, 40, 43, 120, 207, 240, 260
Serbia, ix, 17, 19, 21, 23–28, 33–41, 43–50, 52–56, 58–59, 61–64, 67–68, 70, 72–73, 151–53, 220–21, 258, 262–64, 271–72, 278–82, 294–95
Serbian Government, 26, 35, 40, 48–49, 51, 74, 151, 190
Seres, vi, 66, 68, 69, 91, 100-01, 126–27, 128, 178, 201-02, 228
Seres Road, 56, 66, 68–69, 78, 101, 103, 105, 128, 192
Skouloudis, Stephanos, 55, 72, 79, 107
Skopje, ix, 13, 18–19, 48–49, 60–61, 225–26, 228, 247, 249–52, 255–58, 261, 263–65, 271–72
Skra di Legen, 145, 181, 205–7, 212, 218, 221, 227, 229, 231, 240, 279
Sofia, 46, 48, 119, 143, 223, 228, 231, 246, 250, 253, 261–65, 271, 273
Sokol, Mt.,146–47, 219, 222, 230, 232–35
Spahis, 257–58
Stepanović, Voivode Stepa, 29, 48, 74, 146, 155, 221, 224
Stip, 59–60, 125, 127, 223, 228, 249, 252–54
Struma, 66, 76, 90–94, 100–101, 103–6, 119, 141, 173, 178–79, 192–93, 198, 202–4, 207, 227–28, 249–50, 252–53, 278
Struma Front, 79, 100–101, 103, 105, 126, 128, 130, 132, 141, 143, 176–78, 190, 192, 196–98, 237
Struma valley, 63, 69, 79, 81, 90, 94, 119, 126, 178–79, 186, 188, 198, 200–201
Strumitsa, 60–61, 125, 202, 228–29, 245, 253, 261-63
Strumitsa valley, 201–2, 220, 246–47, 249, 251–52, 258, 261, 263
Supreme War Council,(SWC), 189–90, 199, 200, 205, 211–14, 216, 224, 231, 248, 263, 266, 269, 272-73, 279, 286

Tetovo, 24, 49, 121, 125, 226, 228, 256, 263

Thessaly, vii, 15–18, 21, 105, 108, 111–12, 115–18, 144, 156–59, 162, 164
Third Balkan War, 23, 25, 27, 29, 38, 150, 153
Thrace, 13, 16–18, 34, 107, 110
Todorov, General Giorgi, 249–50, 253, 255–56, 263
Transylvania, 18, 36, 82–86, 92, 114
Treaty of Berlin 1878, 17–19, 21, 82, 120
Tsar Ferdinand of Bulgaria, 20, 43, 211, 227, 213, 249-50, 255, 260–62, 265, 271, 293
Tservena, 129, 144-50
Turkey, 14, 21, 34–38, 40, 44, 46, 54, 73, 105, 119–20, 161–62, 266–68, 270, 273–74, 276–77, 279, 282–83, 285–86

Udovo, 24, 48, 59, 125, 131, 225-26, 228, 247, 251, 254, 258

Valona, 24, 50–51, 83, 116, 121–23, 180–81, 190, 204, 208, 218, 228
Vardar, ix, 38, 59–63, 65–67, 76, 90–91, 94–95, 100–103, 105–6, 125–27, 132–33, 143–48, 161, 196–98, 201–08, 220–23, 225, 227, 231–32, 238–49, 251–54, 261–63, 269–72, 278
Veles, 24, 48, 59–61, 125, 228, 251–52, 255–58, 263, 271

Venizelos, Eleutherios, 34, 41, 43–44, 52–53, 55, 65, 72, 110–12, 157–58, 160–61, 175, 181, 285
Vetrenik, Mt., 125, 147, 219, 222, 224, 230, 232–33, 235, 248, 251
Villari, Luigi, 45, 78, 80–81, 92–94, 98, 103, 105–6, 122–23, 131, 146, 166–68, 197, 204–6, 256, 261–62, 264–65

Wakefield, Alan, 65, 67–68, 103–4, 131, 133, 135, 137, 140, 239–45, 253, 263
Western Front, 37, 39, 73–74, 148–49, 163, 166–67, 182, 186–89, 193–96, 199, 202–3, 248, 250, 277–78, 281–82
Wilhelm, Kaiser, 27, 34-35, 48, 118, 161, 227, 250, 262, 265, 270-71
Wilson, General Sir Henry, CIGS, 196, 238, 246, 252, 268
Wilson, General Maitland, 77, 116, 133, 135, 139, 240

Yenikoi, 101, 103, 176, 178
Yugoslavia, 13, 153–54, 253, 285

Zaimis, Alexandros, 159–60
Zouaves, 71, 94–95, 97, 244–46, 253

INDEX OF FORMATIONS

French Army

French Army, 73, 75, 89, 94, 166–67, 173, 183, 193–94, 220, 225, 286
French First Group, 193, 197, 225, 236, 240, 245, 247–53, 255, 258, 261, 263
AFO (French Army of the Orient), 191–92, 203, 209, 215, 225–26, 228, 241, 247–49, 251–52, 255–56, 258, 265, 267

156th Division, 43, 53, 56-62, 76, 90–95, 126, 129, 144, 166, 180, 204, 284
57th Division, 44, 58–62, 76, 90, 94–95, 97, 126, 129-30, 144–46, 166, 180, 284
122nd Division, 44, 60–62, 76, 90, 94–95, 144–45, 148, 183, 196, 206, 222, 224, 232–34, 273–75, 284
17th Division Colonial, 53, 76, 90–91, 94–95, 100, 126, 144, 222, 224, 232–34, 248, 254, 284
11th Division Colonial, 106, 126, 144, 146, 182, 255–56, 284
16th Division Colonial, 106, 126, 144, 146, 284
76th Division, 123–24, 126, 128–29, 144–45, 148, 180, 182, 195, 284
30th Division, 124, 126, 144, 182, 195, 204, 284

British Army

British Army, x, 74, 139, 185–86, 239, 241, 280, 286
BSF (British Salonica Force), 56–58, 64–65, 68–69, 77–79, 87, 89–91, 100, 102–3, 106, 119, 140–41, 143–45, 168, 170–72, 191–94, 196–98, 220, 237–40, 249, 251–53
British Army Group, 225, 237, 239, 245, 247, 249, 252, 255, 258, 261

XII Corps, 56, 77, 90, 98, 102-3, 114, 132–33, 141, 145, 168, 176, 191, 198, 204, 239–41, 244-45, 252-53
XVI Corps, 56, 68, 77, 90, 98, 100, 102-105, 114, 132, 141, 145, 176, 178-79, 191–92, 198, 204, 240, 243–44, 252-54

10th Division, 43, 53, 56, 61-64, 67, 103-04, 132, 141, 157, 163-64, 172, 176, 284
22nd Division, 44, 54, 62-63, 65–66, 78, 91, 94-95, 102-04, 132–33, 136-37, 140, 176, 198, 239–43, 252, 284
26th Division, 44, 57, 63, 65–66, 130, 132-3, 136-37, 139–41, 176, 198, 239–44, 253, 273, 284

27th Division, 44, 57, 63, 65-66, 103-05, 132, 137, 172, 176, 178-79, 198, 204, 225, 231, 239, 252, 284
28th Division, 44, 57, 65-66, 77-78, 104, 132, 141, 173, 176, 198, 204, 240, 243-44, 253, 273-75, 284
60th Division, 106, 132-33, 140, 157, 163-64, 176, 284

29th Brigade, 141
30th Brigade, 63, 141
31st Brigade, 63
65th Brigade, 63, 242
66th Brigade, 132, 137, 148, 241, 243
67th Brigade, 241-43
77th Brigade, 140, 244
78th Brigade, 133, 137, 139-40
79th Brigade, 133, 136-37, 139
81st Brigade, 103
82nd Brigade, 103,
83rd Brigade, 198, 240
84th Brigade, 198, 240
85th Brigade, 141, 198, 240, 244
228th Brigade, 132, 176, 177, 179, 198, 200, 244, 253
7th Mounted Brigade, 93, 100. 104, 141, 148, 157, 176, 178
8th Mounted Brigade, 115, 141, 148, 157, 176, 178

Serbian Army
Serbian Army, 23, 27–29, 45, 47–51, 55, 74–75, 89, 98, 105, 119, 122, 126–27, 138, 141, 145–47, 150–55, 197, 202, 204, 208–9, 220–25, 227, 229–30, 233, 237, 239, 248–50, 266, 258, 271–73, 278–79
First Serbian Army, 28, 47–48, 91-92, 97, 144, 146–47, 154, 220–22, 230, 235, 248–49, 251-52, 255, 257-58, 261–62, 267, 271-72
Second Serbian Army, 27, 48, 90, 144, 146–47, 222, 226, 229–30, 234–35, 250–52, 254–55, 263, 267, 272
Third Serbian Army, 47, 92–93, 95–97, 154

Danube Division, 74, 92, 154, 219, 222, 234-35, 271, 284
Drina Division, 74, 154, 219, 222, 234-35, 284
Morava Division, 74, 154, 219, 222, 235-36, 284
Sumadija Division, 74, 147, 154, 219, 222, 224, 233-34, 248, 284
Timok Division, 74, 154, 219, 222, 224, 233-36, 248, 254, 284
Vardar Division, 74, 92, 154, 197, 284
Yugoslav Division, 74, 197, 219, 222-25, 233-36, 248, 254, 271, 284

Italian Army
XVI Corps, 35, 51, 116, 122-23, 128, 167, 180, 190, 204-05, 208, 218, 271, 279

35th Division, 51, 77, 89, 94, 97-98, 100, 103, 105, 114, 119, 123-24, 131, 144, 166-67, 177, 191-93, 226, 255, 267, 275, 284

Russian Army
2nd and 4th Brigades, 76, 89-90, 94-95, 124, 144-45, 160, 193, 195, 230, 284

Greek Army
Greek Army, 55–57, 62–63, 73, 76, 92, 107, 109, 111, 160–61, 177, 189–91, 194, 202-04, 207, 215–16, 225-26, 239-40, 278-79
National Corps, 119, 182, 191, 193
Royalist Corps, 198, 200, 207-08, 227

Crete Division, 77, 145, 167, 197-98, 206, 225, 240, 243-44, 246, 252-53, 284
Seres Division, 144-45, 148, 197, 206, 225, 234, 239-40, 241-44, 246, 252, 284
Archipelago Division, 145, 197, 206, 254, 284
Larissa Division, 196, 198, 204, 240-41, 246, 284
Calchis Division, 198, 241, 284
Athens Division, 198, 241, 284

Bulgarian Army
Bulgarian Army, 47–49, 51, 62–63, 85–86, 91–92, 147–48, 150–51, 153, 211, 221–23, 236–37, 253, 264–65, 269–70, 278–80
German Army Support, 46, 48-9, 64, 73, 79, 92, 105, 107-08, 120, 130-01, 146, 148, 203, 211, 217, 227, 235, 249, 250, 261-02, 265, 271,
First Bulgarian Army, 47, 48, 63, 68, 220, 227, 231, 240, 245, 249, 252-54
Second Bulgarian Army, 47-50, 54, 59, 62-64, 91–92, 94, 154, 220, 227, 249, 262
Fourth Bulgarian Army, 227, 229
Eleventh Germano-Bulgarian Army, 47, 107, 223, 226-27, 231, 249, 251, 255-56
LXI Corps, 255-56, 258, 263
LXII Corps, 129, 255-56, 258

1st Division, 146, 228
2nd Division, 102, 219, 228, 235, 241, 248, 250, 255, 269
3rd Division, 147, 219, 228, 235-36, 250, 255, 261, 269-70
4th Division, 219, 228, 236, 248, 250, 255, 257
7th Division, 92
8th Division, 93
9th (Plevna) Division, 102, 228, 239
302nd Division, 228, 219